Wireless# Guide to
Wireless Communications
Second Edition

By Jorge Olenewa
and
Mark Ciampa

COURSE TECHNOLOGY
CENGAGE Learning

Australia • Brazil • Japan • Korea • Mexico • Singapore • Spain • United Kingdom • United States

COURSE TECHNOLOGY
CENGAGE Learning

Wireless# Guide to Wireless Communications, Second Edition
Jorge Olenewa and Mark Ciampa

Vice President, Technology and Trades:
Dave Garza

Acquisitions Editor: Nick Lombardi

Quality Assurance Coordinator: Christian
Kunciw

Marketing Director: Deborah Yarnell

Cover Design: Abby Scholz

Copyeditor: Harold Johnson

Proofreader: Christine Grace Clark

Indexer: Liz Cunningham

Editorial Director: Sandy Clark

Product Managers: Amy Lyon, Donna Gridley

Technical Editor: John Tucker

Senior Channel Marketing Manager: Dennis
Williams

Text Design: GEX Publishing Services

Development Editor: Amanda Brodkin

Executive Editor: Stephen Helba

Production Editor: Daphne Barbas

Manufacturing Coordinator: Susan Carroll

Senior Editorial Assistant: Dawn Daugherty

Compositor: GEX Publishing Services

Photo Research Editor: Abby Reip

For product information and technology assistance, contact us at
Cengage Learning Customer & Sales Support, 1-800-354-9706

For permission to use material from this text or product, submit all requests online at **www.cengage.com/permissions**
Further permission questions can be emailed to
permissionrequest@cengage.com

ISBN-13: 978-1-4188-3699-3
ISBN-10: 1-4188-3699-0

Course Technology
20 Channel Center Street
Boston, Massachusetts, 02210
USA

Cengage Learning is a leading provider of customized learning solutions with office locations around the globe, including Singapore, the United Kingdom, Australia, Mexico, Brazil, and Japan. Locate your local office at:
international.cengage.com/region

Cengage Learning products are represented in Canada by Nelson Education, Ltd.

Disclaimer: Course Technology reserves the right to revise this publication and make changes from time to time in its content without notice.

The Web addresses in this book are subject to change from time to time as necessary without notice.

For your lifelong learning solutions, visit **course.cengage.com**

Purchase any of our products at your local college store or at our preferred online store **www.ichapters.com**

Printed in the United States of America
6 7 8 9 10

BRIEF Contents

TABLE OF
Contents

CHAPTER TWELVE
Wireless Communications in Business   421

APPENDIX A
Wireless# Certification Exam Objectives   447

Introduction

The whole world is going wireless! The new technologies and new standards that have been published in the past three years mean that almost every thing we touch, every aspect of our lives nowadays, has a wireless component to it. From cordless phones in the home to cellular phones that are used throughout the world—often replacing the traditional wired telephone line to wireless local, metropolitan, and wide area networks—to wirelessly counting the inventory of products on store shelves and paying for your purchases without using hard currency, wireless data communications are everywhere today. Many towns and cities are installing wireless networks that allow residents and visitors to access the Internet from everywhere, using notebook computers and handheld devices. Whether you are a manager involved in the implementation of any type of wireless communication devices, a technician looking to enhance your understanding of the field of wireless communications, or a student taking an introductory course, *Wireless# Guide to Wireless Communications, Second Edition* will provide you with the background and a solid overview of the entire range of wireless data communications technologies. This book will also be of assistance to students and technicians looking to obtain the Wireless# (Wireless Sharp) entry-level certification from Planet3 Wireless, the organization that is the leader in vendor-neutral wireless certifications. This book and the Wireless# certification will help you gain the necessary knowledge and skills to get started and to confidently take courses that are more advanced.

Approach

Since the introduction of infrared interfaces in notebook computers in mid-1995, which allowed two computers to communicate without wires, and the publication of wireless local area network standards in 1997, the field of wireless data communications has expanded dramatically. Many new technologies have been developed and new standards published. This book takes you on a virtual tour of all these technologies, covering the basics of radio frequency transmissions, antennas, infrared, the now-popular Bluetooth, the new IEEE 802.15.4 (ZigBee) standard for low-rate wireless personal area networks, the IEEE 802.15.3 high-rate wireless personal area network standard and the proposed ultra wide band (UWB) enhancements, low-speed and high-speed wireless local area networks, IEEE 802.16 (WiMAX), free-space optics, LMDS and MMDS wireless metropolitan area networks, cellular and satellite wireless wide area networks, and, finally, radio frequency identification (RFID). In addition, the text addresses coexistence, security, and the basics of implementation issues for each technology, as well as their application in business.

Using straightforward language, the text provides an introduction to the most important technical aspects of each technology. As such, the book is easy to read and can be used either in classroom settings or in distance education. Hands-on activities can be performed in the lab or at home and use inexpensive, consumer-class equipment manufactured by Linksys and D-Link, as well as freeware and demo versions of popular software. The text also includes extensive Web site links where you can find additional materials as well as individual and team-based research projects that help expand your knowledge of the technologies discussed and direct the student to locate additional learning resources. Please note that the addresses of these Web sites were accurate at the time this book was printed. However, due to the changeable nature of the Web, some of the addresses referred to here may no longer be available.

Intended Audience

This book is intended to meet the needs of students and professionals who want to gain a better understanding of the full range of wireless data communications technologies. A basic knowledge of computers and networks at a CompTIA A+ and Net+ level are required to use this book. Those seeking to take the Planet3 Wireless, Inc., Wireless# exam will find the text's approach and coverage of certification objectives very helpful. For more information on Wireless# certification, visit the Planet3 Wireless, Inc., Web site at *www.cwnp.com*. *Wireless# Guide to Wireless Communications, Second Edition* is much more than just an examination preparation book: it provides a solid, in-depth coverage of a wide range of wireless data communications technologies, far more than is required for the exam, and helps professionals and students truly understand the scope and penetration of these technologies. The book's pedagogical features are designed to provide a realistic, interactive learning experience to help prepare you for the challenges of working in the field of wireless data communications.

Chapter Descriptions

A summary of the topics covered in each chapter of this book follows:

Chapter 1, "Introduction to Wireless Communications," provides an overview of a range of applications of wireless data communications in personal, local, metropolitan, and wide area networks. The chapter follows the way the industry is classifying wireless data communications today and looks at the advantages and disadvantages of wireless data communications.

Chapter 2, "Wireless Data Transmission," introduces you to wireless data transmission techniques by discussing various techniques used with infrared light and radio waves to transmit data without wires.

Chapter 3, "Understanding Radio Frequency Communications," looks at the individual components and design of radio systems, and how they are used to transmit data. It also provides an overview of standards and their role in the wireless data communications industry.

Chapter 4, "How Antennas Work," takes a simplified but in-depth look at antennas and the important role that they have in the successful implementation of a wireless data communications system.

Chapter 5, "Low Rate Wireless Personal Area Networks," looks at the first three technologies developed for short-range wireless data communications: IrDA infrared, Bluetooth, and ZigBee (IEEE 802.15.4).

Chapter 6, "High Rate Wireless Personal Area Networks," wraps up the discussion of short-range wireless data communications with WiMedia (IEEE 802.15.3), a technology developed for interconnecting multimedia devices and entertainment systems in homes and businesses, and also looks at ultra wide band (UWB) technology and the impact it can have in wireless communications in general.

Chapter 7, "Low-Speed Wireless Local Area Networks," covers the basic details of IEEE 802.11 WLAN technology, including its infrared variant, for transmission at up to 11 megabits-per-second.

Chapter 8, "High-Speed WLANs and WLAN Security," discusses IEEE 802.11a as well as all the enhancements to 802.11 technology designed to boost its data transmission speed and usability. An in-depth introduction to the security techniques and issues in WLANs is also included in this chapter.

Chapter 9, "Wireless Metropolitan Area Networks," addresses medium-range wireless data communications from infrared free-space optics to the latest WiMAX (IEEE 802.16) technology.

Chapter 10, "Wireless Wide Area Networks," takes a look at cellular and satellite technologies and how they are used to extend the reach of wireless data communications networks to cover the entire world.

Chapter 11, "Radio Frequency Identification," describes the fascinating technology that is being used to help identify, count, and track everything from small packaged products to the entire contents of large warehouses automatically and without wires.

Chapter 12, "Wireless Communications in Business," outlines the advantages and challenges of wireless data communications and discusses the steps that a typical business must go through to identify, evaluate, and implement the wireless data communications technology that is the best solution for its needs.

The two appendices at the end of this book serve as references for the wireless networking student and professional:

Appendix A, "Wireless# Certification Examination Objectives," provides a complete listing of the Planet3 Wireless, Inc., Wireless# certification exam objectives and shows which chapters and sections in the book cover material associated with each objective.

Appendix B, "History of Wireless Communications," details the history of wireless communications, in addition to television, radar, and cellular technologies.

New To This Edition

This edition covers a number of new standards and technologies that were not available when the first edition was published, and also includes coverage of several new topics, including:

- Decibels, gain and loss calculations (simplified)
- Antennas
- IEEE 802.11g, IEEE 802.11n, IEEE 802.11r, IEEE 802.11s, IEEE 802.11i, and IEEE 802.1X
- IEEE 802.15.4 and ZigBee
- IEEE 802.15.3 and WiMedia
- IEEE 802.16 and WiMAX
- Expanded coverage of cellular technologies such as CDMA 1xRTT and 1xEV-DO, EDGE, W-CDMA, and HSDPA
- Expanded coverage of satellite communications, including Ka Band and transmission techniques
- RFID technology
- Wi-Fi site surveys

Features

To aid you in fully understanding wireless data communications technology, this book includes many features designed to enhance your learning experience.

- **Chapter Objectives.** Each chapter begins with a detailed list of the concepts to be mastered within that chapter. This list provides you with both a quick reference to the chapter's contents and a useful study aid.

- **Illustrations and Tables.** Numerous illustrations of wireless LAN concepts and technologies help you visualize theories and concepts. In addition, the many tables provide details and comparisons of practical and theoretical information.

- **Chapter Summaries.** Each chapter's text is followed by a summary of the concepts introduced in that chapter. These summaries provide a helpful way to review the ideas covered in each chapter.

- **Key Terms.** The important terminology introduced in each chapter is summarized in a list at the end of each chapter. The key term list includes definitions for each term.

- **Review Questions.** The end-of-chapter assessment begins with a set of review questions, including multiple choice, fill-in, and True/False, that reinforce the ideas introduced in each chapter. These questions help you evaluate and apply the material you have learned. Answering these questions will ensure that you have mastered the important concepts and provide valuable practice for taking the Wireless# certification exam.

- **Hands-On Projects.** Although it is important to understand the theory behind wireless networking technology, nothing can improve on real-world experience. To this end, each chapter provides several Hands-On Projects aimed at providing you with a practical wireless network experience. Some of these projects require Internet and library research to investigate concepts covered in the chapter, while other projects let you put into practice the chapter's content using Linksys and D-Link equipment and the Windows XP operating systems as well as software downloaded from the Internet.

- **Case Projects.** Located at the end of each chapter are several Case Projects. In these extensive exercises, you implement the skills and knowledge gained in the chapter through real design and implementation scenarios.

Text and Graphic Conventions

Wherever appropriate, additional information and exercises have been added to this book to help you better understand the topic at hand. Icons throughout the text alert you to additional materials. The icons used in this textbook are described below.

The Note icon draws your attention to additional helpful material related to the subject being described.

NOTE

Tips based on the author's experience provide extra information about how to attack a problem or what to do in real-world situations.

TIP

The Caution icons warn you about potential mistakes or problems and explain how to avoid them.

Each hands-on activity in this book is preceded by the Hands-On icon and a description of the exercise that follows.

Case Project icons mark Case Projects, which are scenario-based assignments. In these extensive case examples, you are asked to implement independently what you have learned.

INSTRUCTOR'S MATERIALS

The following additional materials are available when this book is used in a classroom setting. All of the supplements available with this book are provided to the instructor on a single CD-ROM. You can also retrieve these supplemental materials from the Cengage Web site, *www.cengage.com*, by going to the page for this book, under "Download Instructor Files & Teaching Tools."

Electronic Instructor's Manual. The Instructor's Manual that accompanies this textbook includes additional instructional material to assist in class preparation, including suggestions for lecture topics, recommended lab activities, tips on setting up a lab for the Hands-On Projects, and solutions to all end-of-chapter materials.

ExamView Test Bank. This cutting-edge Windows-based testing software helps instructors design and administer tests and pretests. In addition to generating tests that can be printed and administered, this full-featured program has an online testing component that allows students to take tests at the computer and have their exams graded automatically.

PowerPoint Presentations. This book comes with a set of Microsoft PowerPoint slides for each chapter. These slides are meant to be used as a teaching aid for classroom presentations, to be made available to students on the network for chapter review, or to be printed for classroom distribution. Instructors are also at liberty to add their own slides for other topics introduced.

LAB REQUIREMENTS

To the User

This book is designed to be read in sequence, from beginning to end. Each chapter builds on preceding chapters to provide a solid understanding of wireless data communications. You can also use this book to prepare for Planet3 Wireless Inc.'s Wireless# certification exam. The summary grid on the inside front cover of the book and Appendix A pinpoint the chapters that cover each exam objective.

Hardware and Software Requirements

Following are the hardware and software requirements needed to perform the end-of-chapter Hands-On Projects:

■ D-Link DBT-120 USB Bluetooth adapter or equivalent (the adapter should optionally be supported by Windows XP; see Microsoft Technet article 841803 for a list of supported devices)

■ Linksys G Wireless-G router or Linksys Wireless-G access point

■ Wi-Fi certified IEEE 802.11b, a, or g wireless network adapter (the adapter standard must match that of the access point or wireless router). To use AirMagnet demo software, the adapter must be also appear on the list of supported hardware. See *www.airmagnet.com*

■ Windows XP Professional or Home Edition

■ An Internet connection and Web browser (i.e., Internet Explorer)

Specialized Requirements

Whenever possible, the need for specialized equipment was kept to a minimum. The following chapter features specialized hardware:

■ Chapter 5: Notebook computers with IrDA and USB version 1.1 or 2.0 ports

Free downloadable software is required in the following chapters. Instructions for downloading the software are given in the chapters:

■ Chapter 4: Cisco Link Budget calculation spreadsheet

■ Chapter 5: AirMagnet Bluesweep

■ Chapter 8: QCheck

■ Chapter 12: AirMagnet Laptop Analyzer

ACKNOWLEDGMENTS

As I began writing this book, I did not fully appreciate how many people played a role and how much work was involved in this kind of undertaking. As Mark Ciampa thoughtfully put it, a book is not created by an author alone but is the work of an entire team, and the team at Cengage is undoubtedly the very best. Acquisitions Editor Nick Lombardi again demonstrated his excellent vision and insight by crafting the direction of the book to meet the needs of the readers. Product Managers Amy Lyon and Donna Gridley were once again wonderful in keeping this project on track and always being so helpful and supportive. Developmental Editor Amanda Brodkin deserves full credit for helping to turn my thoughts into readable text. Amanda's help was instrumental throughout the process with probing questions and insightful suggestions. Production Editor Daphne Barbas was great in finding my mistakes and also making excellent suggestions. A very special thank you is also due to Professor Khalid Danok of George Brown College in Toronto, Ontario, Canada, for his review and suggestions for Chapter 4, Mark Tauschek from Wireless Friendly Inc. in Newmarket, Ontario, Canada, for his review and assistance with the case studies and hands-on projects, Henry White of Bell Mobility in Mississauga, Ontario, Canada, for his help with several of the figures throughout the book, and Jeff Mulvey of Redline Communications Inc. of Markham, Ontario, Canada, for his assistance with the WiMAX material. The Editorial Team would like to thank the Technical Editor John Tucker and the Quality Assurance testers who carefully reviewed the book: Peter Stefanis, Danielle Shaw, and Susan Whalen. In addition, we would like to thank our team of peer reviewers who evaluated each chapter and provided very helpful suggestions and contributions:

Phillip Coleman	Western Kentucky University
Keith Conn	Cleveland Institute of Electronics
Alireza Fazelpour	Palm Beach Community College
Beau Sanders	Greenville Technical College

The entire Cengage staff was always helpful and worked very hard to create this finished product. I feel privileged and honored to be part of such an outstanding group of professionals, and to these people and everyone on the team I extend a very sincere thank you.

I also want to thank my son Ricardo for his encouragement and support, in spite of being so busy after he and wife Jennifer graced me with my first grandson, Tristan, just when I was getting ready to write the first chapter. Ricardo's continuing interest in and offers of assistance for this project meant very much to me. Finally, I want to thank my fiancée Elisabeth and our dog Charlie, whose love and patience are reflected in literally every page of this text. I could not have finished this work without Elisabeth's unstoppable insistence that I get back to work on the book and leave everything else to her, as well as Charlie's constant companionship and undying affection.

DEDICATION

To my ever loving and caring fiancée Elisabeth and our faithful toy poodle, Charlie, and to my first grandson, Tristan.

PHOTO CREDITS

Figure	Caption	Credit
Figure 2-6	Infrared wireless notebook	Copyright © 2001 NEC Computers Inc. All rights reserved.
Figure 4-14	Phased array antenna	Courtesy of Applied Radar Inc.
Figure 7-2	CF card wireless NIC and SD card wireless NIC	Courtesy of SanDisk and Pretect
Figure 9-3	FSO transceiver	Courtesy of Terabeam Corporation
Figure 9-11	Pizza box antenna	Courtesy of Alan Herrell, LemurZone Design, Phoenix, Arizona
Figure 11-3	RFID tag	Courtesy of R. Moroz Ltd.
Figure 11-4	RFID tags and antennas	Courtesy of Symbol Technologies

1

INTRODUCTION TO WIRELESS COMMUNICATIONS

After reading this chapter and completing the exercises, you will be able to:

♦ Explain how the major wireless technologies are used today

♦ Describe various applications of wireless communications technology

♦ Explain the advantages and disadvantages of wireless communications technology

♦ List several different wireless technologies

Information technology experts seldom agree on anything. Each has his or her own opinion on which software is the best, which brand of personal computer is superior, and which operating system should run every computer. However, there is one point on which IT professionals all agree: wireless communications technology has had a huge impact on most of the developed world and a large number of developing countries. Wireless communications affects almost every aspect of our daily lives. From the ubiquitous cordless phone to automated counting of inventory in large retail stores to remote wireless sensors installed in locations that are difficult to access, wireless technologies play a role. Furthermore, wireless communications technology, or, simply, wireless, is poised to continue expanding at a very fast pace.

Wireless communications is revolutionizing the way we live—just as personal computers in the 1980s forever altered how we work, and the Internet in the 1990s dramatically changed how we acquire information. Using wireless communications to send and receive messages, browse the Internet, and access corporate databases from any location in the world has already become commonplace. A wide array of devices ranging from computers to digital cameras, laser printers, and even refrigerators can already communicate without wires. Users will soon be able to access the digital resources that they need at any time, no matter where they may find themselves. The IT industry and consumer marketplace are already seeing dramatic changes based on wireless technologies. It is truly becoming a wireless world.

How Wireless Technology Is Used

Before we continue, we need to define precisely what we mean by *wireless communications*. The term *wireless* is often used to describe all types of devices and technologies that are not connected by a wire. A garage door opener, a television remote control, and a pager all can be called "wireless," but they have little in common with the technologies discussed in this book. Because the term wireless today is sometimes used to refer to any device that has no connecting wires, users tend to be puzzled about the exact meaning of wireless communications. While a cordless phone is also a communications device—for human voice communications, that is—for the purposes of this book, **wireless communications** is defined as the transmission of user data without the use of wires. In addition to digital data, user data may include e-mail messages, spreadsheets, and telephone voice messages. Cordless phones that use a computer network to transmit voice conversations are also included here.

This section addresses the various forms that wireless data communications can take. You will learn about Bluetooth, Ultra Wide Band, satellite, cellular, wireless LAN, fixed broadband, and wireless WAN communications technologies. The specific details of each of these technologies are covered in later chapters. A day in the life of a typical couple, Joseph and Ann Kirkpatrick, provides a good overview of today's wireless communications and how they are applied in a real-world scenario.

A Wireless World

Joseph and Ann, both employees of a delivery service company, get ready for a typical day. Before Ann leaves home for the office, she must first print a copy of a spreadsheet that she finished working on late last night. Because there are several computers in their house, the Kirkpatricks have set up a wireless network that uses a specific networking standard to allow all the digital data-enabled devices around the house to communicate with each other. Computers and other devices that are compatible with the standards can be as far as 300 feet (90 meters) apart from each other and can send and receive data at up to 54 million bits per second (54 megabits per second or Mbps), depending on which specific standard they are compatible with. The devices that can be part of the network include not only computer equipment but also **Voice over Internet Protocol (VoIP)** telephones, which carry digitized voice over the Internet, and home entertainment and gaming equipment.

Ann sits down at the desktop computer upstairs and retrieves the spreadsheet. She then selects the print command. A device called a **wireless network interface card** (or **wireless NIC**) is connected to the computer. This interface card sends the data over radio waves to the computer downstairs, which has both a wireless network interface card and a laser printer connected to it. This wireless network is ideal for the Kirkpatricks. They can have all their home computing and electronic devices interconnected without the expense of installing cables; this network enables the devices to share printers, files, and even an Internet connection. Figure 1-1 illustrates the home wireless network.

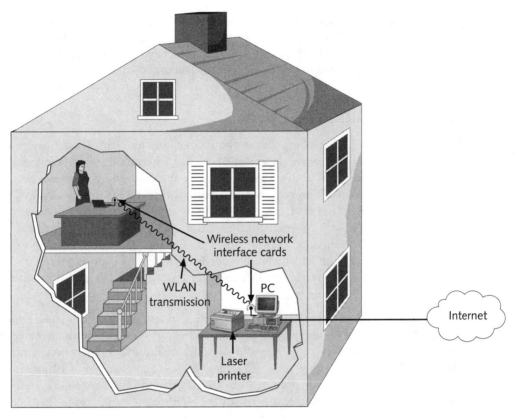

Figure 1-1 Home wireless network (WLAN)

Ann places a call to her office to pick up her messages using her **Smartphone**, a combination mobile phone and **personal digital assistant (PDA)**, which is a small handheld device used for keeping an appointment calendar, to-do list, phone book, and notepad. Some PDAs can connect to other devices such as personal computers and other PDAs to transfer files, or they can electronically store business cards or similar information. A few of the more sophisticated models can even connect directly to a wireless network. Since Ann is inside the home, the Smartphone automatically connects to the wireless network. Very small devices plugged in around the house keep the couple's mobile phones connected to a central receiver, which in turn connects them to the main house telephone line. While inside the home or office, the mobile phones automatically disconnect from the cellular network and connect to the local wireless network. As soon as Joseph and Ann leave home, their mobile phones again automatically disconnect from the house line and connect to the cellular network.

NOTE

Runners in the Boston Marathon cover the 26.2-mile course with tiny wireless transponder chips clipped to their shoelaces. The chips are used to track the times of all runners and also to e-mail updates to friends and relatives regarding the runners' location and progress. You can find several articles on this application by searching the Internet using keywords "boston marathon wireless."

Bluetooth and Ultra Wide Band

Shortly after finishing their breakfast in the kitchen, Joseph hears a short beep and notices that a shopping list has been downloaded to his Smartphone from the refrigerator. A computer system installed in the refrigerator door automatically generates a grocery list by scanning the **radio frequency identification device (RFID)** tags attached to almost every product package. RFID tags are small chips containing radio transponders that can be used to track inventory. At predetermined dates and times, the refrigerator computer compares the remaining food items with a list of the minimum allowable quantity of products. The items in short supply get added to the list. As soon as Joseph's Smartphone comes within range, the refrigerator's computer transmits the shopping list to the phone using Bluetooth wireless technology.

Bluetooth and **Ultra Wide Band (UWB)** are wireless standards designed for very short ranges—typically only a few inches or feet. Their purpose is to eliminate cables between devices such as PDAs and computers, allowing for synchronization between printers, mobile telephone headsets, and other devices. Figure 1-2 shows an example of a Bluetooth headset that can be used with mobile phones. Both Bluetooth and UWB communicate using small, low-power transceivers called **radio modules** built onto tiny microprocessor chips. Bluetooth devices use a **link manager**, which is special software that helps identify other Bluetooth devices, creates a link between them, and sends and receives data.

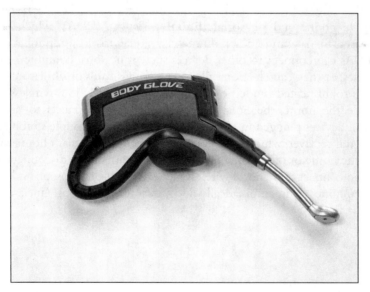

Figure 1-2   A Bluetooth headset

UWB technology is capable of doing everything that Bluetooth can, but it can handle a lot more data at higher speeds. For example, UWB can send CD-quality sound to receivers around the house at the same time that it is sending several other transmissions. Bluetooth has the capacity of transferring a maximum of about 1 Mbps at distances of up to 33 feet (10 meters). UWB can transfer data from 100 Mbps to 2 Gbps at equivalent distances. UWB has a transmit and receive range of up to 150 feet (50 meters), at lower speeds. Bluetooth and UWB can send data through physical barriers, like walls, to one of many different devices all at the same time. These devices don't even have to be aimed at each other. Over 1,500 different computer, telephone, and peripheral vendors have agreed to create products based on the Bluetooth standard.

Joseph and Ann both work for Federated Package Express (FPE), a package delivery service. When a customer wants to send a package, he telephones the local FPE call center. An FPE customer service representative receives the call using her mobile phone and a Bluetooth telephone headset. As the customer service representative walks into her cubicle to answer the phone, several things instantly occur. Her Bluetooth device automatically establishes a connection with the telephone. She can immediately start talking without having to pick up the telephone receiver. In addition, the notebook computer she is carrying automatically synchronizes with her desktop computer. The address list and calendar that she updated last night at home are transmitted to the desktop computer, and the information is immediately refreshed.

In the case of Bluetooth, the automatic connection between various Bluetooth devices creates a **piconet**, also called a **wireless personal area network (WPAN)**. A piconet consists of two or more Bluetooth devices that are exchanging data with each other.

The customer service representative answers the call while she is moving around her cubicle without being tethered by telephone wires. She then sits down and enters the pick-up information on her computer. Figure 1-3 illustrates a Bluetooth wireless network.

Figure 1-3   Bluetooth network (piconet) or WPAN

Bluetooth is named after the 10th century Danish King Harald Bluetooth, who was responsible for unifying Scandinavia.

NOTE

Satellite Networks

FPE's connectivity needs go far beyond the walls of its headquarters building. The company uses a satellite-based wireless network to stay in touch with its delivery vehicles while they are on the road.

After the FPE customer service representative has entered the pick-up information into the computer, the data needs to get to the pick-up driver, in this case, Joseph. FPE's satellite network is responsible for this data transmission. From the customer service rep's computer, the pick-up data is then transmitted to a satellite orbiting the Earth.

In satellite communications, a device called a **repeater** is located in the satellite itself. A repeater simply "repeats" the same signal to another location. An earth station transmits to the satellite at one frequency band, and the satellite regenerates and transmits (repeats) the signal back to Earth on another frequency. The transmission time needed to repeat a signal from one Earth station to another is approximately 250 milliseconds. This relay is illustrated in Figure 1-4.

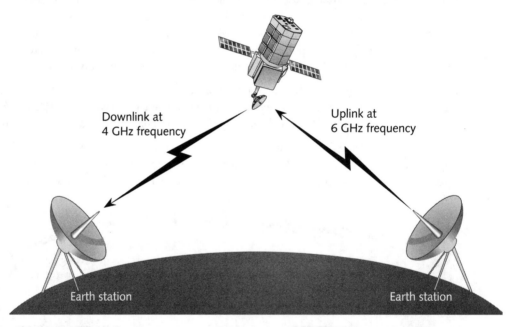

Downlink at
4 GHz frequency

Uplink at
6 GHz frequency

Earth station   Earth station

Figure 1-4   A satellite repeats a signal to another Earth station

Federated Package Express uses a vendor that provides international satellite communications. Although trucking companies have used satellite systems to track the location of fleets of trucks for several years, FPE is one of the first companies to use this system to relay customer data directly to its trucks.

Joseph's FPE delivery truck is equipped with a smart wireless computer terminal that is embedded into the hub of the steering wheel. The satellite transmits the pick-up order to the terminal in Joseph's van. The satellite can also send time-sensitive information, such as route alerts to warn of traffic delays or changes in pick-up schedules. The van's own onboard computer, which monitors engine performance and other vehicle systems, can perform diagnostic checks and transmit the results back to FPE over the satellite connection. The satellite network that FPE uses is illustrated in Figure 1-5.

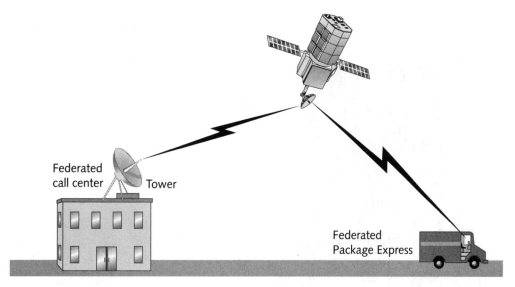

Figure 1-5   Satellite network

The first satellite to orbit Earth successfully was called Sputnik, launched by the Soviet Union in 1957.

NOTE

Cellular Networks

Cellular digital technology provides another link between the various components that make up the FPE package pick-up process. A modern cellular telephone network is built around the concept of low power transmitters with each "cell" handling a number of users. Many transmission towers are then spread throughout a geographical area; the same radio frequency channels can be reused by another tower located a few miles away to avoid interference. This concept maximizes the use of a limited range of frequency channels and is made possible by digital transmission technology. This topic is discussed in detail in Chapter 8, Wireless Wide Area Networks.

As the pick-up order is transmitted through the satellite onto the terminal in the van, Joseph swings onto the highway and reaches the address in about 15 minutes. Joseph leaves the van carrying his Smartphone, shown in Figure 1-6. Joseph walks into the building to retrieve the package. The sender has already filled out a form called a waybill that includes the sender's information as well as the recipient's name, address, and other information. A unique,

12-digit tracking number is printed on the waybill along with a bar code that corresponds to the tracking number. Using the PDA functionality of his Smartphone, which includes a bar code scanner and keyboard, Joseph scans the bar code on the waybill and then types in the destination of the package, the type of service delivery (such as Priority or Standard Overnight), and the delivery deadline. The Smartphone then connects to the van's terminal and prints out a detailed routing label that contains all of this information, which Joseph affixes to the package before placing it in the back of the truck.

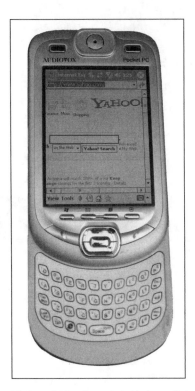

Figure 1-6   Smartphone—cellular telephone and PDA device

The information Joseph enters on his Smartphone is immediately transmitted back to the terminal in his van using wireless digital cellular technology. The data from Joseph's PDA is actually transmitted to a cellular tower, which then retransmits the data back to the van. This technology is based on a standard known as **3G (third generation)** technology, which uses 100% digital transmission for both voice and data.

3G sends data at rates of up to 2 Mbps when stationary, 384 Kbps for slow-moving pedestrians, and up to 144 Kbps from a moving vehicle. 3G is expected to eventually synchronize all of the different digital cellular specifications used around the world into one universal standard. However, 3G may not be widely available in North America yet, so FPE is currently using the interim technology known as **2.5G**, which has a maximum data transmission rate of up to 384 Kbps. A digital cellular network is illustrated in Figure 1-7.

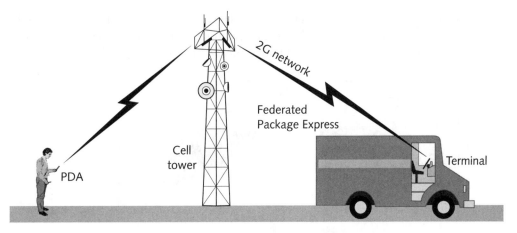

Figure 1-7   Digital cellular network

In a moving automobile, the 3G bandwidth can be 144 Kbps or higher, according to the FCC (Federal Communications Commission).

NOTE

An older generation of cellular technology, called 2G, could transmit data at a maximum rate of about 14.4 Kbps.

NOTE

As Joseph steps into the van, the information from the PDA has been transmitted to the terminal in his vehicle. The package pick-up process repeats until Joseph is ready to return to FPE with a load of packages.

Wireless Local Area Networks

Joseph pulls his van into the FPE distribution warehouse where packages are unloaded and sorted for delivery. The terminal in his van contains a large amount of important data, including shipping receipts and electronic customer signatures for deliveries. As soon as Joseph pulls the van up to the loading dock, the terminal in the van begins communicating with the computer network in the warehouse through a **wireless local area network (WLAN)**. A WLAN is an extension of a wired LAN, connecting to it through a device called a **wireless access point**. The access point (AP) relays data signals between all of the devices in the network, including file servers, printers, and even other access points (and the wireless devices connected to them). Each computer on the WLAN has a wireless network interface card (NIC). This card performs the same basic functions and looks similar to a traditional NIC except that it does not have a cable that connects it to a network jack in the wall. Instead, the wireless NIC has an antenna built into it. The access point is fixed in one place, although it can be moved when necessary, while the computing devices with wireless NICs have the freedom to move around. An access point and wireless NIC are illustrated in Figure 1-8.

Figure 1-8   Access point (upper-left) and wireless NICs

WLANs operate based on networking standards established by the Institute of Electrical and Electronic Engineers (IEEE). The IEEE has published a series of standards, including **IEEE 802.11a**, **IEEE 802.11b**, and **IEEE 802.11g**, which vary in their data transmission speeds and distances. Depending on the standard used, WLANs can transmit at speeds anywhere from 11 Mbps up to 54 Mbps and at distances of up to 375 feet (112 meters). See Table 1-1 later in this chapter for a breakdown of the standards and their capabilities.

Federated Package Express currently uses an 802.11b network and is in the process of updating its WLAN to the higher capacity 802.11a standard. The transmission of data from the van's terminal, which includes all of the important information regarding each pick-up, is completed before the first package is unloaded from Joseph's van. See Figure 1-9.

Joseph's wife Ann, who also works for FPE, uses WLANs at her office too. Ann does not have a desktop computer in her cubicle on which to work. Instead, FPE provides employees with portable notebook computers that they use while traveling, at home, and in the office. None of the notebook computers in the office are connected to the local area network by cables or wires. Instead, a WLAN supplies connectivity between devices.

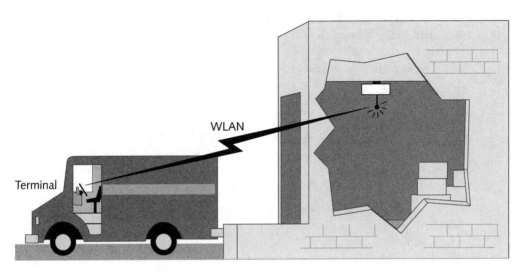

Figure 1-9   Warehouse WLAN

The WLAN provides FPE employees with portability of their various devices. Ann turns on her notebook computer at her desk, and then establishes a connection with the AP. She can now perform any network activity as if she were connected to the network with a cable. She can bring her notebook to a conference room for meetings. Once there, her notebook is still connected to the network, as are the notebooks of the other five staff members in the meeting. Figure 1-10 illustrates the office WLAN.

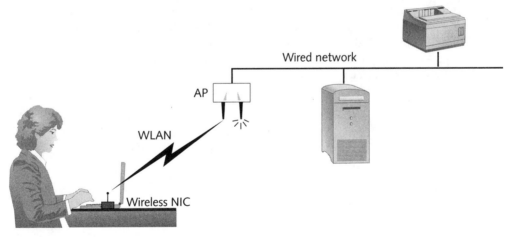

Figure 1-10   Office WLAN

Fixed Broadband Wireless

FPE's offices are spread over three locations: the main office is downtown, the warehouse is in a small industrial park, and the call center is at the edge of town. Through the years FPE has tried a variety of connection types to link the three sites. Initially, FPE used telephone modems, but these soon proved to be too slow. Next, expensive transmission lines were leased from the local telephone company. These **Integrated Services Digital Networks (ISDN)** lines, which transmit at 256 Kbps over regular phone lines, were soon replaced with **T1** lines, which transmit at 1.544 Mbps. However, T1 lines cost several thousand dollars per month. Technologies such as **cable modems**, which use a television cable connection, and **digital subscriber lines (DSL)**, which use special telephone lines, are generally only available in residential areas, and even if they are available, the maximum transmission speed that can be achieved with these technologies is only about 8 Mbps.

Recently, FPE started using a **wireless metropolitan area network (WMAN)**. A single WMAN link covers a distance of up to 35 miles and can be used to carry data, digitized voice, and video signals. WMANs are based on the **IEEE 802.16 Fixed Broadband Wireless** standard and use wireless transmissions for data communications. These networks use small custom antennas on the roof of each building in the WMAN. The signal is transmitted to the antenna of the receiving building, which can be as far as 35 miles (56 kilometers) away. The transmission speed can be as high as 75 Mbps at distances of up to 4 miles (6.4 km), and 17 to 50 Mbps (depending on link quality) at distances over 6 miles (10 km). The use of the antennas substantially reduces the cost over traditional wired connections, which require installation of the infrastructure under city roads, are more prone to damage, and are more expensive to maintain.

NOTE

Spectators can watch live online coverage of the Ironman triathlon, which occurs in various locations and covers a geographical area as large as a city. In some of these events, an IEEE 802.16 WMAN connects cameras along the race route to the competition's Web site and sends several channels of video, allowing enthusiasts to check what is happening at different race checkpoints simultaneously. For more information, read the article at http://www.intel.com/business/casestudies/ironman.pdf.

Federated Package Express has an antenna on each of its three buildings in the area. Once the data from Joseph's van is transmitted to the network in the warehouse, it is then sent to the main office by fixed broadband wireless. This process is illustrated in Figure 1-11.

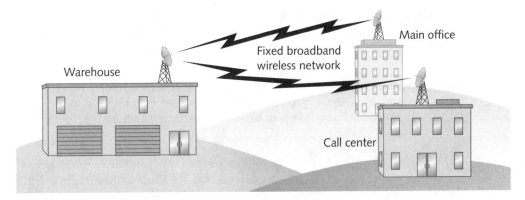

Figure 1-11   IEEE 802.16 Wireless metropolitan area network (WMAN)

Wireless Wide Area Network

Personal computers use Web browsers to display Internet data. Based on user input, a Web browser requests Web pages to be displayed on the user's computer screen. The requested page is transmitted from a file server to the user's Web browser in **Hypertext Markup Language (HTML)**, the standard language for displaying content from the Internet. This model is illustrated in Figure 1-12.

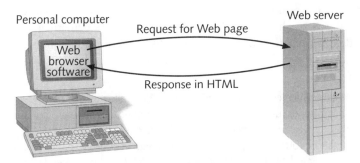

Figure 1-12   Browsing the World Wide Web on a PC

As Joseph's van is unloaded, he takes his afternoon break. Joseph pulls out his Smartphone to surf the Internet. He can do this because his phone includes a **microbrowser**, a miniaturized version of a Web browser program that is based on version 2.0 of the **Wireless Application Protocol (WAP)**. Wireless Application Protocol version 2.0 (**WAP2**) provides a standard way to transmit, format, and display Internet data for small wireless devices such as cell phones.

WAP2 follows the standard Internet model, allowing compatible cellular phones to display Internet content directly. The microbrowser in a WAP2-compatible cell phone is a tiny program much like the browser on a PC, but the Web pages can be reformatted by the microbrowser for cellular phone screens, which usually have much less space. WAP2 is compatible with HTTP, the protocol used by Web server software to format data into Web pages, but it uses an earlier, simpler version (1.1) of HTTP than the current version (4.1) in use by today's full-featured browsers.

NOTE   When a Web server sends a Web page back to a PC, it is sending HTML code and any files (such as graphics) required to assemble the page; the Web browser application program is responsible for interpreting the code and displaying the results on the screen.

Some new cellular phones have capabilities that go far beyond those of devices shipped only a couple of years ago. While these mobile phones are already common in other parts of the world, they are just beginning to appear in North America. These devices can display live television and can also be used for a variety of business applications. Two competing software programming languages—**BREW (Binary Run–Time Environment for Wireless)** and **J2ME (Java 2 Micro Edition)**—are designed and optimized to display text, graphics, and even animations on the small screen of a cellular phone, as seen in Figure 1-13. Business applications, such as Microsoft Excel, can be automatically downloaded to the mobile device or can be available on demand. Using cellular phone technologies, companies can create a **Wireless Wide Area Network (WWAN)** that enables employees to access corporate data and applications from virtually anywhere, across the country, an entire continent or, depending on the technology used, anywhere around the world.

Joseph uses his cell phone to connect to a Web server. The cell phone connects to the nearest cell tower, which connects to the local telephone company, which in turn calls his local Internet provider and completes the connection to the Web server. The contents of the Web page are then sent back to Joseph's phone.

NOTE   A previous version of Wireless Application Protocol (WAP) allowed Web browsing from cellular phones using text only, and it required a gateway server between the Web server and the cellular phone. In the original version of WAP, the text information (but not the images) contained in a Web page was extracted and translated by the WAP gateway (or WAP proxy) server from HTTP into a WAP-specific format called Wireless Markup Language (WML) and broken down into a series of pages called "cards." These cards could be displayed on the small screen of a cellular phone, one at a time. Newer cellular phones with much larger screens and PDAs almost always include browsers that can support HTML code directly, without requiring the use of WAP or WAP2.

Older Wireless Technologies

Before IEEE 802.11 became a standard, various older technologies were introduced by some manufacturers. One of them is outlined below, for historical reasons.

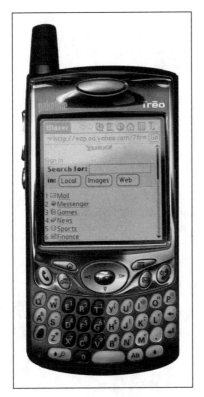

Figure 1-13   Displaying Web content on a Smartphone or cell phone

SWAP and HomeRF

The Shared Wireless Access Protocol (SWAP) defined a set of specifications for wireless data and voice communications around the home. Devices could be as far as 150 feet (45 meters) apart and could send and receive data up to 10 Mbps. The devices that could be part of the network included not only computer equipment but also cordless telephones and home entertainment equipment. SWAP was established by the HomeRF Working Group, which was made up of over 50 different companies from the personal computer, consumer electronics, communications, and software industries. The HomeRF Working Group is no longer in existence due to competition and price reductions in IEEE 802.11 WLAN hardware.

The Wireless Landscape

The Kirkpatricks use wireless technology throughout the day in a variety of ways. Most of the activities in Joe and Ann's typical day could not have been completed—much less attempted—without wireless technology. It's clear that wireless communication is no longer reserved only for high-end users. Instead, it has become a standard means of communication for people in many occupations and circumstances, as illustrated in Figure 1-14. As new wireless communications technologies are introduced, they will become even more integral to our lifestyle and will continue to change how we live. Table 1-1 summarizes these technologies, while Figure 1-15 shows a comparison of their capabilities.

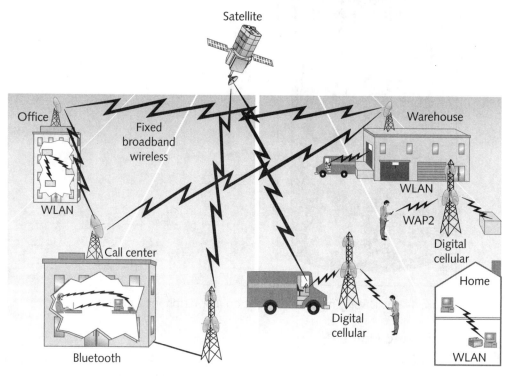

Figure 1-14   Wireless communications

Table 1-1   Wireless data communications technologies

Wireless Technology	Range (Transmission Distance)	Speed
RFID	1 inch (2.5 centimeters) to 300 feet (100 meters) depending on frequency and tag	Usually a few thousand bits-per-second (Kbps)
Bluetooth	33 feet (10 meters)	1 Mbps
UWB	150 feet (50 meters)	100 Mbps
WLAN 802.11b	375 feet (112 meters)	11 Mbps
WLAN 802.11g	300 feet (90 meters)	54 Mbps
WMAN 802.16 WiMax	35 miles (56 kilometers)	75 Mbps
2.5G digital cellular	Nationwide	384 Kbps
3G digital cellular	Nationwide	2 Mbps
Satellite	Worldwide	250 millisecond delay

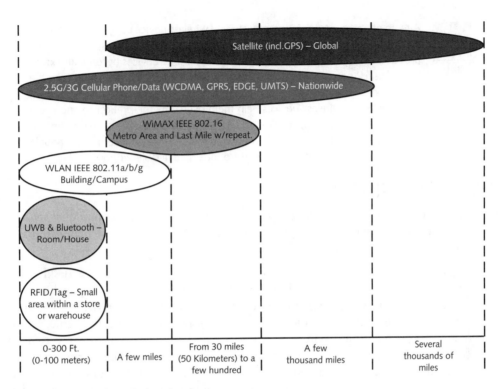

Figure 1-15 The wireless landscape

Just as the number of wireless devices will dramatically increase, so will the number of job opportunities to support this new technology. Professionals such as wireless engineers, wireless local area network managers, and wireless technical support personnel will be needed to build wireless networks and assist wireless users. The job market for these new careers is already exploding.

NOTE Worldwide expansion of wireless has surpassed all expectations. This has made it difficult for market research companies to provide accurate estimates of growth. In areas of central Africa for example, where banking systems and a communications infrastructure practically do not exist, customers do not have a credit history, and the majority of the population survives on less than $1 a day, a cellular phone operator estimated it might have 36,000 customers by the end of one year; it instead had 38,000 subscribers in three weeks.

NOTE
A team of anthropologists recently studied wireless device usage among people around the world. They noted several cultural differences in how wireless products were perceived. In Sweden, wireless phone devices become an extension of users' personalities. In France, users are more concerned about how the phone looks than the underlying technology or what it can do. In Great Britain, shy people find wireless devices help them overcome their reticence and reach out to others. In Japan, wireless usage helps citizens hurdle social barriers, a common issue in that culture. In the United States, there's concern about people suffering from information overload from being available 24 hours a day.

Digital Convergence

Users are constantly demanding more functionality from their computers, and, as a result, wireless devices such as cellular phones, PDAs, and Smartphones are being combined into a single device.

Digital convergence refers to the power of digital devices—such as desktop computers and wireless handhelds—to combine voice, video, and text processing capabilities, as well as to be connected to business and home networks and to the Internet. The same concept applies to development of Voice over IP networks, which use the same protocols and media—both wired and wireless—that once carried only data, to carry two-way voice conversations. Wireless networks play an important part in digital convergence as users demand to be connected to their data and voice networks at all times—wherever they may be. Cellular providers in North America are beginning to introduce TV programming; soon we will have access to on-demand movies from our phones.

Both the recent and short-term future advances in wireless technology and standards discussed in this book will enable an ever-wider range of applications for wireless devices. The day of the single handheld device that incorporates all voice and data communications, in addition to entertainment functions and the ability to make payments and debit directly from a bank or a special account, is not far off.

NOTE
In China, more people are purchasing cellular phones than computers to access the Internet and e-mail, watch news reports, and even enjoy movies.

WIRELESS APPLICATIONS

Almost every type of business needs a computer network, but many are unable to install traditional cabled networks because of the physical limitations of such systems. Wireless networks can go where regular wired networks cannot. Wireless applications—the use of wireless communications technologies in conducting day-to-day business activities—can be found in any industry whose employees need the mobility and freedom to conduct business without being confined to a specific location. Industries and fields such as education, construction, and health care are among those using wireless technologies to make a number of activities occur more quickly and conveniently.

Education

Wireless technology is an ideal application for colleges and schools. An instructor can create a classroom presentation on the notebook computer in his home or school office and then carry that computer right into the classroom. He does not have to plug and unplug cables to attach to the campus network. Instead, the notebook automatically connects to the classroom network as soon as the instructor walks into the room. Teachers can also distribute handouts directly to students who have brought their own wireless devices to class.

The wireless connection also frees students from having to go to a specific computer lab or the library to get on the school's computer network. They can access the school network "wirelessly" from almost any location on campus. As students move to different classrooms in different buildings, they remain connected to the network. Many schools that require students to own a notebook computer are now requiring that those same computers have wireless network connections. This wireless education model makes computing resources available to students from anywhere and at any time.

Wireless technology translates into a cost savings for colleges as well. Traditional classrooms now become fully accessible computer labs without the expense of additional wiring and infrastructure. And colleges no longer have to consider the expense of adding open computer labs for students, since everyone can access the resources from any building on campus, and in some cases even outdoors.

Home Entertainment

Several large computer manufacturers are introducing specialized media PCs that enable movie and audio enthusiasts to download, distribute, and control all forms of digital entertainment from anywhere in the house. These PCs are equipped with wireless net-working software and hardware to simplify processing of sound, video, and pictures. Some of these systems also have the ability to control lights, air conditioners, and other household devices. You can send music, movies, or pictures to a stereo receiver, portable device, or PC located anywhere in the house. Begin watching a movie in the family room, if you wish, then move to the bedroom and finish watching the show from there. You can also download the files to your digital media portable devices, such as MP3 and video players, that can be used while roaming throughout the house.

Health Care

Administering medication in a hospital setting is a major problem area for the health care industry. According to some estimates, incorrectly dispensed medication results in hundreds of thousands of medical emergencies annually. Typically, printouts of prescribed medications are posted at the medication area. As medications are given, they are crossed off the list and initialed. However, since the paper record cannot always be updated immediately, there is a possibility that a patient could get an extra dose of medication before an order for a new or changed medication is processed. This problem also requires duplicate documentation, with nurses first checking the medication printout to determine the medication to be given, then noting on paper that the medication was actually given, and later entering the data into the hospital's database.

Wireless point-of-care computer systems allow medical staff to access and update patient records immediately. Many hospitals are using notebook computers on mobile carts or handheld PDAs with bar code scanners and a wireless connection. Health care professionals can document a patient's medication administration immediately in the computer as they move from room to room without connecting and disconnecting cables. Nurses first identify themselves to the computer system by scanning their own personal bar-coded ID badge. The patient's bar-coded armband is then scanned and all medications that are currently due for that particular patient are brought up on the screen. The medications to be administered are sealed in bar-coded pouches. Nurses scan this bar code before opening the package. An alert immediately appears on the screen if the wrong medication or incorrect amount is identified. After administration, the nurse indicates through the wireless network that the medication has been given, essentially electronically signing the distribution form. A hard copy can be printed out as needed.

The system immediately verifies that medication is being administered to the correct patient in the correct dosage, which eliminates potential errors and documentation inefficiencies. The documentation process now takes place at the bedside where care is delivered, which improves accuracy. In addition, all hospital personnel now have real-time access to the latest medication and patient status information.

NOTE
Select medical groups are now beginning to provide their physicians with a PDA, printer, and prescription-writing software. This technology is intended to reduce errors associated with illegible handwritten prescriptions.

Even telephones are now being connected to hospital IEEE 802.11 WLANs, employing VoIP technology. Doctors and nurses no longer have to be paged over the PA system, or be in an office or nursing station to be contacted by phone or access information regarding lab results for patients. Doctors can also consult with specialists while at a patient's bedside—and the specialists can be more easily reached, no matter where they are in the hospital. Cellular phones cannot be used in health care facilities, but handsets that can connect to an IEEE 802.11 WLAN and use VoIP are allowed and are making hospitals far more efficient.

Government

The city of Corpus Christi, Texas is deploying a broadband wireless network that lets city employees and contractors at remote sites access data stored in a central database. For example, building inspectors can update permit data while at the construction site. City employees can locate and monitor municipal vehicles anywhere in the 147-square mile network, helping the city to dispatch work crews to problem sites more efficiently. Police officers can both download and upload streaming video to help them fight crime.

Allegany County in western Maryland has been reaping the benefits of an IEEE 802.16 network since before the 802.16 standards were ratified. The county's $4.7 million AllCo-Net2 project uses 16 radio towers configured in a ring to deliver broadband connectivity to schools, libraries, and government buildings. A few Internet service providers resell excess capacity of the county's broadband network at a reduced rate to commercial users, which stimulates economic development in the region.

Many other cities use wireless technology to provide free Internet access to residents and to attract visitors and businesspeople. The city of Fredericton in the province of New Brunswick, Canada deployed a system that covers the entire downtown business district and uses a mix of technologies; IEEE 802.16 wireless broadband connects all the major points and IEEE 802.11 is available in the major downtown streets as well as in restaurants, bars, and many other retail businesses. These options provide residents with free Internet access from notebook computers and PDAs. The city recently won a major award for innovation as a result of this project. The city of Hamilton in Ontario, Canada uses an IEEE 802.11 network to read smart electrical meters. These meters monitor business and residential hourly electricity consumption and report back to the city's utilities commission.

Military

The U.S. military has created a Universal Handset, a 1.5-pound device that will be delivered to over 300,000 soldiers. It allows military personnel in the field to communicate through a variety of methods using wireless technologies. Using cellular and satellite communications, soldiers can talk, access the Internet, and receive full-motion video through their Universal Handset. Military personnel can also connect with other wireless devices using the Bluetooth wireless protocol, or to a WLAN using the IEEE 802.11b standard. The military is currently working on preventing enemies from eavesdropping on or jamming the signal.

Office Environments

Thanks to wireless technologies, employees in all lines of work no longer have to be away from the data they need to help them make decisions. In addition to the accessibility of networked data, wireless technologies allow businesses to create an office where the traditional infrastructure doesn't already exist. Typically, an office space must be wired with computer cables for network connections and telephone wires for telephones. With wireless technologies such as WLAN and Bluetooth, that expensive cabling infrastructure is no longer necessary. This means that an office can be created in a very short period of time with minimum expense. For example, a hotel conference room that may not have the infrastructure to support a wired network can quickly be turned into a wireless networked office environment. During office renovations or reorganization, employees can move to another location in the building and be connected immediately, also saving businesses the expense of rewiring the entire office.

Event Management

Managing spectators attending a sporting event or concert can be a daunting task. Each attendee has a ticket, and there are special passes for the press and team officials. However, tickets can be lost, stolen, or counterfeited. Attempting to identify a stolen or counterfeit ticket as thousands of spectators are waiting to be admitted has until now been almost impossible. But several large arenas and stadiums are now turning to wireless systems to facilitate this process.

Event tickets are printed with a unique bar code that is then scanned at the venue's point of entry using handheld or integrated turnstile hardware, which is connected to a wireless network. The network instantly validates the ticket and then sends a signal back to the turnstile that either permits or prohibits the entry of the patron into the arena. This check prevents the use of counterfeit tickets, and it also can be used to identify stolen tickets.

The wireless point-of-entry turnstiles can also give a real-time look at traffic flow, helping a venue more effectively manage its staff and determine where additional people are needed. Data about who is entering at which gate can even be used by advertisers to tailor their marketing efforts.

In addition, wireless technologies are changing the entertainment experience itself. In several major stadiums, wireless transmissions of in-progress game statistics are available to any fan in the stadium with a wireless device such as a notebook computer or PDA. Fans can also view instant replays of the event they are attending or watch replays from other games around the country. In the Arizona Cardinals' football stadium, fans can use their wireless devices to play fantasy football or order concessions and have them delivered to their seats.

Travel

Because wireless technology creates mobility, the travel industry was one of the first to embrace wireless technologies. Wireless global positioning systems (GPS) that tie into emergency roadside assistance services have become standard features on many automobiles sold today. **Satellite radio** transmission of over 150 music and talk stations solves the problem of losing a station outside of its transmission range. Satellite radio is a subscription service, meaning that users pay a monthly fee for the privilege of listening to the stations without any commercial advertising interruptions.

Airport terminals are likewise turning to wireless technologies. Most large airport terminals in North America transmit wireless signals that passengers can pick up on their wireless notebook computers or PDAs while waiting for their flights. For a nominal fee, they can also surf the Internet or read e-mail.

Even the airplanes themselves are being equipped with wireless data access. Several large airlines, including Lufthansa, Scandinavian Airlines System, Singapore Airlines, China Airlines, Korean Air, and many others, are offering wireless Internet capabilities to passengers on flights. Like their Earth-bound counterparts, these passengers can access the Internet or view their corporate data from their seats, while in flight. Although demand for this technology is high in North America, U.S. airlines have been slow to implement this capability.

Construction

Although at first glance the construction industry may not seem to be a prime candidate for wireless technologies, in reality it benefits greatly. One challenge for builders is that each construction phase must be completed before the next can begin. For example, if the concrete footings for a new building cannot be poured, then the entire project must be put on hold. This series of events often means idle construction employees and last-minute schedule adjustments. Information from the job site, such as a tardy subcontractor or a problem with materials, could be relayed back to the main office for rescheduling of workers to other sites to prevent idle time.

Because foremen are often at multiple sites during a day's work, filing daily payroll paperwork can be a challenge. Payroll clerks often wrestle with scrawled or illegible notes and are unable to contact the foreman on the job for clarification. The paperwork problems can be eliminated when foremen enter time sheet information on a notebook computer and transmit it to the main office.

Construction equipment such as bulldozers and earth graders also participate in wireless networks by being fitted with wireless terminals, turning them into "smart" equipment. A global positioning system on a bulldozer can provide location information accurate to within feet. The exact location of the dig coordinates can be transmitted to a terminal on the bulldozer, which displays a color-coded map to guide the operator as it digs. Smart equipment can be connected through wireless transmissions back to the home office, which tracks engine hours and equipment location. Wireless terminals in the engine's diagnostic system can send an alert when the oil needs to be changed or other maintenance operations are due.

Warehouse Management

Managing a warehouse stocked with inventory can be a nightmare. New products arrive continually and must be inventoried and stored. When products are shipped out of the warehouse, they must be located and then transferred to the correct loading dock so they can be placed on the right truck. Then, employees must update the stock database to reflect the outgoing shipment. A mistake in any one of these steps can result in a warehouse stocked with products that it cannot locate, irate customers receiving the wrong items, or a store running out of goods to sell.

Implementing wireless technology is key for many warehouse operations. By equipping all of the warehouse's machinery and personnel with wireless networking devices, managers can use warehouse management system (WMS) software to manage all of the activities from receiving through shipping. And since this network is tied into the front office computer system, managers can have statistics that are always current.

Pallet loads arriving from locations outside the receiving warehouse come with bar-coded pallet labels. The bar coding includes product identification numbers, product code dates or expiration dates, originating plants and lines of manufacture, and sequentially assigned serial numbers. As pallets arrive, a forklift operator scans the bar code label with his portable wireless device. This device sends the data to the wireless network, where the warehouse software immediately designates a storage location for the pallet and relays the information back to the computer on the forklift. A warehouse employee prints out a bar code and affixes it to the pallet. The forklift operator then transports the pallet to the designated storage location. A bar code label suspended from the ceiling for floor locations or attached to a rack face identifies every storage location. The operator scans that bar code to confirm that the pallets are being put in the correct location before depositing the load.

In the front office, orders for merchandise to ship out are received and entered into the computer that connects to the WLAN in the warehouse. The WMS software manages order picking, balances workloads, and selects pick sequences for forklift operators. The dock control module of the WMS then releases orders for picking. A forklift operator locates the correct storage location, scans the bar code of the pallet, and then ferries it to the shipping dock to be loaded onto a truck.

In the near future, most of the bar code functions, including inventory counting, will be replaced by RFID tags, avoiding the need for printing and affixing labels. Many large retailers already have instructed their suppliers to implement RFID in all the products they purchase. Some highly sophisticated warehouses are operating with fully automated pallet machines and forklifts that can process the storing and retrieving of products completely without human intervention.

Environmental Research

One of the most challenging aspects of documenting outdoor research while in the field is that it is difficult and dangerous to extend long cables or install heavy equipment inside deep caves or on mountaintops. Scientists are now using small, battery- or solar-cell-powered WLAN sensors in places that were previously difficult to access and monitor. For example, transmitter-equipped sensors located at the tops of tall trees monitor the effects that ultraviolet rays are having on our forests due to the holes in the ozone layer. The computer equipment that records the sensor readings can be installed in a much more accessible location nearby, along with large, heavy batteries or generators, and can communicate with the sensors using wireless technology. This capability has proven to be a major breakthrough

1

in many different scientific fields and helped collect data that, until recently, was very difficult—if not impossible—to record.

Industrial Control

Because of their size and complexity, large manufacturing facilities, such as automotive assembly plants, find that it is often impossible to install a full-featured network using very long cables. If machines need to be monitored, it can take hours or even days for a technician to access every machine and record or download the status of each piece of equipment. Wireless networking can solve that problem. Remote sensors called **motes** can connect to a WLAN, then collect data and transmit it to a central location. Manufacturing managers can monitor their equipment from an office, detecting problems instantly. Technicians in a control room can monitor the status of every machine or device and dispatch a technician to perform work on the equipment when necessary.

WIRELESS ADVANTAGES AND DISADVANTAGES

As with any new technology, wireless communications offers both advantages and disadvantages.

Advantages of Wireless Networking

There are many advantages to using wireless technology compared to wired networks. These include mobility, ease of installation and lower cost, increased reliability, and more rapid disaster recovery.

Mobility

The freedom to move about without being tethered by wires is certainly the primary advantage of a wireless network. Mobility enables users to stay connected to the network no matter where they go within the network's range. Many occupations that require workers to be mobile instead of tied to a desk, such as police officers and inventory clerks, are finding that wireless communications are becoming vital.

Wireless technology is also permitting many industries to shift toward an increasingly mobile workforce. Many employees spend large portions of their time away from a desk—whether they are in meetings, working on a hospital floor, or conducting research. Notebook computers and other portable devices allow these employees added convenience; however, immediate access to the company network is an even greater convenience. WLANs fit well in this work environment, giving mobile workers the freedom they require but still allowing them to access the network resources that they need.

Another characteristic of the business world of today is "flatter" organizations, meaning there are fewer management levels between top executives and other workers. Much work is done in teams that cross functional and organizational boundaries, requiring many team meetings away from individuals' desks. The need for immediate access to network resources exists even while these meetings are taking place. WLANs are again the solution to the problem. They give team-based workers the ability to access the network resources that they need while collaborating in a team environment.

Easier and Less Expensive Installation

Installing network cabling in older buildings can be a difficult, slow, and costly task. Facilities constructed prior to the mid-1980s were built without any thought given to running computer wiring in each room. Thick masonry walls and plaster ceilings are difficult (and messy and loud) to drill holes through and snake cabling around. Sometimes an older building may have asbestos—a potentially carcinogenic insulation material—that would first have to be completely removed before cabling could be installed. And often restrictions exist on modifying older facilities that have historical value.

In all these instances a wireless LAN is the ideal solution. Historical buildings would be preserved, harmful asbestos would not be disturbed, and difficult drilling could be avoided by using a wireless system. And of course, eliminating the need to install cabling results in a significant cost savings.

Wireless networks also make it easier for any office—in either an old or new building—to be modified with new cubicles or furniture. No longer does the design for a remodeled office first have to consider the location of the computer jack in the wall when relocating furniture. Instead, the focus can be on creating the most effective work environment for the employees.

Also, the time required to install network cabling is generally significant. Installers must pull wires through the ceiling and then drop cables down walls to network outlets. This can take days or even weeks to complete. During that time, employees must somehow continue their work in the midst of the construction zone, which is often difficult to do. Using a wireless LAN eliminates such disruption.

Increased Reliability

Network cable failures may be the most common source of network problems. Moisture from a leak during a thunderstorm or a coffee spill can erode metallic conductors. A user who shifts the computer on her desk may break the network connection. A cable splice that is done incorrectly can cause problems that result in unexplainable errors and are very difficult to identify. Using wireless technology eliminates these types of cable failures and increases the overall reliability of the network.

Disaster Recovery

Accidents happen every day: fires, tornados, and floods can occur with little, if any, warning. Any organization that is not prepared to recover from such disasters will find itself quickly out of business. A documented disaster recovery plan is vital to every business if it is to get back to work quickly after a calamity.

Because the computer network is such a vital part of the daily operation of a business, the ability to have the network up and working after a disaster is critical. Many businesses are turning to WLANs as a major piece of their disaster recovery plans. Savvy planners keep laptop computers with wireless NICs and access points in reserve along with backup network servers. Then, in the event of a disaster, managers can quickly relocate the office, without needing to find a new facility with network wiring. Instead, the network servers are installed in the building along with the access points, and the laptop computers are distributed to the resettled employees.

Disadvantages of Wireless Networking

Along with the many advantages of wireless technology, there are likewise disadvantages and concerns, including radio signal interference, security issues, and health risks.

Radio Signal Interference

Because wireless devices operate using radio signals, the potential for two types of signal interference exists. Signals from other devices can disrupt what a wireless device is trying to transmit, or a wireless device may itself be a source of interference for other devices.

Several common office devices transmit radio signals that may interfere with a WLAN. These devices include microwave ovens, elevator motors, and other heavy electrical equipment, such as manufacturing machines, photocopiers, certain types of outdoor lighting systems, theft protection systems, and cordless telephones. These may cause errors to occur in the transmission between a wireless device and an access point. In addition, Bluetooth and WLAN 802.11b/g devices both operate in the same radio frequency, potentially resulting in interference between such devices.

Interference is nothing new for a computer data network. Even when using cables to connect network devices, interference from fluorescent light fixtures and electric motors can sometimes disrupt the transmission of data. The solution for wireless devices is the same as that for standard cabled network devices: locate the source of the interference and eliminate it. This usually is solved by moving a photocopier or microwave oven across the room or to another room. In addition, many wireless devices can identify that an error has occurred in the transmission and retransmit the data as necessary.

 Outside interference from AM or FM radio stations, TV broadcast stations, or other large-scale transmitters does not occur since these stations and WLANs operate at different frequencies and power levels.

NOTE

Security

Because a wireless device transmits radio signals over a broad area, security becomes a major concern. It is possible for an intruder to be lurking outdoors with a notebook computer and wireless NIC with the intent of intercepting the signals from a nearby wireless network.

Because much of a business' network traffic may contain sensitive information, this is a real concern for many users.

However, some wireless technologies can provide added levels of security. A special coded number can be programmed into every authorized wireless device, and the device must transmit the special number prior to gaining access to the network; otherwise it is denied access. Network managers can also limit access to a wireless network by programming it with a list of approved wireless devices. Only those devices on the list will be allowed access. As a further protection, data transmitted between the access point and the wireless device can also be encrypted or encoded in such a way that only the recipient can decode the message. If an unauthorized user were to intercept the radio signals being transmitted, he or she could not read the messages being sent.

Health Risks

Wireless devices contain radio transmitters and receivers that emit radio frequency (RF) energy. Typically, these wireless devices emit low levels of RF while being used. Scientists know that high levels of RF can produce biological damage through heating effects (this is how a microwave oven is able to cook food). However, it is not known if lower levels of RF can cause adverse health effects. Although some research has been done to address these questions, no clear picture of the biological effects of this type of radiation has emerged to date.

 NOTE   Most wireless devices also emit very low levels of RF energy when in the stand-by mode. However, these levels are considered insignificant and do not appear to have health consequences.

In the United States, the Food and Drug Administration (FDA) and the Federal Communications Commission (FCC) set policies and procedures for some wireless devices, such as cellular telephones. The latest FDA update stated that "the available science does not allow us to conclude that (wireless devices) are absolutely safe, or that they are unsafe." However, the report went on to say that "the available scientific evidence does not demonstrate any adverse health effects associated with the use of (wireless devices)." At the present time, no scientific studies have revealed health problems associated with the absorption of low-level RF energy by the human body.

The FCC and FDA, along with the Environmental Protection Agency (EPA), established RF exposure safety guidelines for wireless phones in 1996. Before a wireless phone is available for sale to the public, it must be tested by the manufacturer and certified that it does not exceed specific limits. One of the limits is expressed as a Specific Absorption Rate (SAR). SAR relates to the measurement of the rate of absorption of RF energy by a wireless phone user. The FCC requires that the SAR of handheld wireless phones not exceed 1.6 watts per kilogram, averaged over 1 gram of tissue.

NOTE

Questions exist regarding the safety of handheld cellular phones, the kind with a built-in antenna that is positioned close to the user's head during normal telephone conversation. These types of mobile phones are of concern because of the short distance between the phone's antenna—the primary source of the RF—and the person's head. The safety of "cordless phones," which have a base unit connected to the telephone wiring in a house and which operate at far lower power levels and frequencies, has not been questioned.

Thus, the available science does not permit a conclusion either way about the safety of wireless mobile devices. However, no proof exists to demonstrate any adverse health effects associated with the use of mobile wireless devices. Although there is no evidence regarding any health risks associated with using any wireless device, it is always wise to be aware of the concern and to monitor ongoing scientific research.

CHAPTER SUMMARY

- ❑ Wireless communications have become commonplace today and are becoming the standard in the business world. Remote wireless Internet connections and entire wireless computer networks are making many network-based business activities faster and more convenient.

- ❑ Wireless networks and devices are found in all circles of life today. Home users can implement wireless local area networks (WLANs) to connect different devices, while Bluetooth and UWB can connect devices over short distances. The WAP2 protocol is used along with programming languages such as BREW and J2ME to access Web sites and private networks from cellular phones. WLANs are also becoming a fixture of business networks. Fixed broadband wireless is used to transmit data at distances up to 35 miles (56 kilometers), while satellite transmissions can send data around the world. Digital cellular networks are used to transmit data at up to 2 Mbps.

- ❑ Wireless wide area networks will enable companies of all sizes to interconnect their offices without the high cost charged by telephone carriers for their landline connections.

- ❑ WLAN applications are found in a wide variety of industries and organizations, including the military, education, business, entertainment, travel, construction, warehouse management, and health care.

- ❑ Remote sensors capable of communicating using wireless technologies are used in large manufacturing facilities to monitor equipment and for scientific research.

- ❑ Mobility, or the freedom to move without being connected to the network by a cable, is the primary advantage of a WLAN. Other advantages include easier and less expensive installation, increased network reliability, and support for disaster recovery.

- ❑ Radio signal interference, security issues, and health risks are all potential disadvantages of WLANs.

KEY TERMS

2.5G — A digital cellular technology that sends data at a maximum of 384 Kbps.

3G (third generation) — A digital cellular technology that sends data at up to 2 Mbps and is expected to synchronize all of the different specifications used around the world into one universal standard.

Bluetooth — A wireless standard that enables devices to transmit data at up to 1 Mbps over a maximum distance of 33 feet.

BREW (Binary Run-Time Environment for Wireless) — A programming language used to display text, graphics, and animations on cellular telephone screens.

cable modems — A technology used to transmit data over a television cable connection.

digital convergence — The power of digital devices, such as desktop computers and wireless handhelds, to combine voice, video, and text-processing capabilities, as well as to be connected to business and home networks and to the Internet.

digital subscriber lines (DSL) — A technology used to transmit data over a telephone line.

Hypertext Markup Language (HTML) — The standard language for displaying Web pages.

IEEE 802.11a/b/g standards — A group of standards developed by the Institute of Electrical and Electronic Engineers that allows WLAN computers to transmit data at speeds ranging from 1 Mbps to a maximum of 54 Mbps. 802.11a transmits at 1 or 2 Mbps; 802.11b at up to 11 Mbps; 802.11g at 54 Mbps. These transmit in the 2.4 GHz unlicensed frequency band. 802.11a also transmits at up to 54 Mbps but in the less crowded frequency band of 5 GHz.

IEEE 802.16 Fixed Broadband Wireless — A set of standards, some established and some still under development, for fixed and mobile broadband wireless communications that allows computers to communicate at up to 75 Mbps and at distances of up to 35 miles (56 km) in a point-to-point configuration. This group of standards also allows the use of both licensed and unlicensed frequencies.

Integrated Services Digital Networks (ISDN) — A technology that transmits data over telephone lines at a maximum of 256 Kbps.

J2ME (Java 2 Micro Edition) — A variation of the Java programming language designed for use in portable devices such as PDAs and cellular phones.

link manager — Special software in Bluetooth devices that helps identify other Bluetooth devices, creates the links between them, and sends and receives data.

microbrowser — A tiny browser program that runs on a WAP or WAP2 cell phone.

motes — Remote sensors used for collecting data from manufacturing equipment or for scientific research that can communicate using wireless technology.

personal digital assistant (PDA) — A handheld computer device used for taking notes, making appointments, creating to-do lists, and communicating with other devices.

piconet — A small network composed of two or more Bluetooth devices that are exchanging data with each other.

radio frequency identification device (RFID) — A small tag placed on product packaging and boxes that can be remotely activated and read by remote sensors. The data about the product is then transferred directly to an information-processing system for inventory control, location, and counting.

radio modules — Small radio transceivers built onto microprocessor chips that are embedded into Bluetooth devices and enable them to communicate.

repeater — A device commonly used in satellite communications that simply "repeats" the signal to another location.

satellite radio — A pay-for-service high-quality radio broadcast system that transmits digital programming directly from satellites to a network of ground-based repeaters and that holds the signal regardless of the listener's location.

Smartphone — A device that combines a cellular phone with the capabilities of a personal digital assistant (PDA). These devices provide the user with the ability to enter appointments in a calendar, write notes, send and receive e-mail, and browse Web sites, among other functions.

T1 — A technology to transmit data over special telephone lines at 1.544 Mbps.

Ultra Wide Band (UWB) — A wireless communications technology that allows devices to transmit data at hundreds of megabits per second at short distances (up to a few feet) and at up to 150 feet (50 meters) at lower speeds.

Voice over Internet Protocol (VoIP) — A technology that allows voice telephone calls to be carried over the same network used to carry computer data.

wireless access point (access point or AP) — A device that receives and transmits signals back to wireless network interface cards.

Wireless Application Protocol (WAP or WAP2) — A standard for transmitting, formatting, and displaying Internet data on cellular phones. WAP can display only text. WAP2 supports HTML and can display color and pictures.

wireless communications — The transmission of user data without the use of wires between devices.

wireless local area network (WLAN) — A local area network that is not connected by wires but instead uses wireless technology. Its range extends to approximately 100 meters and has a maximum data rate of 54 Mbps, by current standards. Today's WLANs are based on IEEE 802.11a/b/g standards.

wireless metropolitan area network (WMAN) — A wireless network that covers a large geographical area such as a city or suburb. The technology is usually based on the IEEE 802.16 set of standards, and can span an entire city, covering distances of up to 35 miles (56 km) between transmitters and receivers or repeaters.

wireless network interface card (wireless NIC) — A device that connects to a PC to transmit and receive network data over radio waves. It includes an antenna for wireless communication between networked devices.

wireless personal area network (WPAN) — A very small network that typically extends to 33 feet (10 meters) or less. Due to their limited range, WPAN technology is used mainly as a replacement for cables. *See also* piconet and UWB.

wireless wide area network (WWAN) — A WAN that uses cellular phone technologies and encompasses any geographical region, including the entire globe.

REVIEW QUESTIONS

1. Ultra Wide Band technology is used primarily for _____ .
   a. displaying Web pages on a cellular phone
   b. connecting devices inside the home at very high speeds
   c. finding the location of a car within a city
   d. transmitting data at distances of up to 35 miles

2. Bluetooth devices communicate using small radio transceivers called _____ that are built onto microprocessor chips.
   a. receivers
   b. transponders
   c. radio modules
   d. link managers

3. _____ provides a standard way to transmit, format, and display Internet data on cell phones.
   a. WLAN
   b. WAP
   c. HTML
   d. WML

4. IEEE 802.11g devices can be as far as 300 feet apart and can send and receive data at rates up to _____ million bits per second (Mbps).
   a. 75
   b. 10
   c. 100
   d. 54

5. Each Bluetooth device uses a _____ , which is special software that helps identify other Bluetooth devices.
   a. frame
   b. link manager
   c. repeater
   d. bridge

6. Bluetooth can send data through physical barriers, like walls. True or False?

7. A Bluetooth device can transmit data at up to 1 Mbps over a distance of 33 feet (10 meters). True or False?

8. A wireless network interface card performs basically the same functions and looks identical to a traditional network interface card (NIC) card. True or False?

9. An earth station transmits to a satellite at one frequency, and the satellite regenerates and transmits the signal back to earth at another frequency. True or False?

10. Eliminating installation costs is a disadvantage of a WLAN. True or False?

11. The automatic connection between various Bluetooth devices creates a network called a(n) _____ .

12. The new third generation (3G) cellular technology will allow data to be transmitted at a maximum speed of up to _____ Mbps.

13. The wireless NIC sends its signals through invisible radio waves to a(n) _____ .

14. _____ uses wireless transmissions for data communications as much as 35 miles apart.

15. "WAP" stands for _____ Application Protocol.

16. Explain the role of an access point in a WLAN.

17. Explain how a WAP cell phone works to send and receive Internet data.

18. Explain how a WLAN can be used in a classroom.

19. Describe how wireless networks can reduce installation time.

20. Explain how implementing a wireless network can be helpful in case of disaster recovery.

HANDS-ON PROJECTS

Project 1-1

Write a one-page paper outlining the differences and similarities between UWB and Bluetooth. Use the Internet as well as material from UWB and Bluetooth forums and vendors. Include their advantages and disadvantages. When would you use UWB instead of Bluetooth, and vice versa? What limitations have kept Bluetooth from gaining more market share? In your opinion, will UWB ever replace IEEE 802.11b WLANs? Explain your position.

Project 1-2

Research the differences between BREW and J2ME. How are they similar? How are they different? What types of mobile phones are available that can display Web pages? Write a one-page paper on your findings and provide examples or links from manufacturer Web pages. Be sure to include phones that have PDA capabilities as well as some that don't.

Project 1-3

Use local news services on the Internet to locate a school, hospital, manufacturing plant, warehouse, or other business that is switching to wireless devices. Interview appropriate people to determine why they are making the change. Ask what benefits and drawbacks they considered. Write a one-page paper on your findings.

Project 1-4

Because a wireless device transmits radio signals over a broad area, security becomes a major concern. What are the security concerns with using a WLAN? Why are some experts claiming that the security built into an IEEE 802.11b WLAN is insufficient? What other security options are available? Write a one-page paper that addresses these concerns. Use the Internet and information from hardware and security vendors as additional resources.

Project 1-5

Using the Internet, find the latest information about health concerns using wireless technologies. What studies are currently under way? What issues are of concern? What are the official positions of the FCC, the FDA, and the EPA? Write a one-page paper about your findings.

CASE PROJECT

Project 1-1

You are employed by The Baypoint Group (TBG), a company of 50 consultants that assists organizations and businesses with issues involving network planning, design, implementation, and problem solving. You have recently been hired by TBG to work with one of their new clients, Vincent Medical Center (VMC), a large health care facility, concerning their wireless needs.

Each day, VMC doctors and nurses throughout the facility attend to thousands of patients, update medical records, issue prescriptions, and order medical exams. VMC deployed a sophisticated suite of medical software that stores all patient records, exam results, and diagnoses. The system is also fully integrated with VMC's pharmacy and can process purchase orders, payments, and receipts as well as inventory and shipments. However, all data entry and processing currently requires that a staff member be at a nursing station or office to access the application and central VMC database.

1. VMC is interested in learning about the possibilities of upgrading all of its infrastructure and deploying a wireless network to allow doctors, nurses, and all staff to access information from anywhere within the entire medical facility (two buildings). VMC does not want to spend money installing additional network cabling connections to every patient room. VMC has asked you to make a presentation to its administrator

regarding the use of a WLAN. Create a presentation to deliver to the staff about WLANs. Be sure to cover the following points:

- Greater mobility for doctors and nurses

- Ease and cost of installation

- Easier network modifications

- Increased network reliability

- Radio signal interference

- Security

2. The physicians and nurses at the facility are concerned about the potential health impact that the wireless equipment may have on themselves as well as on the patients. In addition, VMC would like to know about potential interference that medical equipment such as X-ray machines and CT and MRI scanners might cause on the WLAN. Prepare a report addressing their concerns that you will present to the hospital administrators.

3. After your presentation, the physicians and nurses seem very interested in the potential of the WLAN. However, VMC also has an outdated telephone system that provides mobile cordless handsets but is no longer supported by the manufacturer. Without the ability to use voice communications from anywhere in the facility, the staff cannot see how a wireless network alone will solve their dilemma. Create a presentation that expands on your first one and proposes a solution to VMC.

4. While some doctors have notebook computers already equipped with wireless NICs, VMC is also interested in providing other staff members with portable data communication equipment, but at a lower cost than notebooks. The devices should be able to transmit prescriptions directly to the central system. The pharmacy would then deliver medications to patients right away. VMC would also like to be able to check on the status of these pharmacy orders. VMC administrators have asked your opinion regarding using cellular telephones or wireless PDAs and have told you that their software can handle these requirements through a Web server or using an application called DrugMagnet that runs on PDAs. Prepare to present your recommendations to VMC's management team.

OPTIONAL TEAM CASE PROJECT

A syndicated magazine is writing an article about Bluetooth technology and has asked The Baypoint Group for information. Form a team of or three or four consultants and research Bluetooth technology. Focus on the future of Bluetooth. Provide information regarding its problems and concerns by some vendors. Also provide estimates regarding how you envision Bluetooth or any other proposed technology will be used in home, office, and personal applications.

2

WIRELESS DATA TRANSMISSION

> **After reading this chapter and completing the exercises, you will be able to:**
>
> ◆ Explain how network data is represented using binary notation
> ◆ List and explain the two types of wireless transmission
> ◆ Illustrate the basic concepts and techniques through which data can be transmitted by radio waves

Consider the wireless cellular telephone that may be in your pocket or on your desk. If you were to take that telephone apart, you would find an array of pieces: a microphone, a loudspeaker, resistors, capacitors, and a variety of other parts. Yet much more than that single telephone is needed to complete a call. Some of the other elements involved are the cellular towers, the equipment that manages your call as you move from one cell to another, and all the equipment at the telephone company's central office that directs your call to the correct recipient. Moreover, suppose you were calling someone overseas—additional equipment, such as satellites or underwater cables, might be used to complete the international connection.

The number of parts that make up a modern communications system is truly mind-boggling. Making sense of it all can often be confusing simply because of the sheer number of components that are involved. How can we begin to understand how it all works?

One approach is the *bottom-up* method. This approach looks first at the individual elements or components that make up a system, and then it ties them all together to show how the system works. This chapter uses the bottom-up approach to set the foundation for our exploration of wireless communications and networks. You will apply the concepts covered in Chapter 2 to more specific technologies discussed in later chapters. First, you will learn how data is represented. Then, you will see how the various types of wireless signals are used to transmit data. Finally, we'll delve a little deeper into how radio data is transmitted.

How Data Is Represented

When exploring wireless data communications, a good first step is to understand how the data itself is represented in digital form. Digital data for wireless communications is represented in the same way as standard computer data, using the two binary digits 0 and 1.

The Decimal Number System

Before getting into the binary system, it is helpful to review how numbers are represented as we know them in the decimal system.

Consider the number 639. This number can be defined as follows:

6	3	9
100s	10s	1s

or

6 x 100 + 3 x 10 + 9 x 1 = 639

The number 639 is six 100s plus three 10s plus nine 1s. This way of representing numbers is based on the **decimal** or **Base 10 number system**. It's known as the Base 10 because there are 10 different symbols that are used to represent each digit: 0, 1, 2, 3, 4, 5, 6, 7, 8, and 9; this means that with a single digit we can represent any value from zero to nine. The rightmost column is the units (10^0 or 1s) position, the next column to the left is the tens (10^1 or 10s) position, the next is the hundreds (10^2 or 100s) position, and so on. Take a look again at the representation of the number 639:

10^2	10^1	10^0
6	3	9
(100s)	(10s)	(1s)

$6 \times 10^2\text{s} + 3 \times 10^1\text{s} + 9 \times 10^0\text{s} = 639$

Whenever more than nine units need to be represented, the number in the second rightmost column (to the left of the units) is increased by one and the symbol in the units column goes back to zero (0). Now with two digits and the 10 symbols available for use in each position, we can represent values up to 99. If you add 1 to 639, the next higher number is represented as follows:

10^2	10^1	10^0
6	4	0
(100s)	(10s)	(1s)

$6 \times 10^2\text{s} + 4 \times 10^1\text{s} + 0 \times 10^0\text{s} = 640$

No additional symbols (beyond 0-9) are needed to represent any number in decimal.

This is pretty basic information, but it shows how suitable the decimal number system is for humans to use (because humans have 10 fingers for counting that correspond to the base number of 10 in decimal).

2

The Binary Number System

The decimal number system is not good for a computer or for data transmissions. Computers and data transmission equipment are better suited for a base of 2 instead of 10, because these devices are electrical and a value stored in a computer circuit can be represented only by the presence of an electrical signal (1) or the absence of an electrical signal (0). An electrical signal has only two basic states: on or off. Since computers and data transmission equipment are electrical devices, and electricity has two states, these devices use the **Base 2** or **binary number system**. Binary uses a base number of 2 instead of 10. There are only two symbols used to represent a digit in binary, the symbols 0 and 1. The following decimal digits are represented in binary like this:

2^3	2^2	2^1	2^0	Decimal Value
(8)	(4)	(2)	(1)	
0	0	0	0	= 0
0	0	0	1	= 1
0	0	1	0	= 2
0	0	1	1	= 3
0	1	0	0	= 4
0	1	0	1	= 5
0	1	1	0	= 6
0	1	1	1	= 7
1	0	0	0	= 8
1	0	0	1	= 9

Any number can be represented in binary by only using the digits 0 and 1. The digits 0 and 1 are known as **bits** (BInary digiTS). Eight binary digits grouped together form a **byte**.

But how can letters of the alphabet or symbols like a dollar sign be represented in a Base 2 system? The solution is that every character or symbol is assigned a number based on a specific scheme. One of these schemes uses the numbers from 0 to 255 and is called the **American Standard Code for Information Interchange** (or **ASCII** code). Table 2-1 shows part of the ASCII code. The uppercase letter A for example, has been assigned the number 65 in ASCII. To store the letter A, it is first converted to its ASCII (decimal) equivalent (65) and then that number is stored as a byte (8 bits) in binary code (01000001).

NOTE In addition to letters of the alphabet and symbols, numbers such as a street number used in an address, or any numbers that are not used in calculations, can be stored as text (that is, as character data without numerical value). In this case, the number is stored in ASCII code. For example, the number 47 is not stored as its binary equivalent (00101111). Instead, the ASCII value of the digit 4, which is 52, is stored as one byte (00110100) and the digit 7 (ASCII 55) is stored as another byte (00110111).

NOTE One of the limitations of ASCII is that there are not enough codes for all the symbols used by foreign languages. Another coding scheme called Unicode can represent 65,535 different characters because it is 16 bits in length instead of only 8 bits. In addition, when one bit out of every byte is used for error control (parity), the ASCII code can only be used to represent 128 different codes.

Table 2-1 Partial ASCII code table

ASCII (Decimal)	Symbol	ASCII (Decimal)	Symbol
65	A	78	N
66	B	79	O
67	C	80	P
68	D	81	Q
69	E	82	R
70	F	83	S
71	G	84	T
72	H	85	U
73	I	86	V
74	J	87	W
75	K	88	X
76	L	89	Y
77	M	90	Z

WIRELESS SIGNALS

Traditional wired communications use copper wires or fiber-optic cables to send and receive data. Wireless transmissions, of course, do not use these or any other visible media. Instead, data signals travel on electromagnetic waves. All forms of electromagnetic energy, from gamma rays to radio waves, travel through space in waves. Light from a flashlight or heat from a fire both move through space as a special type of wave known as electromagnetic waves. These waves require no special medium for movement. They travel freely through space at the speed of light, or 186,000 miles per second (300,000 kilometers per second).

Figure 2-1 illustrates the electromagnetic spectrum. The top section shows the length of the wave, as measured from the beginning of one wave to the beginning of the next, and compares it to the size of some common objects. The middle portion of the figure shows the commonly used names of waves of a particular length. The bottom half shows how many waves occur in one second.

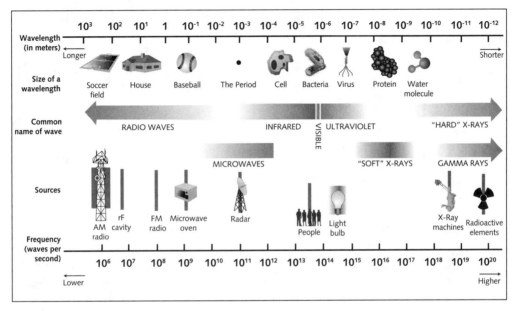

Figure 2-1 Electromagnetic spectrum

TIP   Many people, when asked what type of medium is used to send and receive wireless transmissions, answer "air." If this were the case, radio signals would not propagate in space, where there is no air. Wireless transmissions use electromagnetic waves as the medium, not air or empty space.

There are two basic types of waves by which wireless data are sent and received: infrared light and radio waves.

Infrared Light

Flashes of light have been used for centuries to transmit information. Bonfires set on top of hills were used in early America to relay messages. Ocean vessels sent signals from ship-to-ship or ship-to-shore using light. Even Alexander Graham Bell in 1880 demonstrated an invention called the photophone, which used the concept of light waves to transmit voice information. Transmitting modern computer or network data using light follows the same basic principle.

Because computers and data communication equipment use binary code, it is easy to transmit information with light. Just as binary code uses only two digits (0 and 1), light has only two properties (off and on). To send a 1 in binary code could result in a light quickly flashing on; to send a 0, the light would remain off. For example, the letter "A" (ASCII 65 or 01000001) could be transmitted by light as *off-on-off-off-off-off-off-on*. This concept is illustrated in Figure 2-2.

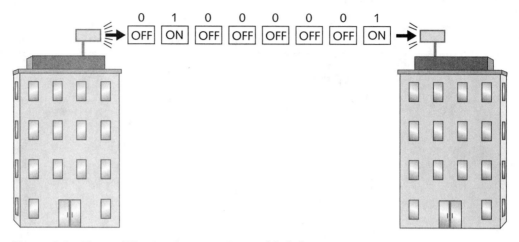

Figure 2-2   Transmitting a message using visible light

What type of light should be used to transmit these signals? To transmit data by visible light flashes, such as a strobe light, would be very unreliable, because other lights could be mistaken for the transmission signal or another bright light could wash out the light flashes. Visible light is not a reliable medium for data transmissions.

However, visible light is only one type of light. All the different types of light that travel from the Sun to the Earth make up the **light spectrum**. Visible light is just a small part of that entire spectrum. Some of the other forms of energy within the light spectrum, such as x-rays, ultraviolet rays, and microwaves, are invisible to the human eye. **Infrared light**, although invisible, has many of the same characteristics as visible light because it is adjacent to visible light on the light spectrum but is a much better medium for data transmission, because it is less susceptible to interference from other sources of visible light.

NOTE   Each frequency has a particular wavelength, which is measured as the distance between any point in one wave cycle and the same point in the next wave cycle. In turn, each wavelength within the spectrum of visible light represents a particular color. This is because the differing wavelengths of light waves bend at a different angle when passed through a prism, which in turn produces different colors. The colors that visible light produces are red (R), orange (O), yellow (Y), green (G), blue (B), indigo (I), and violet (V). Visible light is sometimes referred to as ROYGBIV.

Infrared wireless systems require that each device have two components: an **emitter** that transmits a signal, and a **detector** that receives the signal (these two components are sometimes combined into one device). An emitter is usually a laser diode or a light emitting diode (LED). Infrared wireless systems send data by the intensity of the light wave instead of *on-off* signals of light. To transmit a 1 the emitter increases the intensity of the electrical current, which indicates a pulse to the receiver, using infrared light. The detector senses the higher intensity pulse of light and produces a proportional electrical current. See Figure 2-3.

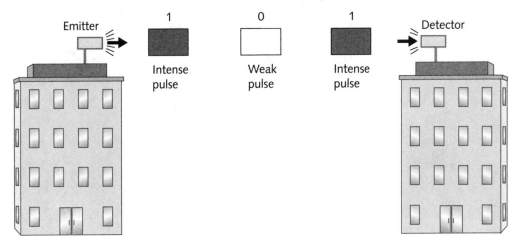

Figure 2-3 Light pulses

Infrared wireless transmission can be either directed or diffused. A **directed transmission** requires that the emitter and detector be directly aimed at one another (called **line-of-sight** or **LOS**), as seen in Figure 2-4. The emitter sends a narrowly focused beam of infrared light. The detector has a small receiving or viewing area. A television remote control, for example, uses directed transmission.

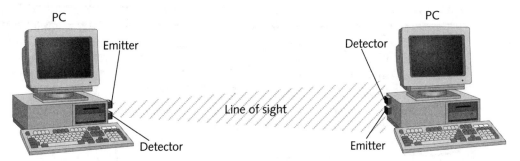

Figure 2-4 Directed transmission

A **diffused transmission** relies on reflected light. The emitters on diffused transmissions have a wide-focused beam instead of a narrow beam. The emitter is pointed at the ceiling of a room and uses it as a reflection point. When the emitter transmits an infrared signal, the signal bounces off the ceiling and fills the room with the signal. The detectors are also pointed at the same reflection point and can detect the reflected signal, as seen in Figure 2-5.

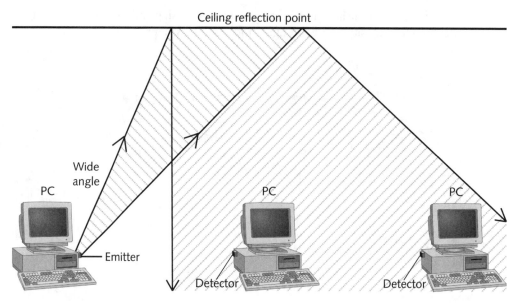

Figure 2-5   Diffused transmission

Infrared wireless systems have several advantages. Infrared light neither interferes with other types of communications signals such as radio signals, nor is it affected by other signals, except light. In addition, because infrared light does not penetrate walls, the signals are kept inside a room. This makes it impossible for someone elsewhere to listen in on the transmitted signal.

However, there are several serious limitations to infrared wireless systems. The first limitation involves the lack of mobility. Directed infrared wireless systems use a line-of-sight principle, which makes it impossible for mobile users to use it since the alignment between the emitter and the detector would have to be continually adjusted. The second limitation is the range of coverage. Directed infrared systems, which require line-of-sight, cannot be placed in an environment where there is the possibility that anything could get in the way of the infrared beam (think of someone standing in front of your remote control while you are trying to change TV channels). This means devices using infrared transmissions must be placed close enough to one another to eliminate the possibility of something moving between them. Due to the angle of deflection, diffused infrared can cover a range of only 50 feet (15 meters). And because diffused infrared requires a reflection point, it can be used only indoors. These restrictions limit the range of coverage.

Another significant limitation of an infrared system is the speed of transmission. Diffused infrared can send data at only up to 4 Mbps. This is because the wide angle of the beam loses energy as it reflects. The loss of energy results in a weakening signal. The weak signal cannot be transmitted over long distances nor does it have sufficient energy to maintain a high transmission speed, resulting in a lower data rate.

Because of these limitations, infrared wireless systems are generally used in specialized applications, such as data transfers between notebook computers, digital cameras, handheld data collection devices, PDAs, electronic books, and other similar mobile devices. A device using an infrared wireless system is illustrated in Figure 2-6.

Infrared port

Figure 2-6 Notebook computers are often equipped with infrared wireless ports

Some specialized wireless local area networks are based on the infrared method of transmitting data signals. These are used in situations where radio signals would interfere with other equipment, such as in hospital operating rooms, or when security is a concern, such as in secure government buildings.

Infrared light, like other types of electromagnetic waves such as visible light and heat, has limitations regarding its movement. Light waves, for example, cannot penetrate through materials like wood or concrete, and heat rays are absorbed by most objects, including human skin (we feel these waves as heat). Thus, the distance that light and infrared waves can travel is limited. See Figure 2-7.

Is there a wave in the electromagnetic spectrum that does not have the distance limitations of light or infrared? The answer is yes: radio waves.

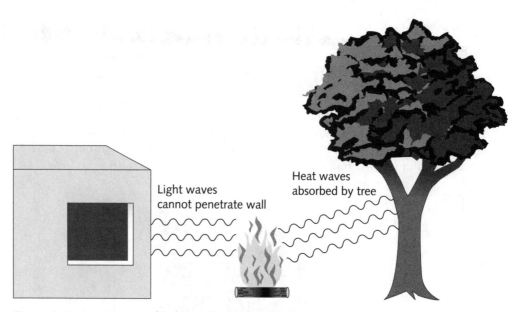

Figure 2-7   Limitations of light and heat waves

Radio Waves

The second means of transmitting a wireless signal is by using radio transmission. Radio waves provide the most common and effective means of wireless communications today. To understand the basic properties of radio waves, imagine that you are standing out in your yard with a garden hose in your hand watering the lawn. As you move your hand up and down, the water creates what looks like waves that move up and down, as shown in Figure 2-8.

Figure 2-8   Simulating radio waves with a garden hose

The waves created by the garden hose are similar to electromagnetic waves. Recall that energy travels through space or air in electromagnetic waves. Infrared light, visible light from a flashlight, and heat from a fire move through space or air as electromagnetic waves. These waves require no physical medium for movement.

Another type of electromagnetic wave that travels in this fashion is called a **radio (radiotelephony) wave**. When an electric current passes through a wire, it creates a magnetic field in the space around the wire. As this magnetic field radiates or moves out, it creates radio waves. Because radio waves, like light and heat waves, are electromagnetic waves, they radiate outward, usually in all directions.

Radio waves are free of some of the limitations that light and heat experience. Unlike heat waves, radio waves can travel great distances. Radio waves can also penetrate nonmetallic objects, unlike light waves. Visible light waves and heat waves can be seen and felt, but radio waves are invisible. These characteristics are illustrated in Figure 2-9. Because of these characteristics, radio waves are an excellent means to transmit data without wires.

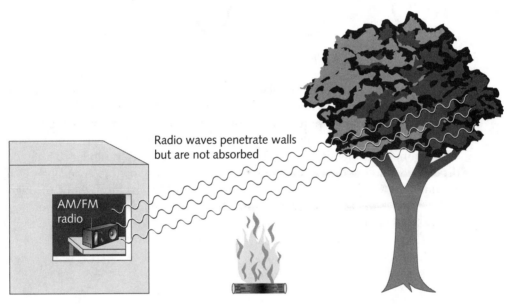

Radio waves penetrate walls but are not absorbed

AM/FM radio

Figure 2-9   Radio waves penetrate most solid objects

HOW RADIO DATA IS TRANSMITTED

Radio waves can be used to transmit data over long distances without the need for wires. To understand the method by which these waves can transport data requires an understanding of several different concepts. We will start by discussing the ways that analog and digital data are transmitted over radio waves.

Analog and Digital

Consider again standing out in your yard creating waves of water with a garden hose. The waves are continuous as long as the water is turned on. These waves represent an analog signal. An **analog signal** is one in which the intensity (voltage or amplitude) varies and is broadcast continuously, in other words, the signal has no breaks in it. Figure 2-10 illustrates an analog signal. Audio, video, voice, and even light are all examples of analog signals. An audio signal that contains a tone or a song is continuously flowing and doesn't start and stop until the tone or song is over.

Figure 2-10   Analog signal

Now, using the garden hose simulation again, suppose that instead of moving the hose up and down, you were to hold it steady, place your thumb over the end of the garden hose for a second and then remove it. Water would stop flowing (while your thumb was over the hose) and then would start flowing out of the hose again (when you removed your thumb). This example is shown in Figure 2-11. This on-off activity is similar to a digital signal. A **digital signal** consists of discrete or separate *pulses*, as opposed to an analog signal, which is continuous. A digital signal has numerous starts and stops throughout the signal stream. Morse code with its series of dots and dashes is an example of a kind of digital signal. Figure 2-12 illustrates a digital signal.

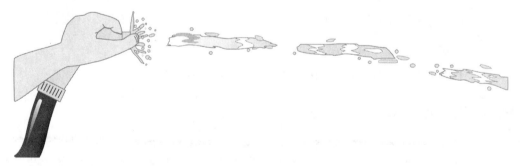

Figure 2-11   Simulating a digital signal with a garden hose

Computers operate using digital signals. If analog data, such as a video image or an audio sound, needs to be stored on the computer, it must be converted into a digital format before it can be stored and processed or interpreted by a computer.

Figure 2-12   Digital signal

NOTE
Various techniques are used to convert different types of analog data to digital data. For CD-quality music, for example, the analog signal must be measured (sampled) at the rate of 44,100 times per second; each sample taken is then stored in a digital format, using a minimum of 16 bits per sample. Computers also compress digitized signals through a number of other techniques to minimize the total amount of storage space or the amount of data that needs to be transmitted.

When a digital signal needs to be transmitted over an analog medium, such as when a computer needs to send digital signals over an analog telephone line or TV cable, a device known as a **modem** (for MOdulator/DEModulator) is used. A modem converts the distinct digital signals from a computer and encodes them into a continuous analog signal for transmission over analog phone lines. The process of encoding the digital signals (bits) onto an analog wave is called **modulation**. The modem at the other end of the connection then reverses the process by receiving an analog signal, decoding it, and converting it back into a digital signal.

Frequency

Now think about standing in your yard with a garden hose and moving your hand up and down slowly. You will create long waves, like in Figure 2-13. If you move your hand up and down rapidly, the waves become shorter, as shown in Figure 2-14. Depending on how fast you move your hand up and down, the peaks of the waves will be closer together or farther apart.

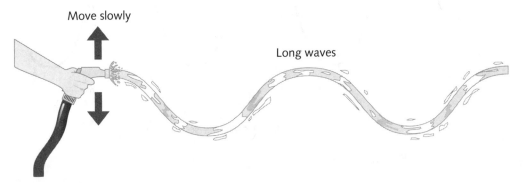

Move slowly

Long waves

Figure 2-13   Long waves

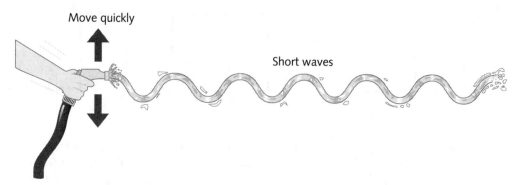

Figure 2-14   Short waves

The same variations occur with radio waves. The rate at which a radio circuit creates the waves (like moving the garden hose up and down faster or slower) will result in a different number of radio waves being created each second (the peaks will be either closer or farther apart). This rate is a radio wave's **frequency**. That is, the number of times a **cycle** (which is composed of one top [positive] and one bottom [negative] peak) occurs within one second equals the frequency of a wave.

Radio transmitters send what is known as a **carrier signal**. This is a continuous wave (CW) of constant amplitude (also called **voltage**) and frequency. This carrier signal wave is essentially an up-and-down wave called an **oscillating signal** or a **sine wave** and is illustrated in Figure 2-15. The carrier signal (or carrier wave) carries no useful information by itself. Only after it is modulated does it contain some kind of information signal such as music, voice, or data.

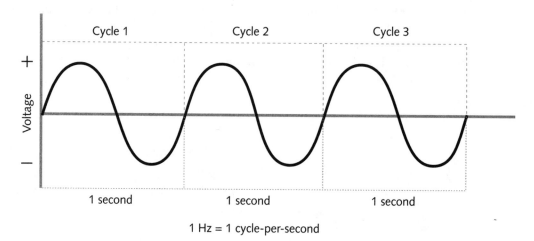

Figure 2-15   Sine wave

Notice in Figure 2-15 that the wave starts at zero, moves up to the maximum voltage (+), then down to the minimum voltage (-), and finally returns back to its starting point (0) before beginning all over again. Whenever the wave completes its trip up, then down, and returns back to the starting point, it has finished one cycle. Recall that frequency is defined as the number of times that a wave completes a cycle, in one second.

Figure 2-16 illustrates two different frequencies. Notice that the lower frequency and the higher frequency both alternate to the same maximum and minimum voltage. A change in voltage does not create a change in frequency. Instead, changes in frequency result from how long it takes to reach the maximum, fall back to the minimum, and then return to neutral to complete a cycle.

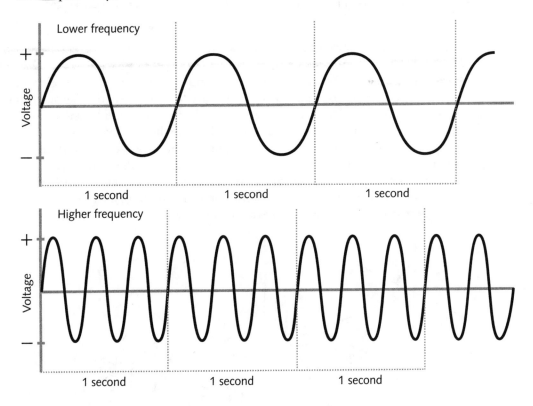

Figure 2-16 Low-frequency and high-frequency signals

NOTE In electrical terms, the cycle produces what is known as an alternating current (AC) because it flows between negative (-) and positive (+). AC is the type of current that runs to the electrical outlets in a house. Direct current (DC) is found in batteries. With DC, the current flows only from one terminal (-) to the other (+) and does not alternate.

Although frequencies are measured by counting the number of complete wave cycles that occur in one second, the term **Hertz (Hz)** is used instead of cycles-per-second. A radio wave measured as 710,000 Hz means that its frequency is 710,000 cycles per second. Because of the high number of cycles required, metric prefixes are generally used when referring to frequencies. A **Kilohertz (KHz)** is 1,000 Hertz, a **Megahertz (MHz)** is 1,000,000 Hertz, and a **Gigahertz (GHz)** is 1,000,000,000 Hertz. The wave measured as 710,000 Hz is referred to as 710 KHz.

NOTE Frequency is an important part of music also. The frequency of the musical note A is 440 Hz and middle C is 262 Hz. This means that when middle C is played, 262 pockets of higher air pressure pound against your eardrum each second.

Radio waves are usually transmitted and received using an antenna. An **antenna** is a length of copper wire, or similar material, with one end free and the other end connected to a receiver or transmitter. When transmitting, the radio waves created by the electronic circuit of the transmitter strike this antenna wire (the most common length of an antenna is usually about 1/2 of the wavelength). This sets up an electrical pressure (voltage) along the wire, which will cause a small electrical current to flow into the antenna. This causes a movement back and forth of the electricity in the antenna at the same frequency as the radio waves. When the electricity moves back and forth in the antenna at the same frequency as the radio waves, it creates a magnetic field around the antenna. This continuous (analog) combination of magnetism and electrical pressure moves (propagates) through air or space, and the result is an **electromagnetic wave (EM wave)**, as illustrated in Figure 2-17.

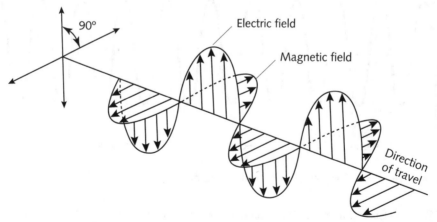

Figure 2-17   Electromagnetic wave consisting of electrical and magnetic fields

Antennas are also used to pick up transmitted radio signals. A very small amount of electricity moves back and forth in the receiving antenna in response to the radio signal (EM wave) reaching it. This results in a very small amount of current flowing from the antenna into the receiver, as shown in Figure 2-18.

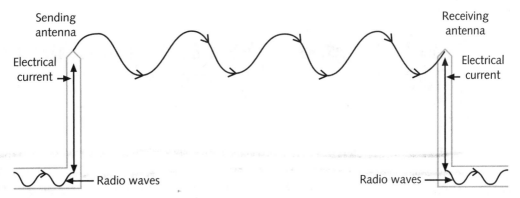

Figure 2-18   Radio antennas transmit and receive

Transmission Speed

Several different terms are used when referring to the transmission speed of radio waves. The electromagnetic waves themselves always travel at the speed of light, or 186,000 miles per second (300,000 kilometers per second). When data is transmitted using radio waves, the speed of transmission is usually shown in **bits per second (bps)**, since the primary concern is how efficiently the data can be moved from one place to another.

Another term used in measuring the speed of radio transmission is baud rate. Recall that radio transmissions send out a carrier signal, and this signal can be changed or modulated. A **baud** is a change in that signal, and every time the signal changes, in amplitude, frequency, phase, or a combination of these, it defines the boundary of a signal unit. **Baud rate**, then, refers to the number of signal units per second that are required to represent the bits transmitted. As you will learn below, the fewer signal units required, the better the system works, since the range of frequencies required for transmitting the signal is smaller.

Sometimes the terms *bps* and *baud rate* are used interchangeably, although the terms are not synonymous. This confusion originated with early computer modems. The first modems had speeds of 300, 600, and 1200 Baud. These early modems used a simple modulation technique and were capable of transmitting at a maximum of one signal unit per bit transmitted, therefore their speed in bps was the same as the baud rate, or 300, 600, and 1200 bps. For example, to transmit the letter U (85 ASCII or 01010101) it would take 8 signal changes, one for each bit. Thus, the number of bits transmitted per signal unit (baud) was 1.

However, with later modems it became possible to have a change in signal (a baud) represent more than 1 bit. A signal can be changed in several different ways, as explained a little later in the text; different changes result in different combinations of two bits (there can be up to four), each being assigned to one of four different signal changes. This is illustrated in Table 2-2.

Table 2-2   Bit representation of four signal changes

Signal Change (Baud)	Bit Combination Represented
Signal W	00
Signal X	01
Signal Y	10
Signal Z	11

Today's analog modems transmit at a maximum rate of 4,800 baud, which is the maximum number of signal changes per second that a phone line can support. However, by using more complex modulation techniques, along with compression of the data, current modems can achieve transmission speeds of up to 33,600 bps.

NOTE   56 Kbps modems are a little different from 33.6 Kbps modems, requiring that one end of the connection be a digital connection. To achieve 56 Kbps download speed from the ISP, the signal conversion from analog-to-digital or digital-to-analog must only happen at one end of the phone line. Because of this limitation, these modems achieve a high downstream speed of 56 Kbps. The maximum speed from the modem side to the ISP side, or upstream, is 33.6 Kbps.

A signal unit that represents two bits is known as a **dibit**. When a signal unit can represent three bits, it is called a **tribit**. If 16 different signal units are used, then a four-bit-per-signal unit could be represented (known as a **quadbit**). These characteristics are summarized in Table 2-3.

Table 2-3   Signal changes (baud) vs. number of bits represented

Name	Number of Signal Units Needed	Number of Bits Encoded per Signal Unit
Standard	1	1
Dibit	4	2
Tribit	8	3
Quadbit	16	4

Another term used when referring to transmission speed is **bandwidth**. Although this term is often used to refer to the maximum data transmission capacity, this is accurate only when referring to purely digital systems. Strictly speaking, in analog systems, bandwidth is defined as the range of frequencies that can be transmitted by a particular system or medium. In simple terms, bandwidth is the difference between the higher frequency and the lower frequency. Suppose a transmission for voice could be sent between 3,400 Hz and 300 Hz. The difference between the two frequencies (3,400 Hz − 300 Hz) is 3,100 Hz, which happens to be the bandwidth of a telephone conversation.

NOTE

Digital Subscriber Line (DSL) modems can transmit at speeds ranging from a few Kbps to about 9 Mbps on a telephone line, at a distance of up to 2.5 miles (4 kilometers). The usable bandwidth of the pair of copper wires in a modern phone line is about 1 Megahertz. DSL takes advantage of the higher frequencies that can be transmitted on a phone line but are not used for voice (above 4,000 Hz), divides these frequencies up into a large number of channels, and transmits data bits at a few bps over several channels at the same time, resulting in the high data rates described earlier. Full coverage of DSL technology is beyond the scope of this book. See the following Web link: http://computer.howstuffworks.com/dsl5.htm.

Analog Modulation

The carrier signal sent in analog radio transmissions is simply a continuous electrical signal. It carries no information. **Analog modulation** is the representation of analog information by an analog signal. There are three types of modulation that can be applied to an analog signal to enable it to carry information: the height of the signal, the frequency of the signal, and the relative starting point, or **phase**, of the signal. To understand this concept, let's look at each type of modulation separately.

NOTE

The height, frequency, and relative starting point of a signal (phase) are sometimes called the "three degrees of freedom."

Amplitude Modulation (AM)

The height of a carrier wave is known as the **amplitude** and can be measured in volts (electrical pressure). This is illustrated in Figure 2-19 with a typical sine wave. In **amplitude modulation (AM)**, the height of the carrier wave is changed in accordance with the height of another analog signal, called the modulating signal. In the case of an AM radio station, the modulating signal is the voice of the announcer or the music, which is an analog signal. The carrier wave's frequency and phase remain constant. Figure 2-20 shows an example of a carrier wave and a sine wave used to modulate the carrier. The bottom diagram shows the resulting carrier wave after it has been modulated.

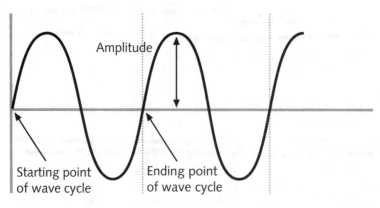

Figure 2-19 The amplitude of a signal

Amplitude modulation is used by broadcast radio stations. Because pure AM is very susceptible to interference from outside sources, such as lightning, it is not generally used for data transmissions.

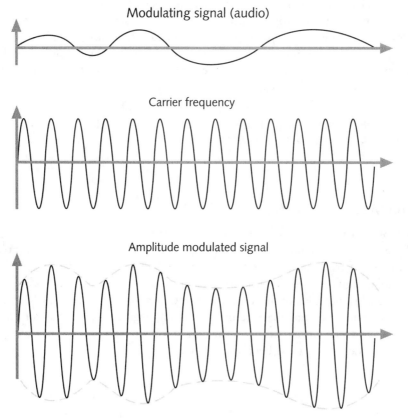

Figure 2-20 Amplitude modulation (AM)

Frequency Modulation (FM)

In **frequency modulation (FM)** the number of waves that occur in one second change based on the amplitude of the modulating signal, while the amplitude and phase of the carrier remain constant. Figure 2-21 illustrates an FM signal and a simple modulating sine wave. The bottom diagram shows the result of modulating the FM carrier in frequency.

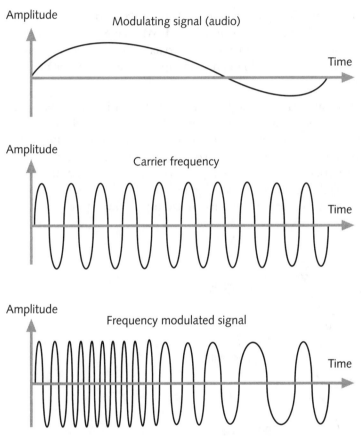

Figure 2-21   Frequency modulation (FM)

Like amplitude modulation, frequency modulation is often used by broadcast radio stations. However, unlike AM, FM is not as susceptible to interference from outside sources and is most commonly used to broadcast music programs. In addition, an FM carrier has a wider bandwidth, which allows it to carry Hi-Fi as well as stereophonic signals, with two sound channels.

NOTE

FM radio stations broadcast between 88 MHz and 108 MHz, while AM stations transmit between 535 KHz and 1,700 KHz.

Phase Modulation (PM)

In contrast to AM, which changes the height of the wave, and FM, which increases the number of waves per cycle, **phase modulation (PM)** changes the starting point of the cycle, while the amplitude and frequency of the carrier remain constant. Phase modulation is not generally used to represent analog signals, except for the color information transmitted with television signals.

A signal composed of sine waves has a phase associated with it. This phase is measured in degrees, and one complete wave cycle covers 360 degrees. A phase change is always measured with reference to some other signal. Since it would be very difficult to ensure that the wave cycles of a reference signal in two separate devices—the transmitter and the receiver—remained perfectly synchronized (in phase), PM systems almost always use the previous wave cycle as the reference signal. Figure 2-22 shows an example of four different phase shifts, with respect to a reference signal at the top of the figure.

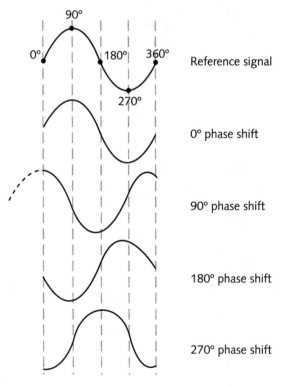

Figure 2-22   Visual example of phase shift

NOTE Although radio broadcasts use either amplitude modulation (AM) or frequency modulation (FM), television broadcasts actually use AM, FM, and phase modulation (PM). A television video signal uses amplitude modulation, the sound uses frequency modulation, and the color information uses phase modulation.

Digital Modulation

How then can digital data be transmitted by an analog carrier signal, when the medium used for transmission cannot be used with digital signals? The simple answer is: by modulating the analog signal or changing it to represent a 1 bit or a 0 bit.

Most modern wireless systems use **digital modulation**, which is the method of encoding a digital signal onto an analog wave for transmission over a medium that does not support digital signals, such as the atmosphere. In an analog system, the carrier signal is continuous, and amplitude, frequency, and phase changes also occur continuously because the input or modulating signal is still analog, and therefore continuous. However, in a digital system, the changes are distinct using binary signals, which exist in one of two states, a 1 or a 0, a constant positive or negative (or zero) voltage, on or off. For a computer to be able to understand these signals, each bit must have a fixed duration to represent a 1 or a 0 (more on digital signals later). Otherwise the computer would not be able to determine when one bit ends and another one begins.

There are four primary advantages of digital modulation over analog modulation:

- It makes better use of the bandwidth available.
- It requires less power to transmit.
- It performs better when the signal experiences interference from other signals.
- Its error-correcting techniques are more compatible with other digital systems.

With digital modulation, like analog modulation, there are three basic types of modulations, or changes, to the signal that can be made to enable it to carry information: the height, the frequency, and the relative starting point (phase) of the signal. However, as users demand more transmission speed, more binary signals (or bits) have to be crammed into the same number of wave cycles. The result is that in wireless communications today there are dozens of different types of modulation. For the most sophisticated modulations it can be difficult, if not impossible, to show a graphic example of what the signals look like. This chapter covers a few basic types of digital modulation; these methods serve as the basis for more sophisticated modulation techniques.

Binary Signals

Recall that with an analog signal the carrier wave alternates between the positive and negative voltage in a continuous cycle; that is, it doesn't stop. A binary signal likewise alternates between positive and zero volts, or alternatively between positive and negative voltage. However, data transmissions are typically sent in bursts of bits, meaning that some bits are transmitted and then the transmission stops. When there are no bits to be transmitted, no signal is transmitted. In analog systems, even when a radio station is not transmitting any sound, the carrier wave continues to be transmitted; in this case, your radio receiver simply does not detect any modulation of the carrier, and therefore does not extract the original signal and, consequently, does not reproduce any sound.

Three types of binary signaling techniques can be used. The **return-to-zero (RZ)** technique calls for the signal to rise (voltage to increase) to represent a 1 bit. A 0 bit is represented by the absence of voltage, or zero volts. This is illustrated in Figure 2-23. Notice that the voltage is reduced to zero before the end of the period for transmitting a 1 bit. Also notice that the signal does not quite fill the bit period; this gap is used for synchronization purposes.

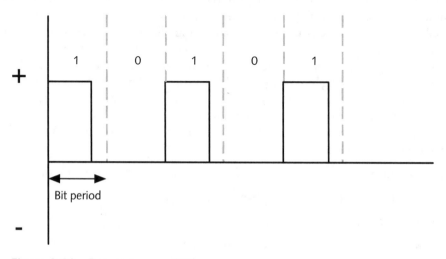

Figure 2-23   Return-to-zero (RZ)

The second method is known as the **non–return-to-zero (NRZ)** technique. With non–return-to-zero, the voltage signal remains positive, or high, for the entire length of the bit period. In addition, if the next bit to be transmitted is the same as the previous bit, the signal does not change, remaining high for a 1 and low (0 volts or negative, depending on the method used) for a 0. This effectively reduces the number of signal transitions (baud) required to transmit the message. Like in RZ, there is no voltage when transmitting a 0 bit. This is illustrated in Figure 2-24.

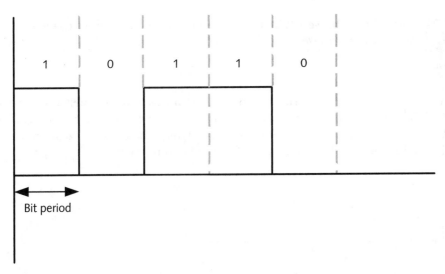

Figure 2-24   Non-return-to-zero (NRZ)

The final technique, **polar non–return–to–zero (polar NRZ)**, raises the signal (increases the voltage) to represent a 1 bit, but drops the signal (reduces the voltage to a negative amount) to represent a 0 bit. This technique is more commonly referred to as **non–return–to–zero–level (NRZ-L)** since the signal never returns to the zero volts level. NRZ-L is illustrated in Figure 2-25.

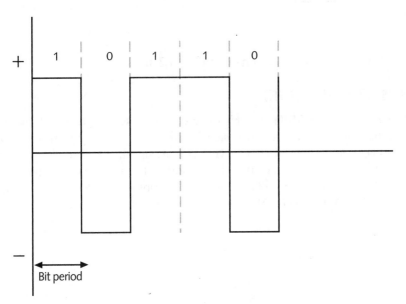

Figure 2-25   Polar non-return-to-zero (polar NRZ or NRZ-L)

The difference between NRZ and polar NRZ is that polar uses two voltage levels (positive and negative).

NOTE

A variation on a non–return–to–zero–level is **non–return–to–zero, invert–on–ones (NRZ–I)**. This is also used to reduce the baud rate required to transmit a digital signal. In NRZ–I, a change in voltage level represents a 1 bit, whereas no change in voltage level indicates that the next bit is a 0. NRZ–I is illustrated in Figure 2-26.

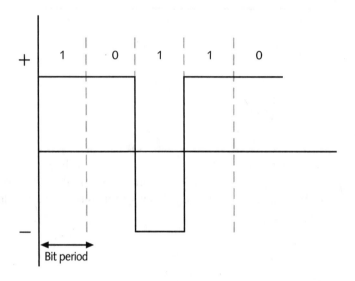

Figure 2-26   Non-return-to-zero-invert-on-ones (NRZ-I)

Amplitude Shift Keying (ASK)

Amplitude shift keying (ASK) is a binary modulation technique similar to amplitude modulation, in that the height of the carrier signal can be changed to represent a 1 bit or a 0 bit. However, instead of both a 1 bit and a 0 bit having a carrier signal, as with amplitude modulation, ASK uses NRZ coding. This means that .the presence of a carrier signal represents a 1 bit (positive voltage), while the absence of a carrier signal means a 0 bit (zero voltage). Figure 2-27 illustrates the letter A (ASCII 65 or 01000001) being transmitted by ASK.

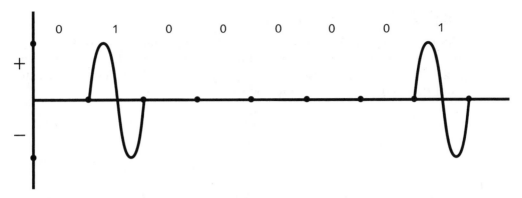

Figure 2-27   Amplitude shift keying (ASK)

NOTE   The signals for transmission using digital binary modulation are still shown here as sine waves since wireless transmissions use a medium (electromagnetic waves) that can only support analog signals. Note that the direct transmission of digital signals can only be done using a medium that conducts electricity, such as copper wiring. A full discussion of this concept is beyond the scope of this book.

Frequency Shift Keying (FSK)

In a way that is similar to frequency modulation, **frequency shift keying (FSK)** is a binary modulation technique that changes the frequency of the carrier signal. Because it is sending a binary signal, the carrier signal does start and stop as the data transmission stops. When using FSK, more wave cycles are needed to represent a 1 bit and respectively, fewer wave cycles are needed to represent a 0 bit. Figure 2-28 illustrates the letter A (ASCII 65 or 01000001) being transmitted using FSK. Note that in this example, the number of wave cycles used to represent a 1 bit is double that of the number of wave cycles used to represent a 0 bit.

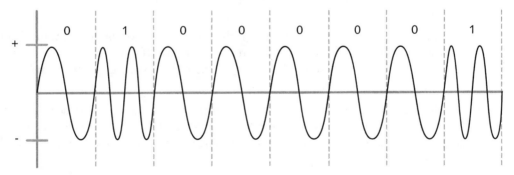

Figure 2-28   Frequency shift keying

Phase Shift Keying (PSK)

Phase shift keying (PSK) is a binary modulation technique, similar to phase modulation, in which the transmitter varies the starting point of the wave. The difference is that the PSK signal starts and stops because it is a binary signal. Figure 2-29 illustrates the letter A (ASCII 65 or 01000001) being transmitted by PSK.

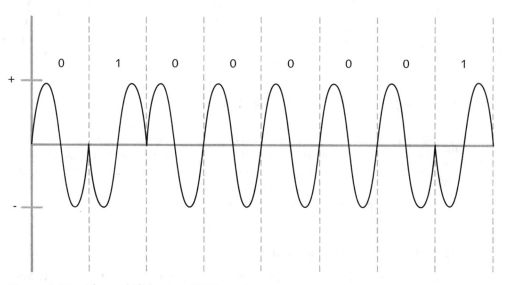

Figure 2-29   Phase shift keying (PSK)

Notice that whenever a bit being transmitted changes from 1 to 0 (or 0 to 1), the starting point, or direction of the wave changes. For example, after the first 0 bit is represented by a "normal" carrier wave cycle, the next bit is a 1 bit. However, instead of this being indicated by another normal carrier wave cycle where the signal advances into the positive range (goes up on the sine wave), it instead starts by going down into the negative range. The change in starting point (going down instead of going up) represents a change in the bit being transmitted (0 to 1).

In the preceding example, the change in the starting point of the wave means that the wave will start moving in the opposite direction, in this case 180 degrees away from the original direction. Note that phase modulation can change the starting point at various points, or angles, as Figure 2-30 illustrates.

In this case there are eight possible starting points for a signal (0 degrees, 45 degrees, 90 degrees, 135 degrees, 180 degrees, 225 degrees, 270 degrees, and 335 degrees), with each dot in the figure representing a different starting point. You will recall that with a tribit, eight

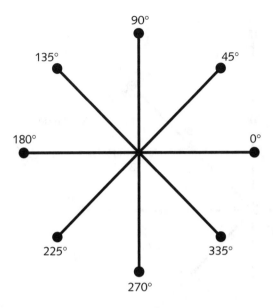

Figure 2-30   Phase modulation angles

different signals are needed. Using phase modulation with 45-degree angles can result in eight different signals. However, in wireless communications today, phase modulation is combined with amplitude modulation, which is easier for receivers to detect than very small phase changes, and can provide 16 or more different signals.

In Figure 2-31, each dot represents a different signal for a total of 16 different combinations, which can be used to transmit quadbits. This technique of combining amplitude and phase modulation is called **quadrature amplitude modulation (QAM)**. Due to the potential complexity of the resulting signal, most graphic representations of QAM only show the starting point of each wave with a dot. This representation is called a **constellation diagram**.

In the presence of background electromagnetic noise (interference), receivers can detect phase changes much more reliably than a frequency or amplitude change. Noise may be detected as a spike or sudden change in the amplitude of the signal and also can be detected as a change to a higher frequency at a particular point, although the latter happens less frequently. Since the phase of a signal is always referenced to the phase of the last wave cycle that was correctly detected, it is much less likely that noise will occur at the exact time in a wave, and at the correct amplitude level. These benefits make PSK-based systems more attractive for high-speed wireless communications.

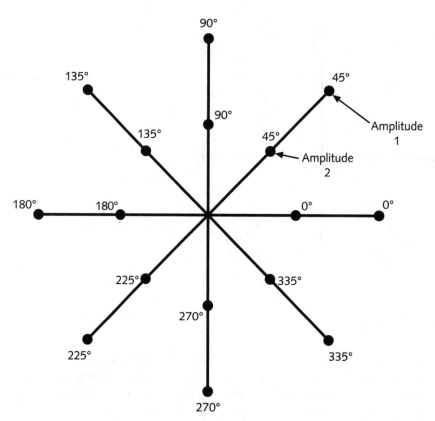

Figure 2-31   Constellation diagram (QAM)

A variation of the PSK modulation technique previously described combines amplitude modulation with PSK. This variation, called **quadrature phase shift keying (QPSK)**, can be used to transmit dibits (four signal changes). Figure 2-32 shows an example of the resulting waveform of this modulation technique for sending a series of 10 bits.

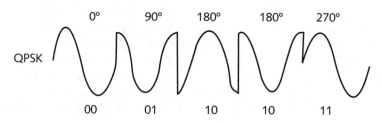

Figure 2-32   Transmitting dibits using QPSK

SPREAD SPECTRUM

Radio signal transmissions are, by nature, **narrow–band transmissions**. This means that each signal transmits on one radio frequency or a very narrow range of frequencies. FM broadcast radio stations, for example, tell their listeners to "tune to 90.3 MHz" because this is the frequency on which they broadcast. The next lower station frequency that listeners would be able to tune on the dial would be 90.1 MHz, and 90.5 MHz would be the frequency of the next higher station. This ensures that the station at 90.3 MHz can broadcast roughly between 90.2 and 90.4 MHz without interfering with other stations. The actual bandwidth used by FM stations is less than the difference between 90.2 and 90.4 MHz, allowing for some unused "frequency space" between the highest frequency used by the next station on the lower end of the dial, the station you are tuned to, and the next station at the higher end of the FM band.

Narrow-band transmissions are vulnerable to outside interference from another signal. Another signal that is transmitted at or near the broadcast frequency, 90.3 in this case, can easily render the radio signal inoperable or make it difficult to detect and decode the information contained in the signal.

NOTE Broadcast radio stations work effectively with narrow-band transmissions because each station is allowed to transmit on only one frequency in one specific area. Radio stations broadcast using high-powered transmitters and use different frequencies, which are licensed by the Federal Communications Commission. In contrast, most WLAN devices use the same frequency band but transmit at very low power levels. This means that the signals have a short useful range, helping to ensure that minimum interference occurs.

An alternative to narrow-band transmission is **spread spectrum transmission**. Spread spectrum is a technique that takes a narrow band signal and spreads it over a broader portion of the radio frequency band, as seen in Figure 2-33. Spread spectrum transmissions are more resistant to outside interference, because any noise is likely to affect only a small portion of the signal instead of impacting the entire signal. As an analogy, although an accident in one lane of an eight-lane freeway is inconvenient, there are still seven other lanes traffic can use to move around it and keep going. Spread spectrum likewise results in less interference and fewer errors. Two common methods used in spread spectrum transmissions are frequency hopping and direct sequence.

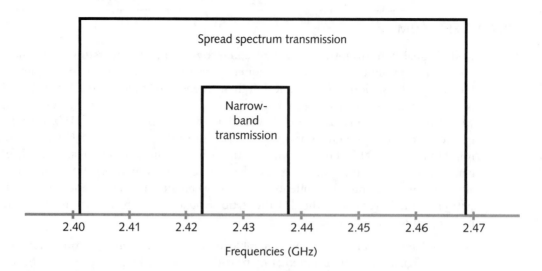

Figure 2-33   Spread spectrum vs. narrow-band transmissions

Frequency Hopping Spread Spectrum (FHSS)

The first method is called **frequency hopping spread spectrum (FHSS)**. Instead of transmitting on just one frequency, frequency hopping uses a range of frequencies and changes frequencies several times during the transmission. With FHSS, a short burst is transmitted at one frequency and then a short burst is transmitted at another frequency, and so on until the transmission is completed.

NOTE   Hedy Lamarr, a well-known film actress during the 1940s, and George Antheil, who had experience synchronizing the sounds of music scores with motion pictures, originally conceived the idea of frequency hopping spread spectrum during the early part of World War II. Their goal was to keep the Germans from jamming the radios that guided U.S. torpedoes against German warships. Lamarr and Antheil received a U.S. patent in 1942 for their idea.

Figure 2-34 shows how an FHSS transmission starts by sending a burst of data at the 2.44 GHz frequency for 1 microsecond. Then the transmission switches to the 2.41 GHz frequency and transmits for the next microsecond. During the third microsecond, the transmission takes place at the 2.42 GHz frequency. This continual switching of frequencies takes place until the entire transmission is complete. The sequence of changing frequencies is called the **hopping code**. In Figure 2-34, the hopping code is 2.44-2.41-2.42-2.40-2.43. The receiving station must also know the hopping code in order to correctly receive the transmission. The hopping codes are predefined and are usually part of the standard that defines how the radio circuit will be designed and implemented. Hopping codes can change so that multiple radios can each use a different sequence of frequencies within the same area and never interfere with each other, but the transmitter and receiver have to agree beforehand on which sequence to use.

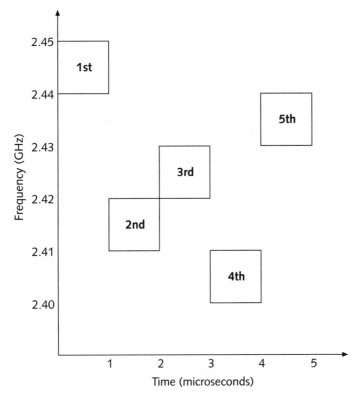

Figure 2-34 FHSS transmission

While transmitting with FHSS, if interference is encountered on a frequency, only a small part of the message is lost. Figure 2-35 shows an example in which the second transmission received interference. Each block of data transmitted in FHSS is only about 400 bytes long, and FHSS systems can detect errors at the lower protocol layers and request retransmission before passing the data to higher protocol layers. Some technologies make use of forward error correction (FEC), which is a technique that sends redundant data to minimize the need for retransmission of the messages. Error handling and error detection and correction at the lower protocol layers are discussed in later chapters.

Frequency hopping can reduce the impact of interference from other radio signals. An interfering signal will affect the FHSS signal only when both are transmitting at the same frequency and at the same time. Because FHSS transmits short bursts over a wide range of frequencies, the extent of any interference will be very small, the error can be detected through error checking, and the message can be easily retransmitted. In addition, FHSS signals exert minimal interference on other signals. To an unintended receiver, FHSS transmissions appear to be of a very short duration (similar to noise), and, unless the receiver knows the exact hopping sequence of frequencies, it is extremely difficult to eavesdrop on the message.

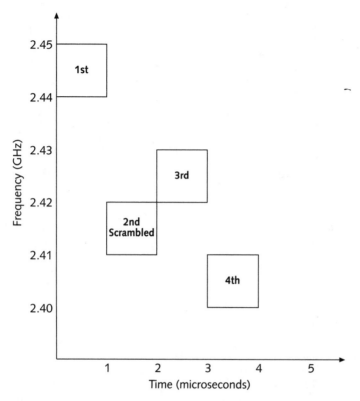

Figure 2-35   FHSS error detection

A variety of devices use FHSS. Several of these devices are consumer-oriented products, because FHSS devices are relatively inexpensive to manufacture. Cordless phones, including multi-handset units for small businesses, typically use FHSS. Bluetooth, which is covered in Chapter 5, also uses FHSS.

Direct Sequence Spread Spectrum (DSSS)

The other type of spread spectrum technology is **direct sequence spread spectrum (DSSS)**. DSSS uses an expanded redundant code to transmit each data bit and then a modulation technique such as QPSK. This means that a DSSS signal is effectively modulated twice. The first step for transmission is shown in Figure 2-36. At the top of the figure are two original data bits to be transmitted: a 0 and a 1.

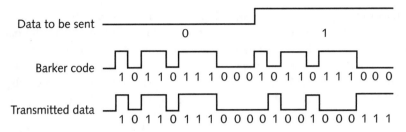

Figure 2-36   DSSS transmission

However, instead of simply encoding these two bits over a carrier wave for transmission, the value of each data bit is first added to each individual 1 and 0 in a sequence of binary digits called a Barker code. A **Barker code** (or **chipping code**) is a particular sequence of 1s and 0s that has properties that make it ideal for modulating radio waves, as well as for being detected correctly by the receiver. These 1s and 0s are called "chips" instead of bits, to avoid confusing them with the actual data bits. The chipping code is also called a **pseudo-random code** since it is usually derived through a number of mathematical calculations as well as practical experimentation.

The term "Barker code" is correctly used only when referring to 802.11 transmissions at 1 and 2 Mbps. When referring to most other spreading codes used in DSSS-based systems, such as CDMA cellular phones, the terms "pseudo-random code," "PN code," "spreading code," and "chipping code" may be used interchangeably.

The next step before transmission is to add the original data bit to the chipping code, as seen in the bottom line of Figure 2-36, to create the signal that is actually sent. If a 1 bit is to be transmitted, then a 1 is added to each bit of the chipping code:

Bit to be transmitted: 1	1	1	1	1	1	1	1	1	1	1	1
Add Barker code:		1	0	1	1	0	1	1	1	0	0	0
Resulting signal sent:		0	1	0	0	1	0	0	0	1	1	1

If a 0 data bit is to be transmitted, then a 0 is added to each bit of the chipping code:

Bit to be transmitted: 0	0	0	0	0	0	0	0	0	0	0	0
Add Barker code:		1	0	1	1	0	1	1	1	0	0	0
Resulting signal sent:		1	0	1	1	0	1	1	1	0	0	0

The adding of the chipping code and the value to add to the chipping code is accomplished by the Boolean operation of exclusive or (XOR), on a bit by bit basis, which is equivalent to a modulo 2 addition. In modulo 2 addition there is no carryover, which means that 1 + 1 = 0 and a 1 is not carried over to the next digit to the left. Other than that, a modulo 2 addition works exactly like a normal sum of two digits. See Boolean operations, Exclusive Or, at http://www.cplusplus.com/doc/papers/boolean.html.

Instead of transmitting a single 1 or 0, a DSSS system transmits these combinations of multiple chips. The 11 chips are transmitted at a rate 11 times faster than the data rate; in other words, the data rate does not change. However, the result of transmitting at a higher rate is the spreading of the signal over a much wider frequency band than that of the channel. In the case of 802.11, to continue with the example given earlier, the signal is spread 11 MHz to each side of the center frequency and ends up occupying a total bandwidth of 22 MHz. Figure 2-37 illustrates the results.

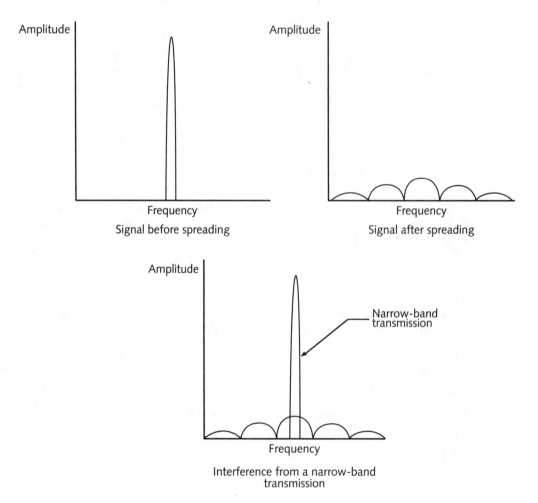

Figure 2-37   Spreading the signal over a wider range of frequencies

This spread signal has three important characteristics:

- The frequency of the digital component of the signal is much higher than that of the original data (chip rate).

- A plot of the frequency spectrum of this signal would look similar to random noise.

- All of the information contained in the original signal (a 0 or a 1 bit) is still there!

The most important aspect of this, however, is not the spreading of the signal but the fact that the power level (amplitude), *at any given frequency*, has dropped significantly. In similar fashion to FHSS, a DSSS signal appears to an unintended narrow-band receiver to be low-powered noise, which is one major advantage of this method.

At the receiver, the signal is first demodulated and then de-spread. One of the techniques the receiver uses to detect which bit was transmitted is to count the number of 0 chips. If the pattern of chips received contains six 0s, the bit is has a value of 1. Conversely, if the pattern contains six 1s, the value of the bit is a 0.

Another major advantage of using DSSS with a chipping code is that in conventional narrow-band transmissions, any interference, even if it caused the loss of only one bit, would require the entire message to be re-sent, which takes time. In DSSS, if there is any noise or other type of narrow-band interference that may cause some of the chips to change value, the receiver can employ embedded statistical techniques, mathematical algorithms that are used to recover the original data bit, thus avoiding the need for retransmission.

Devices that use DSSS are typically higher-end products because they are more expensive to manufacture than FHSS systems, but they also have many advantages over FHSS, as previously described. High-end office-based wireless local area networks use DSSS, along with products to connect networks between several buildings in a campus setting such as schools, large corporations, manufacturing plants, and convention centers.

FHSS and DSSS are not the only transmission techniques used for spread spectrum transmission. There are other techniques that are even more resistant to interference and different kinds of phenomena that can cause data loss or reduce the performance of this type of wireless transmission. Some of the techniques are based on variations of DSSS, and some others are completely different. Later chapters of this book include discussions of more sophisticated techniques as well as types of problems that can affect wireless transmissions.

CHAPTER SUMMARY

- Humans use the decimal or Base 10 number system. However, the decimal number system is not suitable for a computer or for data transmissions. Because computers are electrical devices, and electricity has basically two states (on or off), these devices use the binary or Base 2 number system instead. The only digits used to represent a number in binary are the digits 0 and 1. Every character or symbol that is stored or transmitted is assigned an arbitrary number based on a specific standardized coding scheme.

❑ One of these arbitrary coding schemes uses the numbers from 0 to 255 and is called the American Standard Code for Information Interchange (ASCII). A character that will be stored or transmitted by the computer is first converted to its ASCII equivalent, and then that number is stored as a byte in binary code.

❑ Whereas traditional wired communications use copper wires or fiber-optic cables to send and receive data, wireless transmissions do not use these or any other visible media. Instead, they travel on electromagnetic waves. There are two basic types of waves by which wireless signals are sent and received: infrared light and radio waves. Infrared light, next to visible light on the light spectrum, has many of the same characteristics as visible light.

❑ Infrared wireless transmission can be either directed or diffused. A directed transmission sends a narrowly focused beam of infrared light from the emitter to the detector. A diffused transmission relies on reflected light. The second means of transmitting a wireless signal is by using radio transmission. Radio waves provide the most common and effective means of wireless communications today. Radio waves have fewer limitations than light waves.

❑ Radio transmissions use a carrier signal, which is a continuous wave (CW) of constant amplitude (voltage) and frequency. This signal is essentially an up-and-down wave called an oscillating signal or a sine wave. The carrier signal sent by analog radio transmissions is simply a continuous electrical signal that carries no information.

❑ The carrier signal can undergo three types of modulation, or change, to enable it to carry information: the height of the signal, the frequency of the signal, and the relative starting point. Changing the signal height is known as amplitude modulation (AM). Frequency modulation (FM) changes the number of wave cycles that occur in one second. Phase modulation (PM) changes the starting point of the cycle.

❑ In digital modulation, there are also three types of changes that can be made to the carrier to enable it to carry information: the height of the signal, the frequency of the signal, or the relative starting point. Amplitude shift keying (ASK) changes the height of the carrier to represent a 1 bit or a 0 bit. A carrier is transmitted for a 1 bit and no signal is transmitted for a 0 bit. Frequency shift keying (FSK) is a modulation technique that changes the frequency of the carrier signal. Phase shift keying (PSK) is a modulation technique similar to phase modulation. The difference is that the PSK signal starts and stops because it is a binary signal.

❑ Radio signals are by nature a narrow-band type of transmission, which means that they transmit on one radio frequency or a very narrow spectrum of frequencies. An alternative to narrow-band transmissions is spread spectrum transmission. Spread spectrum is a technique that takes a narrow signal and spreads it over a broader portion of the radio frequency band.

❑ One of the most common spread spectrum methods is frequency hopping spread spectrum (FHSS). Instead of sending on just one frequency, frequency hopping uses a range of frequencies and changes frequencies during the transmission. The other method is direct sequence spread spectrum (DSSS). DSSS uses an expanded redundant code to transmit each data bit.

Key Terms

American Standard Code for Information Interchange (ASCII) — An arbitrary coding scheme that uses the numbers from 0 to 255.

amplitude — The height of a carrier wave.

amplitude modulation (AM) — A change in the height of the cycle.

amplitude shift keying (ASK) — A binary modulation technique whereby 1 bit has a carrier signal while a 0 bit has no signal.

analog modulation — A method of encoding an analog signal onto a carrier wave.

analog signal — A signal in which the intensity (amplitude or voltage) varies continuously and smoothly, over a period of time.

antenna — A copper wire, rod, or similar device that has one end up in the air and the other end connected to the ground through a receiver.

bandwidth — The range of frequencies that can be transmitted.

Barker code (chipping code) — A bit pattern used in a DSSS transmission. The term "chipping code" is used because a single radio bit is commonly referred to as a "chip."

Base 2 number system — See binary number system.

Base 10 number system — See decimal number system.

baud — A change in a carrier signal.

baud rate — The number of times that a carrier signal changes per second.

binary number system — A numbering system commonly used by computers that has a base number of 2 and uses the digits 0 and 1.

bit — A binary digit; an electronic 0 or a 1 based on the binary number system.

bits per second (bps) — The number of bits that can be transmitted per second.

byte — Eight binary digits (bits).

carrier signal — A transmission over a radio frequency that carries no useful information.

constellation diagram — a graphical representation that makes it easier to visualize signals using complex modulation techniques such as QAM. It is generally used in laboratory and field diagnostic instruments and analyzers to aid in design and troubleshooting of wireless communications devices.

cycle — An oscillating sine wave that completes one full series of movements.

decimal number system — A numbering system that has a base number of 10 and uses the digits 0-9.

detector — A diode that receives a light-based transmission signal.

dibit — A signal unit that represents two bits.

diffused transmission — A light-based transmission that relies on reflected light.

digital modulation — A method of encoding a digital signal onto an analog carrier wave for transmission over media that does not support direct digital signal transmission.

digital signal — Data that is discrete or separate.

direct sequence spread spectrum (DSSS) — A spread spectrum technique that uses an expanded, redundant code to transmit each data bit.

directed transmission — A light-based transmission that requires the emitter and detector to be directly aimed at one another.

electromagnetic wave (EM wave) — A signal composed of electrical and magnetic forces that in radio transmission usually propagates from an antenna and can be modulated to carry information.

emitter — A laser diode or a light-emitting diode that transmits a light-based signal.

frequency — A measurement of radio waves that is determined by how frequently a cycle occurs.

frequency hopping spread spectrum (FHSS) — A spread spectrum technique that uses a range of frequencies and changes frequencies during the transmission.

frequency modulation (FM) — A change of the number of waves used to represent one cycle.

frequency shift keying (FSK) — A binary modulation technique that changes the frequency of the carrier signal.

Gigahertz (GHz) — 1,000,000,000 Hertz.

Hertz (Hz) — The number of cycles per second.

hopping code — The sequence of changing frequencies used in FHSS.

infrared light — Light that is next to visible light on the light spectrum that has many of the same characteristics as visible light.

Kilohertz (KHz) — 1,000 Hertz.

light spectrum — All the different types of light that travel from the Sun to the Earth.

line of sight (LOS) — The direct alignment as required in a directed transmission.

Megahertz (MHz) — 1,000,000 Hertz.

modem (MOdulator/DEModulator) — A device used to convert digital signals into an analog format, and vice versa.

modulation — The process of changing a carrier signal.

narrow-band transmissions — Transmissions that use one radio frequency or a very narrow portion of the frequency spectrum.

non-return-to-zero (NRZ) — A binary signaling technique that increases the voltage to represent a 1 bit, but provides no voltage for a 0 bit.

non-return-to-zero, invert-on-ones (NRZ-I) — A binary signaling technique that changes the voltage level only when the bit to be represented is a 1.

non-return-to-zero-level (NRZ-L) — See polar non-return to zero.

oscillating signal — A wave that illustrates the change in a carrier signal.

phase — The relative starting point of a wave, in degrees, beginning at zero degrees.

phase modulation (PM) — A change in the starting point of a cycle.

phase shift keying (PSK) — A binary modulation technique that changes the starting point of the cycle.

polar non-return-to-zero (polar NRZ) — A binary signaling technique that increases the voltage to represent a 1 bit, but drops to negative voltage to represent a 0 bit.

pseudo-random code — A code that is usually derived through a number of mathematical calculations as well as practical experimentation.

quadbit — A signal unit that represents four bits.

quadrature amplitude modulation (QAM) — A combination of phase modulation with amplitude modulation to produce 16 different signals.

2

quadrature phase shift keying (QPSK) — A digital modulation technique that combines quadrature amplitude modulation with phase shift keying.

radio wave (radiotelephony) — An electromagnetic wave created when an electric current passes through a wire and creates a magnetic field in the space around the wire.

return-to-zero (RZ) — A binary signaling technique that increases the voltage to represent a 1 bit, but the voltage is reduced to zero before the end of the period for transmitting the 1 bit, and there is no voltage for a 0 bit.

sine wave — A wave that illustrates the change in a carrier signal.

spread spectrum transmission — A technique that takes a narrow signal and spreads it over a broader portion of the radio frequency band.

tribit — A signal unit that represents three bits.

voltage — Electrical pressure.

REVIEW QUESTIONS

1. The Base 10 number system is also known as _____ .

   a. octal

   b. decimal

   c. binary

   d. hexadecimal

2. With the Base 2 number system, the base number 2 is increased by power(s) of _____ as you move from one column to the next (right to left).

   a. one

   b. two

   c. three

   d. ten

3. The only digits used to represent a number in binary are the digits _____ .

   a. 1-10

   b. 2, 4, 6, and 8

   c. 1, 2, 4, 6, and 8

   d. 0 and 1

4. The reason computers and data transmission equipment use binary is:

   a. They are electrical devices and electricity has two states.

   b. Base 2 is too difficult to use.

   c. Base 10 was developed before binary.

   d. Binary is the next step above quadecimal.

5. Eight binary digits grouped together form a _____ .

   a. byte

   b. bit

   c. binary

   d. 2x quad

6. The American Standard Code for Information Interchange (ASCII) can represent up to 1024 characters. True or False?

7. Letters of the alphabet and symbols are stored based on the ASCII code, but not numbers to be used in calculations. True or False?

8. Infrared light, although invisible, has many of the same characteristics as visible light. True or False?

9. Infrared wireless systems require that each device needs to have only one component: either an emitter that transmits a signal, or a detector that receives the signal. True or False?

10. Infrared wireless systems send data by the intensity of the light wave instead of "on-off" signals of light. True or False?

11. Infrared wireless transmission can be either directed or _____ .

12. Radiotelephony or radio travels in waves known as _____ waves.

13. Unlike a digital signal, a(n) _____ signal is a continuous signal with no "breaks" in it.

14. Changing a signal is known as _____ .

15. The changing event that creates the different radio frequencies is a(n) _____ .

16. Explain how a radio antenna works when transmitting a signal.

17. Explain the difference between bps, baud, and baud rate.

18. Explain the difference between amplitude modulation, frequency modulation, and phase modulation.

19. What is quadrature amplitude modulation (QAM) and how does it work?

20. List and describe the three different types of binary signaling techniques.

HANDS-ON PROJECTS

Project 2-1

Locate an ASCII chart on the Internet or in a book. Using the letters of your first and last name, look up the ASCII value for each of these letters. The values will range from 65 to 122. Note that there is a difference between uppercase and lowercase letters. After having determined the ASCII value, convert each value to binary code. Because all ASCII values are between 0-255, the number of bits needed to represent any ASCII code is eight. The binary equivalents are:

2^7	2^6	2^5	2^4	2^3	2^2	2^1	2^0
(128)	(64)	(32)	(16)	(8)	(4)	(2)	(1)

For example, the name "Li Smith" contains the ASCII value of uppercase "L," which is 76, and the binary equivalent of "L" is 010001100.

Project 2-2

Telephone dial-up modems are fading in popularity among home computer users, and digital subscriber line (DSL) modems are becoming the transmission method of choice. Using the Internet, research DSL. Explain how each type of connectivity works. (*Hint*: Think about different frequencies over a telephone line.) How can a telephone line be used when a DSL connection is active but cannot be used when a standard data dial-up modem is being used? Determine the top speeds for broadband cable (Internet over cable TV) and ADSL. What are the advantages and disadvantages of each?

Project 2-3

TV remote controls were some of the first devices to use infrared signals generated by light-emitting diodes. TV remote controls date back to 1950 when Zenith introduced the first remote control, the Lazy Bones. Using the Internet and printed sources, trace the development of the TV remote control as one of the pioneers of infrared technology. Explain how other technologies, such as radio frequency and ultrasonics, were proposed but rejected for use in remote controls. What are the capabilities and limitations of today's infrared remotes?

Project 2-4

Using the information obtained from Hands-on Project 1, take the first letter of your first name in binary and draw a sine wave showing how it would appear in each of the following modulations:

- ❏ Amplitude shift keying (ASK)
- ❏ Frequency shift keying (FSK)
- ❏ Phase shift keying (PSK)

Project 2-5

Amplitude modulation (AM), frequency modulation (FM), and phase modulation (PM) all have strengths and weaknesses. Research these three types of modulations and develop a chart indicating the advantages, disadvantages, and how each modulation is currently being used. Also, include a list of at least two devices that use the technology.

CASE PROJECT

Project 2-1

The Baypoint Group (TBG), a company of 50 consultants who assist organizations and businesses with issues involving network planning and design, has again hired you as a consultant. One of their oldest clients, Woodruff Medical Group, needs your help.

Woodruff Medical has been approached by a vendor who is trying to sell it an infrared wireless local area network for its office. Although none of the networking equipment will be around any sensitive medical equipment, the office manager is worried that "stray infrared signals" could "leak out" of the third-floor office area into the x-ray lab on the ground floor. Your job is to explain the technology.

1. Prepare a PowerPoint presentation outlining how infrared and radio wireless transmissions work. This will be presented to the office manager, who is not technically inclined, and the local area network manager, who has a strong technology background. Be sure to list the advantages and disadvantages of both. The presentation should contain at least 12 slides.

2. After listening to your presentation, the office manager has several questions. One of the questions involves wireless transmission speeds. The office manager has a "good 14,400 baud" dial-up data modem at home and wants to know how its transmission speed compares with that of an infrared WLAN. He also says that baud and bps are the same, because when his Windows 3.11 computer asks for information about his modem it wants him to enter the baud rate. This time the office manager wants a written report instead of a presentation. Write a one-page summary regarding different transmission speeds. Be sure to include information about the difference between bps, baud, baud rate, and bandwidth. Also, show how bps is not always identical to baud.

OPTIONAL TEAM CASE PROJECT

A local community college has contacted The Baypoint Group for information about modulation for a networking class, and TBG has passed this request on to you. Form a team of two or three consultants and research AM, FM, PM, ASK, FSK, and PSK. Specifically pay attention to how they are used as well as their strengths and weaknesses. Provide an opinion regarding which technology will become the dominant player in the future of wireless.

3

UNDERSTANDING RADIO FREQUENCY COMMUNICATIONS

After reading this chapter and completing the exercises, you will be able to:

♦ List the components of a radio system

♦ Describe how different factors affect the design of a radio system

♦ Discuss why standards are beneficial and list the major telecommunications standards organizations

♦ Explain the radio frequency spectrum

Radio frequency (RF) communications is the most common type of wireless communications. RF comprises all types of radio communications using radio frequency waves, from telegraph to radio broadcasting and wireless computer networks as well. In the context of this book, however, as explained in Chapter 1, we focus primarily on wireless data communications. Due to the convergence of many technologies such as data transmission over cellular phones and satellites, these types of RF communications are also covered in this book.

Unlike light-based communications, such as infrared, RF communications can travel long distances and are not always impeded by surrounding objects. Radio communications is also a mature technology, with the first radio transmission taking place over 100 years ago.

RF communications can be very complex. This chapter attempts to demystify this topic. The first part of the chapter explores the different basic components that are necessary for radio frequency communications. Then we look at the issues regarding the design and performance of an RF system, concluding the chapter by exploring the national and international organizations that create and enforce radio frequency standards and examining the radio frequency spectrum allocation.

COMPONENTS OF A RADIO SYSTEM

Several hardware components are essential for communicating using RF. These components are common to all radio systems, even though the function and purpose of the radio systems may vary. The components include filters, mixers, amplifiers, and antennas. The first three are covered in this chapter. The latter is important enough to warrant a dedicated chapter, especially given the accelerated pace of development and growth in the wireless data communications field. We introduce antennas in this chapter, but they are addressed in depth in Chapter 4.

Filters

A **filter** does exactly what its name indicates. It gets rid of all the RF signals that are not wanted. The world around us is filled with RF signals covering every frequency imaginable (take another look at Figure 2-1, in Chapter 2). Most of these signals are generated by transmission equipment such as cellular phones, communications satellites, and radio and television station transmitters, but some even reach us from outer space. Radio receivers pick up all of these RF waves "flying" around us, and the filter sifts out the extra frequencies that we do not want to receive. Think of a water filter used in a home that removes particles and other impurities, or an automotive oil filter that prevents large contaminants from reaching the engine while allowing the oil itself to pass through. An RF filter either passes or rejects a signal based on the signal's frequency. The block diagram symbol for a filter is illustrated in Figure 3-1.

 NOTE   The block diagram symbols are universal and are commonly used to illustrate radio frequency as well as microwave components.

Figure 3-1   Filter symbol

There are three types of RF filters: low-pass, bandpass, and high-pass. With a **low-pass filter**, a maximum frequency threshold is set and all signals below that value are allowed to pass through, as seen in Figure 3-2.

Maximum threshold: 900 MHz

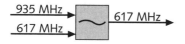

Figure 3-2   Low-pass filter

The second type of filter is a **high-pass filter**. Instead of setting a maximum frequency threshold level, as with a low-pass filter, a minimum frequency threshold is set. All signals that are above the minimum threshold are allowed to pass through, while those below the minimum threshold are blocked. This is illustrated in Figure 3-3.

Minimum threshold: 2.4 GHz

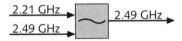

Figure 3-3   High-pass filter

A bandpass filter is the third type of RF filter. Instead of setting either a minimum or maximum frequency threshold, a **bandpass filter** sets a range called a **passband**, which includes both a minimum and a maximum threshold. Signals that fall within the passband are allowed through the bandpass filter. This is seen in Figure 3-4.

Passband: 300 Hz to 3400 Hz

Figure 3-4   Bandpass filter

Filters are also found in transmitters, where they are used to eliminate some unwanted frequencies that result from the process of modulating the signal before transmission. The function of a filter can be seen in Figure 3-5, which is a partial block diagram of a radio transmitter. The input data is the information that needs to be sent, and can exist in the form of audio, video, or data. The transmitter takes the input data and modulates the signal (through analog or digital modulation) by changing the amplitude, frequency, or phase of the sine wave (review Chapter 2, if necessary, to refresh your memory on RF signal modulation). The resulting output from the modulation process is known as the **intermediate frequency (IF)** signal. The output signal from the modulator (the IF) includes the frequencies between 8 MHz and 112 MHz. The IF signal is then filtered through a bandpass filter to remove any undesired high or low frequency signals and produce an output with a range of frequencies between 10 MHz and 100 MHz.

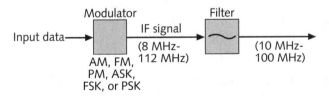

Figure 3-5   Filter function in a radio transmitter

Mixers

The purpose of a **mixer** is to combine two radio frequency inputs to create a single output. Its symbol is shown in Figure 3-6. The single output of a mixer is in the range of the highest sum and the lowest difference of the two frequencies. In Figure 3-7, the input signal is 300 Hz to 3400 Hz and the frequency mixed in is 20,000 Hz.

Figure 3-6 Mixer symbol

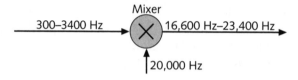

Figure 3-7 Mixer output

The mixer adds the input frequencies to the mixed-in frequency to produce the sums:

20,000 Hz	20,000 Hz
+ 300 Hz	+3,400 Hz
20,300 Hz	23,400 Hz

In this example, 23,400 Hz is the highest sum. The mixer also determines the lowest difference between the input frequencies and the mixed-in frequency, for example:

20,000 Hz	20,000 Hz
- 300 Hz	-3,400 Hz
19,700 Hz	16,600 Hz

In the example above, the lowest difference frequency would be 16,600 Hz. Therefore, the output from the mixer would be a frequency from 16,600 Hz to 23,400 Hz. The sum and the differences are known as the **sidebands** of the frequency carrier. These serve as buffer spaces around the frequency of the transmitted signal to shield it from "stray" signals that may invade the frequency. Such interference comes from radio stations transmitting at the next lower or higher frequency.

One way to illustrate sidebands is by considering AM radio signals. AM broadcast radio is confined to a frequency range of 535 KHz to 1605 KHz. In an AM broadcast radio signal, the sidebands are typically 7.5 KHz wide, so a radio station on the AM dial requires about 15 KHz of bandwidth. This is illustrated in Figure 3-8.

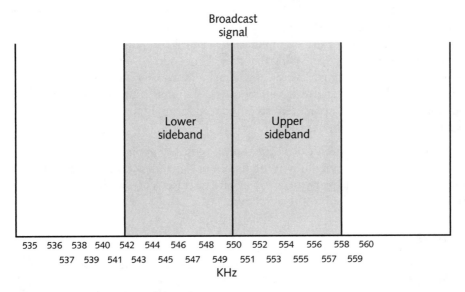

Figure 3-8   AM radio sidebands

Mixers are used to convert an input frequency to a specific desired output frequency. Figure 3-9 shows the symbol for an amplifier. Amplifiers, described in the next section, affect RF signals. Figure 3-10 illustrates how a mixer functions in a radio transmitter. The transmitter takes the input data and modulates the signal to produce an IF signal. In this example, the output from the modulator was 8 MHz to 112 MHz. This signal was then put through a bandpass filter to produce the desired IF signal range of 10 MHz to 100 MHz. This IF signal then becomes the input to the mixer along with the desired frequency of 800 MHz. This creates a signal with a frequency of 698 MHz to 903 MHz, which is then run through another bandpass filter to remove any stray frequencies.

Figure 3-9   Amplifier symbol

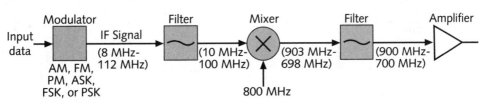

Figure 3-10   Mixer and amplifier function in a radio transmitter

Amplifiers

The next item on our list, the **amplifier**, essentially increases the amplitude of an RF signal. In Figure 3-10, the amplifier boosts the power of the signal received from the filter before it is transmitted. RF signals tend to lose intensity (amplitude) when they move through circuits, or through air or space; amplifiers are critical components in RF circuits. Filters and mixers are passive devices, meaning that they do not add power to a signal, instead, they take power away from the signal. Likewise, when an electromagnetic wave carrying a modulated signal leaves the antenna and travels from the transmitter to the receiver antenna, a large portion of its power is lost or attenuated (reduced in amplitude) when it is absorbed by water particles in the air, walls, trees, and so on.

The amplifier is an active device. To work, it must be supplied with electricity. It increases a signal's intensity or strength by using the input signal to control a circuit that "shapes" the output to reflect the shape of the input signal exactly, except that the signal will be re-created using the power supplied to the amplifier.

Antennas

For an RF signal to be transmitted or received, the transmitter or receiver must always be connected to an antenna. Figure 3-11 illustrates the symbol for an antenna, and Table 3-1 shows the complete list of these major components along with the block diagram figures.

Figure 3-11   Antenna symbol

Table 3-1   Radio components and their symbols

Component Name	Function	Block Diagram Symbol
Filter	Accept or block RF signal	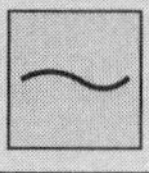
Mixer	Combine two radio frequency inputs to create a single output	
Amplifier	Boost signal strength	
Antenna	Send or receive electromagnetic wave	

DESIGN OF A RADIO SYSTEM

Filters, mixers, amplifiers, and antennas are necessary components of all radio equipment, but designers of radio communications systems also need to consider how the systems will be used. For example, in radio signal broadcasting, the considerations may be as straightforward as the size and location of the antenna, along with a signal that is strong enough to cover a very large area. However, in radio systems that incorporate two-way communications such as cellular phones and wireless networks, there are other considerations, including multiple user access, transmission direction, switching, and signal strength.

Multiple Access

Because only a limited number of frequencies are available for radio transmission, conserving the use of frequencies is important. One way to conserve is by sharing a frequency among several individual users. Instead of giving each user his or her own frequency, it is possible to "divide" or share one frequency among multiple users, which reduces the number of frequencies needed. Imagine a group of people using walkie-talkies and all of them using the same channel. See Figure 3-12. If the three people on the left all transmitted at the same time, the three on the right would not be able to understand the message. In this case, the only way for them to share a single channel would be if they each took a turn transmitting.

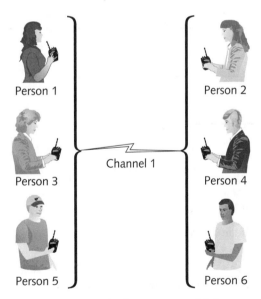

Person 1   Person 2

Channel 1

Person 3   Person 4

Person 5   Person 6

Figure 3-12 Multiple access: multiple users sharing the same frequency for communication

Another example of multiple access is when a company sends multiple envelopes or packages from different people in one office to another office. All of the envelopes and packages shipped at the same time share space in the same courier truck, on the same trip (multiple access). When the truck arrives at the other office, the envelopes and packages are separated and delivered to their respective recipients.

Several methods allow multiple access; the most significant in terms of wireless communications are Frequency Division Multiple Access (FDMA), Time Division Multiple Access (TDMA), and Code Division Multiple Access (CDMA).

Frequency Division Multiple Access (FDMA)

Frequency Division Multiple Access (FDMA) divides the bandwidth of a channel (a range of frequencies) into several smaller frequencies bands (narrower ranges of frequencies, or channels). For example, a transmission band with a 50,000 Hz bandwidth can be divided into 1,000 channels, each with a bandwidth of 50 Hz. Each channel is dedicated to one specific user. This concept is illustrated in Figure 3-13. FDMA is most often used with analog transmissions.

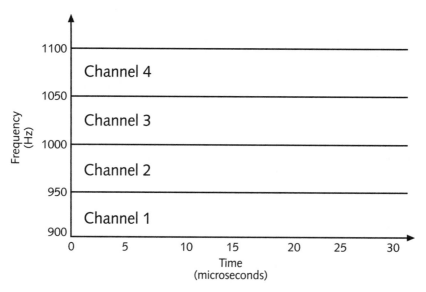

Figure 3-13   Frequency Division Multiple Access (FDMA)

Cable television is transmitted using FDMA over coaxial cable. Each analog television signal uses 6 MHz of the 500 MHz bandwidth of the cable.

NOTE

Think back to the example in Figure 3-12. If the three people on the left each use a different portion of the same frequency band, by selecting a different channel on the walkie-talkie, and the three people on the right each selected one of the three transmitting channels, the people on the left can all transmit simultaneously and each person on the right will then receive a different transmission.

FDMA does, however, have some drawbacks. One is that when signals are sent at frequencies that are grouped closely together, an errant signal from one frequency may encroach on its neighbor's frequency. This phenomenon, known as **crosstalk**, causes interference on the other frequency and may disrupt the transmission.

Time Division Multiple Access (TDMA)

To overcome the problem of crosstalk, **Time Division Multiple Access (TDMA)** was developed. Whereas FDMA divides the bandwidth into several frequencies, TDMA divides the transmission time into several slots. Each user is assigned the entire frequency for the transmission for a fraction of time on a fixed, rotating basis. Because the duration of each time slot is short, the delays that occur while others use the frequency are not noticeable. Figure 3-14 illustrates TDMA for seven users. TDMA is most often used with digital transmissions.

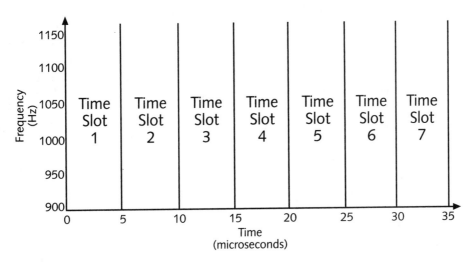

Figure 3-14   Time Division Multiple Access (TDMA)

If a user has no data to transmit during his or her assigned time slot with TDMA, the frequency remains idle.

NOTE

This concept is similar to the walkie-talkie example from Figure 3-12. Instead of each person on the left waiting their turn to transmit, their radios would be designed in way that they could synchronize with each other and each radio would transmit for only a short period of time. The time slots would rotate very quickly so each of the people transmitting could talk continuously, without having to wait their turn. The receivers would pick up only the portion of the transmission assigned to each of them. With TDMA, all of the transmissions are taking place at the same frequency, but one at a time.

NOTE   Cellular phones based on GSM technology transmit using the TDMA method.

TDMA has several advantages over FDMA. TDMA uses the bandwidth more efficiently. Studies indicate that when using a 25 MHz bandwidth, TDMA can achieve over 20 times the capacity of FDMA, meaning it can handle a much larger number of transmitters sharing the same frequency band than FDMA. Also, TDMA allows both data and voice transmissions to be mixed using the same frequency.

Code Division Multiple Access (CDMA)

Code Division Multiple Access (CDMA) is used primarily for cellular telephone communications and is unlike TDMA or FDMA. CDMA uses direct sequence spread spectrum (DSSS) technology with a unique digital spreading code (**PN code**), rather than separate RF frequencies or channels, to differentiate between the multiple transmissions in the same frequency range. Before transmission occurs, the high-rate PN code is combined with the data to be sent; this step spreads the signal over a wide frequency band. The technique is very similar to the one described in the section on spread spectrum in Chapter 2, except that to implement multiple access, the transmission to each different user begins on a subsequent chip of the PN code. Recall that in DSSS the 1s and 0s of the spreading code are referred to as "chips," to avoid confusing them with the data bits. This approach essentially imprints a unique address on the data. Each "address" is then only used by one of the receivers sharing the same frequency. Figure 3-15 illustrates the concept of the spreading code.

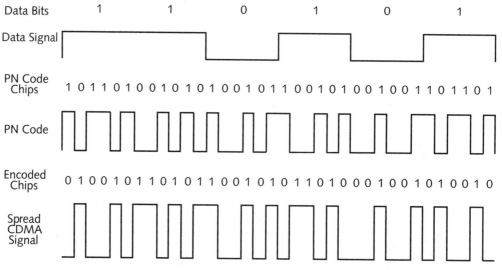

Figure 3-15   CDMA spreading of a data signal by a PN code

The unique "address" concept works as shown below:

Channel 1:   1 0 0 1 1 0 1
Channel 2:   0 0 1 1 0 1 1
Channel 3:   0 1 1 0 1 1 0

and so on, until the sequence of chips wraps around.

Note that each of the codes above starts on a different chip of the same sequence of 1s and 0s. The code for channel 2 begins on the second chip of channel 1. The code for channel 3 begins on the second chip of channel 2, and so on, until there are no more unique codes available and the sequence of chips wraps around. The longer the code is, the more users will be able to share the same channel. In the preceding example, there are seven chips per code, which allows for seven unique codes.

The number of chips in the code determines the amount of spreading or bandwidth that the transmitted signal will occupy. Since the amount of spreading is limited by the bandwidth allocated to the system, the length of the spreading code also determines the number of unique code sequences and, consequently, the number of users that can share that frequency band.

In CDMA technology, the spreading code is called a pseudo-random code (PN code), because the code appears to be a random sequence of 1s and 0s but it actually repeats itself over and over.

The spreading process is reversed at the receiver, and the code is de-spread to extract the original data bit transmitted. Since all receivers are on the same frequency, they all receive the same transmissions. The PN code is designed so that when a receiver picks up a signal that was spread with the PN code being used by another receiver, and attempts to recover the original data, the decoded signal still looks like a high-frequency signal, instead of data, so it is ignored. Figure 3-16 illustrates the decoding of the data in CDMA, and Figure 3-17 shows an example of what happens when a receiver attempts to de-spread another receiver's signal and recover the data bits.

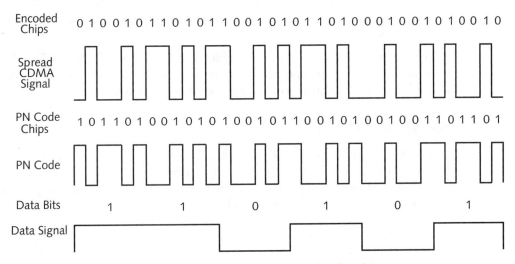

Figure 3-16   De-spreading a CDMA signal to recover the data bits

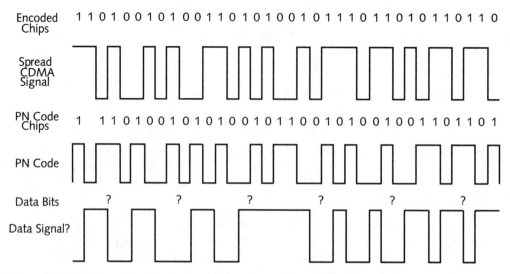

Encoded Chips   1 1 0 1 0 0 1 0 1 0 0 1 1 0 1 0 1 0 0 1 0 1 1 1 0 1 1 0 1 0 1 1 0 1 1 0

Spread CDMA Signal

PN Code Chips   1   1 1 0 1 0 0 1 0 1 0 1 0 0 1 0 1 1 0 0 1 0 1 0 0 1 0 0 1 1 0 1 1 0 1

PN Code

Data Bits   ?   ?   ?   ?   ?   ?

Data Signal?

Figure 3-17   Attempting to de-spread another receiver's CDMA signal

To understand CDMA, imagine a room full of 20 people trying to have 10 simultaneous conversations. Suppose that each pair talks at the same time but they all use a different language. Because none of the listeners understands any language other than that of the individual with whom they are speaking, the other nine conversations don't bother them.

There are several advantages to CDMA:

- CDMA can carry up to three times the amount of data as TDMA.

- Transmissions are much harder to eavesdrop on, since a listener would have difficulty picking out a single conversation spread across the entire spectrum.

- A would-be eavesdropper must also know the exact chip in which the transmission starts.

CDMA-based cellular technology is extremely complex. Since the focus of this book is not specifically on CDMA technology, the preceding description and examples are included here merely to provide an overview of this method of multiple access.

Transmission Direction

In most wireless communications systems, data must flow in both directions between transmitter and receiver. The flow must be controlled so that the sending and receiving devices know when data will arrive or when it needs to be transmitted. There are three types of data flow: simplex, half-duplex, and full-duplex.

Simplex transmission occurs in only one direction, from device 1 to device 2, as seen in Figure 3-18. A broadcast radio station is an example of simplex transmission: the signal goes from the radio transmitter to the listener's radio, but the listener has no way of communicating back to the station using the same radio signal. Simplex is rarely used in wireless communication today except for broadcast radio and television. The reason is that the receiver is unable to give the sender any feedback regarding the transmission, such as whether it was received correctly, or if it needs to be re-sent. Such reliability is essential for successful data exchange.

Figure 3-18   Simplex transmission

Half-duplex transmission sends data in both directions, but only one way at a time, as seen in Figure 3-19. Half-duplex transmission is used in consumer devices such as citizens band (CB) radios or walkie-talkies. In order for User A to transmit a message to User B, he must hold down the "talk" button while speaking. While the button is being pressed, User B can only listen and not talk. User A must release the "talk" button before User B can press his "talk" button. Both parties can send and receive information, but only one at a time.

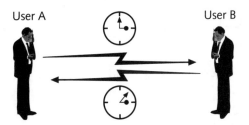

Figure 3-19   Half-duplex transmission

Full-duplex transmissions allow data to flow in both directions simultaneously, as seen in Figure 3-20. A telephone system is an example of a type of full-duplex transmission. Both parties on a telephone call can speak at the same time and they are able to hear each other. Most modern wireless systems such as cellular telephones use full-duplex transmission.

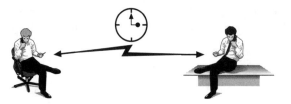

Figure 3-20   Full-duplex transmission

If the same antenna is used for wireless transmission and reception, a filter can be used to handle full-duplex transmissions. Wireless communications equipment that works in full-duplex mode sends and receives on different frequencies. A transmission picked up by the antenna on the receive frequency passes through a filter and is sent to the receiver, while the transmission signal on the send frequency is passed on to the antenna. This is illustrated in Figure 3-21.

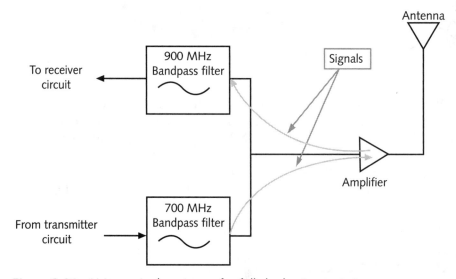

Figure 3-21   Using a single antenna for full-duplex transmission

Switching

The concept of **switching** is essential to all types of telecommunications, wireless as well as wired. Switching involves moving the signal from one wire or frequency to another. Consider for a moment the telephone in your home. You can use that one telephone to call a friend across the street, a classmate in another town, a store in a distant state, or anyone else around the world who also has a phone. How can one single telephone be used to call all other telephones on the earth? This is accomplished through a switch at the telephone company's central office. The signal from your phone goes out your telephone's wire and is then switched or moved to the wire of the telephone that belongs to your friend across the street. This is illustrated in Figure 3-22.

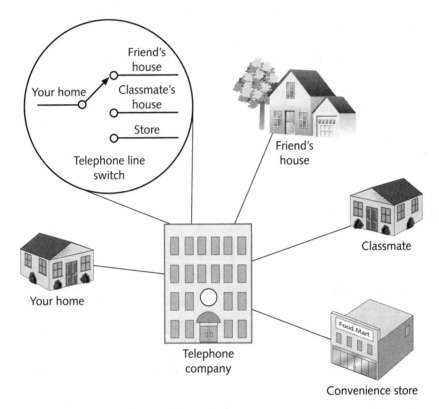

Figure 3-22 Telephone call switching

NOTE The first telephone switches were not automatic. The switching was done manually on switchboards by human operators. Today the telephone system is officially known as the Public Switched Telephone Network (PSTN), and the collection of equipment used in this network is commonly referred to in the data communications field as the Plain Old Telephone System (POTS).

As an example, imagine a telephone network where each telephone must be wired to every other telephone. If your network had 500 telephones, this would require 499 cables for each telephone and a total of 124,750 cables to connect all of the telephones. Try to draw a simple network of only five telephones on a piece of paper and you will quickly realize that you need 10 cables to interconnect all of them. This type of connection is called a "mesh network."

TIP   You can quickly calculate how many cables would be required to interconnect several telephones or computers in a mesh network by using the formula n(n-1)/2, where n is the total number of devices you want to connect. Of course, this is not a very practical solution.

Telephone systems use a type of switching known as **circuit switching**. When a telephone call is placed, a dedicated and direct physical connection is made between the caller and the recipient of the call through the switch. While the telephone conversation is taking place, the connection is "dedicated" and remains open between only these two users. Ignoring for a moment some of the advanced features available today in telephone networks, basically no other calls can be made from the two connected phones while the first conversation is going on, and anyone who calls that phone will receive a busy signal. This direct connection lasts until the end of the call, at which time the switch drops the connection.

NOTE   Circuit switching is used for both wired and cellular wireless telephone systems.

Circuit switching is ideal for voice communications. However, circuit switching is not efficient for transmitting data, because data transmissions occur in "bursts" with periods of delay in between. The delay would result in time wasted while nothing was being transmitted. Instead of using circuit switching, data networks use **packet switching**. Packet switching requires that the data transmission be broken into small units called **packets**. Each packet is then sent independently through the network to reach the destination, as shown in Figure 3-23.

Packet switching has several advantages for data transmissions. First, it allows better utilization of the network. Circuit switching ties up the communications line until the transmission is complete, whereas packet switching allows multiple computers to share the same line or frequency. That's because packets from several different computers can be intermingled while being sent. Another advantage is in the area of error correction. If a transmission error occurs, it usually affects only one or a few packets. Only those packets affected must be re-sent, not the entire message.

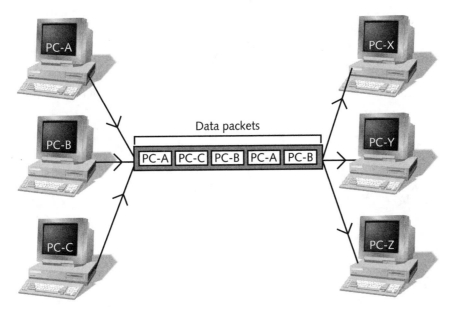

Figure 3-23   Packet switching

Signal Strength

The strength of the signal in a radio system must be sufficient for the signal to reach its destination with enough amplitude to be picked up by the antenna and for the information to be extracted from it. It is much more complicated to manage the strength of the signal in a wireless system than in a wired network. Because the signal is not confined to a pair of wires in an office building but may be transmitted in the open air space across town, many types of interference can wreak havoc with a wireless transmission. In addition, many types of objects, both stationary and moving, can impact the signal. Examples include high-voltage power lines, various types of radiation emitted by the sun, and lightning. See Figure 3-24.

One factor that affects radio signal strength is **electromagnetic interference (EMI)**, also called **noise**. Consider a room full of 20 people with 10 one-on-one conversations taking place. If everyone is talking freely, there is a great deal of "racket" or background noise with which to contend. With radio waves, background electromagnetic "noise" of various types can impede a signal.

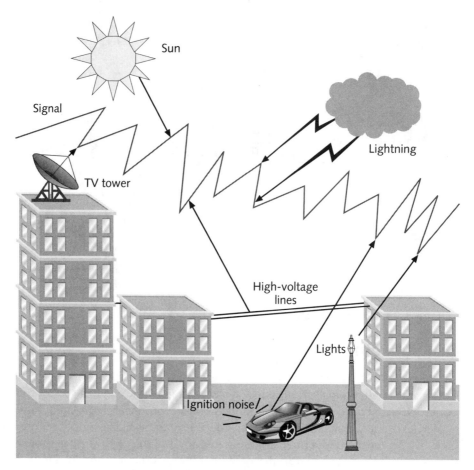

Figure 3-24   Sources of EMI or noise (interference)

A measurement called **signal-to-noise ratio (SNR)** compares the signal strength with the background noise. See Figure 3-25. When signal strength falls close to or below the level of noise, interference can take place. However, when the strength of the signal is high, it is well above the noise, and interference can be easily filtered out. Consider again the example of the room full of people trying to carry on a conversation. If someone moves closer to her partner so that she can be heard above the background noise, she is trying to achieve a higher SNR.

There are a variety of ways to attempt to reduce the interference of noise and create an acceptable SNR. Boosting the strength of the signal through the use of more powerful amplifiers in the transmitter is one common method. The use of filters when receiving the signal is another way to reduce noise. Also, techniques such as frequency hopping spread spectrum can reduce the impact of noise on a signal.

3

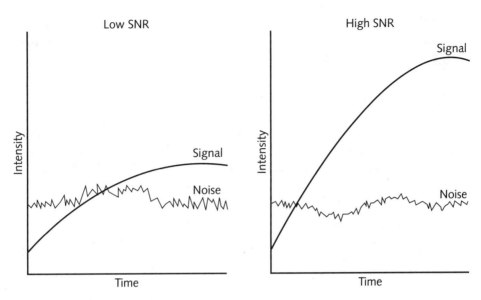

Figure 3-25 Signal-to-noise ratio (SNR)

NOTE

With a highly complex and expensive device, such as a radio telescope, the temperature of the circuits is lowered to −459 degrees Fahrenheit to maximize the performance and minimize the noise and attenuation that is generated by the circuits themselves. Recall that filters and mixers are passive devices that tend to reduce the amplitude or strength of the signal. Cooling these circuits down to -459 degrees Fahrenheit virtually eliminates the attenuation and dramatically reduces the noise. However, it is not practical to do this in a handheld transmitting device.

A loss of signal strength is known as **attenuation**. Attenuation can be caused by a variety of factors. Objects in the path of the signal generally cause the most attenuation. Man-made objects, such as walls and buildings, can decrease the strength of a signal. Table 3-2 shows examples of different building materials and their effect on radio transmissions. Amplifying a signal both before it is transmitted (to increase the power level) and after it is received helps to minimize attenuation.

Table 3-2 Materials and their effect on radio waves

Type of Material	Use in a Building	Impact on Radio Waves
Wood	Office partition	Low
Plaster	Inner walls	Low
Glass	Windows	Low
Bricks	Outer walls	Medium
Concrete	Floors and outer walls	High
Metal	Elevator shafts and cars	Very high

NOTE Attenuation can also be caused by precipitation, such as rain or snow, at certain frequencies. Consequently, attenuation decreases as the altitude increases because of the decrease in air and water vapor density at higher altitudes.

As a radio signal is transmitted, the electromagnetic waves spread out. Some of these waves may reflect off distant surfaces and continue toward the receiver. This results in the same signal being received not only from several different directions but also at different times, since it takes longer for the wave that bounced off a distant surface to reach the receiver. This phenomenon, known as **multipath distortion**, is illustrated in Figure 3-26.

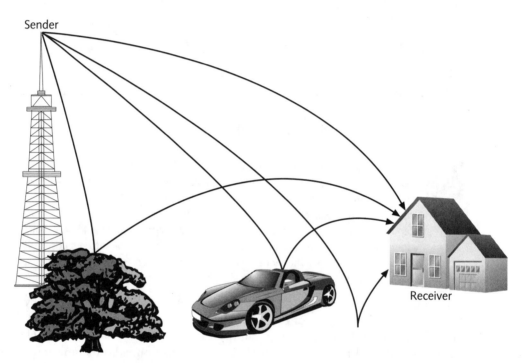

Figure 3-26   Multipath distortion

Multipath distortion can cause reduction in the strength of the signal and prevent the receiver from picking up a signal strong enough for reliable reception. See Figure 3-27.

NOTE Multipath distortion gets its name from the fact that as waves arrive at different times, and therefore out of phase with one another, the resulting signal at the input of the receiver gets distorted since the amplitudes of both signals get added to each other or subtracted from one another.

3

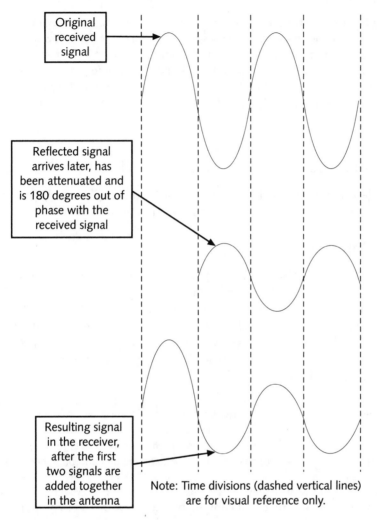

Original received signal

Reflected signal arrives later, has been attenuated and is 180 degrees out of phase with the received signal

Resulting signal in the receiver, after the first two signals are added together in the antenna

Note: Time divisions (dashed vertical lines) are for visual reference only.

Figure 3-27   Effect of multipath distortion; reflected signal received later

Several steps can be taken to minimize multipath distortion. These include using a **directional antenna** where possible or changing the height of the transmitter antenna to provide a clear line of sight to the receiver's antenna. A directional antenna radiates the electromagnetic waves in one direction only and can help reduce or eliminate the effect of multipath distortion if there is a clear line of sight between the two antennas. Other methods include using an amplifier in front of the receiver to increase the SNR or transmitting the same signal on separate frequencies (see OFDM in Chapter 8). Multipath distortion is particularly problematic in cities with large buildings and structures where the receiver is in constant motion, such as in cellular telephony.

NOTE

Multipath distortion affects FM reception as well, particularly in the downtown districts of metropolitan areas. FM stations are usually free from noise; however, if you have ever been riding in an automobile in the downtown area of a large city you may have noticed occasional static-like noise while listening to an FM station. This noise is caused by the signal reflecting off large buildings and reaching the receiver out of phase, sometimes canceling the signal for very brief moments.

UNDERSTANDING STANDARDS

Standards for telecommunications have been in place almost since the beginning of the industry. They have played an important role in the rapid growth of communications.

The Need for Standards

The role that standards—which are commonly accepted technical specifications—play in a particular industry varies widely. Mention the word "standards" to someone who works in information technology (IT) and you may receive a strong negative response. This is because some in that industry believe that standards set for computer technologies stifle growth in this fast-paced field. They maintain that waiting for standards to catch up to the rapid changes in IT only slows everything down. Nevertheless, standards in any industry do ultimately benefit both industry and consumers.

NOTE

The world's first telecommunications standard was published by the International Telegraph Union (ITU) in 1885. The standard originated from a desire by the governments of many different nations to have compatible telegraph operation. It took 20 years for the first standard to be created and published.

Standards for telecommunications have been essential since the very beginning. The very nature of the industry, in which pieces of equipment interact with other equipment, requires that standards exist for the design, implementation, and operation of the equipment. A lack of standards between devices would prevent communications from taking place. Telecommunications experts rely on standards for the industry to function. Telecommunications would essentially be impossible without standards.

Advantages and Disadvantages of Standards

Despite what any proponent or detractor of standards may say, there are both pros and cons to developing and applying standards in the telecommunications industry. Advantages relate to interoperability and corporate competition, while disadvantages are primarily political in nature.

Advantages of Standards

The advantages of standards primarily include the guarantee that telecommunications devices from one vendor will interoperate with those from other vendors. Devices that are not based on standards may not be able to connect and communicate with similar devices from other vendors. Standards ensure that a transmitter purchased from Vendor A can be seamlessly integrated into a communications network that contains a receiver from Vendor B.

A second benefit of standards is that they create competition. Standards are open to everyone; any vendor who wants to enter a marketplace can do so. Thus, standards can result in competition between vendors; and competition has several advantages. Competition results in lower costs for consumers and improvements in products developed by vendors. A vendor who has created a proprietary device gains no benefit in reducing his prices because he has no competition. Instead, because he has a captive market, he may raise prices at will. However, vendors making the same product based on the same standards may reduce their prices below the competition's prices. The competition between vendors, due to standards, usually results in lower costs to consumers.

Competition also results in lower costs for manufacturers. Because standards have already been established, manufacturers do not have to invest large amounts of capital in research and development. Instead, they can use the standards as a blueprint for their manufacturing. This reduces startup costs as well as the amount of time needed to bring a product to the market. Also, because standards increase the market for products that follow the standard, manufacturers tend to deploy mass production techniques and gain economies of scale in manufacturing and engineering. As a result, production costs stay low, and these savings are passed on to the consumer.

A third benefit is that standards help consumers protect their investment in equipment. It is not uncommon for a manufacturer of a proprietary device to phase out a product line of equipment. Businesses that purchased that line are left with two choices. They can continue to support this now-obsolete legacy system into the foreseeable future. However, the costs will dramatically escalate as replacement parts—and support specialists—become more difficult to locate. The second option is to throw everything away and buy a new up-to-date system. Both choices are very expensive.

Standards, however, can help create a migration path. The body that is responsible for creating initial standards will continue to incorporate new technologies into regularly revised standards. Generally these new standards are backward-compatible, reducing the risk of obsolete "orphan" systems that are incompatible with newer technologies.

Disadvantages of Standards

There are disadvantages to standards as well. International standards can be a threat to industries in large countries, because their domestic markets become subject to overseas competition. Manufacturers in foreign nations may have lower overhead costs and can produce the device cheaper than manufacturers in-country. Standards allow foreign manufacturers to produce and sell their products abroad, often threatening a domestic manufacturer's market share. However, this also means that standards can be a benefit to industries in smaller countries.

Another disadvantage to standards is that although they are intended to create unity, they can have the opposite effect. Periodically, a specific nation will create a standard and offer it for consideration to other nations as a global standard. However, due to opposing political interests (which may have nothing to do with technology), a particular nation may reject that standard and attempt to create its own. This division can result in each nation creating its own standards and decreasing the value of global communications. Television broadcasting standards is an example; many nations around the world have approved different standards as a way of protecting their internal markets as well as their culture. With the advent of the Internet and global commerce, this type of protectionist thinking has been mostly wiped out, but multiple TV standards continue to be in effect, forcing many manufacturers to design and produce television sets and video recorders that can support multiple standards. The consumer ultimately has to pay the cost to purchase and maintain these more complex devices.

Most experts agree that the advantages of standards far outweigh the disadvantages, and that standards are vital in industries such as telecommunications.

Types of Standards

There are two major types of standards in the telecommunications industry: de facto and de jure. A third emerging type of standard, by consortia, is increasingly influencing how standards are set.

De Facto

De facto standards are not really standards at all. Rather, they are common practices that the industry follows for various reasons. The reasons range from ease of use to tradition to what the majority of the users do. For the most part, de facto standards are established by success in the marketplace. For example, most industry experts would agree that Microsoft Windows has become the de facto standard operating system today for personal computers and network servers. This is because as of October 2005, 77% of the computer users worldwide have elected to install and run Windows on their computers. There was no standards body that proclaimed Windows as the standard; its widespread use in the industry has created what amounts to a standard.

NOTE   The term de facto comes from Latin and means "from the fact." As it applies to computer and communications technologies, those technologies that are adopted by the market voluntarily become known as a de facto standard. One of the best examples of this is the TCP/IP protocol. See www.ietf.org.

De Jure

The second major type of standard is known as a **de jure standard** also called **official standard**. De jure standards are those that are controlled by an organization or body that has been entrusted with that task; different standards groups have different rules regarding membership. You will read about some of these groups in the next section.

The process for creating standards can be very involved. Generally, the organization develops subcommittees responsible for a specific technology. Each subcommittee is composed of different working groups, which are teams of industry experts who are given the task to create the initial draft of a standard's documentation. The draft is then published to the members, both individuals and companies, and requests for comments are solicited (these members may be developers, potential users, and other people with general interest in the field). The original committee reviews the comments and revises the draft. This final draft is then reviewed by the entire organization and usually is put to a vote before the final standards are officially published and made available to the public. There may be a cost associated with obtaining a copy of the official published standard.

De facto standards sometimes become de jure standards by being approved by a committee. Ethernet is one example of a de facto standard that later became an official standard.

NOTE

Consortia

One of the major complaints against de jure standards is the amount of time it takes for a standard to be completed. For example, the initial standard for wireless local area networks took seven years to complete. In the telecommunications and IT industries, this represents an extremely long period of time before products can be brought to the marketplace.

In reaction to this criticism, consortia are often used today to create standards. **Consortia** are usually industry-sponsored organizations that have the goal of promoting a specific technology. Unlike de jure standards bodies, membership in consortia is not open to everyone. Instead, specific high-profile companies create and serve on consortia. The goal of consortia is to develop a standard that promotes their specific technology in a shorter period of time than the official standards organizations.

One of the most famous consortia is the World Wide Web Consortium (W3C), which is composed of industry giants such as Microsoft, Netscape, Sun, and IBM. The W3C is responsible for creating the standards that are widely used on the Internet today, including hypertext markup language (HTML), cascading style sheets (CSS), and the Document Object Model (DOM).

Telecommunications Standards Organizations

The need for standards in telecommunications is apparent. Several different national, multinational, and international standards organizations establish standards.

United States Standards Groups

In the United States, there are several standards organizations, each of which plays a role in setting telecommunications standards. The **American National Standards Institute (ANSI)** functions largely as a clearinghouse for all kinds of standards development in the United States. Most ANSI standards are developed by one of its 271 affiliated organizations, which include diverse groups such as the Water Quality Association and the Air Movement and Control Association.

One of the ANSI-affiliated organizations is the **Electronic Industries Alliance (EIA)**. The EIA is made up of industry vendors from four areas: electronic components, consumer electronics, electronic information, and telecommunications. Working with vendors, the EIA publishes "Recommended Standards" (RS) for the industry to follow. For example, the EIA developed and published a standard that defines how a computer's serial port, connector pin-outs, and electrical signaling should function. This standard is generally known as EIA RS-232. More information on the EIA can be found at www.eia.org.

A companion organization is known as the **Telecommunications Industries Association (TIA)**. The TIA comprises more than 1,100 members that manufacture or supply the products and services used in global communications. The function of the TIA is to advocate policy issues to legislative bodies and to establish standards in five areas: user premises equipment, network equipment, wireless communications, fiber optics, and satellite communications. You can visit the TIA Web site at www.tiaonline.org.

Two other organizations play a role in establishing national standards for telecommunications technology. The **Internet Engineering Task Force (IETF)** focuses on the lower levels of telecommunications technologies. The IETF is the protocol engineering and development arm of the Internet. It is a large, open, international community of network designers, operators, vendors, and researchers concerned with the evolution of the Internet architecture and the smooth operation of the Internet. The IETF existed informally for many years, and it was not an official standards body until 1986, when the IETF was formalized by the **Internet Architecture Board (IAB)**. The IAB is responsible for defining the overall architecture of the Internet and also serves as the technology advisory group to the **Internet Society (ISOC)**, a professional membership organization of Internet experts that comments on policies and practices and oversees a number of other boards and task forces dealing with network policy issues. You can find out more about the development of the Internet and the other IETF parent organizations mentioned above by visiting www.ietf.org.

The **Institute of Electrical and Electronics Engineers (IEEE)**, like the IETF, establishes standards for telecommunications as well. However, the IEEE also covers a wide range of IT standards. Some of its most well known standards are the IEEE 802.3, which is the standard for local area network Ethernet transmissions, and the IEEE 802.11b, which is standard for wireless local area network transmissions.

You can learn about the IEEE at www.ieee.org. You can also obtain a no-cost copy of IEEE 802 standards that relate to networking and wireless networking, provided that these have been published for longer than six months, by visiting the following Web site: standards.ieee.org/getieee802/portfolio.html.

Multinational Standards Groups

There are several standards organizations that span more than one nation. Many of these multinational standards organizations are found in Europe. The **European Telecommunications Standards Institute (ETSI)** develops telecommunications standards for use throughout Europe. Its membership is made up primarily of European companies and European government agencies. The ETSI site is at www.etsi.org.

International Standards Groups

Because telecommunications technology is truly global, there are also global organizations that set industry standards. The best known is the **International Telecommunications Union (ITU)**, which is an agency of the United Nations that is responsible for telecommunications. The ITU is composed of over 200 governments and private sector companies that coordinate global telecommunications networks and services. Unlike other bodies that set standards, the ITU is actually a treaty organization. The regulations set by the ITU are legally binding on the nations that have signed the treaty.

Two of the ITU's subsidiary organizations prepare recommendations on telecommunications standards. The ITU-T is responsible for establishing standards for telecommunications networks, while the ITU-R sets standards for radio-based communications, such as radio frequencies and standards for radio systems. Although these recommendations are not mandatory standards, and are not binding on the nations that have signed other treaties, almost all of the nations elect to follow the ITU recommendations, and these actually function as worldwide standards. The ITU can be found at www.itu.org.

The ITU-T recently replaced a standards body known as the CCITT, whose origins date back to work on standards for telegraphs in the 1860s.

The **International Organization for Standardization (ISO)** is based in Geneva, Switzerland. (Note that they use the ISO acronym, instead of their initials, IOS. This was selected because "iso" means "equal" in Greek.) Started in 1947, the ISO's goal is to promote international cooperation and standards in the areas of science, technology, and economics. Today, groups from over 100 countries belong to the ISO. You can visit the ISO at www.iso.org.

NOTE   Several of the groups that belong to the ISO are actually national standards bodies. For example, the EIA plays a role in the ISO.

Although it would seem that there are too many standards organizations, in the interest of worldwide standardization, all of these organizations, including the many organizations in the United States, tend to cooperate with each other and seldom step over each other's authority or geographical jurisdiction. You will read about some examples of this cooperation in the upcoming chapters. Table 3-3 summarizes those organizations.

Table 3-3   Telecommunications standards organizations

Organization Name	Jurisdiction
American National Standards Institute (ANSI)	National
Electronic Industries Association (EIA)	National
Telecommunications Industries Association (TIA)	National
Internet Engineering Task Force (IETF)	National
Institute of Electrical and Electronics Engineers (IEEE)	National
European Telecommunications Standards Institute (ETSI)	Multinational
International Telecommunications Union (ITU)	International
International Organization for Standardization (ISO)	International

Regulatory Agencies

Although setting standards is important for telecommunications, enforcing telecommunications regulations is equally important. In a sense, the nature of national and international commerce enforces some standards. A company that refuses to abide by standards for cellular telephone transmissions will find that nobody buys its products. Telecommunications regulations, however, must be enforced by an outside regulatory agency, whose role is to ensure that all participants adhere to the prescribed standards. These regulations typically involve defining who can use a specific frequency when broadcasting a signal. Almost all nations have a national organization that functions as the regulatory agency to determine and enforce telecommunications policies.

In the United States, the **Federal Communications Commission (FCC)** serves as the primary regulatory agency for telecommunications. The FCC is an independent government agency that is directly responsible to Congress. The FCC was established by the

Communications Act of 1934 and is charged with regulating interstate and international communications by radio, television, wire, satellite, and cable. The FCC's jurisdiction covers the 50 states, the District of Columbia, and U.S. territories.

NOTE   In order to preserve its independence, the FCC is directed by five commissioners who are appointed by the President and confirmed by the Senate for five-year terms. Only three commissioners may be members of the same political party, and none of them can have a financial interest in any FCC-related business.

The FCC's responsibilities are very broad. In addition to developing and implementing regulatory programs, it also processes applications for licenses and other filings, analyzes complaints, conducts investigations, and takes part in congressional hearings. The FCC also represents the United States in negotiations with foreign nations about telecommunications issues.

The FCC plays an important role in wireless communications. It regulates radio and television broadcast stations as well as cable and satellite stations. It also oversees the licensing, compliance, implementation, and other aspects of cellular telephones, pagers, and two-way radios. The FCC regulates the use of radio frequencies to fulfill the communications needs of businesses, local and state governments, public safety service providers, aircraft and ship operators, and individuals.

The RF spectrum is a limited resource, meaning that only a certain range of frequencies can be used for radio transmissions. Because of this limitation, frequencies are often licensed by regulatory agencies in the different countries around the world. In the United States, the regulatory agency is the FCC, which has the power to allocate portions of the spectrum. Broadcasters are required to transmit only in the frequency or frequencies for which they obtained a license. Commercial companies such as radio and television stations must pay fees (which are sometimes quite large) for the right to use a frequency, and, naturally, they do not want anyone else to be allowed to transmit on the same frequency within their coverage area. The FCC and other country agencies continually monitor transmissions to ensure that no one is using a frequency without a license or is transmitting with more power than their license allows.

RADIO FREQUENCY SPECTRUM

The **radio frequency spectrum** is the entire range of all radio frequencies that exist. This range extends from 10 KHz to over 30 GHz, as seen in Figure 3-28. The spectrum is divided into 450 different sections, or **bands**. Table 3-4 lists the major bands, their corresponding frequencies, and some typical uses.

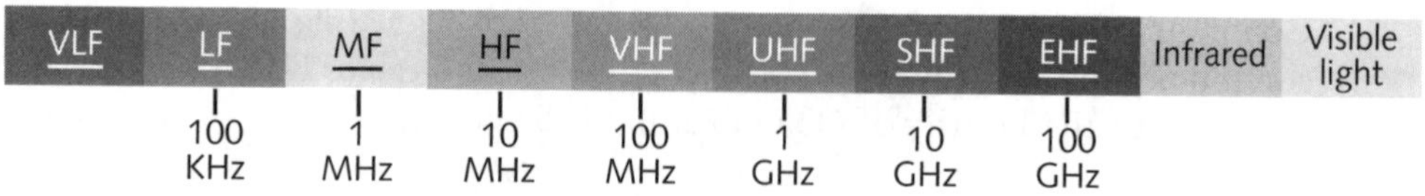

Figure 3-28   Radio frequency spectrum

Table 3-4   Radio frequency bands

Band	Frequency	Common Uses for These Frequencies
Very Low Frequency (VLF)	10 KHz to 30 KHz	Maritime ship-to-shore
Low Frequency (LF)	30 KHz to 300 KHz	Radio location such as LORAN (Long Range Navigation) Time signals for clock synchronization (WWVB)
Medium Frequency (MF)	300 KHz to 3 MHz	AM radio
High Frequency (HF)	3 MHz to 30 MHz	Short wave radio, CB radio
Very High Frequency (VHF)	30 MHz to 144 MHz 144 MHz to 174 MHz 174 MHz to 328.6 MHz	TV channels 2-6, FM radio Taxi radios TV channels 7-13
Ultra High Frequency (UHF)	328.6 MHz to 806 MHz 806 MHz to 960 MHz 960 MHz to 2.3 GHz 2.3 GHz to 2.9 GHz	Public safety: Fire, Police, etc. Cellular telephones Air traffic control radar WLANs (802.11b)
Super High Frequency (SHF)	2.9 GHz to 30 GHz	WLANs (802.11a)
Extremely High Frequency (EHF)	30 GHz and above	Radio astronomy

Radio frequencies of other common devices include:

- Garage door openers, alarm systems: 40 MHz
- Baby monitors: 49 MHz
- Radio-controlled airplanes: 72 MHz
- Radio-controlled cars: 75 MHz
- Wildlife tracking collars: 215 MHz–220 MHz
- Global positioning system (GPS): 1.227 GHz and 1.575 GHz

The United States is obligated to comply with the international spectrum allocations established by the ITU. However, the U.S. domestic spectrum uses may differ from the international allocations if these domestic uses do not conflict with international regulations or agreements.

3

NOTE Until 1993, the ITU held conferences at 20-year intervals to review the international spectrum allocations. Since then, ITU conferences are convened every two to three years.

NOTE The U.S. Commerce Department's National Telecommunications and Information Administration (NTIA) serves as the principal advisor to the president on domestic and international communications and information issues. It also represents the views of the executive branch before the Congress, the Federal Communications Commission, foreign governments, and international organizations.

Although a license is normally required from the FCC to send and receive on a specific frequency, there is a notable exception. This is known as the **license exempt spectrum**, or unregulated bands. Unregulated bands are, in effect, radio spectra that are available nationwide without charge to any users without a license. Devices that use these bands can be either fixed or mobile devices. The FCC says that it designated the **unregulated bands** to "foster the development of a broad range of new devices, stimulate the growth of new industries, and promote the ability of U.S. manufacturers to compete globally by enabling them to develop unlicensed digital products for the world market."

There are some negative features of the unregulated bands. Because they are not regulated and licensed, devices from different vendors may attempt to use the same frequency. This conflict can cause the signals from different devices to interfere with each other, preventing them from functioning properly. Thus the performance of devices using unregulated bands may be unpredictable.

NOTE The FCC does impose power limits on devices using the unregulated bands, which in effect reduces their range. This prevents manufacturers of devices such as long-range walkie-talkies from using these frequencies instead of the regulated frequencies intended for these products.

Table 3-5 outlines the unregulated bands. One unregulated band is the **Industrial, Scientific and Medical (ISM) band**, which was approved by the FCC in 1985. Devices such as WLANs that transmit at 11 Mbps use this band. Another unlicensed band is the **Unlicensed National Information Infrastructure (U–NII)**, approved in 1996. The U-NII band is intended for devices that provide short-range, high-speed wireless digital communications. U-NII devices may provide a means for educational institutions, libraries, and health care providers to connect to basic and advanced telecommunications services. Wireless networks working in unlicensed frequency bands are already helping to improve the quality and reduce the cost of medical care by allowing medical staff to obtain on-the-spot patient data, X-rays, and medical charts, and by giving health care workers access to telecommunications services.

Table 3-5 Unregulated bands

Unlicensed Band	Frequency	Total Bandwidth	Common Uses
Industrial, Scientific and Medical (ISM)	902-928 MHz 2.4-2.4835 GHz 5.725-5.85 GHz	234.5 MHz	Cordless phones, WLANs, wireless public branch exchanges
Unlicensed Personal Communications Systems	1910-1930 MHz 2390-2400 MHz	30 MHz	WLANs, wireless public branch exchanges
Unlicensed National Information Infrastructure (U-NII)	5.15-5.25 GHz 5.25-5.35 GHz 5.725-5.825 GHz	300 MHz	WLANs, wireless public branch exchanges, campus applications, long outdoor links
Millimeter Wave	59-64 GHz	5 GHz	Home networking applications

Two recent developments have had an impact on the crowded radio frequency spectrum. The first involves the direction of radio signals. Currently, when radio signals leave the sender's antenna, they spread or radiate out (the word "radio" comes from the term "radiated energy") and can be picked up by multiple recipients. A new technique known as **adaptive array processing** replaces a traditional antenna with an array of antenna elements. These elements deliver RF signals to one specific user instead of sending signals out in a scattered pattern. This helps prevent eavesdropping by unapproved listeners and also allows more transmissions to take place in a given range of frequencies.

The second development is known as **ultra-wideband transmission (UWB)**. UWB does not use a traditional radio signal carrier sending signals in the regulated frequency spectrum. Instead, UWB uses low-power, precisely timed pulses of energy that operate in the same frequency spectrum as low-end noise, such as that emitted by computer chips, TV monitors, automobile ignitions, and fans. UWB is currently used in limited radar and position-location devices; however, IEEE standards should be approved within a year or two for its use in wireless network communications.

CHAPTER SUMMARY

❑ Several hardware components are essential for communicating using radio frequencies (RF): filters, mixers, amplifiers, and antennas. A version of each of these components is found on all radio systems.

❑ A filter is used either to accept or to block a radio frequency signal. With a low-pass filter, a maximum frequency threshold is set. All signals that are below that maximum threshold are allowed to pass through. Instead of setting a maximum frequency threshold, as with a low-pass filter, a high-pass filter sets a minimum frequency threshold. All signals that are

3

above the minimum threshold are allowed to pass through, while those below the minimum threshold are turned away. A bandpass filter sets a passband, which is both a minimum and maximum threshold.

- The purpose of a mixer is to combine two inputs to create a single output. The single output is the highest sum and the lowest difference of the frequencies.

- An amplifier increases a signal's intensity or strength, while an antenna is used to convert an RF signal from the transmitter into an electromagnetic wave, which carries the information through the air or empty space.

- Although filters, mixers, amplifiers, and antennas are all necessary components for a radio system, there are other design considerations that must be taken into account when creating a radio system. Because there are only a limited number of frequencies available, conserving the use of frequencies is important. One way to conserve is by sharing a frequency among several individual users.

- Frequency Division Multiple Access (FDMA) divides the bandwidth of the frequency into several narrower frequencies. Time Division Multiple Access (TDMA) divides the bandwidth into several time slots. Each user is assigned the entire frequency for their transmission but only for a small fraction of time on a fixed, rotating basis. Code Division Multiple Access (CDMA) uses spread spectrum technology and unique digital spreading codes called PN codes, rather than separate RF frequencies or channels, to differentiate between the different transmissions.

- The direction in which data travels on a wireless network is important. There are three types of data flow. Simplex occurs in only one direction. Half-duplex transmission sends data in both directions, but only one way at a time, while full-duplex transmissions enable data to flow in both directions simultaneously.

- Switching involves moving the signal from one wire or frequency to another. Telephone systems use a type of switching known as circuit switching. When a telephone call is made, a dedicated and direct physical connection is made between the caller and the recipient of the call through the switch. Instead of using circuit switching, data networks use packet switching. Packet switching requires that the data transmission be broken into smaller units called packets, and each packet is then sent independently through the network to reach the destination.

- In a wireless system, it is much more complicated to manage the strength of the signal than in a wired network. Electromagnetic interference (EMI), sometimes called noise, can come from a variety of man-made and natural sources. The signal-to-noise ratio (SNR) refers to the measure of signal strength relative to the background noise. A loss of signal strength is known as attenuation. Attenuation can be caused by a variety of factors, such as walls and buildings that can decrease the strength of the signal. As a radio signal is transmitted, the electromagnetic waves spread out. Some of these waves may reflect off of surfaces and slow down. This results in the same signal being received not only from several different directions but also at different times. This is known as multipath distortion.

❏ Standards for telecommunications have been in place almost since the beginning of the industry. They have played an important role in the rapid growth of communications. There are several advantages of standards, including interoperability, lower costs, and a migration path. De facto standards are not really standards but are "common practices" that the industry follows. Official standards (also called de jure standards) are those that are controlled by an organization or body that has been entrusted with that task. Consortia are often used today to create standards. Consortia are usually industry-sponsored organizations that have the goal of promoting a specific technology. There are also standards organizations that span more than one nation. Because telecommunications is truly global, there are also multinational organizations that set standards. In the United States, the Federal Communications Commission (FCC) serves as the primary regulatory agency for telecommunications. The FCC is an independent government agency that is directly responsible to Congress.

❏ The radio frequency spectrum is the entire range of all radio frequencies that exist. This range extends from 10 KHz to over 30 GHz and is divided into 450 different bands. Although a license is normally required from the FCC to send and receive on a specific frequency, unregulated bands are available for use without a license in the United States and many other countries. Two unregulated bands are the Industrial, Scientific and Medical (ISM) band and the Unlicensed National Information Infrastructure (U–NII).

❏ Two recent developments have had an impact on the crowded radio frequency spectrum. A new technique known as adaptive array processing replaces a traditional antenna with an array of antenna elements. These elements deliver RF signals to one specific user instead of sending signals out in a scattered pattern. Ultra-wideband transmission (UWB) does not use a traditional radio signal carrier sending signals in the regulated frequency spectrum. Instead, UWB uses low-power, precisely timed pulses of energy that operate in the same frequency spectrum as low-end noise such as that emitted by computer chips and TV monitors.

KEY TERMS

adaptive array processing — A radio transmission technique that replaces a traditional antenna with an array of antenna elements.

American National Standards Institute (ANSI) — A clearinghouse for standards development in the United States.

amplifier — A component that increases a signal's intensity.

attenuation — A loss of signal strength.

bandpass filter — A filter that passes all signals that are between the maximum and minimum threshold.

bands — Sections of the radio frequency spectrum.

circuit switching — A dedicated and direct physical connection is made between two transmitting devices.

Code Division Multiple Access (CDMA) — A technique that uses spread spectrum technology and unique digital codes to send and receive radio transmissions.

consortia — Industry-sponsored organizations that have the goal of promoting a specific technology.

crosstalk — Signals from close frequencies that may interfere with other signals.

de facto standards — Common practices that the industry follows for various reasons.

de jure standards — Standards that are controlled by an organization or body.

directional antenna — An antenna that radiates the electromagnetic waves in one direction only. As a result, it can help reduce or eliminate the effect of multipath distortion, if there is a clear line of sight between the two antennas.

electromagnetic interference (EMI) — Interference with a radio signal; also called noise.

Electronic Industries Alliance (EIA) — U.S. industry vendors from four areas: electronic components, consumer electronics, electronic information, and telecommunications.

European Telecommunications Standards Institute (ETSI) — A standards body that is designed to develop telecommunications standards for use throughout Europe.

Federal Communications Commission (FCC) — The primary U.S. regulatory agency for telecommunications.

filter — A component that is used to either accept or to block a radio frequency signal.

Frequency Division Multiple Access (FDMA) — A radio transmission technique that divides the bandwidth of the frequency into several smaller frequency bands.

full-duplex transmission — Transmissions that enable data to flow in either direction simultaneously.

half-duplex transmission — Transmission that occurs in both directions but only one way at a time.

high-pass filter — A filter that passes all signals that are above a maximum threshold.

Industrial, Scientific and Medical (ISM) band — An unregulated radio frequency band approved by the FCC in 1985.

Institute of Electrical and Electronics Engineers (IEEE) — A standards body that establishes standards for telecommunications.

intermediate frequency (IF) — The output signal that results from the modulation process.

International Organization for Standardization (ISO) — An organization to promote international cooperation and standards in the areas of science, technology, and economics.

International Telecommunications Union (ITU) — An agency of the United Nations that sets international telecommunications standards and coordinates global telecommunications networks and services.

Internet Architecture Board (IAB) — The organization responsible for defining the overall architecture of the Internet, providing guidance and broad direction to the IETF. The IAB also serves as the technology advisory group to the Internet Society, and oversees a number of critical activities in support of the Internet.

Internet Engineering Task Force (IETF) — A standards body that focuses on the lower levels of telecommunications technologies.

Internet Society (ISOC) — A professional membership organization of Internet experts that comments on policies and practices and oversees a number of other boards and task forces dealing with network policy issues.

license exempt spectrum — Unregulated radio frequency bands that are available in the United States to any users without a license.

low-pass filter — A filter that passes all signals that are below a maximum threshold.

mixer — A component that combines two inputs to create a single output.

multipath distortion — The same signal being received from several different directions and also at different times.

noise — Interference with a signal.

official standards — See de jure standards.

packet — A smaller segment of the transmitted signal.

packet switching — Data transmission that is broken into smaller units.

passband — A minimum and maximum threshold.

PN code — Pseudo random code; a code that appears to be a random sequence of 1s and 0s but actually repeats itself. Used in CDMA cellular telephone technology.

radio frequency communications (RF) — All types of radio communications that use radio frequency waves.

radio frequency spectrum — The entire range of all radio frequencies that exist.

sidebands — The sum and the differences of the frequency carrier that serve as buffer space around the frequency of the transmitted signal.

signal-to-noise ratio (SNR) — The measure of signal strength relative to the background noise.

simplex transmission — Transmission that occurs in only one direction.

switching — Moving a signal from one wire or frequency to another.

Telecommunications Industries Association (TIA) — A group of more than 1,100 members that manufacture or supply the products and services used in global communications.

Time Division Multiple Access (TDMA) — A transmission technique that divides the bandwidth into several time slots.

ultra-wideband transmission (UWB) — Low-power, precisely timed pulses of energy that operate in the same frequency spectrum as low-end noise, such as that emitted by computer chips and TV monitors.

Unlicensed National Information Infrastructure (U-NII) — An unregulated band approved by the FCC in 1996 to provide for short-range, high-speed wireless digital communications.

unregulated bands — See license exempt spectrum.

REVIEW QUESTIONS

3

1. Each of the following is a type of filter except _____ .
   a. low-pass
   b. high-pass
   c. passband
   d. bandpass

2. The purpose of a(n) _____ is to combine two inputs to create a single output.
   a. mixer
   b. codex
   c. filter
   d. amplifier

3. A(n) _____ actively increases a signal's intensity or strength.
   a. transmitter
   b. demodulator
   c. amplifier
   d. antenna

4. The purpose of the PN code is to _____ .
   a. add a unique address to the signal
   b. spread the signal
   c. mix the signal with the IF
   d. decode the signal

5. _____ is applicable to transmissions where the information is broken up into smaller units.
   a. Error correction
   b. Circuit switching
   c. Electromagnetic interference
   d. Packet switching

6. A passband is both a minimum and maximum threshold. True or False?

7. The resulting output from the modulation process is known as the middle frequency (MF) signal. True or False?

8. The sum and the differences are known as the sidebands of the frequency carrier. True or False?

9. TDMA can carry three times the amount data that CDMA can. True or False?

10. Without switching, _____ cables would be required to interconnect 50 telephones.

11. When using the same antenna for full-duplex communications, a different _____ must be used for transmitting and receiving simultaneously.

12. _____ divides the bandwidth of the frequency into several smaller multiple frequencies.

13. When signals are sent at frequencies that are closely grouped together, an errant signal may encroach on a close frequency, causing _____ .

14. _____ divides the bandwidth into several time slots.

15. A _____ transmission uses spread spectrum technology and unique digital spreading codes.

16. List and describe the three types of data flow.

17. List and discuss the advantages of standards.

18. What is switching? What type of switching is used with telephone transmissions, and what type is used for data transmissions?

19. Explain multipath distortion and how it can be minimized.

20. What does the Federal Communications Commission do?

HANDS-ON PROJECTS

Project 3-1

Draw and label a functional block diagram of a radio transmitter. The frequency of the transmission signal will be 36,000 Hz. Label the frequency of the signal as it moves from one component to the next.

Project 3-2

Write a one-page paper on adaptive array processing systems. What technology barriers does adaptive array processing face? In what applications will it be used? Who is spearheading its development? Use the Internet and other technology sources for your paper.

Project 3-3

Because telecommunications is truly global, the International Telecommunications Union (ITU) has become the predominant international agency that is responsible for telecommunications. Research the history of the ITU and its important subagencies. Who can join? How are its standards enforced? What are some of its most recent decisions? Write a one-page paper on your findings.

Project 3-4

Natural and man-made objects in the path of a radio signal can cause attenuation, or a loss of signal strength. Locate a notebook computer with a wireless local area network that transmits to an access point. Launch the utility that monitors the strength of the signal, and move the computer away from the access point. Determine how far you can be from the access point before the signal is too weak to be useful. Record what objects in the path of the signal have the greatest impact. Also, monitor the strength of the signal while covering the antenna of the wireless NIC (if the NIC is built into the notebook, try covering the back of the screen or the bottom of the notebook computer) with your hand (for a short period of time), a piece of aluminum foil, a sheet of paper, a sheet of plastic (like a shopping bag), a purse or a briefcase containing various items, and a key ring containing many keys. Record the results and write a paper on your findings.

CASE PROJECT

Project 3-1

The Baypoint Group (TBG), a company of 50 consultants who assist organizations and businesses with issues involving network planning and design, has again requested your services as a consultant. The Good Samaritan Center, which assists needy citizens in the area, needs to modernize its office facilities. As part of its community outreach program, TBG has asked you to donate your time to help the Good Samaritan Center.

The Good Samaritan Center wants to install a wireless network in its offices. One local vendor has been trying to sell the center a proprietary system based on five-year-old technology that does not follow any current standards. The price given for the product and its installation is low and is thereby attractive to the center. However, managers at the center have asked TBG for advice. The Baypoint Group has asked you to become involved.

1. Create a PowerPoint slide presentation that outlines the different types of standards, the advantages and disadvantages of standards, and why they are needed. Include examples of products that did not follow standards and have vanished from the marketplace. Because the Good Samaritan Center is on the verge of buying the product, TBG has asked you to be very persuasive in your presentation. You are told that presenting the facts is not enough at this point; you must convince them why they should purchase a product that follows standards before you leave the room.

2. Your presentation casts a shadow of doubt over the vendor's proprietary product, but the Good Samaritan Center is still not completely convinced it should go with a standard product. TBG has just learned that the vendor's proprietary product uses a licensed frequency that will require the Center to secure and pay for a license from the FCC. TBG has asked you to prepare another presentation regarding the advantages of unregulated bands. Because an engineer who sits on the Board of the Good Samaritan Center will be there, this PowerPoint presentation should be detailed and

technical in its scope. Avoid focusing on the disadvantages of the vendor's proposal. Be prepared to answer questions related to potential interference by other wireless network users in nearby offices and what measures can be taken either to avoid such interference altogether or to deal with any problems that may arise.

OPTIONAL TEAM CASE PROJECT

A local engineering user's group has contacted The Baypoint Group requesting a speaker to discuss multiple access technologies (FDMA, TDMA, and CDMA). Form a team of two or three consultants and research these technologies in detail. Specifically, pay attention to how they are used, and address their strengths and weaknesses. Provide an opinion regarding which technology will become the dominant player in the future of wireless.

4

HOW ANTENNAS WORK

After reading this chapter and completing the exercises, you will be able to:

- Define decibels, gain, and loss
- Outline the purpose of an antenna
- List the different antenna types, shapes and sizes, and their applications
- Explain RF signal strength and direction
- Describe how antennas work

So far, we have looked at the properties of radio frequency signals, most of the components that are required to generate these signals, and how to load these signals (modulation) with some kind of meaningful information, whether analog like music or voice, or digital data. The last component required for transmission of these signals is an antenna.

Antennas, a topic that can mystify RF engineers and technicians, are the devices responsible for the "magic" of RF communications. The purpose of an antenna is to convert electricity into electromagnetic waves and radiate these waves into a medium (air or free space) that normally does not conduct electrical signals.

The field of wireless communications is growing at a very fast pace, with new standards and technologies being introduced virtually every week. Service providers are beginning to deploy wireless devices everywhere, from cellular to Internet access at airports, hotels, train stations, restaurants, cafes, shopping malls, and even in public parks. The use of cellular telephones has exploded in the last few years. Employees in all types of industries are being equipped with Smartphones so they can stay in touch through voice and e-mail at all times and from anywhere in the world. Wireless networks and wireless Internet hotspots are becoming commonplace in locations catering to businesspeople and the general public alike. Concerns about security, privacy and interference, especially in devices that use unlicensed bands, are growing. Because all of today's wireless networks use RF communications, they require antennas.

Antennas play a key role in the successful deployment of any kind of wireless connectivity. Proper planning and installation of antennas is required to ensure good signal coverage and to permit user mobility, as well as reduce the impact of additional segmentation on the network resources and minimize or eliminate interference. Cellular service providers spend a great deal of time and effort planning and analyzing utilization and traffic patterns in order to maximize the number of customers that can use the system in a given area and allow for continuous connectivity for both data and voice. In the rush to get wireless networks installed today, many are being deployed with little thought to where the signals originate or how far they reach.

This chapter will take you on a technical tour of antennas, their types, sizes, and applications, as well as some of the implementation issues. First you will learn about power gain and loss, then we will delve into the physical aspects of antennas. Most of the chapter discusses antennas that are used in a limited range of wireless communications technologies. However, the basic concepts of antennas are very similar and the details provided here can be easily extended to other types of antenna system implementation.

Gain and Loss

An understanding of RF signal transmission involves knowing:

- The strength or the power with which the transmitter is sending the signal
- The amount of reduction in signal strength caused by cables, connectors, and other components
- The transmission medium (atmosphere or free-space)
- The minimum strength of the signal required by the receiver to be able to properly recover the data sent by the transmitter

These requirements mean that we need to know how much power the signal loses or gains at various points. For example, an analysis of the signal would determine the power level that was fed into the antenna and how much signal strength was lost in transit.

Consider a wireless cable/DSL router for home networking, which typically sends out a signal with approximately 32 milliwatts (0.032 Watts) of power. The router is on the lower level of the house, and by the time the signal reaches the wireless NIC in a notebook computer in the second floor bedroom, it may only have a strength of about 0.000000001 (10^{-9}) Watts, or 1 microwatt. With received signals being sometimes a *billion* times smaller or larger than the signals that were transmitted, performing calculations is challenging, and it is easy to make a mistake reading, writing, or entering these long numbers in a calculator. Fortunately, mathematicians have the same kind of difficulty with other types of very large or very small numbers, so they came up with a system to simplify these calculations.

Recall from the previous chapter, an amplifier boosts the power of a signal; when this happens, the effect is called a **gain**. Likewise, cables and connectors offer a resistance to the flow of electricity and therefore they tend to decrease the power of a signal. This decrease is called a **loss**. Knowing how much gain or loss occurs in an RF system composed of radio transmitters, receivers, cables, connectors, and antennas is necessary to assist RF engineers and technicians to select the appropriate components and properly install them for successful signal transmission and reception.

Signal power also does not usually change in linear fashion. Instead, it changes *logarithmically*. Figure 4-1 shows an example of two values: one that changes in linear fashion and another that changes in logarithmic fashion.

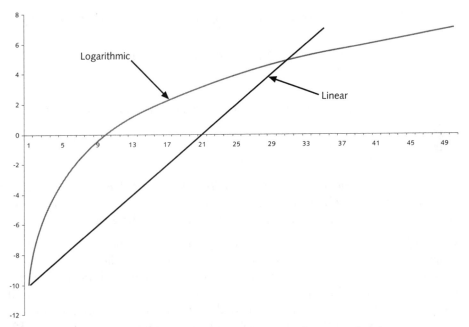

Figure 4-1   Linear vs. logarithmic changes in a signal's power level

Both gain and loss are relative concepts, which means that you need to know the power level of the signal at two different points, such as at the transmitting antenna and at the receiving antenna. Relative concepts are best quantified with relative measurements, such as percentage. To calculate the home network signal loss example using percentages, you would still have to deal with numbers that are difficult to read or type.

The Decibel

Decibel (dB) is a ratio between two signal levels (a relative measurement) that makes it much simpler to express and calculate power gain or loss.

The decibel is so named in honor of Alexander Graham Bell, the inventor of the telephone. That is why the B in dB is written with a capital B.

Before you panic, believing that this chapter is full of math formulas, you should know that in practically all cases, you can calculate gain by only remembering that:

- A gain of 3 dB (+3 dB) means the signal is two times bigger (twice the power).

- A gain of 10 dB (+10 dB) means the signal is 10 times bigger (10 times the power).

What about loss? It is exactly the opposite of gain:

- A loss of 3 dB (-3 dB) means the signal is two times smaller (half the power; divide by 2).

- A loss of 10 dB (-10 dB) means the signal is 10 times smaller (1/10th the power; divide by 10).

To say "a loss of minus 3 dB" (−3 dB) is incorrect. The correct form is to say "a loss of 3 dB."

The rules above are generally known as the *tens and threes of RF mathematics.* As you will see in the examples that follow, you can easily and quickly calculate the gain or loss with a fair amount of accuracy, without using a calculator, by using these simple rules.

Using dB to represent gains and losses means that the only types of calculations required are simple additions and subtractions. There is no need for multiplication, division, or any kind of complex calculation to convert the values to the same unit in order to get a meaningful result. For example, if a transmitter is connected to a cable that has a loss of 4 dB and each connector—one on the transmitter end of the cable and the other on the antenna end of the cable—has a loss of 1 dB, you can simply add the losses together like this: (-4 dB) + (-1 dB) + (-1 dB) = -6 dB, or a total loss of 6 dB.

Although dB is a relative measurement, at some point we have to make a connection between dB and a linear, absolute measurement. One example of this is **dBm**, which is a relative way to indicate an absolute power level in the linear Watt scale:

1 mW = 0 dBm

Although you can add or subtract any value represented in dB (dBm, etc.) using the tens and threes rule, you can also convert a dBm value directly to milliwatts of power. Let's look at some examples:

- +3 dB or 3 dB of gain will double the power: 10 mW + 3 dB = approximately 20 mW

- –3 dB or 3 dB of loss will halve the power: 10 mW – 3 dB = approximately 5 mW

- + 10 dB will increase the power 10 times: 10 mW + 10 dB = approximately 100 mW

- – 10 dB will decrease the power 10 times: 10 mW – 10 dB = approximately 1 mW

 NOTE Converting to mW does not change the relative measurement characteristic of decibel. It simply means that you have a reference point for the values used in the calculations; you can still add or subtract any dB values as if they were all represented in the same units.

Therefore, if you want to know the absolute power level of a particular signal that is supplied by a transmitter and you know from the specifications for this particular unit that the strength of the output signal is +36 dBm, you can calculate the absolute power by breaking down this number like this:

36 dBm = +10 dBm +10 dBm +10 dBm +3 dBm +3 dBm   +3 dm

Since 0 dBm is equal to 1 mW, it follows that: 3 um

- plus 10 dBm will make the signal 10 mW

- plus another 10 dBm will make the signal 100 mW

- plus another 10 dBm will make it 1000 mW or 1 W

- plus another 3 dBm will double the power to 2 W

- plus the last 3 dBm will double the power again to 4 W

 NOTE In situations where using the tens and threes rule will not work, the formula for converting milliwatts (mW) to dBm is $P_{dBm} = 10\log P_{mW}$. Therefore, the formula for converting dBm to mW is: $P_{mW} = \log{-1}(P_{dBm} / 10) = 10$ dBm. These formulas are provided here for your reference only. P_{mW} is power in milliwatts and P_{dBm} is the equivalent figure in dB.

When assigning a dB factor to the gain of an antenna, the measurement must also relate to some absolute value. The most perfect radiator of electromagnetic waves is an isotropic source (a point source). An **isotropic radiator** is a theoretical perfect sphere that radiates power equally in all directions. It is not possible to build a real isotropic radiator since it would need a power or signal cable connected to it at some point on the surface of the sphere. The cable connection means that it would no longer be perfect and would not be able to radiate with equal intensity in all directions. However, an isotropic radiator does provide a reference point for representing the gain of an antenna. The gain of antennas is usually expressed in **dB isotropic (dBi)**, which is the measurement of the gain that any antenna has when compared to the theoretical isotropic radiator.

NOTE The closest thing to an isotropic radiator is the sun. However, even the sun is not perfect because of a phenomenon called sunspots, which are dark areas on the surface of the star that change periodically and radiate energy levels different from the rest of the surface.

For microwave and higher frequency antennas, the gain is usually expressed in **dB dipole (dBd)**. A **dipole** is the smallest, simplest, most practical type of antenna that can be made, but that also exhibits the least amount of gain. A dipole has a fixed gain over that of an isotropic radiator of 2.15 db, so if the gain of an antenna is 5 dBd, to convert to dBi, you simply add 2.15 or: 5 + 2.15 = 7.15 dBi. Table 4-1 shows a summary of the decibel values used in RF communications.

Table 4-1   Decibel values and references

Nomenclature	Description	Refers To:
dBm	dB milliwatts	0 dB = 1 mW of power
dBd	dB dipole	The gain an antenna has over a dipole antenna at the same frequency
dBi	dB isotropic	The gain an antenna has over a theoretical isotropic (point source) radiator

ANTENNA CHARACTERISTICS

Now that you have an understanding of gain and loss, it's time to get acquainted with a few of the other characteristics of antennas, such as types, sizes, and shapes.

NOTE Antennas are reciprocal devices, which means that an antenna that works well for transmitting a signal on a particular range of frequencies is also effective at receiving the same signal.

Antenna Types

Antennas used in wireless communications can be characterized as either passive or active. The various types of antennas include omnidirectional, directional, patch, parabolic dish, and yagi, and each of these types can be constructed as either passive or active; however, most antennas are passive.

Passive Antennas

Passive antennas are the most common type and are constructed of a piece of metal, wire, or similar conductive material. A passive antenna does not amplify the signal in any way; it can only radiate a signal with the same amount of energy that appears at the antenna connector, after any cable and connector losses. However, as you will learn, certain shapes of passive antennas radiate the RF energy supplied by the transmitter in one direction and consequently exhibit an effective gain that is similar to amplification of the signal, and is called **directional gain**. This is equivalent to using a flashlight in which you can focus the beam. The more focused and narrow the beam is, the farther the light will reach. If you spread the beam, you can illuminate a wider area but the light is not as effective at a distance.

Active Antennas

Active antennas are essentially passive antennas with an amplifier built-in. The amplifier is connected directly to the piece of metal that forms the antenna itself. Most active antennas have only one electrical connection. Both the RF signal and the power for the amplifier are supplied on the same conductor. This construction reduces the cost of materials and also makes active antennas easier to install.

Antenna Sizes and Shapes

If you ever looked at the antennas installed on the roofs of buildings and on towers, you may have noticed that antennas come in many sizes and shapes. The size and shape of an antenna depend on three characteristics:

- The frequency (or range of frequencies) on which the antenna will transmit and receive

- The direction of the radiated electromagnetic wave

- The power with which the antenna must transmit or how sensitive it needs to be to receive very weak signals

The size of an antenna is inversely proportional to the wavelength of the signal it is designed to transmit or receive. Lower frequency signals require larger antennas. Conversely, higher frequency signals require shorter antennas. For example, the antenna for an AM radio station transmitting at the frequency of 530 KHz (530,000 Hz) is several hundred feet high whereas that of a cellular telephone operating at a frequency of 900 MHz (900,000,000 Hz) is only about six inches long. Antenna shapes vary according to their specific application.

Omnidirectional Antennas

Omnidirectional antennas are used to transmit and receive signals from all directions with relatively equal intensity. Figure 4-2 shows two examples of omnidirectional antennas for use in IEEE 802.11 wireless networks. On the left is a magnetic mount antenna, with an integrated cable designed for use in WLAN applications. These antennas are useful for improving signal reception over antennas that are built inside notebook computers or permanently attached to a wireless NIC. They can be used in an office environment, placed on top of metal cabinets, and can also be attached to car and truck roofs for mobile applications. The photo on the right shows a "blister" type ceiling mount antenna. Blister antennas are typically used when it is either necessary or desirable to hide the antenna or to make it easily blend with the decor.

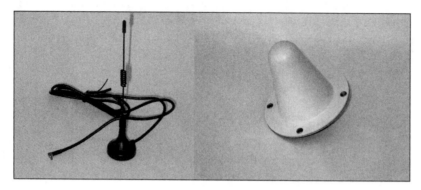

Figure 4-2   Magnetic mount and blister type omnidirectional antennas

Longer omnidirectional antennas have a higher gain but are more difficult to mount and to hide. Later on you will learn how the size of an antenna can affect its gain. Figure 4-3 shows an example of a high-gain antenna of this type.

Figure 4-3   High-gain 8 dBi omnidirectional antenna

NOTE Omnidirectional antennas have a gain because they emit a signal in two dimensions only, not in three dimensions such as an isotropic radiator would emit—that is, if it could be built. When visualized from the side of an omnidirectional antenna, the RF waves form a doughnut shaped pattern with a stick (the antenna) through the center. This means that the energy leaving the antenna is somewhat vertically focused.

4

Directional Antennas

The intended direction of the radiated RF wave also affects the shape of antennas. **Directional antennas** are used when you need to transmit a signal in one direction only. Although this may sound obvious, it represents an important distinction from omnidirectional antennas. Directional antennas, by focusing the RF waves mostly in one direction, will concentrate the energy in (or receive more energy from) a particular direction, and therefore have a higher effective gain than an omnidirectional antenna.

Some types of directional antennas focus the RF energy more or less than others. A **yagi antenna** emits a wider, less focused RF energy beam, while a **parabolic dish antenna** emits a narrow, more concentrated beam of RF energy. Yagi antennas are used for medium-distance—up to about 16 miles (25 km)—outdoor applications, and dish antennas are used for long distance outdoor links. One common application of a dish antenna is to receive satellite signals. Figure 4-4 shows two different models of yagi antennas. The encased model on the left is a 2.4 GHz WLAN antenna, and the open type on the right is used for paging systems.

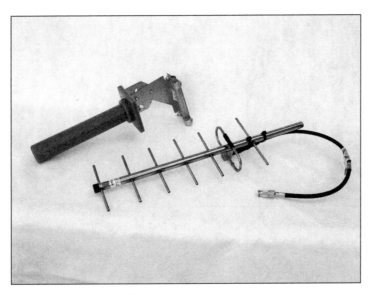

Figure 4-4   Yagi antennas

Patch antennas emit an RF energy beam that is horizontally wide but vertically taller than that of a yagi antenna. Considered a semi-directional antenna, it is often used to send RF energy down a long corridor, although some varieties are designed for installation on the walls of buildings, for example, to send an RF signal in one direction away from the structure. One common application for patch antennas is in cellular telephony. Figure 4-5 illustrates an example of antennas used in a cellular telephone tower, and Figure 4-6 shows a small patch antenna for use indoors.

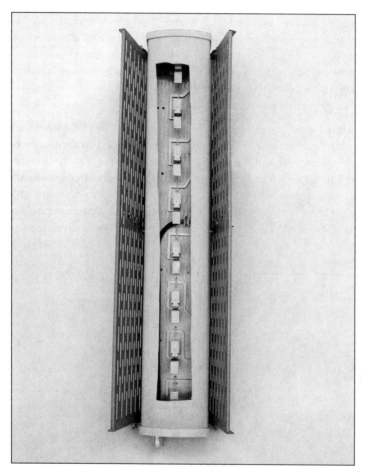

Figure 4-5   Cellular antenna (with cutout to show internal construction)

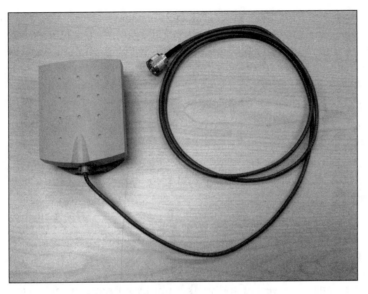

Figure 4-6   Indoor patch antenna

Signal Strength and Direction

The distance between the transmitter and receiver determines the strength of the signal you need to send, which in turn determines what size and shape of antenna you need to use for your application. Recall that most antennas are of the passive type, and that transmitters can only produce a finite amount of RF energy. For most applications, active antennas can be extremely expensive, and licensing restrictions limit the amount of power that may be transmitted.

What is the best solution? An omnidirectional antenna installed high and in a central location works well for sending the signal in all directions, but the strength of the signal is divided more or less equally in a 360-degree circle around the antenna. A directional antenna, on the other hand, sends all of the energy in the direction the antenna is pointed; therefore, the RF wave travels farther than a signal sent from an omnidirectional antenna because the power is concentrated in one direction, an effect similar to the flashlight example described earlier.

This behavior is primarily the result of free space loss. In **free space loss**, RF waves tend to spread away from the source of the signal (the antenna) in much the same way that a circular wave created by throwing a stone in a pond gets wider and wider and moves away from the point where the stone hit the water. The farther the wave moves away, the smaller it gets because the amount of energy the wave originally had when the stone hit the water is distributed over an ever-wider area. Eventually the wave fades to the point that you can no longer see any movement on the surface of the water. If you place two floating objects on the water's surface—one near the point where the stone hits the water and another farther away—the one closer to the center point will move more than the one farther away because less of the wave's energy reaches the farther object. This energy loss is the same thing that happens with a receiver antenna that is located farther away from a transmitter. It receives less of the energy sent by the transmitter because the RF wave is spreading its energy out in all directions. However, if you experiment with dropping a stone into water in a confined space, such as a bathtub, the movement of the wave is contained by the side walls and the energy of the wave will travel much farther away from the point where the stone hits, before it fades.

You can find many free space loss calculator tools on the Internet. Just use one of the common search engines and look for "free space loss calculator."

NOTE   Antenna gain is directional gain—not power gain—due to focusing of the energy in one direction.

Radio stations transmit their signal in all directions to reach the largest number of listeners. Although they transmit with a lot of power, as you travel away from the city where the station is located, the signal gets weaker and weaker until your receiver can no longer detect it and all you may be able to hear are intermittent fragments of the transmission interspersed with noise.

NOTE   Some AM stations in the United States transmit with as much as 50,000 Watts of power, and FM stations may send a signal with as much as 150,000 Watts of power. Higher frequency signals need more power to reach the same distance. In comparison, an average IEEE 802.11b WLAN device sends out a signal with only 100 milliwatts (0.1 Watts) of power.

HOW ANTENNAS WORK

Designing antennas and understanding how they perform the magic of sending RF signals out into air or space requires in-depth knowledge of physics, mathematics, and electronics. The details of the science behind how antennas work are beyond the scope of this book and are probably best left to university courses in electrical and electronics engineering. However, some general coverage of basic antenna functionality should help you develop a better appreciation of the science behind antennas. This section explains how antennas work as transmitters (radiators) and receivers of radio frequency signals.

Wavelength

The length of a single RF sine wave, or the **wavelength**, is what determines the size of an antenna. An antenna transmits and receives a signal most efficiently at a specific frequency when it is as long as the full length of the wave, which is called a **full-wave antenna**. In most cases, this is not practical. For example, a full-wave antenna for an AM station would be about 1,857 feet (over 566 meters) long, while a cellular telephone antenna that transmits or receives at a frequency of 900 MHz (900,000,000 Hz) would have to be over 13 inches (33 centimeters) long. For practical reasons, antennas are more commonly designed to be as long as an exact fraction of the wavelength, and they are called (½) **half-wave antennas**, (¼) **quarter-wave antennas**, or (⅛) **eighth-wave antennas**. While not as efficient as full-wave antennas, these smaller antennas work reasonably well. The AM station antenna could be built as a quarter-wave antenna at about 464 feet (141 meters), which is still quite large, and the cellular antenna, using the same ratio, would only be about 6 ½ inches (8.25 centimeters) long.

When antennas with a higher gain are required, you can increase the size of the antenna to the next bigger fraction. A larger antenna has a higher gain than a shorter antenna. Almost any metallic object or any object that conducts electricity will act as an antenna; but if you use an antenna that is much shorter than the wavelength for a frequency, it will not radiate RF at all. Alternatively, if the antenna is much longer than the wavelength, it will send out some RF energy, just not very efficiently.

NOTE

The wavelength of an RF signal is usually given in metric. The formula for calculating the length of the wave is *wavelength = frequency/speed of light*, since RF waves travel through air or space at the speed of light, 300,000 kilometers per second (300,000,000 meters per second). Using a value in feet-per-second or inches-per-second for the speed of light will yield a result in feet or inches, respectively, for the wavelength. The speed of light in miles-per-second is equal to 186,000.

ANTENNA PERFORMANCE

Antenna performance is a measure of how efficiently an antenna can radiate an RF signal. The design, installation, size, and type of antenna can affect its performance.

Radiation Patterns

In antenna design, certain items such as fasteners, brackets, and support structures can affect the way the antenna emits RF waves. During the antenna testing phase, engineers develop a graphic called an **antenna pattern** by measuring the signal radiating from the antenna. The antenna pattern indicates the direction, width, and shape of the RF signal beam coming from the antenna. An antenna pattern is drawn as a top or side view of the antenna. In the case of directional antennas, sometimes you will see an arrow indicating the direction in which the RF signal is being emitted. Figure 4-7 contains examples of antenna patterns.

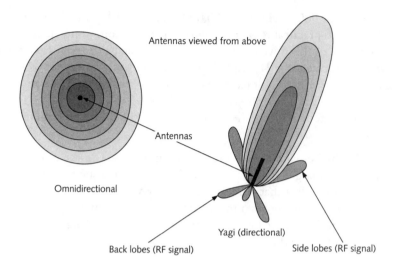

Figure 4-7   Antenna patterns viewed from above

Recall that antennas emit signals in two dimensions—horizontally and vertically. Antenna specifications almost always state the vertical beam angle that a particular antenna emits. Figure 4-8 illustrates the shape of RF waves emitted by an omnidirectional antenna, as viewed from the side.

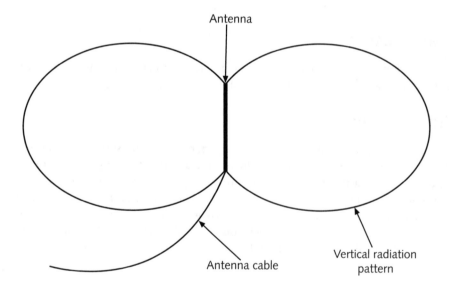

Figure 4-8   Vertical antenna pattern (side view of omnidirectional antenna pattern)

Antenna Polarization

When a signal leaves an antenna, the sine waves have a particular orientation, in other words, they oscillate either horizontally or vertically. The orientation of the wave leaving the antenna is called **antenna polarization**. If you hold a portable cellular phone straight up in your hand, the antenna is positioned vertically. The signal leaving the antenna will be vertically polarized, meaning that the sine waves will travel up and down when leaving the antenna. If you are lying down when talking on the cellular phone, the signal is horizontally polarized, which is to say that the sine waves travel from side to side on a horizontal plane. Cellular base station (tower) antennas are mounted vertically and send out signals that are also vertically polarized. Antenna polarization is important because the most efficient signal transmission and reception is experienced when the sending and receiving antennas are equally polarized, that is, they are both either vertically or horizontally polarized. Figure 4-9 illustrates this concept.

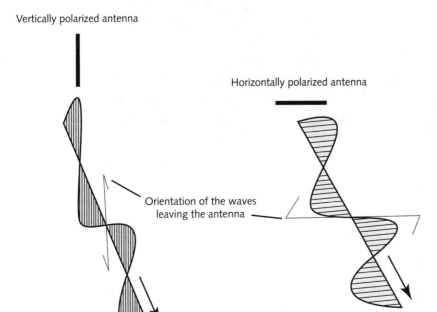

Figure 4-9   Antenna polarization

The add-on wireless NICs used in notebook computers have antennas that stick out of the side of the computers and are horizontally polarized (provided that the notebook computer is used under normal conditions such as on top of a desk or on your lap). The devices that the notebook wireless NIC is transmitting to or receiving from usually have their antennas mounted in a vertical position, which means that the signal is not polarized the same way as the signals emitted or received by the notebook computer. Different polarization between devices can cause poor communication between them. The utility software supplied with wireless NICs can show the strength of the signal. If you experience poor reception, try placing the computer on its side (carefully, of course) while monitoring the strength of the signal. You will most likely see an increase in signal strength due to both antennas having the same polarization. Figure 4-10 shows a notebook computer with an add-on NIC (horizontally mounted antenna) and a wireless router with the antennas mounted vertically.

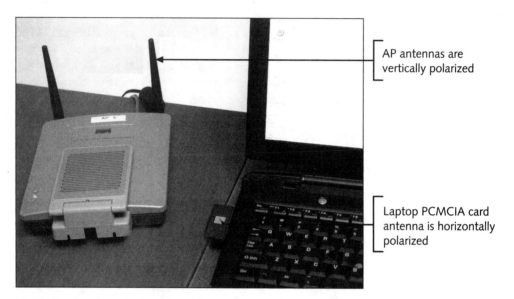

AP antennas are vertically polarized

Laptop PCMCIA card antenna is horizontally polarized

Figure 4-10   Mixed vertical and horizontal antenna polarizations

Antenna Dimensions

The design and construction of an antenna dictates whether it is one-dimensional or two-dimensional in structure.

One-Dimensional Antennas

One-dimensional antennas are basically a length of wire or metal. They can be built as a straight piece or bent in some shape such as the old "rabbit ear" antennas that used to be placed on top of television sets.

A **monopole antenna** is basically a straight piece of wire or metal, usually a quarter of the wavelength, with no reflecting or ground element. As you learned earlier, dipole is the smallest, simplest, most practical type of antenna. Dipoles are commonly built as two monopoles mounted together at the base (the place where the cable(s) connect to the antenna) and laid out in a straight line, with the other ends facing away from each other. Figure 4-11 illustrates an example of a dipole antenna.

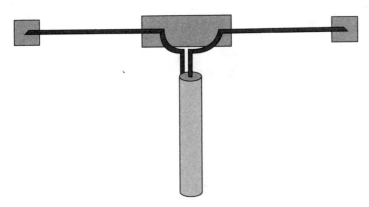

Figure 4-11   Common dipole antenna

A monopole antenna is less efficient than a dipole. Dipoles can be built larger since they are usually laid out horizontally. To work properly, monopole antennas are mounted in such a way that they are practically sticking out of the ground (or very close to it), or another type of large structure that conducts electrical energy. Since the ground is a conductor, it acts as a reflector and this makes the monopole antenna behave like a dipole, making it more efficient. Alternatively, monopoles can be equipped with a large metal base called a **ground–plane**, to simulate the signal-reflecting effect of the ground. The most common application of ground-planes is on boats that have a fiberglass hull. Fiberglass is non-conducting, therefore antennas for nautical radios and radars usually have either a horizontal metal plate near the base or, alternatively, four lengths of wire sticking out horizontally from the base, to act as the ground-plane.

Two-Dimensional Antennas

Antennas organized in a two-dimensional pattern, with both height and width, are known as **two-dimensional antennas**. Examples include patch and satellite dish antennas. A satellite dish works like a signal collector, scooping up any signal that comes in a straight line with the center axis of the antenna. A patch antenna is usually a flat piece of metal, with different heights and widths, depending on the desired radiation angle. Another type of two-dimensional directional antenna is a **horn antenna** such as the one shown in Figure 4-12, which resembles a large horn with the wide end bent to one side. These antennas are common in telephone networks and are used to transmit microwave signals between two distant towers.

Figure 4-12   Telephone transmission tower with two horn antennas

Smart Antennas

A recent development in antenna technology is the smart antenna. Used primarily in mobile or cellular telephony, **smart antennas** "know" where the mobile receiver is, and can track it and focus the RF energy in that particular direction to avoid wasting energy and to prevent interference with other antennas. Instead of sending a signal with a wide beam, smart antennas send a narrow beam of energy toward the receiver. Figure 4-13 illustrates the concept. The illustration on the left is a regular directional antenna. The figure on the right shows a smart antenna tracking a mobile receiver.

There are two classes of smart antennas:

- A switched beam antenna uses several narrow beam antennas pointing in different directions and turns each one on or off, as the receiver moves across the path of the beams.

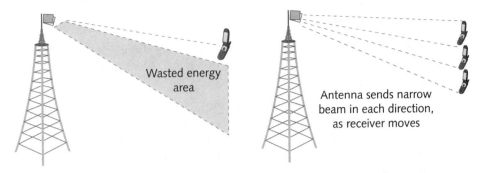

Figure 4-13   Directional antenna vs. smart antenna

■ Adaptive or phased array antennas are similar to patch antennas but, instead of being just a single piece of metal, they are divided into a matrix of radiating elements. A computer-based signal processor controls circuits in the antenna system, turning elements of the matrix on or off as the mobile user moves in front of the antenna.

Phased array antennas are used extensively in ultra-modern radar systems. These antennas are beginning to appear in other applications as well, such as cellular mobile telephony. Figure 4-14 shows an example of a phased array antenna. Note the multiple antenna elements that make up the array.

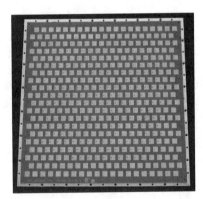

Figure 4-14   Phased array antenna

ANTENNA SYSTEM IMPLEMENTATION

The proper installation of antennas requires knowing the user's requirements and dealing with various challenges, including physical obstacles, municipal building codes, and other regulatory restrictions.

As mentioned at the beginning of this chapter, cellular service providers spend a great deal of time and effort designing and testing their network of antennas in order to provide the best signal coverage, and, hence, the best service to their customers. To have a thorough understanding of their mobile customers' needs, cellular providers also need to know what the user traffic patterns are in a given area. A challenge for these companies is that in North America, obtaining a permit from the government or from private land and building owners to install an antenna or a tower—whether on the ground or at the top of a building—takes longer and is more expensive than in some other countries around the world. As a result, the service providers also need to be smarter and more thorough at both maximizing coverage and minimizing interference.

The ultimate purpose of a single RF antenna or a system consisting of multiple antennas is to serve a group of users and allow them to communicate reliably without wires. The size of the area covered, performance, reliability, and also security are major concerns of the RF technician. This is especially true in today's world of unlicensed frequencies, which are often accompanied by maximum signal power restrictions, lack of support from regulatory agencies in case of conflict or interference, and easy access to a wide range of equipment by untrained and inexperienced users and hackers.

When implementing wireless communications using the antennas that are supplied with the wireless devices, such as when you are setting up a wireless LAN, you are limited to placing the transmitters and receivers in various locations to achieve a good connection. However, when you need to go beyond the standard setup and purchase different antennas to ensure good signal reception in a difficult area or to create a long distance outdoor link, there are a few additional points you need to consider. This section provides an overview of these advanced concepts.

CAUTION

You should not attempt to install towers or antennas outdoors without additional training. Full coverage of tower installation is beyond the scope of this book. The information provided here is intended to provide you with an overview of the process. Lightning storms, for example, can cause severe damage to both equipment and buildings. Safety issues and regulations impact where and how outdoor antennas are installed. Always hire a professional, bonded installer for outdoor antennas with and without towers.

Antenna Cables

Most antennas are connected to the transmitter or receiver using coaxial cable. This type of cable is built in layers of wires (conducting) and insulators (non-conducting). The word coaxial means that both conductors in the cable are laid out along the same axis. Figure 4-15 illustrates the construction of a coaxial cable.

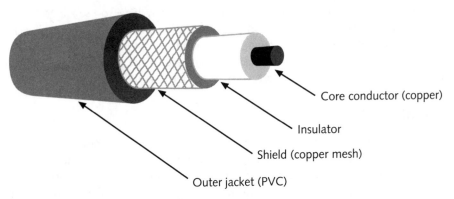

Core conductor (copper)

Insulator

Shield (copper mesh)

Outer jacket (PVC)

Figure 4-15   Coaxial cable construction

Coaxial cables come in many sizes (thicknesses) and specifications. In an RF system, it is very important to use the correct type of cable, per the equipment manufacturer specifications. Among the specifications is the **impedance** of the cable, which is the opposition to the flow of alternating current in a circuit. Represented by the letter "Z" and measured in ohms, impedance is the combination of resistance, inductance, and capacitance of the circuit. The cable's impedance must match that of the transmitter circuit as well as that of the antenna. When you need to connect an external antenna and it is not possible to attach it directly to the transmitter output, you must consider the signal loss caused by the connector and by the cable itself. Almost all conducting materials offer a resistance to the flow of electricity on a wire. This is particularly important in antenna cables and more so in equipment that transmits at very low power, such as those used in IEEE 802.11 WLANs, Bluetooth devices, and others.

Cable loss is measured in relation to the length of the cable. The longer the cable, the more loss occurs. However, you can use special low-loss antenna cables to minimize signal loss. Table 4-2 lists a few examples of LMR low-loss cable and their basic characteristics.

Table 4-2   Low-loss LMR cables

Part Number	Diameter	Loss at 2.4 GHz (per 100 ft.)
LMR-100	$\frac{1}{10}$"	−38.9dB
LMR-240	$\frac{3}{16}$"	−12.7dB
LMR-400	$\frac{3}{8}$"	−6.6dB
LMR-600	$\frac{1}{2}$"	−4.4dB

To calculate the total cable loss, simply divide the loss per 100 feet by 100 and multiply by the required length of your cable. For example, if you needed to install the antenna about 10 feet (3 meters) away from the transmitter, LMR-100 cable will introduce a loss of 3.9 dB (39 dB/100 = 0.39 dB per foot, times 10 = 3.9 dB), which means that significantly more than half of the energy produced at the transmitter output is lost, and that is before adding in the connector losses! Using LMR-400, the loss introduced by the cable will be only about 0.7 dB.

Keep in mind that to keep loss at a minimum, you may have to use a cable that may be too thick for the connector type used in your transmitter, antenna, or both; therefore, the first consideration when deciding to change the manufacturer-provided or equipment-mounted antennas should be the location of the hardware and of the antenna(s). In addition, be aware that LMR cable is far more expensive than regular coaxial cable.

RF Propagation

The way that radio waves propagate, or move, between the transmitter and the receiver through the atmosphere of our planet, depends on the frequency of the signal. RF waves are classified in three groups, as shown in Table 4-3. Ground waves follow the curvature of the earth. Sky waves bounce between the ionosphere and the surface of the earth. RF waves transmitted in frequencies between 30 MHz and 300 GHz require a line-of-sight path between the transmitter and the receiver antennas.

Table 4-3   RF wave propagation groups

Group	Frequencies
Ground waves	from 3 KHz to 2 MHz
Sky waves	from 2 MHz to 30 MHz
Line-of-sight waves	from 30 MHz to 300 GHz

Figure 4-16 illustrates how these different waves propagate through Earth's atmosphere and, consequently, how this affects the implementation of antenna systems.

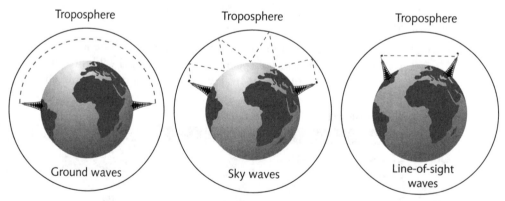

Figure 4-16   How radio waves propagate

Point-to-Multipoint Links

In most wireless communications applications, one transmitter communicates with several mobile clients. This is called a **point-to-multipoint wireless link**. If the receiver is installed in a fixed location, as in the case of a central building in a campus with wireless links to other buildings, it is possible to maximize the signal distance by using an omnidirectional antenna at the central location and directional, higher gain antennas at the remote locations. Figure 4-17 illustrates this type of application.

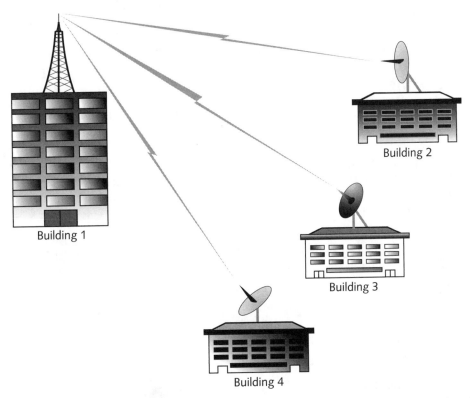

Figure 4-17   Point-to-multipoint links using a combination of omnidirectional and directional antennas

Point-to-Point Links

Two computer networks in different buildings can be connected by a **point-to-point wireless link**. In this case, directional antennas provide the most reliable method of transmitting RF waves. Their narrow beams and high gain ensure that most of the energy of the RF wave will be used between the two antennas. The cost is often much lower and the performance comparable to or higher than that of a digital telephone company line. Telephone companies make extensive use of point-to-point microwave links, instead of cables, for long-distance voice and data communications. Although repeater towers are required, the cost of maintaining a wireless link is usually lower than the cost of installing and maintaining cables, which can be easily damaged and are harder to troubleshoot. Figure 4-18 shows an example of a point-to-point link.

Figure 4-18   Point-to-point link using directional antennas

Fresnel Zone

Although the transmission path for point-to-point links is usually represented by a straight line in a diagram, recall that RF waves have a tendency to spread out. This means that the space between the two antennas would be more accurately represented by something similar to an ellipse, such as that illustrated in Figure 4-19. This elliptical region is called the **Fresnel zone,** and its shape is an important consideration in wireless links. When planning a wireless link, at least 60% of the Fresnel zone must be kept clear of obstructions, which may affect the height of the antenna tower.

NOTE   The name Fresnel (pronounced "Fray-nel") comes from the French physicist Augustin Jean Fresnel, who studied the polarization of light waves.

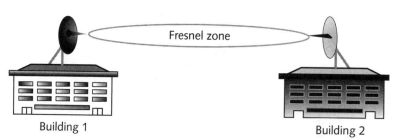

Figure 4-19   Fresnel zone

Link Budgets

Once you have considered the cables, propagation method, link type, and Fresnel zone of your transmission, you still need to calculate whether you will have enough signal strength to meet the receiver's minimum requirements. This calculation is called a **link budget** and is used in every type of wireless link, whether across the road or between a satellite and an earth station.

The process involves all of the variables that you have read about in this chapter. The calculations themselves are not overly complex, but there are many link budgeting tools available on the Internet that you can use. To calculate your link budget, you will need information from the equipment specifications, including the gain of the antennas, cable and connector losses for the receiver and the transmitter, receiver sensitivity, and the free space loss figure.

TIP

You can download a free link budget calculator from the following URL: http://www.cisco.com/application/vnd.ms-excel/en/us/guest/products/ ps458/c1225/ccmigration_09186a00800a912a.xls.

Antenna Alignment

One of the challenges of implementing a point-to-point link is to position the antennas at the same height and point them toward one another to maximize the strength of the signal. Some transmitters and receivers are equipped with tools designed to assist the installers in aligning the two antennas. Others may require the rental or purchase of additional tools to ensure perfect alignment. Some basic tools are essential, such as:

- A compass to position the antenna at the correct angle
- A spotting scope or binoculars, if the other antenna site is within visible range
- A means of communication such as a walkie-talkie or a cellular phone
- If the distance is reasonably short, a light source such as a flashlight

Technicians who perform long-distance link installations often, and who need to align antennas with a great degree of accuracy to ensure maximum reliability, are usually equipped with a spectrum analyzer, such as the one shown in Figure 4-20. This tool displays the signal amplitude and frequency and can also detect interference in a particular frequency or channel. Spectrum analyzers have varying capabilities and are expensive, ranging in price from about $10,000 to over $100,000.

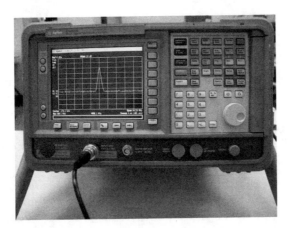

Figure 4-20 Spectrum analyzer

Antenna system implementation, including alignment and troubleshooting, is a topic that can fill an entire book. It demands hours of practical training. Although the subject is beyond the scope of this book, implementation is included here to provide you with an overview of some of the complex issues involved. Before moving on to other more practical aspects of wireless communications, it is useful to know some of the other challenges that can affect implementation, particularly of outdoor links.

Other Challenges of Outdoor Links

Recall that radio waves can reflect, diffract, or be absorbed by some materials. Weather phenomena, such as heavy fog, rain, dust or snow storms; air disturbances like air masses rising quickly from the ground because of the sun heating up the surface in deserts and other very hot areas; even significant differences in temperature at different altitudes that can occur in the morning or evening in deep valleys, can affect the performance and reliability of wireless links. Seasonal changes can impact a wireless link that may have been set up in the winter. When leaves and grass begin to grow in the spring, they can block more than 40% of the Fresnel zone, absorbing most of the RF waves.

While planning an outdoor link, you should always consider the possibility of the link performance being seriously affected or the link going down completely as a result of one or more of the environmental conditions described. Check the history of the region's weather with a local newspaper or weather service. Contact the municipal planning, parks, and building permit departments to identify short and long-term plans that may interfere with your intended link. Always take into account how the positioning of an antenna may be affected by vegetation growth in the spring.

The possibility of another company or person setting up a link in which the RF wave beam interferes with the one you set up is an additional concern. If you are using unlicensed frequencies such as the ISM or U-NII bands, you cannot count on assistance from regulatory agencies or authorities and will have to deal with the situation on your own. Of course, you should always be a good citizen and make sure you are not interfering with anyone else's signal before you set up an outdoor link.

CHAPTER SUMMARY

◻ By the time an RF signal reaches the receiver, it can be a billion times smaller than when it left the transmitter. Cables, connectors, antennas, and the distance between the transmitter and receiver are all factors that affect how much energy a signal has when it is transmitted and when it is received. A gain occurs when a signal is amplified or when most of the signal's energy is focused in one direction. A loss happens when the energy of a signal is decreased.

◻ The decibel (dB) is a relative measurement used by engineers and technicians alike to simplify the calculations of gain and loss as well as to indicate the strength of a signal. A gain of 3 dB doubles the signal power. A loss of 3 dB halves the power of a signal. A gain of 10 dB increases the signal strength 10 times, and a loss of 10 dB decreases the strength of the signal 10 times. Gains and losses expressed in dB can simply be added or subtracted together.

❏ An isotropic radiator is a theoretical perfect sphere that radiates power equally, in all directions. The two most basic types of antennas are the theoretical isotropic radiator, which is only used as a reference since it is not possible to build a working one, and the dipole.

❏ The most common type of antenna is a passive antenna, which is basically a piece of wire or metal and can only radiate a signal with as much power as is provided by the transmitter. Active antennas have a built-in amplifier to boost the signal power.

❏ The size of an antenna depends primarily on the frequency or range of frequencies that it is designed to transmit or receive, and it is proportional to the wavelength of the signal. A longer antenna is required for lower frequencies, and a shorter antenna is used for higher frequencies. To keep antennas a manageable size, most are built as half-wave (½ of the wavelength), quarter-wave (¼ of the wavelength), or eighth-wave (⅛ of the wavelength).

❏ Omnidirectional antennas transmit and receive a signal from all directions. Directional antennas focus the signal energy in one direction only, which has an effect (called directional gain) in passive antennas that is similar to the gain in an amplifier, only without adding any additional electrical power.

❏ Yagi, patch, and dish are different types of directional antennas.

❏ Free space loss is caused by the natural tendency of RF waves to spread out and is a measure of the amount of loss of signal strength between the transmitter antenna and the receiver antenna.

❏ Larger antennas have a higher gain; conversely, smaller antennas have lower gain.

❏ Antennas have a horizontal and a vertical radiation pattern. Antennas emit a signal that is vertically polarized or horizontally polarized. The most efficient communications link is when both the transmitter and the receiver antenna have the same polarization.

❏ There are two basic types of one-dimensional antennas, a monopole and a dipole. The dipole antenna is more efficient than the monopole antenna. Monopoles that are not mounted at or near the ground can make use of an artificial ground-plane. Patch and dish antennas are two-dimensional antennas.

❏ Smart antennas, used mostly in cellular telephone applications, can track a mobile user and send a narrower, more efficient beam of RF energy directed at the user, which also prevents interference with other transmitter antennas. A switched beam antenna uses several narrow beam antennas pointing in different directions. An adaptive array (or phased array) antenna has a matrix of radiating elements and uses a signal processor to enable or disable elements in order to send a focused beam of RF energy in the direction of the mobile user.

❏ Special LMR antenna cables are used to reduce the signal loss between the transmitter and the antenna.

❑ RF waves propagate differently depending on the frequency of the signal. Ground waves follow the curvature of the earth. Sky waves bounce between the ionosphere and the surface of the earth. RF waves transmitted in frequencies between 30 MHz and 300 GHz require line-of-sight path between the transmitter and the receiver antennas.

❑ Directional antennas are used to build point-to-point links to connect two buildings using a wireless link. They are also used by telephone carriers for long distance communications using microwave. Point-to-multipoint links can also be set up using an omnidirectional antenna and multiple directional antennas.

❑ A Fresnel zone is an elliptical area between two directional antennas. When setting up a wireless link in this way, maintaining a reliable connection requires that no more than 40% of the Fresnel zone be blocked by obstructions.

❑ Directional antennas must be aligned with each other to maximize the strength of the signal between the two. Although most wireless equipment manufacturers include built-in tools to facilitate the alignment of antennas, technicians use spectrum analyzers for high reliability, accuracy, and for troubleshooting wireless links.

❑ RF waves can be blocked, partially or completely, by weather phenomena and conditions such as heavy rain, dust, or snow storms. When designing a long distance wireless link, you should always check with the local authorities to make sure that no buildings or trees are planned for the area, since development could interfere with your connection.

KEY TERMS

active antenna — A passive antenna with an amplifier built-in.

antenna pattern — A graphic that shows how a signal radiates out of an antenna.

antenna polarization — An indication of the horizontal or vertical orientation of the sine waves leaving an antenna.

dB dipole (dBd) — The relative measurement of the gain of an antenna when compared to a dipole antenna.

dB isotropic (dBi) — The relative measurement of the gain of an antenna when compared to a theoretical isotropic radiator.

dBm — A relative way to indicate an absolute power level in the linear Watt scale.

decibel (dB) — A ratio between two signal levels.

dipole — An antenna that has a fixed amount of gain over that of an isotropic radiator.

directional antenna — An antenna that focuses RF energy, sending the signal in one direction.

directional gain — The effective gain that a directional antenna achieves by focusing RF energy in one direction.

eighth-wave antenna — An antenna that is ⅛ of the wavelength of the signal it is designed to transmit or receive.

free space loss — The signal loss that occurs as a result of the tendency of RF waves to spread, resulting in less energy at any given point, as the signal moves away from the transmitting antenna.

Fresnel zone — An elliptical region spanning the distance between two directional antennas that must not be blocked more than 40% to prevent interference with the RF signal.

full-wave antenna — An antenna that is as long as the length of the wave it is designed to transmit or receive.

gain — A relative measure of increase in a signal's power level.

ground-plane — A metal disc or two straight wires assembled at 90 degrees used to provide a reflection point for monopole antennas that are not mounted on or near the surface of the ground.

half-wave antenna — An antenna that is half as long as the wavelength of the signal it is designed to transmit or receive.

horn antenna — A two-dimensional directional antenna typically used for microwave transmission; it resembles a large horn with the wide end bent to one side.

impedance — The opposition to the flow of alternating current in a circuit. Represented by the letter "Z" and measured in ohms, impedance is the combination of resistance, inductance, and capacitance of the circuit.

isotropic radiator — A theoretical perfect sphere that radiates power equally in all directions; impossible to construct.

link budget — The process of calculating the signal strength between the transmitter and receiver antennas to ensure that the link can meet the receiver's minimum signal strength requirements.

loss — A relative measure of decrease in a signal's power level.

monopole antenna — An antenna built of a straight piece of wire, usually a quarter of the wavelength with no ground point or reflecting element.

omnidirectional antenna — An antenna that sends out the signal in a uniform pattern in all directions.

one-dimensional antenna — A straight length of wire or metal connected to a transmitter at one end.

parabolic dish antenna — A high-gain directional antenna that emits a narrow, focused beam of energy and is used for long-distance outdoor links.

passive antenna — The most common type of antenna. Passive antennas can only radiate a signal with the same amount of energy that appears at the antenna connector.

patch antenna — A semi-directional antenna that emits a wide horizontal beam and an even wider vertical beam.

point-to-multipoint wireless link — A link in which one central site uses an omnidirectional antenna to transmit to multiple remote sites, which may use omnidirectional antennas or directional antennas to maximize the distance and the quality of the signal.

point-to-point wireless link — The most reliable link between two antenna sites using directional antennas to maximize the distance and the signal quality.

quarter-wave antenna — An antenna that is ¼ as long as the wavelength of the signal it is designed to transmit or receive.

smart antennas — A new type of antenna that uses a signal processor and an array of narrow beam elements to track the user and send most of the RF energy in the direction of the mobile receiver to prevent interference and avoid wasting RF energy.

wavelength — The length of a single RF wave, measured from the starting point of the sine wave to the starting point of the next sine wave or from any point in a wave (usually the peak) to the same point on the next wave.

yagi antenna — A directional antenna that emits a wide, less-focused beam and is used for medium-distance outdoor applications.

REVIEW QUESTIONS

1. The purpose of a(n) _____ is to send an electromagnetic signal into air or space.

   a. antenna

   b. modulator

   c. filter

   d. mixer

2. Decibel is a relative measurement that requires a(n) _____.

   a. distance

   b. antenna

   c. power level

   d. comparison

   e. gain

3. A gain of 6 dB means that the signal level or strength _____.

   a. increases very little

   b. doubles

   c. doubles twice

   d. does not increase at all

4. A transmitter generates a 15 dBm signal and is connected to an antenna using a cable that induces a 3 dB loss. The cable has two connectors that induce a loss of 2 dB each. What is the signal level at the input of the antenna?

   a. 8 dBm

   b. 10 dB

   c. 22 dBm

   d. 3 db

5. The simplest and most practical type of antenna is a _____.

    a. straight wire

    b. dipole

    c. yagi

    d. monopole

    e. passive

6. A(n) _____ antenna transmits a signal in all directions with relatively equal intensity.

    a. multidirectional

    b. phased array

    c. directional

    d. omnidirectional

    e. smart

7. Between the transmitting antenna and the receiving antenna, a signal will always be subject to _____.

    a. gain

    b. amplification

    c. free space loss

    d. reflection

    e. diffraction

8. For the best performance between transmitter and receiver, the two antennas should have the same _____.

    a. size

    b. angle

    c. gain

    d. polarization

9. In a direct, point-to-point link, the Fresnel zone should never be obstructed more than _____.

    a. 40%

    b. 60%

    c. 30%

    d. 50%

10. To work as efficiently as a dipole, a monopole antenna requires a(n) _____.

11. A low frequency signal means the antenna will be _____ whereas higher frequency signal will use a(n) _____ antenna.

12. The gain of an antenna is the measure of how focused the direction of an antenna pattern is. True or False?

13. A directional antenna typically has a low gain. True or False?

14. Passive antennas can increase the strength of a signal. True or False?

15. The _____ of an antenna depends upon the frequency of the RF signal and the gain.

16. When planning a wireless link, you should always prepare a(n) _____ to ensure that the signal that reaches the receiver meets the minimum signal strength requirements.

17. List two types of directional antennas.

18. Discuss how smart antennas function.

19. Explain how sky waves propagate.

20. What happens if someone sets up a pair of antennas that interfere with your point-to-point link between two buildings, which uses an unlicensed frequency?

HANDS-ON PROJECTS

Project 4-1

Write a one-page paper on adaptive array or phased array antenna systems. Other than for cellular telephony and military radar, for what applications is this type of antenna being used? What are the advantages and disadvantages of this type of system? Use the Internet and other technology sources for your paper.

Project 4-2

Write a short paper recommending the type and gain of an antenna that would be required to transmit a signal with 4 W of power from a transmitter that generates a 36 dBm signal to another building across the street. The transmitter will be installed indoors and the antenna on the roof. The cable provided is LMR-400 and is 50 feet long, which is about 10 feet longer than what you need to connect the antenna and transmitter. Show all the steps that you went through to arrive at your answer.

Project 4-3

Using examples from the Internet, draw a diagram that shows the typical horizontal and vertical patterns for the following types of antennas: blister, yagi, dish, and high-gain omnidirectional.

Project 4-4

Do some research on the Internet to learn about home-built antennas for IEEE 802.11 wireless networks, such as the Pringles can antenna, the cantenna, or the wave guide antenna. Using a DSL/cable router or an access point equipped with a removable antenna, build and test one of these low-cost antennas. Write a one-page report showing how much farther you were able to extend your wireless connection using one of these home-built wireless antennas compared to using only the regular antenna provided with the router or access point.

CASE PROJECT

Project 4-1

The Baypoint Group (TBG), a company of 50 consultants who assist organizations and businesses with issues involving network planning and design, has again requested your services as a consultant. Triangle Farms is a farming cooperative that grows vegetables and has two greenhouse locations within six miles of each other on the outskirts of Bennington, Vermont.

Triangle wants to install a wireless network in both locations but also wants to interconnect their two facilities. The local telephone company has proposed to install a dedicated digital line to link Triangle's two locations and has argued that wireless links are not reliable and that they will end up costing more than the $1,500 per month that the dedicated line will cost. Triangle has asked TBG for an opinion. The Baypoint Group has asked you to become involved since you are the expert they always call upon to discuss and recommend antenna systems for wireless links.

TBG is providing the network design and implementation, along with all of the wireless networking equipment required for the connection, except for the antennas linking the two sites. The location of the warehouses allows for line-of-sight access to each other, and the building codes do not allow tall buildings in the area, as they are both near an airport.

Each Triangle location has an office with about 10 staff members. The office area is large and fairly open. Each of the greenhouses has two 500-foot corridors that require wireless access, since staff members perform periodic checks on the planting beds. The farmers would like to be able to upload the updates and harvest predictions directly to the central server, using the wireless network.

Create a PowerPoint slide presentation that outlines the different types of connections and antennas, and the advantages and disadvantages of each. Include examples in the form of pictures and stories about similar successful wireless links. TBG has asked you to be very persuasive in your presentation, because Triangle is on the verge of signing the contract with the phone company. You are told that presenting the facts is not enough at this point; you must convince them why they should select a wireless link.

After your presentation, TBG asked you to prepare another presentation regarding the advantages of unregulated bands. Because an engineer who sits on the Board of Triangle will be there, this PowerPoint presentation should be detailed and technical in its scope.

OPTIONAL TEAM CASE PROJECT

A local engineering user's group has contacted The Baypoint Group requesting a speaker to discuss the merits of different antennas such as dish, yagi, and horn antennas. Form a team of two or three consultants and research these technologies in detail. Specifically, pay attention to how they are used as well as their strengths and weaknesses. Provide an opinion regarding which antenna types will become the dominant players in the future of medium- and long-distance wireless links.

5

LOW RATE WIRELESS PERSONAL AREA NETWORKS

> **After reading this chapter and completing the exercises, you will be able to:**
>
> ♦ Describe a wireless personal area network (WPAN)
> ♦ List the different WPAN standards and their applications
> ♦ Explain how IrDA, Bluetooth, and ZigBee work
> ♦ Describe the security features of low-rate WPAN technology

For many years, few options existed for connecting and synchronizing a PDA, cellular phone, or Smartphone with your laptop or desktop computer. In addition, each new type of peripheral device required consumers to use a different type of cable. One of the first wireless technologies that appeared on the market to replace cable connections between data devices used infrared light (IR), a form of light invisible to the human eye. Although infrared interfaces have been available for quite a long time, the 115,200 bps maximum speed of infrared soon became a limitation, rather than a benefit, for synchronizing portable wireless devices. The IR specification was later enhanced and today it can reach speeds of up to 16 Mbps.

Since the late 1990s many alternative technologies began to eliminate cables and allow data devices and peripherals to communicate without wires. In this chapter, we will briefly explore the still-reliable and easy-to-use IrDA infrared and the now-popular Bluetooth that is available on computers, cellular phones and PDAs, as well as other products. You will also learn about some of the latest developments in short-range, personal area networking.

What Is A WPAN?

A **wireless personal area network (WPAN)** is a group of technologies that are designed for short-range communications, from a few inches to about 33 feet (10 meters), effectively eliminating the need for wires or cables to interconnect multiple devices. Although there is no clear separation between low and high data rates, Bluetooth is included in this chapter since the current versions (1.1 and 1.2) of the specification are limited to 1 Mbps. While this data rate is sufficient to handle up to three simultaneous voice channels, it is not enough to handle most other applications, such as high-quality music and video.

All of these technologies include the ability to network, which means that the devices can communicate with each other. Current and future applications for WPAN technology include:

- Synchronizing PDAs, cellular and Smartphones, cameras, and so on
- Home control systems (smarthome)
- Cordless telephones
- Portable device data exchange
- Industrial control systems
- Location—smart tags used to locate people at home or at the office
- Security systems
- Interactive toys
- Inventory tracking

In addition to helping eliminate wires and cables, WPANs offer two other key advantages. First, because they are designed to communicate at short ranges, WPAN devices use very little power; therefore, the batteries that power the portable devices tend to last a long time. Second, their short range also helps maintain security and privacy, which has long been a concern with other wireless technologies.

Existing and Future Standards

The Institute of Electrical and Electronics Engineers (IEEE), about which you learned in Chapter 3, is currently developing several different standards for WPANs. In this chapter, you will learn about Bluetooth and ZigBee, which are intended to enable connectivity for different types of devices and for different purposes. Because of their differences, you should understand how each standard is implemented.

The IEEE Project P802.15 covers all of the different Working Groups for Wireless Personal Area Networks (WPANs). The last digit in the standard identifies specific working groups such as ".1" for Bluetooth and ".3" for High Rate WPANs.

NOTE

Interoperability

Interoperability in any standard is of utmost importance. The ability to employ standard protocols, such as TCP/IP, is a key factor in the development of any new networking specification. Following the OSI protocol model allows manufacturers to ensure interoperability between their devices and those of other manufacturers and makes their products more attractive to consumers. Throughout the discussion of each of the technologies in the remainder of this chapter, you will notice that the main difference between them is that the layers that change are the **physical layer (PHY)**, which is responsible for converting the data bits into an electromagnetic signal and transmitting it on the medium, and all or part of the **Data Link layer**, the layer responsible for the transfer of data between nodes in the same network segment and that also provides error detection.

Although the OSI model is most often associated with local area networks, it actually is used for all types of data communications.

NOTE

At about the same time that the International Organization for Standardization (ISO) was in the process of creating the Open Systems Interconnect (OSI) model, the IEEE started Project 802 to ensure interoperability among data networking products. Two of the most widely used Project 802 standards are the 802.3 (Ethernet) and 802.5 (Token Ring) networking standards. Project 802 and the OSI model differ in terms of how they are used. The OSI model is a theoretical model of how communications works, while Project 802 sets standards for actual practice.

The IEEE's Project 802 used the OSI conceptual model as a framework for its specifications with some important differences. These are illustrated in Figure 5-1. Project 802 subdivides the OSI model Layer 2, Data Link, into two sublayers: the **Logical Link Control (LLC)**, which is responsible for establishing and maintaining connectivity to the local network, and **Media Access Control (MAC)**, which is responsible for hardware addressing and error detection and correction. The PHY layer performs two basic functions. First, when transmitting, it reformats the data received from the MAC layer into a frame that it can transmit. A **frame** is a data link layer packet that contains the header and trailer required by the physical medium. Second, it listens to the medium to determine when there are no other transmissions, so the data can be sent. The PHY layer also includes the standards for the characteristics of the wireless medium (in the case of wireless networks, IR or RF, as applicable) and defines the method for transmitting and receiving data through that medium. For the purposes of this chapter, you do not need to be concerned about the further project 802 subdivision of the PHY layer, although it will become significant in later chapters on WLANs.

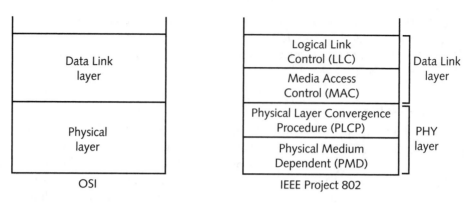

Figure 5-1   OSI model versus IEEE Project 802

INFRARED WPANS (IrDA)

Why consider infrared (IR) wireless technology when today the majority of wireless transmissions are based on radio frequency (RF) technology? The answer is that the low cost and ease-of-use of IR devices mean that many cellular phones and PDAs are equipped with infrared ports that allow them to connect to a computer or another similar device for simple tasks, such as downloading telephone directories and appointment calendars, without cables.

This section explores how IR devices send and receive data and examines the most common use of IR wireless technology, namely those devices that comply with the Infrared Data Association (**IrDA**) specifications (see *www.irda.org*). Unlike other standards discussed in this chapter, IrDA is not an official standard. It has remained as a set of specifications published by the industry association.

Infrared wireless communications dates back over 20 years. The most common infrared connection today is based on the IrDA specifications published by the Infrared Data Association. Infrared ports conforming to the IrDA specifications are also found on some desktop computers, printers, desktop adapters, cameras, phones, overhead projectors, watches, and pagers. The IrDA specifications define both the physical devices and the network protocols they use to communicate with each other. They were originally created because of the need to connect different computer and telecommunications devices without the use of cables.

The goal of the IrDA specifications is to create a data interconnection based on infrared light. IrDA devices have a common set of characteristics:

- They are designed to provide walk-up connectivity. That is, there is a very minimal amount of configuration necessary for two IrDA devices to communicate.

- IrDA devices provide a point-to-point method of data transfer between only two devices at a time.

- Devices following the IrDA standards cover a broad range of computing and communicating devices.

- IrDA is inexpensively implemented because the infrared components are low in cost. In production volumes, the cost of incorporating an IrDA interface on any device today is only about $2 or $3.

There are currently three published versions of the IrDA specifications, plus a fourth currently under development. They are summarized in Table 5-1. Unlike radio frequency (RF) devices that decrease the bandwidth as the distance between devices increases, IrDA devices do not vary the transmission speed. They must be capable of maintaining a constant connection speed. If the distance between two IrDA devices is greater than about 3.3 ft. (1 meter), a connection simply cannot be made or maintained reliably.

Table 5-1 IrDA versions

IrDA Version	Speed
Serial Infrared (SIR)	9,600–115,200 bps
Fast Infrared (FIR)	4 Mbps
Very Fast Infrared (VFIR)	16 Mbps
Ultra Fast Infrared (UFIR)	100 Mbps (under development)

IrDA PHY Layer

IrDA devices communicate using infrared light emitting diodes (LEDs) to send signals and photodiodes to receive. Infrared light can only be modulated in amplitude (intensity), since the frequency of a light beam is predetermined by its color (or wavelength). Because of this, IR interfaces use rather simple modulation techniques.

Serial Infrared (Version 1.0)

SIR was designed to work like the standard serial port on a PC. As such, it uses a **UART (Universal Asynchronous Receiver/Transmitter)**, a microchip that is also used to control a computer's serial interface port. All IrDA devices must support this mode to maintain backward compatibility. To save power and cost, most handheld devices only support SIR.

SIR uses a clock that is 16 times faster than the data rate. To transmit a 0 bit, the UART clock waits for seven clock cycles (pulses) during the bit time (16 clock pulses) and sends an infrared pulse for three clock cycles, and then nothing for six clock cycles. This mechanism is called 7-3-6. Nothing would be sent to transmit a 1 bit during the 16 clock cycles of the bit time. When transmitting at 115,200 bps, the pulses that represent a 0 bit last 1.41 microseconds. The UART chip includes a circuit to provide the 16x clock pulses. An SIR transmission is illustrated in Figure 5-2.

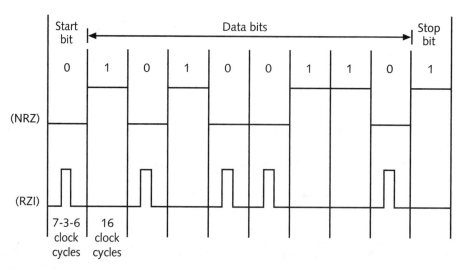

Figure 5-2 IrDA SIR transmission

Fast Infrared (Version 1.1)

The Fast Infrared (FIR) version 1.1 of the IrDA specification extends the data rate to 4 Mbps. When two IrDA devices first communicate, they both transmit using SIR at a speed of only 9600 bps (at 9600 bps, a character arrives once every millisecond). They then exchange basic information, and, if both devices can accommodate the higher FIR speed, they shift to the faster rate.

FIR uses a modulation scheme called **4–pulse position modulation (4–PPM)** in which information is conveyed by the position of a pulse within a time slot. Two bits (or dibits) are transmitted for each pulse: 00, 01, 10, or 11. Depending on which two bits are to be transmitted, a single pulse is placed in either the first, second, third, or fourth part of the 500 ns time slot. This is illustrated in Figure 5–3.

Bit Pattern	Pulse Position	◄ 500 ns ►
00	1000	
01	0100	
10	0010	
11	0001	

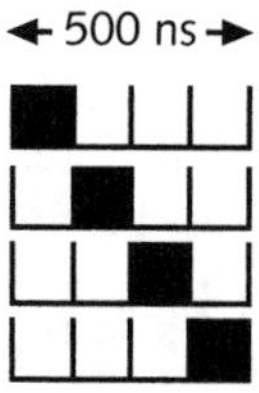

Figure 5-3 IrDA FIR Transmission

NOTE In addition to UFIR, there is an IrDA specification for Medium Infrared (MIR), which supports data rates between 576 Kbps and 1.152 Mbps. MIR is not very common.

Protocols Supported

The IrDA protocol stack supports a variety of other protocols, namely:

- IrDA Physical Layer Protocol (IrPHY) — Controls the hardware that sends and receives the IR pulses through the emitter

- IrDA Link Access Protocol (IrLAP) — Responsible for encapsulating the frames and describes how the devices establish a connection, how they close it, and how are are internally numbered to prevent internal conflicts between devices. IrLAP is similar to the IP protocol.

- IrDA Link Management Protocol (IrLMP) — The status of IrDA devices can change on a regular basis. For example, a user may turn on an IrDA PDA and place it within range of a notebook computer. Every IrDA device somehow must inform all other devices about itself. This is done through the IrLMP protocol. IrLMP's goal is to detect the presence of devices offering a service, to check the data flow, and then act as a multiplexer for the different configurations of the devices. Applications wanting to communicate with IrDA devices would use the IrLMP layer to ask if a specific IrDA device is within range and available.

- IrDA Transport Protocols (Tiny TP) — Manages channels between devices, performs error corrections such as lost packets, divides data into packets, reassembles original data from packets, and defines a reliable way to create a channel. Tiny TP is similar to the TCP protocol.

There are also optional extensions to the protocol stack for specific types of devices and services. These extensions specify how mobile devices transfer information (address books, calendars, dialing control, and so on) over specific networks. One of these extensions is known as IrWWW, which specifies how a wristwatch with an IrDA port can interface with other devices. Another extension is IrTran-P (Infrared Transfer Picture), which is used by digital cameras that have an IrDA port to specifiy how to transfer pictures over the IR interface. Infrared printing (IrLPT) is designed for connecting to printers that are equipped with an IrDA port. Infrared networking is accomplished with IrLAN and IrComm, which enable networking and serial port emulation, respectively.

Some other extensions are IrFM, IrSimple, and IrOBEX. IrFM is a profile that defines the interface with point-of-sale systems (such as cash registers and debit card machines). It enables digital payments from a cellular phone or PDA while cutting costs and simplifying financial transactions for individuals or businesses by using only electronic records. IrSimple is intended to simplify the IrDA protocols, allowing transmission rates from four to ten times that of existing protocols. IrOBEX provides the ability to exchange arbitrary data objects such as vCards and vCalendar between PDAs or between a PDA and a computer.

5

Other IrDA Considerations

There are several factors that must be considered when transmitting with infrared technology:

- Half-duplex transmission — To save space when incorporating IrDA in a device, the transmitter and detector are mounted very close together, which makes it difficult to isolate them optically. This means that IrDA devices cannot transmit and receive at the same time.

- Deflection angle — For IrDA devices to connect reliably, the transmitter and detector must be aligned with each other at a maximum angle of 15 degrees and at a maximum distance of 3.3 ft. (1 meter). At angles between 15 and 30 degrees, IrDA devices must be moved closer together. Communication is not possible at angles greater than 30 degrees.

- Ambient light — IrDA devices will not work in environments where a strong light source interferes with the detector. For example, devices may not function properly or at all when direct sunlight or any other strong light source is aimed directly at the detector.

- Ease of use — One of the advantages of IrDA is that it is very easy to use since there is no need for the users to be concerned about establishing and maintaining a connection. Once it is enabled and provided the devices remain within the maximum distance and deflection angle limitations, the two devices will connect automatically and allow full communications immediately.

- Security — Another advantage is that since only two devices can communicate at a time, and because anyone trying to capture the data transfer would have to be positioned very close to the user and equipment, users don't have to be overly concerned about the security of the link.

- Distance limitation — Any technology that requires devices to be within a very short distance of each other, as well as pointing directly at each other, defeats the purpose of wireless's chief attraction: freedom to roam.

Given some of the preceding advantages mentioned and provided that IrDA continues to be incorporated in popular devices such as cell phones, PDAs, and laptop computers, IR technology may survive for a long time, providing a reliable, easy-to-use, and always-compatible way of linking portable devices.

RF WPANs

The remainder of this chapter looks at RF WPANs, which offer functionality beyond that of IR devices, beginning with Bluetooth and concluding with 802.15.4 (ZigBee).

IEEE 802.15.1 and Bluetooth

Bluetooth is an industry specification that defines small-form-factor, low-cost wireless radio communications. Bluetooth is supported by over 2,500 hardware and software vendors who make up the Bluetooth Special Interest Group (SIG).

The IEEE licensed this wireless technology from the Bluetooth SIG to adapt and copy a portion of the specification as the base material for 802.15.1; the new standard received final approval on March 2, 2002. The approved 802.15.1 standard is essentially the same and is fully compatible with the Bluetooth version 1.1 specification. You can find out more about this and other WPAN technologies by visiting http://www.bluetooth.org and http://ieee802.org/15.

Most new high-end cellular phone models are Bluetooth compatible, enabling users to use headsets that connect without wires, as well as synchronize their phone books with PDAs and computers, and download pictures from a camera-equipped phone. Today you can purchase printers, print servers, GPS devices, computer keyboard and mouse packages, medical equipment, PDAs, and even microwave ovens that are also compatible with Bluetooth, and many new devices will likely become available. Adding Bluetooth capabilities to a computer is as easy as plugging in a small, low-power USB Bluetooth adapter and installing a small amount of software.

NOTE To find out about more products that are Bluetooth enabled, visit http://www.bluetooth.com/products or http://www.palowireless.com/bluetooth/products.asp.

Bluetooth Protocol Stack

Generally speaking, the functions of the stack can be divided into two parts based on how they are implemented. The lower levels of the stack are implemented in the hardware, while the functions of the upper levels of the stack are implemented in software. These functions are discussed in the sections that follow. Figure 5-4 illustrates the Bluetooth protocol stack and compares it to the OSI protocol model.

Bluetooth RF Layer

At the lowest level of the Bluetooth protocol stack is the RF layer. It defines how the basic hardware that controls the radio transmissions functions. At this level, the data bits (0 and 1) are converted into radio signals and transmitted.

Radio Module

At the heart of the Bluetooth RF layer is a single radio transmitter/receiver (transceiver). This single tiny chip is called a **Bluetooth radio module**. Figure 5-5 illustrates the relative

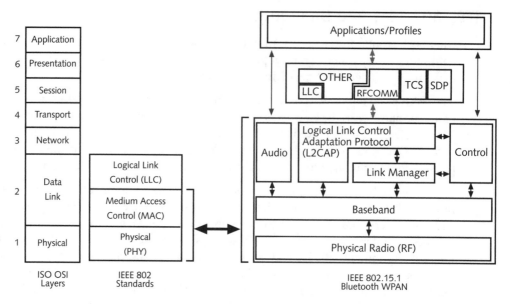

Figure 5-4   Bluetooth protocol stack compared to the OSI protocol model

size of a Bluetooth chip. It is the only hardware that is required for Bluetooth to function. The goals of the original Bluetooth design were for the transceivers to have the basic functions performed by a single chip, be as generic or "mainstream" as possible, be low cost, and require a minimum of supporting off-chip components.

Figure 5-5   Bluetooth transceiver (transmitter/receiver)

The impact of containing Bluetooth hardware on a single chip is significant. Instead of requiring expensive external devices, such as PC cards, to add Bluetooth functionality to a device, the functionality can be built into the product itself by adding a single Bluetooth chip in the manufacturing process. Because devices with a Bluetooth chip include a Bluetooth transceiver, and usually an omnidirectional antenna as well, they are ready to send and receive Bluetooth transmissions the moment the device is powered on.

Bluetooth can transmit at a speed of up to 1 Mbps under the current Bluetooth specification (versions 1.1 and 1.2). Most devices list their maximum data rate as 723 Kbps, since transmission occurs in both directions with some time slots being used for transmission in one direction and some being used for transmission in the other direction. The recently released Bluetooth version 2.0 adds two new modulations that help it achieve data rates of 2 or 3 Mbps while maintaining full backward compatibility with versions 1.1 and 1.2. at 1 Mbps. This new feature is called **enhanced data rate (EDR)**.

Bluetooth has three power classes for transmitting. These determine the communication range between devices and are summarized in Table 5-2. However, keep in mind that because Bluetooth is based on RF transmission, objects such as walls and interference from other sources can affect the range of transmission.

Table 5-2   Power classes

Name	Power Level	Distance
Power Class 1	100 mW	330 feet (100 meters)
Power Class 2	2.5 mW	33 feet (10 meters)
Power Class 3	1 mW	3 inches (10 centimeters)

Modulation Technique

Bluetooth uses a variation of frequency shift keying (FSK), which is a binary modulation technique that changes the frequency of the carrier signal. (You learned about FSK in Chapter 2.) The frequency is higher to send a 1 data bit and lower to send a 0 data bit. The variation of FSK used by Bluetooth is known as **two–level Gaussian frequency shift keying (2–GFSK)**. 2-GFSK uses two different frequencies to indicate whether a 1 or a 0 is being transmitted. The amount that the frequency varies, called the **modulation index**, is between 280 KHz and 350 KHz. This is illustrated in Figure 5-6.

Bluetooth Baseband Layer

The Baseband layer lies on top of the RF layer in the Bluetooth stack. This layer manages physical channels and links, handles packets, and does paging and inquiry to locate other Bluetooth devices in the area.

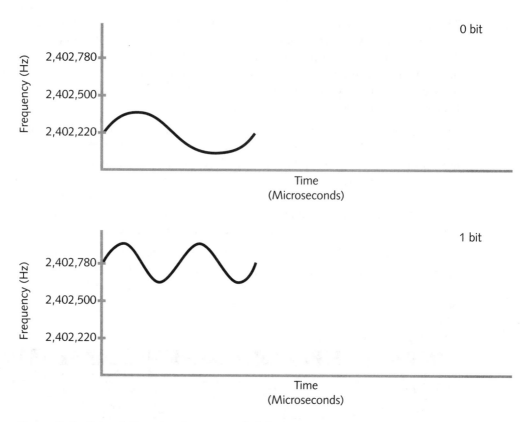

Figure 5-6   2-level Gaussian frequency shift keying (2-GFSK)

Radio Frequency

The part of the spectrum in which Bluetooth operates is the 2.4 GHz Industrial, Scientific, and Medical (ISM) band. Bluetooth divides this 2.4 GHz frequency into 79 different frequencies, called **channels**, spaced 1 MHz apart. Bluetooth uses the frequency hopping spread spectrum (FHSS) technique to send a transmission; the specific sequence of frequencies used, or hopping sequence, is called a channel. This means that the radio frequency hops, or changes rapidly, through the 79 different frequencies during transmission. This is illustrated in Figure 5-7. In just one second of Bluetooth transmission, the frequency changes 1,600 times, or once every 625 microseconds.

NOTE

The Bluetooth hopping sequence is significantly faster than that of most residential cordless telephones that also work in the same 2.4 GHz band and that usually switch frequencies about 100 times per second. The interference caused by cordless phones to a Bluetooth transmission can result in data errors or significant break-ups in a voice stream. This interference has a much longer reach than the Bluetooth transmission itself.

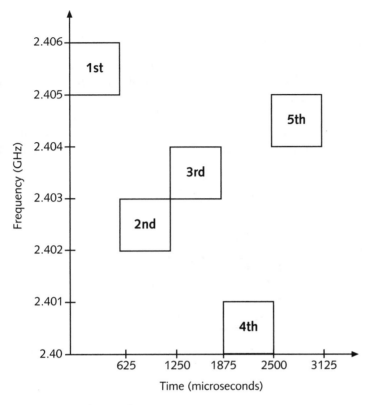

Figure 5-7 Bluetooth FHSS

Bluetooth uses the same frequency as IEEE 802.11b WLANs. Devices that use Bluetooth can interfere with 802.11b WLANs and vice versa. Several solutions are available to avoid this conflict. Special software can be added to the 802.11b WLAN that manages the traffic flow by telling the 802.11b network to be quiet when Bluetooth communications are detected. With the ratification of IEEE 802.15.1, manufacturers following the guidelines of this standard can ensure that 802.11b and Bluetooth will work together with a minimum of interference and disruption. Bluetooth version 1.2 adds a feature called **adaptive frequency hopping (AFH)** that further improves compatibility with 802.11b. Bluetooth accomplishes this by allowing the master in a piconet to change the hopping sequence so that it will not use the frequency channel occupied by 802.11b in the piconet area.

NOTE

Coexistence with other wireless devices operating in unlicensed frequency bands is covered under the IEEE 802.15.2 standard. See http://standards.ieee. org/getieee802/index.html.

Network Topology

There are two types of Bluetooth network topologies: piconet and scatternet.

When two Bluetooth devices come within range of each other, they automatically connect with one another. One device is the **master**, which controls all of the wireless traffic. The other device is known as a **slave**, which takes commands from the master. Slaves can exist in one of several power-saving modes—active, sniff, hold, or parked—described later in this chapter. A Bluetooth network that contains one master and at least one slave and that uses the same channel forms a **piconet**. Examples of piconets are illustrated in Figure 5-8.

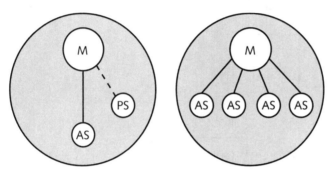

M = Master
AS = Active slave
PS = Parked slave

Figure 5-8   Bluetooth piconets

Each Bluetooth device is preconfigured with an address that is needed when participating or not participating in the piconet. Three of the significant addresses are summarized in Table 5-3.

Table 5-3   Piconet radio module addresses

Name	Description
Bluetooth device address	Unique 48-bit number (IEEE 802 hardware or MAC address), which is preconfigured in the hardware
Active member address	3-bit number valid only as long as device is an active slave in a piconet
Parked member address	8-bit number valid only as long as device is a parked slave; a parked device does not retain the 3-bit active member address

All devices in a piconet must change frequencies both at the same time and in the same sequence in order for communication to take place. The timing (called the phase) in the hopping sequence is determined by the clock of the Bluetooth master. Each active slave is synchronized with the master's clock. The hopping sequence is unique for each piconet and is determined by the Bluetooth device address of the master.

NOTE In a piconet, the master and slave alternatively transmit. The master starts its transmission in even-numbered time slots only, and the slave starts its transmission in odd-numbered time slots only.

A connection between Bluetooth devices is normally a two-step process. The first step is known as the **inquiry procedure**. The inquiry procedure enables a device to discover which devices are in range and determine the addresses and clocks for the devices. When a Bluetooth device enters into the range of other devices, it first attempts to find other devices in the area. The **paging procedure**, during which an actual connection can be established, follows the inquiry procedure. A device that establishes a connection will carry out a paging procedure and will automatically be the master of the connection.

Multiple piconets can cover the same area, and each can contain up to seven slaves. Because each piconet has a different master and hop sequence, the risk of collisions (two devices attempting to send at the same time on the same frequency) is slim. However, if many more piconets are added, the probability of collisions increases. The occurrence of collisions diminishes the performance and throughput of the network.

If multiple piconets cover the same area, a Bluetooth device can be a member of two or more overlapping piconets. A group of piconets in which connections exist between different piconets is called a **scatternet**. A scatternet is illustrated in Figure 5-9. To communicate in each different piconet, the device must use the master device address and clock of that specific piconet.

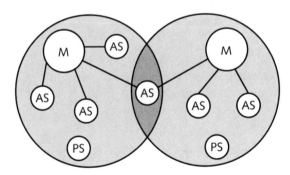

M = Master
AS = Active slave
PS = Parked slave

Figure 5-9   A Bluetooth scatternet

A Bluetooth device can be a slave in several piconets but can be a master in only one piconet. A master and slave can switch roles in a piconet.

Bluetooth Frames

The frame of a Bluetooth transmission is illustrated in Figure 5-10. Each frame consists of three parts:

- Access code (72 bits) — Contains data used for timing synchronization, paging, and inquiry
- Header (54 bits) — Contains information for packet acknowledgment, packet numbering, the slave address, the type of payload, and error checking
- Payload (0-2745 bits) — Can contain data, voice, or both

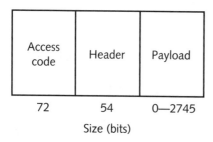

Figure 5-10   A Bluetooth frame

Bluetooth Link Manager Layer

The duties of the Link Manager layer in the Bluetooth stack can be divided into two broad categories: managing the piconet and performing security.

Links Between Bluetooth Devices

Managing the piconet involves such actions as regulating the steps for attaching and detaching slaves from the master as well as overseeing the master-slave switch. This involves establishing different types of links between Bluetooth devices. There are two types of physical links between devices:

- A **synchronous connection-oriented (SCO) link** is a symmetric point-to-point link between a master and a single slave in the piconet. This link functions like a circuit-switched link by using reserved time slots at fixed intervals. A master can support up to three simultaneous SCO links, while slaves can support two or three SCO links. An SCO link carries mainly voice transmissions at a speed of 64 Kbps. These transmissions occur in both directions simultaneously.
- An **asynchronous connectionless (ACL) link** is a packet-switched link that is used for data transmissions. The ACL link is from one master to all the slaves participating on the piconet. It is sometimes called a point-to-multipoint link. A piconet can support only a single ACL link between one master and up to seven slaves. In the time slots not reserved for the SCO links, the master can establish an

ACL and transfer data to any slave. A slave already engaged in an SCO link can also have an ACL link.

Table 5-4 provides an overview of the different types and speed of connections in a piconet. A combined data-voice SCO packet is also defined and can provide 64 Kbps voice and 64 Kbps data transmission in each direction.

Table 5-4 Supported Bluetooth link configurations

Configuration	Max. Transmission Rate Upstream	Max. Transmission Rate Downstream
3 simultaneous voice channels	64 Kbps × 3 channels	64 Kbps × 3 channels
Symmetric data	433.9 Kbps	433.9 Kbps
Asymmetric data	723.2 Kbps or 57.6 Kbps	57.6 Kbps or 723.2 Kbps

NOTE

If an error occurs on an ACL packet, that packet is retransmitted. An SCO packet is never retransmitted.

Error Correction

Another management function of the link manager layer is error correction. There are three kinds of error correction schemes used in the Bluetooth protocol: 1/3 rate Forward Error Correction, 2/3 rate Forward Error Correction, and automatic retransmission request.

- **1/3 rate Forward Error Correction (FEC)** — Repeats every bit three times for redundancy. The maximum data rate is effectively divided by 3, hence the term 1/3 rate.

- **2/3 rate FEC** — Adds extra bits to the data sent for error correction. These extra bits are examined by the receiving device to determine if an error took place in the transmission. For example, if 8 bits of data were to be sent, they would be expanded into 11 bits, which includes the error correction data. The extra bits reduce the maximum data rate that can be achieved for a transmission, but allows the receiver to detect multiple bit errors and correct single bit errors, preventing retransmission of the data.

- **Automatic retransmission request (ARQ)** — Continuously retransmits the data fields of a data-only or a data-voice packet until an acknowledgment is received or a timeout value is exceeded.

Bluetooth Power Usage

Because most Bluetooth devices are designed to be mobile and require battery power from a laptop computer, PDA or similar device, conserving power is essential. The power consumption of Bluetooth devices varies depending on its connection mode. Transmitting voice through a headset uses only 10 milliamps (mA). At this rate, a typical battery would provide 75 hours of use. When data transmissions are occurring, only 6 mA are consumed and a battery can last up to 120 hours before being recharged. When Bluetooth is waiting for a transmission, it only requires 0.3 milliamps, which means the battery can last for up to three months.

 NOTE Although amps and watts are sometimes confusing, think of watts as the measure of the power needed to push the radio signal out while amps is the measure of power that is used to make that push.

Once a Bluetooth device is connected to a piconet, it can be in one of four power-saving modes:

- Active — In **active mode**, the Bluetooth unit actively participates on the channel and consumes an amount of power that corresponds to the type of data that is being transmitted. Over a period of time this amount of power averages out to 2.5 mW in a Power Class 2 device.

- Sniff — In **sniff mode**, a slave device listens to the piconet master at a reduced rate so that it uses less power. The interval is programmable and depends on the application. It is the least efficient of the power-saving modes.

- Hold — The master unit can put slave units into **hold mode**, in which only the slave's internal timer is running. Slave units can also demand to be put into hold mode. Data transfer restarts instantly whenever the slave moves from hold mode back to active mode, but power consumption is kept to a minimum while it is not transmitting.

- Park — **Park mode** is the most efficient of the power-saving modes. In park mode, a device is still synchronized to the piconet but it does not participate in any traffic. These slaves occasionally listen to the traffic of their master in order to resynchronize and check on broadcast messages. Power consumption in this mode is a mere 0.3 mA.

Other Layers and Functions

Some of the remaining layers and parts of the Bluetooth protocol stack play less significant roles than others. Refer back to Figure 5-4. The Logical Link Control Adaptation Protocol (L2CAP) is the Logical Link Control layer that is responsible for segmenting and reassembling data packets. These data packets are then sent through standard data protocols such as TCP/IP for transmission. The RFCOMM data protocol stands for Radio Frequency Virtual Communications Port Emulation. This data protocol provides serial port emulation for Bluetooth data. It packages the data so that it appears as if it were sent through the computer's standard serial port, another feature of Bluetooth.

Control information is also transmitted between devices, such as an instruction for a device to switch from master to slave. This control information comes through the LMP layer but then bypasses the L2CAP layer, which is only used for transmitted data streams.

IEEE 802.15.4—Low Rate WPANs (ZigBee)

The ZigBee standard provides for the connectivity of simple fixed, and mobile devices that require only low data rates between 20 and 250 Kbps, consume a minimum amount of power, and typically connect at distances of 33 feet (10 meters) to 150 feet (50 meters).

The **ZigBee Alliance** was formed in 2002 to create a set of specifications for low-power, cost-effective, wirelessly networked products for monitoring and control, and because there was no global, open standard that enabled manufacturers to build low-cost devices that could interoperate with those manufactured in other countries. The requirements for monitoring sensors, sometimes called *motes*, and control systems are different from those of wireless computer networks.

NOTE The ZigBee specification uses the 802.15.4 standard for the PHY and MAC layers. Both designations are used interchangeably throughout this section. However, keep in mind that the ZigBee Alliance and IEEE are two completely unrelated organizations and that the ZigBee specification goes beyond the IEEE 802.15.4 standard definitions. You can download the ZigBee specification from http://www.zigbee.org. The IEEE 802.15.4 standard is located at http://standards.ieee.org/getieee802/index.html.

The first ZigBee products should begin to appear in 2006 or 2007. Some of the intended applications for ZigBee-compliant devices are:

- Lighting controls
- Automatic meter readers for natural gas, electricity, water, and similar systems
- Wireless smoke and carbon monoxide detectors
- Home security sensors for doors and windows
- Environmental controls for heating and air conditioning systems
- Controls for window blinds, draperies, and shades
- Equipment for medical monitoring
- Universal remote control to a set-top box, including home control
- Industrial and building automation controls for remote machine monitoring

ZigBee Overview

The ZigBee specification is based on the relatively low-level performance requirements of sensors and control systems. ZigBee-compliant devices are designed to remain quiescent (without communicating) for long periods of time.

After a ZigBee device first connects with the network and whenever it is not being used, it can turn itself off, consuming much less power, without having to maintain a constant connection. Devices can wake up any time they need to communicate, follow the network access protocol, and then transmit on the specific network's channel, which is already known (since the device first connected to the network). Once they have performed their required functions, ZigBee devices can return to sleep mode by turning themselves off again. The average duty cycle (the percentage of time ZigBee devices will transmit or receive data) is expected to be between 0.1% and 2% of the time, which means that ZigBee-compliant devices use very little power. A set of AA batteries could last two to five years.

Although ZigBee transmissions are designed to be short in range, both the specification and the 802.15.4 standard includes full mesh networking. Some ZigBee devices have the ability to route packets to other devices. This allows ZigBee devices to reach others beyond their radio range and since each network can simultaneously support up to 65,536 nodes, a ZigBee network can cover a large area such as an entire house, conference center, or manufacturing plant. These characteristics make ZigBee technology ideal for sensors and control applications in large buildings such as factories, warehouses, and even tall office towers.

There are three basic classes of devices in a ZigBee network:

- **Full-function device** — A device that can connect to other full-function devices and has the capability of routing frames to other devices, in addition to connecting to endpoint devices in a parent-child relationship. Full-function devices can maintain a connection to multiple devices.

- **PAN coordinator** — A full-function device that is responsible for starting and maintaining the network. The first full-function device that is turned on in an area assumes the role of PAN coordinator.

- **Reduced-function device** — An endpoint device such as a light switch, or a lamp, that can only connect to one full-function device on the network and only joins the network as a child device. Child devices do not connect to other child devices.

ZigBee Protocol Stack

The protocol stack is based on the OSI seven-layer model but defines only those layers that are relevant to achieving specific functionality required in the ZigBee marketplace. The ZigBee protocol stack is shown in Figure 5-11. Its most important characteristics are:

- Two PHY layers that operate in two separate frequency ranges: 868/915 MHz and 2.4 GHz. The lower frequency PHY layer covers both the 868 MHz European band and the 915 MHz band that is used in countries such as the United States and Australia. The higher frequency PHY layer is used virtually worldwide.

- The MAC sublayer that controls access to the radio channel. Its responsibilities include synchronization and providing a reliable transmission mechanism (error checking).

- The Logical Link Control (LLC) sublayer that complies with the IEEE 802.2 LLC, and is responsible for managing the data-link communication, link addressing, defining service access points, and frame sequencing. A second LLC sublayer is included in the specification to support other protocols and functionality.

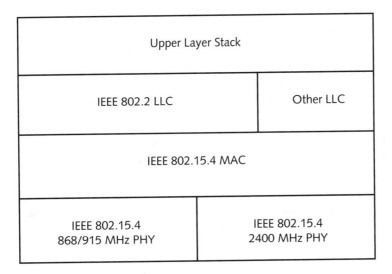

Figure 5-11   ZigBee protocol stack

The upper ZigBee layers include mechanisms used by the devices to join a network, which is called **association**, leave a network (**disassociation**), apply security to frames, and perform routing. These layers are also responsible for device discovery, maintaining routing tables, and storing information about neighbor devices.

The PHY layer in a ZigBee device is responsible for turning the radio transceiver on and off, detecting the presence of an RF signal in the currently selected channel, analyzing and reporting link quality for received packets, assessing whether the channel is clear before initiating a transmission, selecting a frequency channel for operation, and transmitting and receiving data.

There are a total of 27 channels across the different frequency bands. One 600 KHz channel is available in the 868 MHz band, 10 2-MHz-wide channels in the 915 MHz band, and 16 5-MHz-wide channels in the 2,450 MHz band. Table 5-5 summarizes the frequency bands and data rates for 802.15.4 WPANs.

Table 5-5   802.15.4 Frequency bands and data rates

PHY layer (MHz)	Frequency Range (MHz)	Chip Rate (kchips/sec.)	Modulation	Bit Rate (Kbps)
868/915	868 to 868.6	300	BPSK	20
	902 to 928	600	BPSK	40
2,450	2,400 to 2,483.5	2000	O-QPSK	250

Recall from Chapter 2 that binary phase shift keying (BPSK) modulation is a simple scheme that uses just two phase angles to encode the digital signal onto an analog wave. However, since DSSS transmission is used to spread the signal over the bandwidth of the channel, the carrier is modulated with a sequence of 15 chips, instead of the data bits themselves, in both the 868 and 915 MHz bands. To send a binary 1, the sequence 000010100110111 is transmitted and to send a binary 0, the sequence 111101011001000 is transmitted at the chip rates indicated in Table 5-5.

In the 2,450 MHz band, the technique employs 16 different 32-bit chip sequences called **symbols**, which are data units that can represent a single bit or a combination of bits. Each 32-bit chip sequence in this band transmits a different combination of 4-bits.

NOTE

Refer to Table 20, on page 46 of the 802.15.4 standard, for the 16 chip sequences and the corresponding four-bit combinations.

These 32-chip sequences are then modulated using a technique called **offset quadrature phase shift keying (O-QPSK)**, which uses two carrier waves that are exactly 90 degrees out of phase and therefore do not interfere with each other. It modulates some of the chips on one signal and some on the other. Finally, the two signals are combined and transmitted. Figure 5-12 illustrates the modulation of each signal separately; one is called I-Phase for in-phase and the other is called Q-Phase for quadrature signal. Note that the resulting waveform would be far too complex for a graphical example but is similar to QPSK, discussed in Chapter 2.

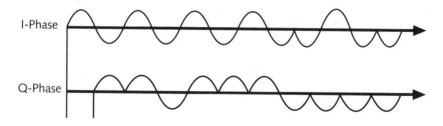

Figure 5-12   Offset quadrature phase shift keying

IEEE 802.15.4 PHY frame format

The PHY frame for IEEE 802.15.4, shown in Figure 5-13, is composed of:

- Preamble (32 binary zeros) — Used for synchronization
- SFD (8-bits) — A fixed pattern of bits that indicates the end of the preamble and the start of the data (SFD)
- Frame length (8-bits) — Indicates the length of the payload (first 7-bits), which can be from one to 127 octets, plus one reserved bit, making this field one octet long
- Payload field (variable) — This field is either five octets long, containing an ACK, or eight to 127 octets long. Frame lengths of zero to four, six, or seven octets are reserved by the standard.

4 octets	1 octet	7 bits	1 bit	Variable
Preamble	**SFD**	Frame Length	Reserved	Payload

Figure 5-13   PHY frame format

802.15.4 MAC layer

The MAC layer in 802.15.4 handles all access from the upper layers to the physical radio channel and is responsible for:

- Generating time synchronization frames if the device is a PAN coordinator
- Synchronizing to the time synchronization frames (described below)
- Association and disassociation
- Device security and support of security mechanisms implemented by the upper layers
- Managing channel access
- Handling and maintaining the guaranteed time slot (GTS) mechanism
- Maintaining a reliable link (error detection); 802.15.4 uses a 16-bit ITU cyclic redundancy check for validating the data

Access to the medium is contention based, which means that all devices must listen to the medium to determine if the channel is free before transmitting. This mechanism is called **carrier sense multiple access with collision avoidance (CSMA/CA)**. 802.15.4 can optionally employ a superframe concept. The **superframe** is a mechanism for managing transmission time in a piconet. It consists of a continuously repeating frame containing contention access periods, but it may also contain **guaranteed time slots (GTS)**, which are reserved periods for critical devices to transmit priority data between two beacons. A superframe always begins with a beacon. A **beacon** signals the beginning of a superframe and contains information about the type and number of time slots contained in the superframe. It is also the time synchronization frame for the network and is required for association. When the network is using superframes, the ZigBee coordinator allocates GTSs but leaves available for use as contention access periods those time slots that are not assigned to other tasks. Each time slot consists of a complete PHY frame, which in turn includes a MAC frame. Figure 5-14 shows an example of an 802.15.4 superframe.

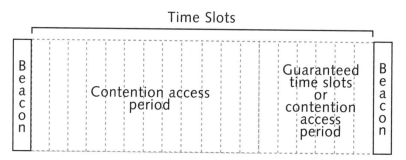

Figure 5-14   802.15.4 superframe

Beacon frames are not required for device-to-device communications, although the PAN coordinator will send beacons periodically since they are required for new devices to associate with the network.

In 802.15.4, all the procedures for associating with and joining a network, routing, and so on, are embedded in the hardware instead of being dependent on client software and driver that may require configuration. This means that in most cases, troubleshooting a ZigBee network is limited to configuring which switch turns on a particular light or group of lights. The only other field troubleshooting function in ZigBee networks is probably determining whether the RF signal from one device is reaching another device so that they can communicate reliably.

ZigBee devices are engineered to automatically associate with and join the network. The network topology is defined during initial installation, depending on the specific needs of the system. When a ZigBee device is powered on for the first time, it will listen for traffic on the network in an attempt to identify which RF channel is being used. Only then will it send a request to join the network. Devices query other devices to identify the location and number of devices that are connected to the network in a process called **device discovery**. Once the devices are associated with the network, they may optionally perform a **service discovery** to identify the capabilities of specific devices of interest that may be members of the WPAN.

Coexistence with Other Standards

Relatively wideband interference, such as that generated by IEEE 802.11b networks, appears like white noise to an IEEE 802.15.4 receiver because only a fraction of the 802.11b power falls within the 802.15.4 receiver bandwidth. Likewise, the impact of interference from

Bluetooth (802.15.1) devices should be minimal due to the much smaller bandwidth of each frequency channel.

802.15.4 devices should only interfere with approximately three out of the 79 hops of a Bluetooth transmission, or approximately 4%. To an IEEE 802.11b receiver, the signal from an 802.15.4 transmitter looks like narrowband interference. In addition, the low duty cycles typical of ZigBee devices further reduce the impact of interference.

Network Addressing

The ZigBee specification defines several different levels of addresses for identifying devices within a PAN: the IEEE address, network (PAN) address, node address, and endpoint address. The IEEE address is a 64-bit static hardware address that is embedded in every radio transmitter and is also called an extended address. The PAN address is a unique 16-bit identifier for each PAN in an area. It is assigned by the PAN coordinator and is only used for a single network or cluster. The node address is a 16-bit address assigned by the PAN coordinator or parent device; this address comes from a group of addresses distributed by the coordinator and is unique for each radio on the network. The node address is used for efficiency, since the extended or IEEE address is 64 bits long. The endpoint address uniquely identifies each endpoint device or service controlled by a single radio.

The best way to understand these multiple levels of addressing is to look at Figure 5-15. The two switches are controlled by a single radio module, as are the three lights on the light fixture. The Switch A, on the left, is used to control the bottom light only. The one on the right, Switch B, controls the two top lights. The ZigBee module controlling the switches can be physically located far away from the light fixture. In this case, for either switch to send a command to the light fixture, they would need to use the network address (since it can be different), the node address to identify the light fixture, and the endpoint address to identify the lamp(s). The process of creating a relationship between the two top lights to Switch B is called **binding**.

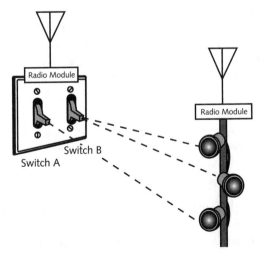

Figure 5-15   Multiple endpoints controlled by a single radio transmitter

Note that not all addresses are used in every frame; the address that is used depends on which two devices are communicating. Although the example in the figure is extremely simple, imagine the application of this same process to controlling endpoint devices in a tall office tower or a large factory.

ZigBee Network Topologies

There are three basic topologies for ZigBee networks—star, tree, and mesh—as illustrated in Figure 5-16.

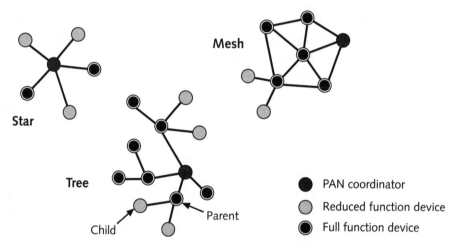

Figure 5-16   Different topologies supported in ZigBee networks

In both tree and mesh topologies, alternate paths may be available for packets, even if a nearby device is turned off or disconnected from the network. However, in cluster tree networks, alternate paths can only be available to a child or a full-function device if another full-function device is within its radio range. If a child device loses the connection with its full-function device, it becomes an orphan. An orphan can rejoin the network by becoming a child of another full-function device that is within range. If a full-function routing device loses the connection to another full-function device, it will automatically use one of its alternate connections, if available, so that it retains its routing capability. These are important considerations when installing a ZigBee network.

NOTE   The IEEE 802.15.4 standard only defines two different topologies: star and peer-to-peer, since a cluster tree network essentially consists of multiple star topology networks.

Figure 5-17 shows multiple paths for packets that are routed in a mesh network. Note that the mesh network itself is made up of full-function devices connected in a peer-to-peer fashion, although these can have other reduced-function child devices connected to them.

Provided that all full-function routing devices are able to connect to each other forming a mesh-like topology, packets can be routed across the entire network.

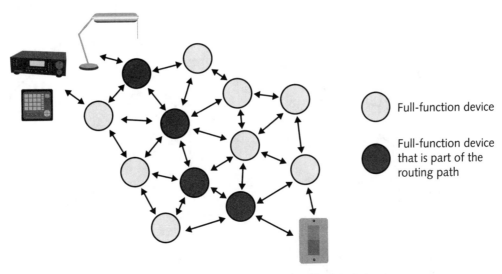

Figure 5-17   Routing of data packets in a ZigBee mesh network

In a star topology, the network is controlled by a single device, the PAN coordinator. All other devices are known as end-nodes, regardless of whether they have additional capabilities. Since most devices are connected to a coordinator, they only communicate directly with the coordinator.

Cluster tree topologies are made up of two or more tree topology networks that are interconnected by full-function devices. Cluster tree networks have a slight advantage over mesh networks. In a mesh network, performance is diminished because each full-function node must maintain a complete routing table and make decisions on the best route to use when forwarding the packets. However, the reliability of a cluster tree network is not as high as that of a mesh network, because the failure of an interconnecting device can prevent an entire cluster tree from communicating with other cluster trees and other devices on the network, perhaps preventing a light switch from turning on a lamp located on another floor.

Figure 5-18 illustrates an example of a larger cluster tree network. Notice the connections between cluster trees; also notice that each cluster tree uses a different channel to communicate between devices. The ZigBee routers must be able to communicate on all channels in order to act as an interface between different cluster trees.

Power Management in ZigBee Networks

Packet routing requires a lot of processing overhead and some additional traffic, which diminishes the power-saving effect of ZigBee devices. In addition, ZigBee devices are designed to be very small, such as a light switch, and for this reason they are more likely to

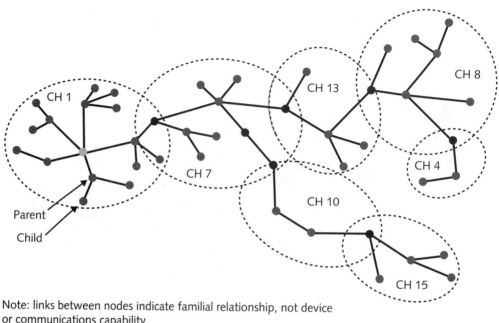

Note: links between nodes indicate familial relationship, not device or communications capability

Figure 5-18   Sample ZigBee cluster tree network

be equipped with low-speed, power-efficient CPUs. In a cluster tree network, only the devices that interconnect each different cluster tree incur overhead, and, consequently, consume more power. The 802.15.4 standard favors battery-powered devices but does not prevent devices from being connected to another power source, such as an electrical outlet. There is also no limitation on devices having additional data processing power. Full-function, routing-capable 802.15.4 devices typically connect to external power sources, although they can run on battery power during outages.

The ZigBee specification includes a number of parameters that must be maintained by devices in case of localized or network-wide power failures or resets. These include the PAN ID, the network address, the address of every associated child device, and the channel in use. Availability of the address information enables a ZigBee network to recover without user intervention. This kind of functionality is crucial for the acceptance of ZigBee devices in the market.

LOW RATE WPAN SECURITY

Although security should be of little concern with WPANs, since most of the transmissions are restricted to a short physical range, hackers will go to almost any length to break into devices and networks. In this section, you will learn about the security models for each of the WPAN technologies discussed in this chapter.

One of the most serious concerns—one that is frequently ignored by end-users—is social engineering. Hackers can target a particular company without anyone knowing why or when. Staff must constantly look for situations that can expose them to security weaknesses. When using equipment outside the office, it must be configured to reject any kind of file transfer without specific user authorization, even when security is used. Stolen or even borrowed equipment also can compromise security, because authorized users may intentionally or unintentionally provide a password or security code to someone else, or change configuration parameters, thereby exposing equipment to unauthorized data transfers. In this case, the security keys must be changed immediately, throughout the organization.

Designing security in WPANs is usually much more difficult than in other networking technologies. Among the reasons for this are that most small devices have only limited processing capabilities, small amounts of memory, and are low-power and low-cost—these factors prevent the implementation of complex security measures. While both the consumer and business markets may be attracted to the concept of being free to roam while remaining connected, they do not want anyone to listen to their telephone conversations, access their private information, steal the signal, or interfere in any way with their systems. This means that a single solution is not likely to meet all the potential security requirements of WPANs.

Banking and electronic funds transactions must be able to verify the user's identity as well as verify the transaction itself by additional methods, such as a **public key infrastructure (PKI)**, which is a unique security code, or key, provided by a certificate authority. A **certificate authority** is a private company that verifies the authenticity of each user to avoid the possibility of fraud. This kind of authentication of devices or users must exist and enjoy widespread use before financial institutions will adopt WPAN technology or support its use by consumers. In addition, the integrity of the data transmission must also be carefully protected to prevent tampering.

Security in Infrared WPANs

Security in IR is limited to the line-of-sight characteristic of this type of connection. The IrDA specification makes no provision for encrypting data or protecting the connection in any other way, although users may encrypt a file before exchanging it between devices.

By default, for data to be transferred between two devices, the recipient must first accept the transfer. However, users can configure IrDA devices so that anyone can transmit files without first notifying the device's owner. This open access can be a major security concern. Both technicians and end users must properly configure their equipment to prevent unauthorized access.

Security in Bluetooth WPANs

Bluetooth provides security at the LMP layer using authentication. Encryption services are also available in Bluetooth networks. **Authentication** in a Bluetooth piconet is based on identifying the device itself, and not who is using the device.

The two major areas in which Bluetooth provides security features are authentication and encryption. Authentication is verifying that the device asking to join the piconet should be allowed to join. The Bluetooth authentication scheme is a **challenge-response strategy** in which a process is used to check if both devices know a shared identical secret key. If both devices have the same response, then the new device is authenticated and allowed to join the piconet.

The second area of security is encryption. **Encryption** is the process of encoding communications and ensures that the transmissions cannot be easily intercepted and decoded. There are three encryption modes:

- Encryption Mode 1 — Nothing is encrypted.
- Encryption Mode 2 — Traffic from the master to one slave is encrypted, but traffic from the master to multiple slaves is not encrypted.
- Encryption Mode 3 — All traffic is encrypted.

The authentication key and the encryption key are two different keys. The reason for separating them is to allow the use of a shorter encryption key without weakening the strength of the authentication key.

There are three levels of Bluetooth security:

- Level 1 — No security. At this level, a Bluetooth device does not initiate any security steps.
- Level 2 — Service-level security. At Level 2, security is established after a connection is made. This is done at the higher levels of the protocol stack.
- Level 3 — Link-level security. Link-level security is performed before a connection is made and is done at the lower levels of the protocol stack.

Security in ZigBee and IEEE 802.15.4 WPANs

ZigBee WPANs use a concept called symmetric key for authentication and encryption. A symmetric key is a sequence of numbers and letters, much like a password, that must be entered by the authorized user on all devices. No automatic key distribution or key rotation is included in the standard, although these options can be implemented by higher protocol layers. The length of the key can be 4, 6, 8, 12, 14, or 16 octets, with longer keys providing more security than shorter ones.

In addition to symmetric key security, the IEEE 802.15.4 standard provides frame integrity, access control, and sequential freshness security services. Frame integrity is a technique that uses a **message integrity code (MIC)**, a sequence of bits based on a subset of the data itself, the length field, and the symmetric key. This code is used by the receiving device to verify that the data has not been tampered with during transmission from the sender to the receiver. In access control, a device maintains a list of other devices with which it wants to communicate. This list is called an **access control list (ACL)**. This technique allows ZigBee devices in a large building, for example, to communicate only with devices belonging to their own network and not with devices in other networks. **Sequential freshness** is a security service used by the receiving device that ensures that the same frames will not be transmitted more than once. The network maintains a sequential number that is continually incremented and tracked by the devices to verify that the arriving data is newer than the last data transmitted. This prevents a frame from being captured and replayed on the network by a hacker who does not have access to the encryption key. For example, a hacker could capture a command frame and replay it on the network to turn off a security system.

There are three security modes in the 802.15.4 standard: unsecured mode, ACL mode (which uses access control), and secured mode (which uses full authentication and encryption). In secured mode, the MAC layer may optionally provide frame integrity and sequential freshness.

5

CHAPTER SUMMARY

- ❑ Computer networks require all the network components to follow certain rules if the network is to work. A network protocol is the set of rules specifying the format and order of the messages exchanged between two or more communication devices. Network protocols are organized into layers. When a set of network protocols is viewed as a whole, the group is called a network protocol stack.

- ❑ The most common infrared connection today is based on the IrDA standard. The primary use for IrDA is to link notebook computers and handheld devices.

- ❑ IrDA transmission requires that the emitter and detector be directly aimed at one another and devices communicate using infrared light emitting diodes (LEDs) to send and photodiodes to receive signals. IrDA devices do not vary the transmission speed. They must be capable of maintaining a constant connection speed ranging from 9,600 bps to 16 Mbps.

- ❑ The IrDA PHY layer can transmit using Serial Infrared (SIR or version 1.0) at up to 115,200 bps, using Fast Infrared (FIR), version 1.1 at up to 4 Mbps, or using VFIR at up to 16 Mbps.

- ❑ IrDA devices cannot send and receive at the same time. Communication between IrDA devices is always in half-duplex mode. When the two devices have a deflection angle of no more than 15 degrees, the distance between devices can be up to 3 feet (1 meter). If the deflection is between 15 and 30 degrees, the devices must be moved closer together. Ambient light can impede an infrared transmission.

- ❑ IrDA is easy to use. Another advantage is security, which is the result of only two devices being able to communicate at a time. IrDA does limit physical distance of transmissions.

❏ Bluetooth is a wireless technology that uses short-range radio frequency (RF) transmissions and enables users to connect to a wide range of devices without cables. Bluetooth can also be used to create a small network.

❏ Bluetooth is supported by over 2,500 hardware and software vendors who make up the Bluetooth Special Interest Group (SIG). The IEEE obtained the right to copy a portion of the specification to use as the base material for the 802.15.1 standard. The standard is fully compatible with Bluetooth version 1.1.

❏ The Bluetooth protocol stack functions can be divided into two parts based on how they are implemented: the lower levels of the stack are implemented in hardware, while the functions of the upper levels of the stack are implemented in software. At the lowest level of the Bluetooth protocol stack is the RF layer. It defines how the basic hardware that controls the radio transmissions functions. At the heart of Bluetooth is a single radio transmitter/receiver (transceiver) that performs all of the necessary functions. Bluetooth can transmit at a speed of 1 Mbps and has three different power classes for transmitting.

❏ Bluetooth uses two-level Gaussian frequency shift keying (2-GFSK) modulation and operates in the 2.4 GHz Industrial, Scientific, and Medical (ISM) band. Bluetooth uses the frequency hopping spread spectrum (FHSS) technique to send a transmission.

❏ When two Bluetooth devices come within range of each other, they automatically connect with one another. One device is the master and the other device is a slave. A Bluetooth network that contains one master and at least one slave using the same channel forms a piconet. A Bluetooth device can be a member of two or more piconets in the same area. A group of piconets in which connections exist between different piconets is called a scatternet.

❏ There are three kinds of error correction schemes used in the Bluetooth protocol: 1/3 rate Forward Error Correction (FEC), 2/3 rate FEC, and the automatic retransmission request (ARQ).

❏ Devices in a piconet can be in active, hold, sniff, or park modes; device activity is lowered during the power-saving modes.

❏ ZigBee is a specification for low-rate WPANs created by the ZigBee alliance to promote the creation of a global standard for small, low-power, cost-effective, wirelessly networked products for monitoring and control.

❏ ZigBee technology is geared toward devices such as lighting controls, wireless smoke and carbon monoxide detectors, thermostats and other environmental controls, medical sensors, remote controls, and industrial and building automation.

❏ The ZigBee specification includes full mesh networking capability to allow networks to encompass large buildings. Full-function devices can route frames across the network to remote devices. Reduced function devices are an endpoint device such as a light switch or lamp.

❏ There are three possible ZigBee network topologies: star, tree, and mesh.

❏ The IEEE 802.15.4 standard defines three frequency bands: 868 MHz, 915 MHz, and the 2.4 GHz–ISM band. The protocol stack has two PHY layers. One supports 868/915 MHz and the other supports 2.4 GHz. There are a total of 27 channels across the three bands. Modulation is BPSK for 868/915 MHz. For 2.4 GHz, it uses O–QPSK modulation with a fixed set of 16 chipping codes each representing a 4-bit data pattern or symbol.

❏ 802.15.4 is designed to coexist easily with other WPAN and WLAN technologies transmitting in the same frequency range. Access to the medium is contention based, but support for guaranteed time slots is also provided through the use of superframes.

❏ Security in Bluetooth supports only device authentication and limited encryption. Secure key distribution is not provided in the standard. ZigBee supports message integrity at the MAC layer and can also check for the freshness of the message to ensure that the same frame will not be transmitted more than once in a piconet.

5

KEY TERMS

1/3 rate Forward Error Correction (FEC) — An error correction scheme that repeats each bit three times for redundancy.

2/3 rate FEC — An error correction scheme that uses a mathematical formula to add extra error correction bits to the data sent.

4-pulse position modulation (4-PPM) — A modulation technique that translates two data bits into four light impulses.

access control list (ACL) — A list of addresses of other devices from which the device that maintains the list expects to receive frames.

active mode — A state in which the Bluetooth device actively participates on the channel.

adaptive frequency hopping (AFH) — A feature added by Bluetooth version 1.2 that further improves compatibility with 802.11b by allowing the master in a piconet to change the hopping sequence so that it will not use the frequency channel occupied by 802.11b in the piconet area.

association — A mechanism for a device to join a network.

asynchronous connectionless (ACL) link — A packet-switched link that is used for data transmissions.

authentication — The process of verifying that the device asking to join the piconet should be allowed to join.

automatic retransmission request (ARQ) — An error correction scheme that continuously retransmits until an acknowledgment is received or timeout value is exceeded.

beacon — A frame that signals the beginning of a superframe and contains information about the type and number of time slots contained in the superframe.

binding — The process of establishing a relationship between endpoints in a ZigBee network.

Bluetooth radio module — A single radio transmitter/receiver (transceiver) that performs all of the necessary transmission functions.

carrier sense multiple access with collision avoidance (CSMA/CA) — A device access mechanism in which all devices must listen to the medium to determine if the channel is free before transmitting.

certificate authority — An organization that supplies security keys and authenticates users.

challenge-response strategy — A process used to check if the other device knows a shared identical secret key.

channels — Another name for frequencies.

Data Link layer — The layer responsible for the transfer of data between nodes in the same network segment and that also provides error detection.

device discovery — The process of querying other devices on the network to identify their location and the number of devices connected.

disassociation — A mechanism used by devices to leave a network.

encryption — The process of encoding communications to ensure that the transmissions cannot be easily intercepted and decoded.

enhanced data rate (EDR) — A feature of the Bluetooth version 2.0 specification that allows it to support data rates of 2 and 3 Mbps by adding two new modulations, while remaining fully backward compatible with Bluetooth versions 1.1 and 1.2.

frame — A Data Link layer packet that contains the header and trailer required by the physical medium.

full-function device — A device used in 802.15.4 (ZigBee) networks that can connect to other full-function devices and has the capability of routing frames to other devices in a ZigBee network. It can also connect to endpoint or child devices. Full-function devices can maintain a connection to multiple devices.

guaranteed time slots — Reserved periods for critical devices to transmit priority data.

hold mode — A state in which the Bluetooth device can put slave units into a mode in which only the slave's internal timer is running.

inquiry procedure — A process that enables a device to discover which devices are in range and determine the addresses and clocks for the devices.

IrDA — An acronym for the Infrared Data Association and also a set of specifications for wireless infrared communications.

Logical Link Control (LLC) — One of the two sublayers of the IEEE Project 802 Data Link layer.

master — A device on a Bluetooth piconet that controls all of the wireless traffic.

Media Access Control (MAC) — One of the two sublayers of the IEEE Project 802 Data Link layer.

message integrity code (MIC) — A code composed of a subset of the data, the length of the data, and the symmetric key, used by the receiving device to verify that the data has not been tampered with during transmission.

modulation index — The amount that the frequency varies.

offset quadrature phase shift keying (O-QPSK) — A transmission technique used in 802.15.4 that uses two carrier waves of the same frequency but with a phase difference of 90 degrees between them. This technique modulates even numbered chips in the in-phase wave and odd numbered chips in the other (Q-Phase), using quadrature amplitude modulation, before combining the waves for transmission.

paging procedure — A process that enables a device to make an actual connection to a piconet.

PAN coordinator — The 802.15.4 device that controls access to the piconet and optionally the timing as well.

5

park mode — A state in which the Bluetooth device is still synchronized to the piconet but it does not participate in the traffic.

physical layer (PHY) — The layer that is responsible for converting the data bits into an electromagnetic signal and transmitting it on the medium.

piconet — A Bluetooth network that contains one master and at least one slave that use the same channel.

public key infrastructure (PKI) — A unique security code that can verify the authenticity of a user.

reduced-function device — In ZigBee networks, a device such as a light switch, or lamp that can only connect to one full-function device at a time and can only join the network as a child device.

scatternet — A group of piconets in which connections exist between different piconets.

sequential freshness — A security service available in 802.15.4 used by the receiving device that ensures that the same frames will not be transmitted more than once.

service discovery — The process of sending a query to other devices on the network to identify their capabilities.

slave — A device on a Bluetooth piconet that takes commands from the master.

sniff mode — A state in which the Bluetooth device listens to the piconet master at a reduced rate so that it uses less power.

superframe — A mechanism for managing transmissions in a piconet. The superframe is a continually repeating frame containing a beacon, contention access periods, channel time allocation periods, and management time allocation periods. Using the superframe is optional in 802.15.4 WPANs.

symbol — A data unit that can represent one or more bits.

synchronous connection-oriented (SCO) link — A symmetric point-to-point link between a master and a single slave in the piconet that functions like a circuit-switched link by using reserved slots at regular intervals.

two-level Gaussian frequency shift keying (2-GFSK) — A binary signaling technique that uses two different frequencies to indicate whether a 1 or a 0 is being transmitted in addition to varying the number of waves.

UART (Universal Asynchronous Receiver/Transmitter) — A microchip that controls a computer's interface to its attached serial devices through a serial port or IrDA port.

wireless personal area network (WPAN) — A group of technologies that are designed for short range communications, from a few inches to about 33 feet (10 meters).

ZigBee Alliance — An association of manufacturers and interested organizations formed to promote the creation of a global standard for wireless devices used in monitoring and control applications.

Review Questions

1. The Bluetooth _____ listens to the medium to determine when the data can be sent.
   a. Physical Layer Convergence Procedure (PLCP)
   b. IEEE 802.x
   c. Logical Link Control (LLC)
   d. Data Link layer

2. Each of the following is an example of a Bluetooth communication except:
   a. cell phone to PDA
   b. notebook computer to PDA cradle
   c. hard drive to memory
   d. notebook computer to GPS

3. Which of the following is not an advantage of infrared over Bluetooth?
   a. Narrow angle
   b. Master controls slave
   c. Short range
   d. Low power

4. The organization that develops and promotes Bluetooth is known as _____ .
   a. Bluetooth SIG
   b. IEEE Bluetooth Task Group
   c. Bluetooth TIA
   d. Bluetooth Standards Organization

5. The lower levels of WPAN communication protocol stacks are implemented in the _____ .
   a. software
   b. hardware
   c. IR
   d. Data Link layer

6. At the lowest level of the Bluetooth protocol stack is the _____ layer.

   a. RF

   b. LMP

   c. TCP/IP

   d. IR

7. One of the advantages of Bluetooth over IrDA is that IrDA requires _____ .

   a. batteries

   b. the devices to be pointed at each other

   c. a wall from which the signals can reflect

   d. an electronic business card

8. The _____ period is when ZigBee devices have time reserved for priority transmissions.

   a. contention access

   b. guaranteed time slot

   c. beacon

   d. time synchronization

9. Two-level Gaussian frequency shift keying (2-GFSK) uses _____ different frequencies to indicate whether a 1 or a 0 is being transmitted.

10. The amount that the Bluetooth frequency varies is called _____ and is between 280 KHz and 350 KHz.

11. Bluetooth divides the 2.4 GHz frequency into 79 different frequencies called _____ that are spaced 1 MHz apart.

12. A ZigBee coordinator cannot allocate guaranteed time slots for devices to transmit data. True or False?

13. Bluetooth has seven different power classes for transmitting. True or False?

14. Objects such as walls and interference from other sources do not affect the range of Bluetooth transmissions. True or False?

15. Bluetooth devices are usually not mobile, so conserving power is not necessary. True or False?

16. How does IrDA FIR modulation work?

17. Why do ZigBee networks transmit data so slowly? Could ZigBee networks benefit from much higher speeds? Discuss the reasons why or why not.

18. Discuss an application for ZigBee devices that was not included in the chapter. How would this application be implemented and why would you implement it using ZigBee?

5

19. In Bluetooth, what is the difference between a piconet and a scatternet?

20. What type of security can be provided in ZigBee networks?

HANDS-ON PROJECTS

Project 5-1: Using IrDA

Setting up and using an infrared port on computers and other devices is a very simple task. Extensive instructions on how to accomplish this are available in the Windows XP help files.

1. Transfer a file between a notebook computer and a PDA or camera-equipped cellular phone, and check the speed of the transfer. Picture phones can usually send and receive files in JPEG format.

2. What was the speed of the transfer? What type of IrDA transmission (SIR or FIR) did the system use to transfer a file to the PDA? Why were this type of link and speed used? Record your answers on a piece of paper, label them "Computer to PDA," and save them for the next step.

3. Transfer the same file between two notebook computers and check the speed of the transmission. What was the speed of the transfer? What type of IrDA transmission (SIR, FIR, or VFIR) did the system use to transfer a file to the other computer? Compare the transfer speed with the PDA transfer in Step 2. Was the transfer speed different? Why were this type of link and speed used for this transfer?

NOTE   To check the speed of data transfer in Windows, you must do so while the transfer is going on between the two devices. Point your mouse cursor to the IrDA icon but do not click. You will see a pop-up help bubble displaying the text "Wireless link with <name of other computer> at <number> bps".

4. Using two notebook computers or other devices with infrared ports, experiment with the angle, distance, and ambient light between them. Use a variety of settings and conditions. What are the practical limits of infrared transmission? What guidelines would you establish for infrared use? What troubleshooting tips can you give? Write a one-page paper on your findings.

Project 5-2: Using Bluetooth

NOTE   Different Bluetooth products have different software and procedures. These project instructions and illustrations are for devices that use DLink DBT-120 hardware and software. If necessary, adjust the specific steps to fit the software for your Bluetooth device(s).

1. Install a Bluetooth USB interface in a notebook computer.

NOTE You may need to uninstall the Microsoft drivers and reinstall the vendor software. Go to http://support.microsoft.com/kb/889814/en-us and follow the instructions on the page.

5

    a. Follow the manufacturer instructions to install the DLink DBT-120 USB Bluetooth adapter in Windows XP. For most USB devices, the software must be installed first. At some point in the installation, the instructions will guide you to insert the Bluetooth USB adapter in the USB connector.

    b. There may be additional vendor software to install. Follow the installation instructions on the screen or check the documentation that came with your Bluetooth card.

2. Locate another Bluetooth-enabled computer.

    a. Position two Bluetooth devices 33 feet (10 meters) from each other. Select one of the devices as the master that is trying to actively join the piconet and the other as the slave that will accept the new device.

    b. On both the master and slave, start the specific vendor Bluetooth software by double-clicking the Bluetooth icon in the system tray. This will display the Initial Bluetooth Configuration Wizard, as shown in Figure 5-19. Click **Next** to accept the defaults. Have another team member perform this and Steps C through F simultaneously on the slave.

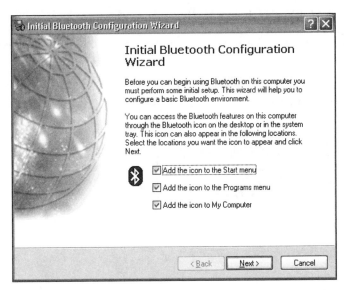

Figure 5-19 Bluetooth Configuration Wizard

    c. Now you will see a dialog box, as shown in Figure 5-20. The text boxes contain the name and type of your computer. Click **Next** to accept the defaults, and then click **Next** again to begin the configuration.

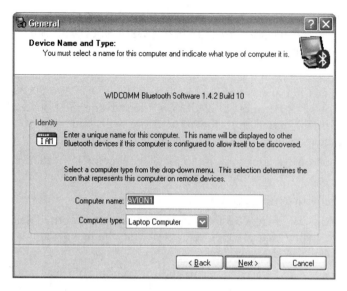

Figure 5-20   Name and type of computer

    d. Now select which Bluetooth services your computer will offer to other computers. Although you can leave all the default options selected, for the purposes of these exercises, it is recommended that you only leave the File Transfer and Network Access boxes checked. Clear the check boxes next to the other services. Remember to scroll down and deselect the other services. See Figure 5-21. Click **Next**.

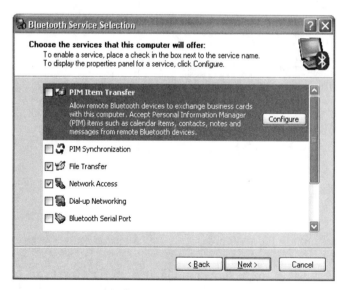

Figure 5-21   Bluetooth services configuration

e. After about a minute, the selected services will be installed. When you see the Configuration Wizard dialog box again, click the Skip button to end the configuration process. Then click the Finish button at the bottom of the final dialog box.

f. Double-click the Bluetooth icon in the system tray or the My Bluetooth Places icon on the Windows desktop to open My Bluetooth Places.

g. By default, Bluetooth devices cannot be seen by other devices. In the left pane of the master, click View devices in range. A moving searchlight will appear while the software scans the area for other devices. After a few seconds, as seen in Figure 5-22, an icon will appear displaying a notebook computer with the name of the other computer beside it. Repeat this step on the slave. Both devices should now have discovered each other on the Bluetooth piconet.

5

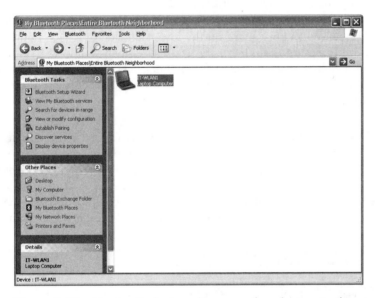

Figure 5-22   Bluetooth devices discover other devices in the piconet

h. Keep the My Bluetooth Places screen open on both devices for the next activity.

3. Transfer files between devices.

a. After the slave has been located, a connection between it and the master must be made. The easiest way to accomplish this is to first pair the two computers. Right-click the slave icon on the master to display the context menu and select Pair Device. The Bluetooth PIN Code Request dialog box opens. You must enter a PIN. Enter **12345678** in the text box, as shown in Figure 5-23, and then click the **OK** button. A bubble will pop up on the slave, next to the system tray. Click the bubble once to open the Bluetooth PIN Code Request dialog box and enter the same PIN to finish pairing the two computers.

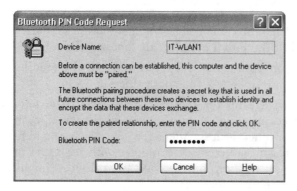

Figure 5-23   Entering the PIN code to pair the devices

   b. You should now see a check mark on the lower-left side of the computer icons in My Bluetooth Places on both the master and slave. Open Windows Explorer on the slave. Select a text, image, or media file. Right-click the file and select Send To, Bluetooth, and Other. In the Select Device dialog box, select the master computer and click **OK**.

   c. In a few seconds, the slave will begin an FTP transfer to the master. You will see a file transfer confirmation bubble appear on the master. Click the bubble once to open the Bluetooth File Transfer Access Authorization dialog box. As shown in Figure 5-24, click the check box next to For the current task to authorize the transfer, and then click OK. A progress dialog box appears. When the file transfer is completed, in My Bluetooth Places on the master, click **Bluetooth Exchange Folder** on the left pane. You should see a copy of the file you just sent from the slave.

Figure 5-24   Accepting a Bluetooth file transfer

   d. Close all open windows.

4. Experiment with Bluetooth networking. If your computer is equipped with a microphone and speakers or a headset, set up the audio gateway and hold a wireless conversation with a fellow student in an adjacent room using Bluetooth.

5. Now compare Bluetooth and IrDA. In which situations is one better than the other? Write a one-page report outlining your conclusions.

CASE PROJECT

5

CASE PROJECTS

Project 5-1: Comparing IrDA and Bluetooth

The Baypoint Group (TBG) has once again requested your services as a consultant. A regional restaurant chain, Thomas' Italian Grill, wants to speed up its service. The management of Thomas' Italian Grill has identified a bottleneck in its order process. Servers write down the customer's order and then must go to a central computer to enter the orders. On nights when the restaurant is very busy, the servers may have to wait in line at the central computer to enter their orders.

TBG has proposed that servers be provided PDAs with IrDA ports. The proposal specifies that as the servers take the orders, they tap them into the PDA. Several infrared ports will be installed at different locations around the restaurant. Servers will only need to point their PDA devices at the IrDA port to transmit the customer's order into the computer system.

Because this technology is so new to Thomas' Italian Grill, the restaurant group is reluctant to go along with the proposal. TBG has asked you to become involved.

1. Create a PowerPoint slide presentation that outlines how infrared technology works. Be sure to include information about IrDA standards, the advantages and disadvantages, and why IrDA would be the best solution for this project.

2. Your presentation convinced Thomas' Italian Grill management that using PDAs would be a good solution. However, the management at Thomas' Italian Grill uses a variety of lighting (incandescent lighting and fluorescent lighting) and has large glass areas that let in sunlight during the daytime hours. Management is concerned about the reliability and convenience of the system for the servers; one of the managers has heard that Bluetooth technology would avoid lighting and distance issues, although there may be interference considerations. TBG has asked you to be involved in a demonstration of both technologies to the client. You should prepare a practical demonstration using two notebooks or one notebook and one PDA, showing a file transfer between the two devices. Be sure to demonstrate what happens when you cannot remain stationary while using IrDA and Bluetooth.

OPTIONAL TEAM CASE PROJECT

Microsoft has included Bluetooth support in Windows XP Service Pack 2 for many devices. To install the Bluetooth software on a computer using the Microsoft driver, you will have to uninstall the vendor-supplied software, remove the Bluetooth USB adapter, reboot the computer, then insert the Bluetooth USB adapter again. Windows XP will automatically detect the adapter and install all of the required software and drivers.

AirMagnet is a company that supplies WLAN analyzer software. AirMagnet also provides a free unsupported utility called BlueSweep that helps you identify nearby Bluetooth devices and services. Download and install this utility, after installing the Bluetooth USB adapter using the Microsoft drivers available in Windows XP. The utility only works with these drivers and in Windows XP Service Pack 2.

Run AirMagnet BlueSweep while other Bluetooth devices are active in the surrounding area. Let the utility run for a few minutes to identify all of the nearby devices and the Bluetooth services they are providing. You may also be able to identify cellular phones, PDAs, and other devices that have Bluetooth capabilities, if any of these are available. Save the file and print a report listing the devices and services you were able to identify. This utility may prove useful in a field technical support situation. Consult the documentation, which is also available online from AirMagnet.

Write a one-page report outlining how you could use BlueSweep to assist you in the field in solving a connectivity or service availability problem for a customer.

NOTE   If you wish to uninstall the Microsoft drivers and reinstall the vendor software, check Microsoft tech support article no. 889814. Go to http://www.microsoft.com/technet and click Troubleshooting & Support on the left side of the page. Scroll down and select the Microsoft Knowledge Base and How-To link. Search the Support Knowledge Base (KB) box by typing the article number and clicking the right arrow to the right of the search box or pressing Enter. Follow the instructions in the article to remove the Microsoft drivers and rename the .inf files. Reboot the machine one more time and then reinstall the vendor software for the Bluetooth USB adapter.

HIGH RATE WIRELESS PERSONAL AREA NETWORKS

After reading this chapter and completing the exercises, you will be able to:

♦ Define a high rate wireless personal area network (HR WPAN)

♦ List the different HR WPAN standards and their applications

♦ Explain how WiMedia and UWB work

♦ Outline the issues facing WPAN technologies

♦ Describe the security features of each HR WPAN technology

In Chapter 5, you learned about two technologies for low rate personal area networks (WPANs), Bluetooth and ZigBee, which address the market need for devices that do not require fast communications. In this chapter, you will learn about standards and technologies—some of which are still under development—that will make it possible for businesses and home users to deploy entertainment systems delivering wireless video, voice, and music throughout an office or home. These networks will be capable of transferring data between computers and peripherals at speeds ranging from the current maximum of 55 Mbps to a future rate of up to 2 Gbps.

These technologies will offer stiff competition to Bluetooth, and may eventually displace other technologies that currently exist for wireless LANs. Consumer electronic equipment, such as digital and high-definition television, gaming, and similar types of entertainment systems, are likely to be the first applications of these HR networks. The first HR wireless devices will likely be available to consumers in 2008.

HIGH RATE WPAN STANDARDS

The Institute of Electrical and Electronics Engineers (IEEE) is currently working on two additional standards for WPANs. The IEEE 802.15.3 and 802.15.5 wireless standards will enable connectivity for devices and purposes different from those provided by IrDA, Bluetooth, and ZigBee, covered in Chapter 5.

NOTE The IEEE Project P802.15 covers all of the different Working Groups for Wireless Personal Area Networks (WPANs). The standards are listed as IEEE 802.x.x and the projects as IEEE P802.x.x. The last digit in the standard identifies specific working or task groups, such as ".1" for Bluetooth and ".3" for High Rate WPANs.

The IEEE 802.15.3 standard defines the specifications for HR WPANs supporting speeds of 11, 22, 33, and up to 55 Mbps in the 2.4 GHz ISM band. It enables multimedia connectivity between portable and fixed consumer devices within the home and can link more than 200 wireless devices using a low-cost and low-power radio module. Data rates vary with connection distance; 802.15.3 provides for up to 55 Mbps at up to 164 feet (50 meters) for multimedia and large file transfers, while audio can be transferred at up to 22 Mbps at distances of up to 330 feet (100 meters).

802.15.3 HIGH RATE WPANs

You have already learned about infrared, Bluetooth, and ZigBee WPANs. Why is there yet another WPAN technology? The answer is simple. Although technologies such as 802.11 and Bluetooth include MAC and PHY layer optimizations for transmitting multimedia signals, no previous wireless standard has been developed *exclusively* for this market.

Since the IEEE standard only defines the MAC and PHY layers, the **WiMedia Alliance** was formed to support the development of any necessary higher-layer protocols and software specifications for 802.15.3 and to perform various other administrative functions.

Radio frequency spectrum licensing organizations around the world have relaxed the rules for low-power transmissions in several frequency bands. Consequently, potential HR WPAN applications include:

- Connecting digital cameras to printers and kiosks
- Connecting laptop computers to multimedia projectors and sound systems
- Connecting camera-equipped cellular phones and PDAs to laptops and printers
- Connecting speakers in a surround sound system to sound amplifiers and FM receivers
- Distributing video signals from a cable or satellite receiver to televisions in rooms throughout the house

- Sending high-quality music to headphones or speakers from a CD or MP3 player
- Photographing yourself with remote viewfinders for video or digital still cameras

These applications, whether for consumer electronics or for professional use, all share a set of common characteristics:

- They require high throughput, typically over 20 Mbps, to support video and multi-channel, high-quality audio.
- The transceiver should be low-power so that it can be used in handheld, portable, battery-powered devices.
- The cost should be low to allow manufacturers to implement wireless communications features without a significant increase in the end-user price of the devices.
- They require **quality-of-service (QOS)** capabilities, which allow devices to request more channel access time in order to prioritize high-volume, time-sensitive traffic, such as voice stream.
- Connections should be simple and automatic to make, eliminating the need for a technically sophisticated user.
- Devices should be able to connect to multiple other devices without the need for complex installation or configuration; in other words, the devices should be able to inform other devices about their capabilities and performance.
- Security features should be included.

WiMedia Protocol Stack

The WiMedia group defined two different architectures, called application profiles, for the upper layers of the protocol stack. One is used for multimedia audio/visual applications and the other for data transfer applications. Depending on the device or the specific application being used on the device, either version or both will be implemented on the specific device. For example, a cordless phone with limited or no data capabilities only needs to implement the audio/visual version, whereas a PDA with the ability to store and transfer data as well as play video or MP3 files would implement both versions of the protocol stack. Figure 6-1 shows both versions of the protocol stack.

NOTE

You can find out more about WiMedia by visiting the organization's Web site at www.wimedia.org.

The lower two layers of the stack (MAC and PHY), defined by the 802.15.3 standard, are implemented in hardware. Whenever possible, the upper layers may also be implemented in hardware with minimal processing power and memory to keep the cost and complexity low and to minimize the size.

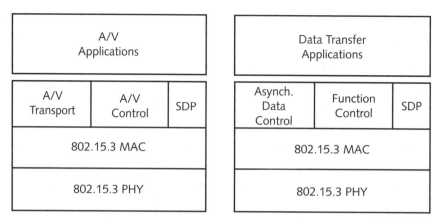

Figure 6-1   WiMedia protocol stack

802.15.3 PHY Layer

As you know, the PHY layer is responsible for converting data bits into a modulated RF signal that can be transmitted over electromagnetic waves. The current 802.15.3 standard uses the ISM 2.4 GHz band and supports two different channel plans:

1. A coexistence channel plan — Three non-overlapping channels to enable better coexistence with 802.11b WLANs in homes and businesses

2. A high-density channel plan — Four non-overlapping channels to support higher-density applications such as hotels and conference centers in which a larger number of WiMedia devices may be installed and no 802.11b networks are within range

In either case, the channels are limited to 15 MHz bandwidth, which accommodates more channels in the 2.4 to 2.4835 GHz band than 802.11 (four usable channels in 802.15.3 instead of only three in 802.11b). Table 6-1 summarizes the frequencies and how the channels are distributed in both the high-density and the coexistence channel plans.

Table 6-1   802.15.3 Channel plan

Channel ID	Center Frequency	High-Density	802.11b Coexistence
1	2.412 GHz	X	X
2	2.428 GHz	X	
3	2.437 GHz		X
4	2.445 GHz	X	
5	2.462 GHz	X	X

The current IEEE 802.15.3 standard specifies five data rates: 11 Mbps, 22 Mbps, 33 Mbps, 44 Mbps, and 55 Mbps. The 22 Mbps rate is considered the base rate. All transmissions are initiated at this rate until synchronization with the network is achieved. The 11, 33, 44, and 55 Mbps data rates use **trellis code modulation (TCM)**, which encodes the digital signal in such a way that single bit errors can be detected and corrected. This is also referred to as forward error correction (FEC), which you learned about in Chapter 5. Multiple bit errors can be detected but only single bit errors can be corrected. The technique saves time because it avoids retransmission of the data when a single bit error occurs.

NOTE   Trellis code modulation was introduced in modems faster than 14.4 Kbps; it was the only way that these early modems could transmit reliably using the existing copper-wire telephone network.

6

Modulation

The RF modulation techniques used for each data rate are listed in Table 6-2. Recall that you learned about the different modulation techniques in Chapter 2. The 22 Mbps data rate is not coded with TCM; this allows all devices in the WPAN to detect traffic without having to spend time decoding the trellis code first.

Table 6-2   802.15.3 modulation

Data Rate	Modulation
11 Mbps	QPSK
22 Mbps	DQPSK
33 Mbps	16-QAM
44 Mbps	32-QAM
55 Mbps	64-QAM

Because 802.15.3 operates in the same 2.4 GHz unlicensed band as other standards, to prevent interference, the PHY layer includes a number of enhancements:

- Passive scanning — Each device scans the channels to detect an existing piconet before joining or starting a new one. The first device to be turned on in an area scans the frequencies to find a channel that is not being used.

- Dynamic channel selection — Once the device locates a channel that is not being used, it selects the channel to be used in the area.

- Ability to request channel quality information — 802.15.3 devices can request channel quality information from other devices. If remote devices cannot use the current channel because of interference, the controlling device can initiate a channel change.

- Link quality and received signal strength indication — An 802.15.3 device can request link quality information between itself and other devices. It also monitors the strength of the received signal from other devices, which is important for power management.

- Transmit power control — Upon receiving information about the channel quality and link quality, devices may be able to decrease or increase the transmit power to improve the quality of the link and the received signal.

- An 802.11 coexistence channel plan — This minimizes channel overlap by providing a 25 MHz passband between channels.

- Lower transmit power — Sharing of the 2.4 GHz unlicensed band is enhanced by the lower transmit power of 802.15.3 radios.

- Neighbor piconet capability — 802.15.3 allows the formation of dependent piconets in the same area; these piconets rely on the device that controls the original piconet to allocate channel time for communications. This feature permits multiple piconets to exist in the same area.

802.15.3 Network Topology

The first device in an area assumes the role of **piconet coordinator (PNC)**, which is the device that provides all of the basic communications timing in a piconet. To do this, the PNC sends a beacon. Recall that a beacon is a frame containing information about the piconet, such as the piconet's unique identification. The beacon also indicates when devices are allowed to transmit and for how long. The piconet is peer-to-peer and devices can transmit data directly to each other, but they can only do so based on the timing instructions sent in the beacon by the PNC.

NOTE Only some 802.15.3 devices must be capable of being a PNC. Devices such as audio speakers do not need the capability of being a PNC. Portable devices that are battery powered and need to be switched off periodically should not usually assume the role of PNC.

The PNC is also responsible for managing QoS. QoS is necessary for voice and sound transmissions because, for example, breaks or interruptions in a continuous voice conversation are unacceptable to users. A small number of breaks can usually be tolerated in video transmissions (a few dropped frames per second). Figure 6-2 illustrates an 802.15.3 piconet and the communication between devices. Since the PNC may be turned off or leave the area at any time, the standard provides for the PNC to hand over control of the piconet to another device, which will become the new PNC.

As indicated above, other devices can form a dependent piconet. There are two kinds of dependent piconets:

- **Child piconets** are separate piconets, with their own unique ID, in which the child PNC is a member of the original or parent piconet. The child piconet's PNC can exchange data with any member of the parent or child piconet.

- **Neighbor piconets** are separate piconets that have their own PNC but that depend on the original piconet's PNC to allocate a private block of time when their devices are allowed to transmit. This is done in order to share the frequency spectrum between one or more piconets when there are no other available channels for communication.

6

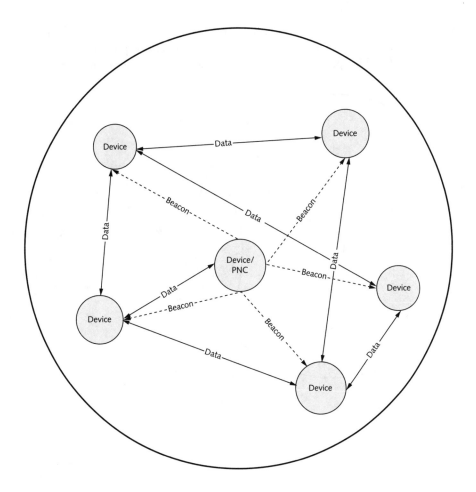

Figure 6-2   An 802.15.3 piconet

Child piconets are useful for extending the coverage of a piconet or for shifting some processing or storage requirements to another device. A piconet can have one or more child piconets. A device in the parent piconet can reach a device in the child piconet by using the child PNC to retransmit the frames directed at the device in the child piconet. A child piconet can also share the same frequency channel as the parent PNC but use a different security key. This situation may happen when a friend comes to visit you and brings along a number of gaming or music devices that both of you want to use, but you want to keep secret your private security key. Alternatively, this may also happen when you purchase and install a new music system that comes preconfigured as a network consisting of the speakers and the player; this network would have its own preconfigured security key.

Neighbor piconets exist mainly to allow coexistence with other piconets in the same area. The parent piconet will only allow the formation of a neighbor piconet if there is sufficient free channel time available. If a set of devices cannot use the same security features of the parent piconet, these devices can still function in the same area, and share the same frequency channel without causing collisions, by becoming a neighbor piconet. Figure 6-3 illustrates the concept of a child piconet, and Figure 6-4 shows a neighbor piconet.

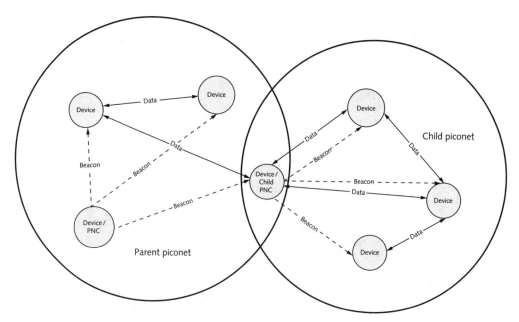

Figure 6-3 Child piconet

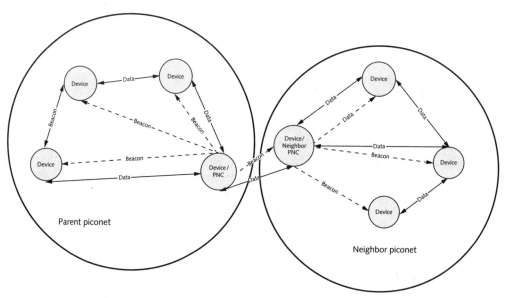

Figure 6-4 Neighbor piconet

Additional MAC Layer Functionality

The IEEE 802.15.3 MAC layer is designed to support the following functionality:

- Connection time (association) is fast, with no complicated setup.

- Devices associated with the piconet can use a short, one-octet device ID to ensure fast connection and access times.

- Devices can obtain information about the capabilities of other devices either during the association process through broadcasts made by the PNC or by querying the PNC about another device. Devices can also advertise their own capabilities to the PNC. The simplicity of this process is what guarantees fast connection times.

- Peer-to-peer (ad hoc) networking allows all devices to communicate directly with each other.

- Data transport with QoS enables the implementation of voice, music, and video.

- Security (covered in the last section of this chapter) is included to ensure privacy.

- Efficient data transfer allows multiple devices to communicate on the same network.

Efficient data transfer in 802.15.3 networks is accomplished using **superframes**. Superframes in 802.15.3 networks function differently from those used in ZigBee networks, as illustrated in Figure 6-5.

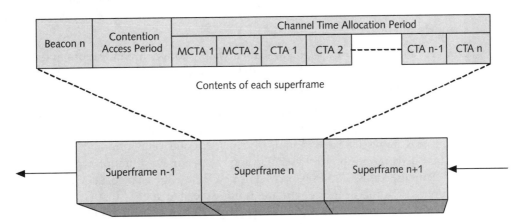

Figure 6-5 The superframe

Each 802.15.3 superframe is composed of three parts:

- A beacon, which is used to set time allocations for the devices in the piconet and to communicate management information for the piconet

- An optional **contention access period (CAP)**, which is used for association, to communicate commands, or for any asynchronous data that may be present in the superframe

- The **channel time allocation period (CTAP)**, which includes **channel time allocations (CTAs)**, the time slots that the PNC allocates to individual devices and that can be used to send commands or data; the CTAP also includes **management channel time allocation (MCTA)** periods, used for communications between the PNC and other devices (devices that don't have CTAs allocated in the current superframe)

Communication in an 802.15.3 piconet is generally accomplished as follows: The beacon frame sent by the PNC includes a variable indicating the end of the CAP. No device—not even the PNC—is allowed to transmit data that can extend past the end of the CAP, into the CTAP. This procedure ensures that all devices have an opportunity to communicate and prevents collisions.

Devices can send asynchronous data in the CAP, if it exists in the current superframe. The CAP is not allocated, so devices will contend for the time using CSMA/CA (refer to Chapter 5). In addition, during the CAP, each device is only allowed to transmit one frame.

Devices can request channel time on a regular basis, such as every superframe or every two or four superframes, in the CTAP from the PNC. The amount of channel time a device will request depends on the type of data the device wants to transmit. The requested channel time is called **isochronous** time, which means a time-dependent or synchronous transmission that must be made every frame or every so many frames to maintain the quality of the connection. Voice or music demand more channel time than video. Video demands more channel time than data files.

Devices can also request channel time for asynchronous communications in the CTAP from the PNC. This can be used to send large data files. Unlike voice streams, delays or interruptions do not affect the quality of data file transmissions.

During the CTAP, communications use a time division multiple access (TDMA) scheme, in which each device gets a *window* of time in which to transmit data or commands. Time in a piconet is always allocated in units of 1 microsecond. The minimum superframe duration is 1000 microseconds or 1 millisecond, and the maximum duration is 65,535 microseconds or 65.5 milliseconds. The PNC may allocate CTAs of any size to a device, provided that the maximum duration of the superframe is not exceeded. Recall that CAPs are optional, so a device may get an allocation that is very large, allowing for the transmission of large blocks of information. In addition, a device may request a change in time allocation from the PNC at any time.

Power Management

One of the best methods to enable 802.15.3 devices to user power efficiently is to allow the devices to turn off completely or at least to reduce power consumption for long periods of time, without losing their association with the piconet. Doing so for a period equal to the duration of one or more superframes results in a significant power-saving opportunity for WPAN devices. The 802.15.3 standard provides for three different power-saving methods:

- Device synchronized power save (DSPS) mode allows devices to sleep for the duration of several superframes but allows them to wake up in the middle of a superframe to transmit or receive data. Other devices in the piconet are informed about which devices in a group (called a DSPS set) are in this mode and when they will awake and be able to receive or transmit data.

- Piconet synchronized power save (PSPS) mode allows devices to sleep during intervals defined by the PNC. The PNC selects beacons to serve as system-wide wake beacons, and indicates the next one to occur in the beacon fields. All devices in PSPS mode are required to wake up and listen to the wake beacons.

- Asynchronous power save (APS) mode allows the devices to sleep for long periods of time until they choose to wake up and listen to a beacon. A device in APS mode must communicate with the PNC before the end of its association time-out period (ATP) in order to maintain its membership in the piconet.

The PNC will always allocate asynchronous CTAs to destination devices that will be in DSPS or PSPS mode in the **wake superframe**. The wake superframe is the superframe designated by the PNC in which devices that are in power save mode wake up and listen for frames addressed to them. Of course, a device that does not rely on battery power, such as a DVD player or sound amplifier, can remain in active mode all the time. Regardless of which power-saving mode a device is in, all devices are allowed to power down during the parts of the superframe when they are not scheduled to transmit or receive. Figure 6-6 illustrates the wake beacons.

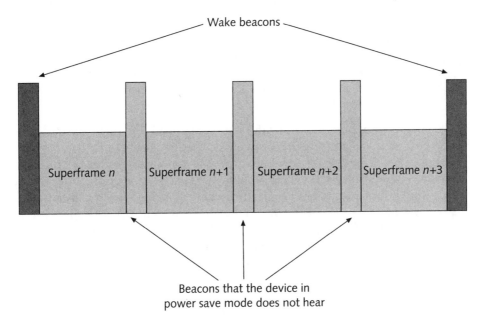

Figure 6-6 Wake beacons

Two additional methods can help devices save power and minimize interference with other wireless networks that share the same frequency channel. In the first method, the PNC can set a maximum transmit power level for associated devices (this feature is not mandatory in the standard, so not all devices may implement it). This method also allows the PNC to save power since the quality of the link between the PNC and other devices defines the coverage area of the piconet. The second method allows devices to request a reduction or an increase in their own transmit power, as long as the device knows that it can maintain a good link with another device.

General MAC Frame Format

This section presents an overview of the general MAC frame format. All MAC frames include a set of fields that are present in the same order in every frame. These are shown in Figure 6-7.

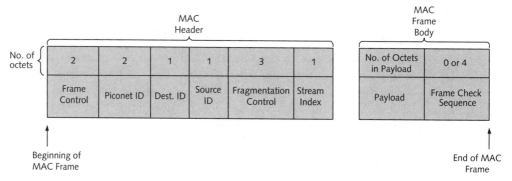

Figure 6-7   General MAC frame format

NOTE   The MAC layer in every device must be able to verify that the data was received without error. The frame check sequence (FCS) field that is present in every MAC frame is responsible for this validation. However, before the PHY passes the frame to the MAC layer, it first checks to make sure that the MAC header was received without errors using the header check sequence (HCS) field.

The frame control field contains information about the protocol version, type of frame, whether it is encrypted, how the receiving device should acknowledge it, whether this is a retransmission of a previously sent frame, and whether the data ends with this frame or more data is to follow. The piconet ID (PNID) field contains a unique identifier for each piconet and confirms that the frames were sent by devices belonging to a specific piconet. The destination and source ID fields contain the unique piconet device identifiers for the sender and receiver. The fragmentation control field is used to assist in the fragmentation and reassembly, in the correct sequence, of parts of a large block of data, such as an MP3 file. It contains the number of the current fragment, the number of the last fragment for this data stream, and a frame number. If a frame is lost, the receiving device can request that the transmitting device resend the fragment so that it will be able to reassemble the complete file. The stream index field is used for managing and uniquely identifying different asynchronous and isochronous streams.

The MAC frame payload is a variable length field that carries the actual information to be transferred between two devices or between one device and a group of devices (multicast or broadcast). The frame check sequence (FCS) is a 32-bit **cyclic redundancy check (CRC)** field, a common technique for detecting data transmission errors.

The general MAC frame format can vary, but the MAC header is standard for all transmissions. The frame body changes to accommodate the different types of payload and the information required in each one. Unlike Bluetooth and 802.11 WLANs, the MAC is implemented in the hardware of the radio module. This minimizes or eliminates most aspects of configuration of the equipment by consumers.

6

Mesh Networking (802.15.5)

IEEE 802.15.5 is a proposed standard for **mesh networking**, in which each device connects to all other devices within range, effectively creating multiple paths for transmission. Recall that the concept of mesh networking is integrated into the 802.15.4 (ZigBee) standard. However, 802.15.5 is a separate standard that applies to 802.15.3, although the idea is basically the same.

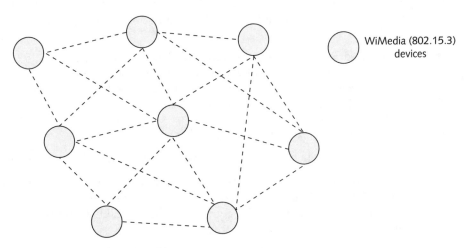

Figure 6-8 Mesh networking

Mesh networking will enable WiMedia networks to span an entire building. The power of 802.15.3 will probably not be fully realized until the 802.15.5 mesh networking standard is published.

It is unlikely that manufacturers will commit a large amount of resources to WiMedia until 802.15.5 is ratified. In addition, as you will discover in the next section, one of the reasons that WiMedia-enabled products are not yet available is that manufacturers are anxiously awaiting the ratification of UWB standards.

Ultra Wide Band (UWB)

Ultra Wide Band (UWB) offers a promising solution to the shortage of frequencies available in the RF spectrum by allowing new transmission techniques based on UWB to coexist with other RF systems, with minimal or no interference. UWB is not really a new technology. It has been used in radar since the 1960s and is a very established technology for ground penetrating radar (see the following Note).

NOTE   Ground-penetrating radar is used to locate pipes, wires, and buried objects under roads and fields, among other applications.

What is new in UWB is the application of this technique to wireless data transmission. Because of the potential to achieve very high data rates, as you will learn in this section, UWB is the only technology capable of handling multiple video streams, including high-definition television with a quality level equivalent to that of a wired system, albeit at short ranges. It may start out as a wireless PAN solution, but industry experts and analysts predict that UWB will expand to full home and business networking as well.

NOTE   In the United States, the FCC has currently allowed UWB transmitters to operate in the 3.1 GHz to 10.6 GHz range at limited power levels of -41 dBm/ MHz (approximately 75 nanowatts of power or 0.000000075 watts for each MHz of bandwidth), which minimizes interference.

UWB for data applications has the following characteristics:

- Unlike ground-penetrating radar, it transmits low-power, short-range signals.

- It transmits using extremely short low-power pulses lasting only about 1 nanosecond (1×10^{-9}, or 1 billionth of a second) or even shorter. These pulses cannot easily be detected by other analog RF equipment; therefore, UWB transmissions do not cause significant interference to other signals.

- UWB transmits over a band that is at least 500 MHz wide, as required by the FCC; such a band is wider than that of any other RF transmission technology in current use, which also helps prevent interference.

- Depending on the frequency band used, if and when approved by the FCC and other countries' regulating authorities, UWB can potentially send data at speeds of up to 2 Gbps. The IEEE is currently exploring the 60 GHz frequency band for this purpose.

How UWB Works

In the next few paragraphs, you will read about the core UWB RF transmission technology. You will not, however, find a section on the MAC layer. This is because, as you may recall, changing the RF layer does not mean that any other changes are required, so the MAC layer and all other higher-layer protocols remain the same.

UWB PHY

In Chapter 2, you learned that in traditional RF data transmission technology a digital signal is modulated over an analog signal using amplitude, frequency, phase, or a combination of amplitude and phase (for example, 64-QAM). In addition, recall that in order to spread the signal over a wide band and to allow for better error detection and correction, digital signals are transmitted using a technique such as frequency hopping spread signal (FHSS) or direct sequence spread spectrum (DSSS). The result of both techniques is to spread the signal over a wide band. In FHSS, signals are transmitted in each of several frequencies for very short periods of time (625 microseconds for Bluetooth). In DSSS, the spreading also has the effect of dividing the signal amplitude across the frequency band, which helps reduce interference.

UWB, on the other hand, is a digital transmission technology. It uses short analog pulses for signaling and does not rely on traditional modulation methods. In UWB, this technique is called **impulse modulation**, meaning that the amplitude, the polarity, or the position of an analog pulse represents either a 1 or a 0. Figure 6-9 illustrates the concept of impulse modulation and compares it with frequency shift keying (FSK) modulation.

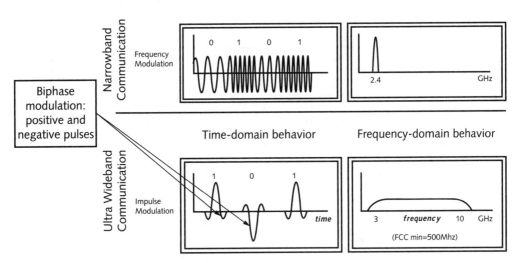

Figure 6-9   UWB impulse modulation

UWB signals can be transmitted using fairly simple techniques by very simple transmitter circuits. Several different types of modulation can be used in UWB, but the most common is **biphase modulation**, which uses a half-cycle positive analog pulse to represent a 1 and a half-cycle negative analog pulse to represent a 0. This kind of modulation is virtually immune to background RF noise and does not cause interference. Biphase modulation requires circuits with two transmitters (one to generate positive pulses and another for negative pulses), which makes it more expensive. The concept of biphase modulation is also shown in the lower-left part of Figure 6-9.

In addition to the modulation schemes mentioned earlier, several different UWB transmission systems were proposed to the IEEE originally. The choices have now been narrowed down to two systems: direct sequence and multiband orthogonal frequency divisional multiplexing.

NOTE   The two UWB RF layer proposals are in technical competition with one another. However, proposals submitted in 2005 to the IEEE for merging the different UWB physical layer techniques should ultimately enable some or all UWB devices to interoperate.

Direct-sequence UWB (DS-UWB) takes advantage of the fact that one of the effects of transmitting pulses that are a nanosecond long—or even shorter—is that the signal naturally spreads over a very wide frequency band, without using any spreading codes. In the UWB case, the signal spreads over a band that is at least 500 MHz wide in the high frequency bands used for this technology. This also spreads the amplitude of the signal across the entire band; as a result, the entire pulse falls below the level of the background noise. Figure 6-10 shows an example of what happens in the frequency domain when a 1-nanosecond pulse is transmitted.

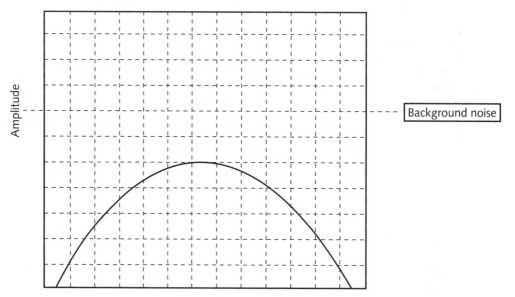

Figure 6-10   A direct-sequence 1-nanosecond UWB pulse

The other method proposed to the IEEE, multiband **orthogonal frequency division multiplexing (OFDM)**, commonly referred to as MB-OFDM, is based on the technique used for 802.11g and 802.11a WLAN transmissions (you will learn more about these in Chapter 8). In MB-OFDM, a frequency band is divided into five groups containing a total of 14 frequency bands, as shown in Table 6-3.

Table 6-3   MB-OFDM frequency band allocation

Band Group	Band ID	Center Frequency (MHz)
1	1	3,432
	2	3,960
	3	4,488
2	4	5,016
	5	5,544
	6	6,072
3	7	6,600
	8	7,128
	9	7,656
4	10	8,184
	11	8,712
	12	9,240
5	13	9,768
	14	10,296

NOTE   The Multiband OFDM Alliance merged with WiMedia. For additional information on MB-OFDM, you can visit the WiMedia Web site at www.wimedia.org.

Each frequency band is 528 MHz wide, which meets FCC requirements, and is further divided into 128 frequency channels. These channels are orthogonal, meaning that they do not interfere with each another. Several data bits are then sent simultaneously (in parallel), one bit over each of these sub-channels, at a low bit rate per channel. Only 122 out of the 128 channels are used for MB-OFDM transmission. Because several data bits are being sent at the same time, each on a different frequency, OFDM can still achieve high data rates by sending the data bits at a slower rate. This technique is comparable to a parallel printer cable that uses one wire for each bit sent to the printer and therefore transfers one byte at a time. MB-OFDM transmits using pulses that are slightly longer than DS-UWB, at 312 nanoseconds long. While these longer pulses are easier to generate with electronic circuits, critics claim that MB-OFDM makes the transmitters very complex.

NOTE   Currently, the MB-OFDM proposal only uses one of the five groups of frequency bands, with frequencies between 3,168 MHz and 4,752 MHz, out of the 3.1 to 10.6 GHz allowed by the FCC. The remaining frequencies are reserved for future expansion.

You can check on the progress of UWB standards and other standards and technologies under development by visiting one of the following Web sites: www.ultrawidebandplanet.com,   www.intel.com/technology/comms/uwb/, www.palowireless.com/uwb, or www.ieee.org.

TIP

IEEE 802.15.3a

The IEEE P802.15.3a project is a proposed enhancement to 802.15.3 that uses UWB technology to support even higher data rates for multimedia and imaging applications. This proposed standard provides excellent channel capacity at short range and will allow data rates greater than 100 Mbps.

In May 2004, the 1394 Trade Association announced the release of a new **Protocol Adaptation Layer (PAL)**, an set of protocol implementation rules that will enable wireless FireWire at 400 Mbps based on an 802.15.3a/WiMedia platform. The USB Forum has also released specifications for wireless USB (WUSB) version 2, based on the WiMedia specifications and transmitting at 480 Mbps at a distance of up to 6 feet (2 meters).

FireWire is a trademark of Apple Computer. This group of standards is designated as IEEE 1394 and is supported by the 1394 Trade Association. Find out more about WUSB and wireless FireWire by visiting the USB Forum at www. usb.org and the 1394 Trade Association at www.1394ta.org.

NOTE

Since USB and FireWire are already familiar to most computer users, this wireless technology should be immediately recognizable in the computer market.

There are approximately 1.5 billion USB ports and 50 million FireWire ports in use worldwide.

NOTE

WPAN CHALLENGES

Now that you have explored WiMedia and UWB WPAN technologies, you will learn about some of the challenges faced by each of these technologies. Along with the topics in this chapter, the next section also discusses technologies, such as Bluetooth and infrared, that were covered in Chapter 5.

Competition Among WPAN Standards

For computer-to-computer and computer-to-handheld devices, you have learned about 802.15.1 Bluetooth and 802.15.3 standards and also how UWB may impact these technologies. Now that Bluetooth products are finally beginning to ship in volume and the technology is being used in some real-world solutions, it is facing some serious threats.

IEEE 802.15.3 and .3a are positioned to compete with Bluetooth for market share because these standards are capable of much higher data rates, something that is always popular with users. While it will take a few years before 802.15.3 products begin to appear on the market, wireless USB and wireless 1394 (FireWire) have the potential to quickly outpace Bluetooth as a cable replacement technology, relegating it to be used primarily for connecting cellular phone headsets. Recall that the Bluetooth SIG has released version 1.2 and version 2.0 of their specifications, which can achieve speeds of up to 3 Mbps and improved audio connections.

HR WPAN Security

Although security should be less of an issue with WPANs than with traditional wired networks, since most of the transmissions are restricted to a short range, as you read in Chapter 5 with Bluetooth, hackers will go to almost any length to break into devices and networks. In this section, we will identify the different security models for each of the WPAN technologies discussed in this chapter.

Bluetooth Security

Hackers are already using Bluetooth to attack mobile devices, and Bluetooth security is becoming an issue. In *Bluejacking*, hackers exploit a Bluetooth device's ability to discover nearby devices and send unsolicited messages. Another type of attack is *Bluesnarfing*, which uses the same discovery ability to access contact lists and other information without the user's knowledge, provided that the user has enabled the server functions on their device. Hackers can also eavesdrop on telephone conversations and use the victim's phone to send data or make calls. **Denial-of-service (DoS)** attacks that flood a Bluetooth device with so many frames that it is unable to communicate are another problem. Bluetooth is also vulnerable to attacks in the form of Trojans, viruses, and worms.

These security risks extend well past PDAs and Smartphones. Some laptops are shipped with Bluetooth technology, potentially creating a back door into a company's network when the computer is connected to the LAN using Ethernet or an 802.11 WLAN. It is both easy and inexpensive for a hacker to surreptitiously add a Bluetooth device to a network. Because of their short-range, low-power signal, devices can remain undetectable for a long period of time, especially when hidden behind a desktop computer case.

Considering these problems, users may prefer the compromise of infrared, which requires line-of-sight communications but can exchange data between laptops or between laptops and printers much faster than using Bluetooth.

Security for IEEE 802.15.3 HR WPANs

Security for this standard is based on the **Advanced Encryption Standard (AES)**, a symmetric key encryption mechanism introduced by the National Institute of Standards and

Technology (NIST) in the United States. In 802.15.3 AES uses a 128-bit key. Its two security modes are:

- Mode 0 — Does not encrypt or protect the data in any way
- Mode 1 — Employs strong cryptography based on AES and supports the protection of commands, beacons, and data frames, as well as secure key distribution for command and data frame protection

The standard defines how any two devices can establish a secure communications session to protect both the information as well as the integrity of communications at the MAC and PHY layers. The security key can be shared by all of the devices in a piconet or by any two devices. In 802.15.3, the key is 13 octets long and is based on a number of parameters such as the source and destination address, the current time token on the network, the frame counter, and the value of the fragmentation control field. This ensures that the key will be unique for each transaction, which makes it almost infinitely harder, if not completely impossible, for a hacker to break. In addition, this standard provides a mechanism for changing or rotating the symmetric key on a periodic basis. The new key is based on the one that was initially entered by the user. Changing keys periodically makes it far more difficult for a hacker to break the key and be able to decode the data.

The authentication key for the piconet is also changed periodically, or every time a device leaves the piconet or stops responding to beacon frames. This new security implementation is far superior to any of the previous methods employed by Bluetooth and 802.11 WLANs.

802.15.3 also supports **message integrity** verification at the MAC layer. Message integrity adds certain encrypted random data to each communications session so that the receiver can verify that the message has not been tampered with during transit. Without message integrity, a would-be hacker could launch a **man-in-the-middle attack** against the piconet by capturing frames, altering them, and retransmitting them to the intended receiver.

Cost of WPAN Components

Because Bluetooth currently supports more devices than other WPAN technologies do, it suffers more from the problem of component cost. Bluetooth radio modules originally cost in excess of $75. However, the cost has decreased to around $15. Yet many industry experts believe that the price must be reduced further—to around $5 per module—for Bluetooth to reach competitive advantage. There are two reasons for this way of thinking. First, adding a $15 chip to a $2,500 notebook computer is irrelevant because the price can easily be absorbed in the total cost. However, adding a $15 chip to a PDA that costs $150 will certainly mean that the price of the PDA would have increase by at least 10% to cover the cost of the Bluetooth chip. Until its price is reduced to the point where it does not have a significant impact on the total cost of the device, Bluetooth's market penetration will be limited.

Also consider the relative cost of the technology Bluetooth replaces. It does not make much economic sense to use a chip that costs $15 to replace a cable that costs $7. Unless the Bluetooth chip cost is equal to or less than connection cables, it will be difficult to justify the expense, and, even then, the lower speed of Bluetooth interfaces may be a compromise that some users are not willing to make. The principal challenge facing 802.15.3 manufacturers then, will be to ensure that the technology is incorporated into their products without significantly increasing the cost for consumers and businesses.

Industry Support for WPAN Technologies

Despite its limitations, IrDA has enjoyed strong industry support for many years. Bluetooth's support in the networking industry, on the other hand, has been, at best, spotty. Many industry experts see Bluetooth as being caught in a Catch-22. Bluetooth is not fully supported by computer hardware and software vendors because of its low market penetration. These vendors do not want to spend the time and money to produce Bluetooth products or provide full technical support for the technology while there are a limited number of Bluetooth users. However, as long as vendors do not support Bluetooth, users will be reluctant to purchase this technology.

Several vendors are attempting to straddle the fence with Bluetooth support, but they only end up confusing users. For example, Microsoft provides Bluetooth support in its version of Pocket PC 2002, which runs on handheld devices. Microsoft also supports Bluetooth in Windows XP Service Pack 2, but only in a very limited way. Until a much larger segment of the industry embraces Bluetooth and provides sufficient support, many experts are unsure how deeply Bluetooth will penetrate the market.

Industry experts predict that new technologies such as 802.15.3 and ZigBee will be more quickly embraced by manufacturers. ZigBee support is likely to come initially from qualified installation technicians, which means that these devices will not likely suffer from the problems that affected Bluetooth from its early days.

Protocol Functionality Limitations

One of the major limitations of the Bluetooth protocol is its lack of hand-off capability between piconets. **Hand-off** is the ability of a device to move from one master or PNC to another without getting disconnected from the network in a network that extends beyond the communications range of each device that controls the communications. Unlike a cell phone that easily switches from one cell to the next as the user drives down the road, when a Bluetooth device moves from one piconet area to the next, the connection is broken and must be restored with a new master. This limitation may be due to consumers expecting something that Bluetooth technology was not originally intended to do, but it may prevent Bluetooth from being adopted as a technology for cordless phones that need to roam throughout the house, for example, which would benefit the market for WiMedia devices that already support communications with neighbor and child piconets. This capability will also be greatly enhanced as soon as the 802.15.5 mesh networking standard is ratified.

Although Bluetooth devices can discover other Bluetooth devices in the area, at present, they cannot automatically determine how the functions of other devices can be used in a cooperative setting; this must be preconfigured by the users. These are concerns that Bluetooth needs to address. Here again, WiMedia devices have a built-in advantage because they can automatically identify the services and capabilities offered by other devices.

In infrared, roaming is a limitation but not a concern, since this technology is designed for peer-to-peer, one-to-one communications anyway. When 802.15.3 networks are combined with 802.15.5 mesh networking, users should be able to roam throughout a building, wherever there are devices installed, without losing the connection to the network.

Although there is no other major protocol limitation with any of the technologies outlined in this chapter, it is important to realize that the drive in the industry is to standardize the protocols as much as possible. In most cases, at higher protocol layers, this means using TCP/IP, and in lower layers it will likely mean using one of the MAC and PHY protocols discussed previously.

Spectrum Conflict

Of all of the issues with WPANs, spectrum conflict is potentially the most damaging. **Spectrum conflict** is the potential for technologies using the same frequency bands to interfere with each other to the extent that they sometimes perform poorly when used within close range of each other. Applying UWB technology to all of the WPAN technologies discussed in this book may significantly reduce or eliminate this issue, but, until then, interference will always be a concern.

For example, today 802.11b/g WLANs perform poorly in environments where a 2.4 GHz cordless phone is also in use. This issue affects all of the technologies that use FHSS and DSSS in the same frequency band. To make their products more attractive and to avoid the technical support issues related to spectrum conflict, manufacturers of cordless phones have been introducing models that transmit at 5.8 GHz instead. This frequency is part of the unlicensed ISM band.

As noted previously, because Bluetooth uses the ISM 2.4 GHz band for its transmissions, it can conflict with other technologies that use the same frequency band. One of the major conflicts comes with IEEE 802.11b and 802.11g WLANs. Using Bluetooth and 802.11b/g devices in close proximity to each other may cause the WLAN to drop the connection if it detects that another device is sharing its frequency. One of the solutions to this problem is to move the Bluetooth device away from the 802.11b/g device. Several vendors have already implemented the recommendations of the IEEE 802.15.1 standard, which lets Bluetooth and 802.11b/g WLANs share the spectrum by first checking to see if the airwaves are clear for transmission. In addition, because the 802.11a WLAN standard uses a different frequency, moving to that standard eliminates the conflict altogether.

UWB can interfere with 802.11a networks. If DS-UWB is selected as the winning proposal to the IEEE, the resulting products will likely still cause interference problems. MB-OFDM-based products, on the other hand, can easily avoid using the 5 MHz band that conflicts with 802.11a.

Extensive tests run by the IEEE indicate that both ZigBee and WiMedia products should be able to coexist with 802.11b/g without any serious problems. However, experience with RF waves suggests that we will not know how well they actually perform until these products have been deployed in large volume and in many different environments.

CHAPTER SUMMARY

□ IEEE 802.15.3-2003 is a WPAN technology optimized for the transmission of multi-media voice and video signals. The promotion of this technology is supported by the WiMedia Alliance, the USB Forum, and the 1394 Trade Alliance (FireWire).

□ The WiMedia protocol stack has two upper layers called application profiles, one for audio/video and one for data transfer applications. Each one is implemented depending on the capabilities of the device. The lower layers of the protocol stack are implemented in hardware with minimal processing power to keep the cost and the complexity low, as well as to keep the size as small as possible.

□ The PHY layer supports two different channel plans, one with three channels to enable better coexistence with 802.11b WLANs and another with four channels for high-density applications. Channels have 15 MHz of bandwidth. Transmission rates are 11, 22, 33, 44, and 55 Mbps. All rates except the 22 Mbps use trellis code modulation, a forward error correction technique that helps make data transmissions more reliable. Data transmitted at 22 Mbps is not coded with TCM to allow devices wishing to join the piconet to detect traffic without having to decode the transmission first.

□ Because the 802.15.3 PHY layer works in the same ISM band as 802.11b WLANs, it includes several methods to prevent interference: passive scanning, dynamic channel selection, the ability to request channel quality information locally as well as link quality and received signal strength from remote devices, a channel plan that minimizes overlap, and transmit power control.

□ For high rate WPANs, there are two new PHY proposals to change the RF technology to Ultra Wide Band. The IEEE 802.15.5 Mesh Networking standard proposal will allow WPANs to extend well past the usual 33 feet (10 meter) maximum distance limitation.

□ 802.15.3 supports peer-to-peer or ad hoc networks, but the timing of transmissions on the piconet is always controlled by the piconet coordinator (PNC). The PNC accomplishes this by sending a periodic beacon containing information about the piconet, such as its unique ID and the time when devices are allowed to transmit. Devices can communicate directly to other devices but can only transmit during the contention access period (CAP) or during the times that the PNC allocates for each device. The PNC is responsible for QoS. Devices can request additional channel time from the PNC. If the PNC leaves the piconet, it can hand over control to another device.

6

❑ 802.15.3 piconets support child and neighbor piconets. The PNC in child piconets is a member of the original piconet. The PNC in a neighbor piconet is not a member of the original piconet but depends on the original piconet's PNC to allocate a private block of time for all devices belonging to the neighbor piconet to transmit. This is done so that the two piconets can share the same frequency, when there are no other channels available. Child piconets are useful for extending the coverage of a piconet or for shifting processing or storage requirements to another device.

❑ Association and disassociation is implemented in hardware to simplify installation and maintenance. The PNC maintains a table of all devices in the piconet. It also broadcasts information about the piconet to all devices. It will only send information about the availability of services when requested by a device.

❑ Efficient data transmission is accomplished by use of the superframe concept, which is the mechanism the PNC uses to allocate CAP; CTAP, which includes MCTAs; and CTAs. For communications during the CAP, devices must use the CSMA/CA mechanism to avoid collisions. Devices listen to the medium for traffic. If the medium is busy, devices must wait before transmitting; this wait time is called a backoff period. The backoff period is never applied to the transmission of beacons. During the CTAP communications period, the piconet uses a TDMA scheme for transmission.

❑ Devices can send asynchronous data in the CAP or can request channel time for asynchronous communications during the CTAP. Normal communications during the CTAP are isochronous or synchronous communications.

❑ In 802.15.3, devices can be in one of several power-saving modes. DSPS allows devices to sleep for several superframes but wake up in the middle to transmit or send data. The PNC informs all devices which one will be the wake superframe for each device. In PSPS mode, devices can sleep during intervals defined by the PNC but all devices must wake up at the same time to listen to system-wide wake beacons. In asynchronous power save mode, devices can sleep for long periods of time and decide when to wake up and listen to a beacon. The PNC can also set a maximum transmit power level for capable devices during the CAP, beacon, and MCTA time periods. This method also allows the PNC to save power.

❑ When the 802.15.5 mesh networking standard is approved, it will extend the capabilities of 802.15.3 networks, enabling them to span a building as large as a conference center.

❑ Ultra Wide Band is a digital transmission technology that will soon support very high-speed transmissions at up to 100+ Mbps in the near term and eventually to 2 Gbps. IEEE 802.15.3a is a proposal for a UWB PHY for WiMedia. Only the PHY layer changes. The MAC layer remains the same. UWB versions of wireless USB and 1394 (FireWire) interfaces will soon be available. These wireless interfaces will transmit at 480 and 400 Mbps, respectively. The Bluetooth SIG has announced that a UWB version of its specification is in the works.

❑ UWB transmissions occupy a bandwidth of at least 500 MHz and transmit using very short pulses. The two proposals currently being evaluated by the IEEE are based on direct sequence and multiband OFDM.

◻ Challenges for WPANs include speed, security, cost, industry support, interference, and protocol limitations. Bluetooth suffers these limitations more than its competing standards do. 802.15.3 has a number of advantages over Bluetooth, including enhanced security and the ability to extend the network through communications with neighbor and child piconets.

◻ WPAN devices that are designed to be small and consume very little power have limited processing capabilities and storage. This makes it difficult to implement sophisticated security mechanisms, a source of concern with WPANs.

KEY TERMS

Advanced Encryption Standard (AES) — A symmetric key encryption mechanism introduced by the U.S. National Institute of Standards and Technology.

biphase modulation — Modulation that uses a half-cycle positive analog pulse to represent a 1 and a half-cycle negative analog pulse to represent a 0.

channel time allocation (CTA) — Periods of time allocated by the PNC to a specific device for prioritizing communications in a WPAN. *See also* management channel time allocation (MCTA).

channel time allocation period (CTAP) — The superframe component used for communications between the PNC and other devices.

child piconets — Separate piconets with their own ID; the child PNC is a member of the original or parent piconet.

contention access period (CAP) — A mechanism used to communicate commands or any asynchronous data that may be present in a superframe. The CAP is also used to allow devices that are not yet part of a piconet to send a request to the PNC to join the piconet.

cyclic redundancy check (CRC) — A common technique for detecting data transmission errors.

denial-of-service (DoS) — A type of security attack on a networked device in which the attacker sends so many frames to a single device that the device is unable to communicate with other devices.

hand-off — The ability of a device to move from one master or PNC to another without getting disconnected from the network in a network that extends beyond the communications range of each device that controls the communications.

impulse modulation — A digital transmission technique employed by UWB in which the polarity of a single analog pulse (one-half of a sine wave) represents a binary digit 1 or 0.

isochronous — The channel time in synchronous transmissions.

management channel time allocation (MCTA) — Time periods used for communication between the devices and the PNC.

man-in-the-middle attack — A security attack in which a hacker captures frames, alters them, and then retransmits them to the intended receiver or another device on the network.

mesh networking — A network topography in which each device connects to all other devices within range.

message integrity — A process of adding certain encrypted random data to each communications session so that the receiver can verify that the message has not been tampered with, after being transmitted.

neighbor piconets — Separate piconets that have their own PNC, but that depend on the original piconet's PNC to allocate a private block of time when their devices are allowed to transmit.

orthogonal frequency division multiplexing (OFDM) — A transmission technique in which the frequency band is divided into a number of frequencies (called sub-frequencies or channels) that do not interfere with each other.

piconet coordinator (PNC) — A device that provides all of the basic communications timing in an 802.15.3 piconet.

Protocol Adaptation Layer (PAL) — A set of protocol implementation rules that will enable wireless FireWire at 400 Mbps based on an 802.15.3a/WiMedia platform.

quality of service (QoS) — A feature of some PANs that allows devices to request more channel access time in order to prioritize high-volume, time-sensitive traffic such as a voice stream.

spectrum conflict — The potential for technologies using the same frequency bands to interfere with each other to the extent that they sometimes perform poorly when used within close range of each other.

superframe — A mechanism for managing transmissions in a piconet. The superframe is a continually repeating frame containing a beacon, contention access periods, channel time allocation periods, and management time allocation periods.

trellis code modulation (TCM) — A method of encoding a digital signal in a way that permits single bit errors to be detected and corrected.

wake superframe — The superframe designated by the PNC in which devices that are in power save mode will wake up and listen for frames addressed to them.

WiMedia Alliance — An association of manufacturers and interested organizations formed to promote the implementation of the IEEE 802.15.3 standard and provide various support activities.

REVIEW QUESTIONS

1. The 802.15.3 PNC is primarily responsible for _____ in a piconet.
   a. timing
   b. acting as the router
   c. switching
   d. Internet connections

2. The 802.15.3 standard was developed to _____ .

    a. compete with Bluetooth technology

    b. provide short-range PC networking

    c. support multimedia

    d. All of the above

3. Which of the following is *not* an advantage of 802.15.3 over Bluetooth?

    a. QoS support

    b. Data transmission rate

    c. Support for child and neighbor piconets sharing the same frequency channel

    d. Security

4. In 802.15.3, the lower levels of the stack are implemented in the

    _____ .

    a. software

    b. hardware

    c. IR

    d. Data Link layer

5. The dual upper layers of the WiMedia protocol stack are the_____ and _____ layers.

    a. RF; MAC

    b. Audio/video; data transfer

    c. TCP/IP; network

    d. PHY; adaptation

6. How many channels are available in 802.15.3?

    a. 2

    b. 14

    c. 4

    d. 11

7. Frame collisions in 802.15.3 can only happen during the _____ .

    a. CTAP

    b. MCTA

    c. CTA

    d. CAP

6

8. In 802.15.3, collisions are prevented by using a method called
   _____ .

   a. CAP

   b. CTAP

   c. CSMA/CA

   d. CSMA/CD

9. A transmission at _____ Mbps is not coded with TCM so that devices can detect piconet traffic without having to decode the signal first.

   a. 53 Mbps

   b. 11 Mbps

   c. 22 Mbps

   d. 44 Mbps

10. In the _____ power save mode, 802.15.3 devices must listen to the system-wide wake beacons.

    a. SPSS

    b. DSPS

    c. PSPS

    d. APS

11. 802.15.3 channels are limited to _____ of bandwidth.

12. The frequencies between _____ and _____ were approved by the FCC for use with UWB technology.

13. The minimum duration of a superframe is _____ millisecond(s).

14. The _____ piconet PNC cannot communicate with the parent piconet's devices.

15. The hardware address is not used when a device communicates in the piconet. Instead, devices use the _____ and the _____ .

16. The beacon carries timing information for the piconet. True or False?

17. Devices in an 802.15.3 piconet can only communicate through the PNC. True or False?

18. CTAPs are optional. True or False?

19. A WiMedia device cannot request more channel time from the PNC. True or False?

20. Discuss the reasons why 802.15.3 devices should be easier for consumers to use.

21. Describe potential interference issues between UWB and 802.11 and how they can be resolved.

22. List three potential applications for WiMedia piconets that are not discussed in the chapter. How would these applications be implemented and why would you implement them using WiMedia?

23. List and describe one type of error control employed in 802.15.3.

24. Explain why mesh networking is an essential enhancement to WiMedia networks.

25. What type of security mechanisms are employed in 802.15.3 networks?

HANDS-ON PROJECTS

HANDS-ON PROJECTS

Project 6-1: Researching Ultra Wide Band Applications

Produce a three-page report on UWB applications. Use the Internet to research potential applications for UWB. You may discuss more than one application but, for each one, be sure to include the following:

1. Who are the target users?

2. What are the benefits to the users?

3. Are there any potential pitfalls, such as interference problems?

4. What are some of the limitations, if any, on who will use it and how?

5. Can you locate any companies that are making or considering making the required equipment?

Write the report in your own words, based on the information you research on the Internet. Your report should include the company names, main Web site links, and product pages, if possible.

HANDS-ON PROJECTS

Project 6-2: Providing Technical Support for WiMedia

Imagine that you work for Multimedia Corporation, a company that is involved in selling multimedia products such as projectors, large display monitors, and audio systems. The company has decided to embrace the new WiMedia technology, but one of its primary concerns is whether it will have the ability to provide technical support to customers during design, installation, and maintenance. Multimedia has asked you to do extensive research on the availability of test and troubleshooting equipment and software. You are to produce a presentation and a report for management.

Use the Internet to research the availability and capabilities of test and troubleshooting equipment for WiMedia. Your report does not have to include cost information at this point, but it should address the following items:

1. What hardware tools exist and what type of measurements they can make?

2. What software tools exist and what is their capability to analyze and assist in troubleshooting the hardware?

3. How portable is the equipment? Can it be used at the customer premises or only in the lab?

4. How much and what type of training would a technician need to be able to use the equipment?

Keep your presentation to a maximum of 10 slides (about 15 to 20 minutes) and your report to about five pages.

CASE PROJECTS

The Bay Cable TV Corp. installs home entertainment systems throughout California. About 100,000 systems are installed, expanded, or upgraded on a yearly basis. Many customers are upgrading their equipment to multiple television sets and high-definition TV. Each time the company sends a van out with a technician or a contractor to a customer's home or business, it costs the company between $150 and $200 in labor alone to install cabling for additional set-top boxes in different rooms of a house or office.

The company's Board of Directors has heard about a new way to deliver this service using wireless networks that would dramatically reduce installation costs. Customers also want to be able to purchase a different movie to watch in each different TV in the home or a different music channel for different offices. They have hired you as a networking expert to help them plan for the expansion of their services over the next five to 10 years.

Project 6-1: Explaining WiMedia Advantages

Create a PowerPoint slide presentation to demonstrate the advantages of WiMedia for the Bay Cable TV Corp. Your presentation should address existing technology and future upgrades.

Project 6-2: Comparing WPAN Technologies

Your presentation convinced the company management, but the Board of Directors is still not convinced about WiMedia. They would like you to draw a comparison between the different WPAN technologies. Create a second PowerPoint presentation that explains the differences, advantages, and disadvantages between the various WPAN alternatives.

OPTIONAL TEAM CASE PROJECT

Microsoft, Hewlett Packard, and many other companies are showcasing hardware that supports the Windows Media Center Edition. Develop a group report that discusses the advantages of adapting these systems to support WiMedia and 802.15.3.

Your report should cover audio, video, and gaming and should focus on WiMedia and 802.15.3. Explain the advantages of adopting a design that can address not only media distribution but also transfer files and provide Internet access throughout the home. Conduct research on the Internet to address the issues of interference from other household appliances, such as microwave ovens and cordless phones.

6

7

LOW-SPEED WIRELESS LOCAL AREA NETWORKS

After reading this chapter and completing the exercises, you will be able to:

♦ Describe how WLANs are used

♦ List the components and modes of a WLAN

♦ Describe how an RF WLAN works

♦ Explain the differences between IR, IEEE 802.11, and IEEE 802.11b WLANs

♦ Outline the user mobility features offered by IEEE 802.11 networks

---

Wireless networks are, without question, one of the technologies that has attracted the most attention since the introduction of the Apple II computer and the IBM PC. The explosive growth of wireless networks all over the world has so far been driven by home and small office sales. In spite of dramatic price reductions, which have benefited the consumer, since 2004 the market has grown by 60% in dollar volume. Growth is expected to continue at the rate of at least 30% per year, reaching $1.6 billion by 2006 and continuing well past 2008. In 2005, the market research firm In-Stat MDR estimated that there are over 75 million wireless networks in use worldwide, with another 40 million more on the way.

As you have learned in previous chapters of this text, WLAN technology supports a very broad spectrum of applications. Most notebook computers are shipped with embedded WLAN interfaces. Very soon it will be difficult to find a coffee shop, fast-food outlet, or hotel anywhere in the world that does not offer wireless Internet access. Public transit buses in the city of Markham, Ontario, offer wireless Internet access to their passengers in a bid to prompt residents to use public transportation. Even airlines offer passengers wireless Internet access.

Chapter 7 begins by reviewing ways in which WLANs are used. The chapter focuses on low-speed WLANs, up to 11 Mbps. This background will help you understand the higher speed technologies and new standards outlined in Chapter 8.

WLAN APPLICATIONS

Wireless networks are increasing in popularity, especially in North America, as computer users seek the freedom to use their notebook computers in various locations throughout their homes or work environments. Installing cabling is inconvenient and very expensive. Also, the locations available for connecting a high-speed cable modem or Digital Subscriber Line (DSL) modem may not be ideal for working or studying. Wireless networks solve these problems. Additionally, with a wireless network, multiple users can easily share a single Internet connection. Some wireless network devices such as a **wireless residential gateway**—a device that combines a router, Ethernet switch, and wireless access point—also allow Internet and printer sharing. A wireless residential gateway provides better security than connecting a computer directly to the Internet.

Wireless LAN applications today are so widespread that we could spend most of the chapter listing different uses and applications. The Internet is packed with information in the form of press releases and white papers about wireless LAN applications. The Web page at http://www.cwnp.com/learning_center/index_applications.html contains many links to this kind of information.

WLAN COMPONENTS

The hardware needed for a WLAN is surprisingly minimal. In addition to a computer and ISP, only wireless network interface cards and access points (APs) are needed for communication to take place.

Wireless Network Interface Card

Recall that the hardware that allows a computer to be connected to a wired network is called a network interface card (NIC), also called a network adapter. A NIC is the device that connects the computer to the network so that it can send and receive data. A wired NIC has a port for a cable connection. The cable connects the NIC to the network, thus establishing the link between the computer and the network.

A wireless NIC performs the same functions as a wired NIC with one major exception: there is no port for a wire connection to the network. In its place is an antenna to send and receive RF signals. Specifically, when wireless NICs transmit, they:

1. Change the computer's internal data from parallel to serial prior to transmission.

2. Divide the data into packets (smaller blocks of data) and attach the sending and receiving computers' addresses.

3. Determine when to send the packet.

4. Transmit the packet.

A wireless NIC is most often a separate card that is inserted into one of the desktop computer's internal expansion slots. For desktop computers, wireless NICs are available for a Peripheral Component Interface (PCI) expansion slot. Another option is an external wireless adapter that can be connected to a computer's Universal Serial Bus (USB) port. These devices are shown in Figure 1-8 in Chapter 1.

For notebook computers, wireless NICs are available in two different formats. The first is for the standard PC Card Type II slot, as seen again in Figure 1-8. Another format is known as the **Mini PCI**. A Mini PCI is a small card that is functionally equivalent to a standard PCI expansion card. It was specifically developed for integrating communications peripherals, such as modems and NICs, onto a notebook computer. When a notebook computer is equipped with a Mini PCI NIC, the antenna is usually embedded in the part of the notebook that surrounds the screen. Figure 7-1 shows a Mini PCI card installed on the underside of a notebook computer.

Figure 7-1   A Mini PCI wireless NIC

Smaller devices, such as PDAs, have two options for wireless NICs. Some offer an optional **sled**, which includes a Type II PC Card slot and an additional battery. This option allows the PDA to accept a standard Type II PC Card wireless NIC, the same card that can also be used in a notebook computer. The second option is a **compact flash (CF) card**, or **secure digital (SD) card**, as seen in Figure 7-2. CF or SD cards consist of a small circuit board that contains a dedicated controller chip and a very small antenna. These wireless NIC cards have two advantages over Type II PC Cards: they are smaller and they consume less power. However, they also transmit and receive with lower power levels than the other types of wireless NICs, and, consequently, may not have the same range.

NOTE At the time this book went to press, PDAs were only capable of supporting 802.11b. Due to their power consumption issues, PDAs may never support faster wireless connections.

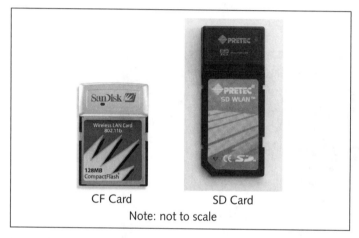

CF Card   SD Card
Note: not to scale

Figure 7-2   CF card wireless NIC and SD card wireless NIC

WLANs are so popular that separate wireless NICs may soon be a thing of the past. Intel has integrated all the functions of a wireless interface into a chipset called Centrino, which is mounted directly on the motherboard. Most notebook computer manufacturers today ship all their models with integrated wireless LAN capabilities, whether using the Intel Centrino chipset or a Mini PCI card.

The software that interfaces between the wireless NIC and the computer can either be part of the operating system or a separate program. Beginning with Microsoft Windows XP, all Microsoft desktop operating systems recognize a wireless NIC without the need for external software drivers; previous versions of Windows required these external drivers. Incorporating them into the operating system eases installation and also provides additional features such as the ability to connect automatically to different WLANs as the user roams, instead of manually configuring the settings. Some wireless NIC vendors include software drivers for other operating systems, such as Linux. Microsoft Pocket PC 2003 also recognizes the most common models of 802.11b wireless NIC cards automatically and requires no additional drivers.

Access Points

As you learned in Chapter 1, an access point (AP), as its name implies, provides wireless LAN devices with a point of access into a wired network. APs consist of three major parts: (1) a radio transmitter/receiver to generate the signals that are used to send and receive wireless data; (2) an antenna to radiate these signals; and (3) an RJ-45 wired network interface port that uses a cable to connect the AP to a standard wired network.

NOTE   It is possible to use a standard PC as an AP by installing a wireless NIC (which functions at the transmitter/receiver), a standard NIC (which serves as the wired network interface), and special software that allows the PC to serve as an AP as well as a security firewall. You can find free public domain versions of this kind of software at the following links: http://www.microtik.com and http://www.m0n0.ch.

An AP has two basic functions. First, the AP acts as the wireless communications base station for the wireless network. All of the devices that have a wireless NIC transmit to the AP, which in turn redirects the signal to the other wireless devices. The second function of an AP is to act as a bridge between the wireless and wired networks. The AP can be connected to the LAN by a network cable, allowing the wireless devices to access the wired network through it, as seen in Figure 7-3.

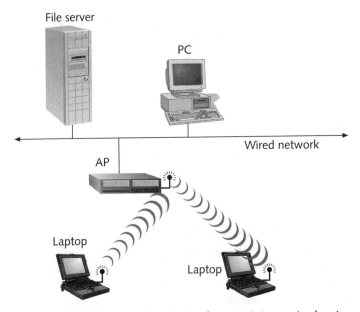

Figure 7-3   The AP is the point of access into a wired network

The range of an AP acting as the base station is approximately 375 feet (115 meters) in an unobstructed office environment. However, the data rate will drop as the signal strength, quality, or both begin to fade. The exact point at which the data rate begins to drop depends on the specific environment, the type and number of obstructions, and any sources of interference. The AP will automatically select the highest possible data rate for transmission, depending on the strength and quality of the signal. This process is called **dynamic rate selection**. This makes testing the signal before implementation an extremely important part of a WLAN deployment. You will learn more about this topic in Chapter 12.

The largest number of users that a single AP can support varies, but is generally over 100. However, because the radio frequency (RF) network signal is shared among users, most vendors recommend one AP per maximum of 50 users if they are only performing basic e-mail, light Web surfing, and occasional transferring of medium-sized files. On the other hand, if the users are mainly transferring large files, the maximum number of users should be kept to about 20 per AP.

APs are typically mounted near the ceiling or a similar area high off the ground to ensure the clearest possible path for the RF signal. However, electrical power outlets are generally not found in these locations and, due to building code restrictions, are expensive to install in these locations. The IEEE has published two enhancements to the 802.3 standard, namely 802.3af and 802.3at, which define how manufacturers may implement the distribution of **power over Ethernet (PoE)** media. Instead of receiving power directly from an AC outlet, DC power is delivered to the AP through the unused wires in a standard unshielded twisted pair (UTP) Ethernet cable that connects the AP to the wired network. This eliminates the need for expensive electrical wiring to be installed in the ceiling and makes the mounting of APs more flexible.

CAUTION Until all manufacturers adopt the standard, the power supplies required to provide power to the APs via Ethernet media should only be purchased from the same manufacturer as the AP itself.

WLAN Modes

In an RF WLAN, data can be sent in one of two connection modes: ad hoc mode and infrastructure mode.

Ad Hoc Mode

The **ad hoc mode** is also known as **peer-to-peer mode**, although its formal name is the **Independent Basic Service Set (IBSS)** mode. In ad hoc mode, wireless clients communicate directly among themselves without using an AP, as seen in Figure 7-4. This mode is useful for a quick and easy setup of a wireless network anywhere that a network infrastructure does not already exist or is not permanently required. Examples of locations that use ad hoc mode WLANs are hotel meeting rooms or convention centers. The drawback is that the wireless clients can only communicate among themselves; there is no access to a wired network.

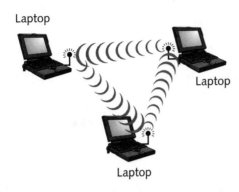

Figure 7-4   Ad hoc mode

Infrastructure Mode

The second wireless network mode is the **infrastructure mode**, also known as the **Basic Service Set (BSS)**. Infrastructure mode consists of wireless clients and an AP. If more users need to be added to the WLAN, or the range of the coverage area needs to be increased, more APs can be added. This creates an **Extended Service Set (ESS)**. An ESS is simply two or more BSS wireless networks installed within the same area, providing users with uninterrupted mobile access to the network, as seen in Figure 7-5.

When multiple APs are used, they create areas of coverage, much like the individual cells in a beehive. However, unlike a beehive, these cells overlap to facilitate roaming. When a mobile user carrying a wireless notebook computer enters into the range of more than one AP, his wireless device chooses an AP with which to associate, usually based on signal strength. Once that device is accepted by the AP, the client device tunes to the radio frequencies at which the AP is set.

On a regular basis, wireless clients will probe all the radio frequencies on the network to determine if a different AP can provide better service. If it finds one (perhaps because the user has moved again), it then associates with the new AP, tuning to the radio frequency to which the AP is set. This transition is called a handoff. To the user, a handoff is seamless because the connection between the wireless device and the wired network is never interrupted.

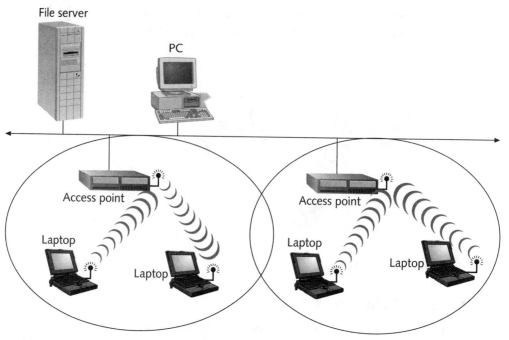

Figure 7-5   Extended service set (ESS)

 Some APs allow you to specify to which AP you want the client device to connect.

NOTE

A drawback of ESS WLANs is that all wireless clients and APs must be part of the same network for users to be able to roam freely between one AP and the other. Sometimes it is difficult to manage one large network. Performance and security may also be adversely affected. Because of this, network managers usually subdivide large networks into units known as **subnets** that contain fewer computers. In an ESS divided into subnets, a mobile user might not be able to freely roam between APs and would need to reconnect each time he moves between subnets, because an IP address belonging to one subnet would not allow him to communicate in another. Some of the business-class network devices that connect these subnets are equipped with special software that allows the wireless device to be accepted in other subnets without changing IP addresses and to maintain the connection. In these cases, the wired switches and routers across the network allow packets to be forwarded transparently to the user's own subnet.

WIRELESS LAN STANDARDS AND OPERATION

In this section, you will learn about the first IEEE standards for wireless LANS. Most WLANs are based on these same initial IEEE 802.11 standards. 802.11a and 802.11g, which are covered in Chapter 8, follow the same basic principles, albeit with a number of enhancements. Each of these standards implements specific transmission technologies based on the differences in the PHY and MAC layers.

IEEE 802.11 Standards

The **802.11 standard** defines a local area network that provides cable-free data access for clients that are either mobile or in a fixed location at a rate of either 1 or 2 Mbps using either diffused infrared or RF transmission. In addition, when using RF technology, this standard also defines the implementation of WLANs using FHSS or DSSS.

The standard specifies that the features of a WLAN be transparent to the upper layers of the TCP/IP protocol stack or the OSI protocol model. That is, the functions of the PHY and MAC layers provide full implementation of all of the WLAN features so that no modifications are needed at any other layers, as illustrated in Figure 7-6. Because all of the WLAN features are isolated in the PHY and MAC layers, any network operating system or LAN application will run on a WLAN without any modification necessary. In order to accomplish this, some features that are usually associated with higher layers are now performed at the MAC layer.

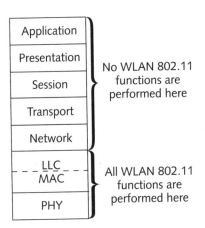

Figure 7-6 WLAN features in PHY and MAC layers

IEEE 802.11 Infrared WLAN Standard

The IEEE 802.11 standards outline the specifications for infrared as well as RF WLANs. The infrared specification is based on diffused transmissions. The PHY layer performs the functions of both reformatting the data received from the upper layers and transmitting the light impulses.

Recall that the PHY layer has two sublayers. The Physical Medium Dependent (PMD) sublayer includes the standards for the characteristics of the wireless medium (IR and RF) and defines the method for transmitting and receiving data through that medium. The second PHY sublayer is the Physical Layer Convergence Procedure (PLCP) sublayer. The PLCP performs two basic functions: it reformats the data received from the MAC layer (when transmitting) into a frame that the PMD sublayer can transmit, as shown in Figure 7-7. Second, it listens to the medium to determine when the data can be sent.

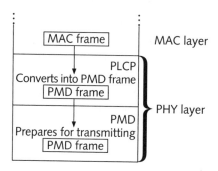

Figure 7-7   PLCP sublayer reformats MAC data

Diffused Infrared PHY Layer Convergence Procedure Standards

The diffused infrared PLCP reformats the data received from the MAC layer (when transmitting) into a frame that the Physical Medium Dependent (PMD) sublayer can transmit. An example of an infrared PLCP frame, including its component parts, is illustrated in Figure 7-8.

Even though it contains data, a frame's size is not measured in bits but in **time slots**, which are periods of time that are predefined in the standard or specification. Infrared wireless systems send data by the intensity of the light wave instead of *on-off* signals of light. To transmit a 1 bit, an infrared emitter increases the intensity of the current and sends a pulse using infrared light. This pulse of infrared light is transmitted in a specific time slot. In the Synchronization field of an infrared PLCP frame the emitter may send between 57 and 73 pulses, each in its own time slot. The receiving device then synchronizes with the incoming signal. The Start frame delimiter is always the same bit pattern and is the part of the frame that defines its beginning. The Start frame delimiter for infrared is always 1001, where 1 represents a high-intensity pulse and 0 is a lower-intensity pulse.

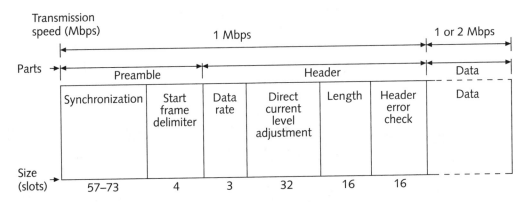

Figure 7-8 Infrared PLCP frame

The Data rate value determines the speed of the transmission. The Direct current level adjustment contains a pattern of infrared pulses that allows the receiving device to determine the signal level. Table 7-1 illustrates the possible values for these fields. The Length field indicates the time needed to transmit the entire frame. Length is used by the receiving device to determine the end of the frame. The Header error check contains a value that the receiving device can use to determine if the data was received correctly. The Data field is the portion of the frame that contains the data and can be from 1 to 20,000 time slots.

Table 7-1 Infrared data rate and direct current level adjustment values

Transmission Speed (Mbps)	Data Rate Values	Direct Current Level Adjustment Values
1.0	000	00000000010000000000000001000000
2.0	001	00100010001000100010001000100010

There are two significant points regarding the transmission speed of the PLCP frame. First, the preamble and header of the PLCP frame are always transmitted at 1 Mbps. This allows for a slower sending device to talk to a faster receiving device because it is using the slowest speed. However, even if both devices are faster and can transmit at a faster rate, the two faster devices must still fall back to the 1 Mbps transmission rate for the preamble and header. Also, the current IEEE 802.11 standards specify that the data can be transmitted only at either 1 or 2 Mbps.

Diffused Infrared Physical Medium Dependent Standards

Once the PLCP has created the frame, it then passes it to the PMD sublayer. The PMD translates the binary 1s and 0s of the frame into light pulses that are used for transmission. To transmit a 1 bit, the emitter increases the intensity of the current and sends a pulse using infrared light. The detector senses the higher intensity signal and produces a proportional electrical current.

The infrared PMD transmits the data using a series of light impulses. For transmissions at 1 Mbps, a **16-pulse position modulation (16-PPM)** is specified. 16-PPM translates four data bits into 16 light impulses, which are then transmitted to the receiving device. This is illustrated in Table 7-2. For transmissions at 2 Mbps, a **4-pulse position modulation (4-PPM)** is used instead, as seen in Table 7-3.

Table 7-2   16-PPM values

Data Bit	16-PPM Value	Data Bit	16-PPM Value
0000	0000000000000001	1100	0000000100000000
0001	0000000000000010	1101	0000001000000000
0011	0000000000000100	1111	0000010000000000
0010	0000000000001000	1110	0000100000000000
0110	0000000000010000	1010	0001000000000000
0111	0000000000100000	1011	0010000000000000
0101	0000000001000000	1001	0100000000000000
0100	0000000010000000	1000	1000000000000000

Table 7-3   4-PPM values

Data Bit	4-PPM Value
00	0001
01	0010
11	0100
10	1000

Each time slot is 250 ns (nanoseconds, or billionths of a second), no matter which transmission speed is being used (1 Mbps or 2 Mbps). If each time slot is the same, how can the 4-PPM transmit at twice the speed? Four times the amount of data is contained in a 4-PPM transmission. Suppose that the data bits 1001 were to be transmitted. Using 16-PPM it would take 16 time slots (0100000000000000) to send the data bits 1001. However, using 4-PPM to transmit the same data bits would only take eight time slots: 10000010 to send the data bits 10, and 0010 to send the data bits 01. Thus 4-PPM can transmit at a maximum rate of 2 Mbps, while 16-PPM can only transmit at 1 Mbps.

The slow maximum bandwidth of only 2 Mbps for the original 802.11 standard is not sufficient for most network applications. As a result, the IEEE body revisited the 802.11 standard shortly after it was released to determine what changes could be made to increase the speed. In 1999, the 802.11b and 802.11a standards were published, increasing the speeds to 11 Mbps and 54 Mbps, respectively. Due to user demand, in 2003, the IEEE published the

802.11g standard, raising the speed of 802.11b-compatible networks to a maximum of 54 Mbps. This drive for more speed has not subsided yet. New standards are in the works to increase the speeds even further, to 108 Mbps and beyond.

IEEE 802.11b Standard

In September 1999 an amendment to the 802.11 standard was published, designated as 802.11b – 1999, Higher Speed Physical Layer Extension in the 2.4 GHz band. The **802.11b standard** added two higher speeds, 5.5 Mbps and 11 Mbps, to the original 1 or 2 Mbps 802.11 standard and specified RF and direct sequence spread spectrum (DSSS) as the only transmission technology. With the faster data rates, 802.11b, also known as **Wi-Fi**, quickly became the standard for RF WLANs.

7

Physical Layer

Recall that the basic purpose of the IEEE PHY layer is to send signals to and receive signals from the network. The 802.11b PHY layer is also divided into two parts, as shown in Figure 7-7, the Physical Medium Dependent (PMD) sublayer and the Physical Layer Convergence Procedure (PLCP) sublayer. The 802.11b standard made changes only to the PHY layer of the original 802.11 standard.

Physical Layer Convergence Procedure Standards

PLCP standards for 802.11b are based on direct sequence spread spectrum (DSSS). The PLCP must reformat the data received from the MAC layer (when transmitting) into a frame that the PMD sublayer can transmit. An example of a PLCP frame is illustrated in Figure 7-9.

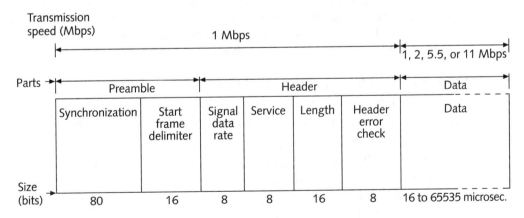

Figure 7-9 PLCP frame

As with infrared, the PLCP frame is made up of three parts: the preamble, the header, and the data. The preamble allows the receiving device to prepare for the rest of the frame. The header provides information about the frame itself. The data portion of the PLCP frame is the information to be transmitted. The fields of the PLCP frame are:

- Synchronization — Consists of alternating 0s and 1s to alert the receiver that a message may be on its way; the receiving device then synchronizes with the incoming signal.

- Start frame delimiter — Always the same bit pattern (1111001110100000); it defines the beginning of a frame.

- Signal data rate — Indicates how fast the data is being sent.

- Service — Most of the bits in this field are reserved for future use and must be set to zero. Bits 2, 3, and 7 are used in combination with the length field for data rates higher than 8 Mbps (see Length below).

- Length — Indicates how long the data portion of the frame (the MAC frame) is in microseconds. The value of the Data field ranges from 16 to 65535. Approximately two pages of the 802.11b standard are devoted to calculating the length of the data. The details are beyond the scope of this book.

- Header error check — Contains a value that the receiving device can use to determine if the data was received correctly.

- Data — Can be up to 4095 bytes (the maximum length of a MAC frame).

The 802.11b PLCP frame preamble and header are always transmitted at 1 Mbps to allow for communication between slower and faster devices. The slow PLCP preamble and header transmission speed permits a slower signal to cover a larger area than a faster signal. The disadvantage of using the lowest common denominator speed is that two faster devices must still fall back to the 1 Mbps transmission rate for the preamble and header. However, the data portion of the frames can be sent at the faster rate.

Physical Medium Dependent Standards

Once the PLCP has created the frame, it then passes it to the PMD sublayer of the PHY layer. Again, the job of the PMD is to translate the binary 1s and 0s of the frame into radio signals that can be used for transmission.

The 802.11b standard uses the Industrial, Scientific, and Medical (ISM) band (an unregulated band that you learned about in Chapter 3) for its transmissions. The 802.11b standard specifies 14 available frequencies, beginning at 2.412 GHz and incrementing by .005 GHz (except for Channel 14). These are listed in Table 7-4.

Table 7-4 802.11b ISM channels

Channel Number	Frequency (GHz)
1	2.412
2	2.417
3	2.422
4	2.427
5	2.432
6	2.437
7	2.442
8	2.447
9	2.452
10	2.457
11	2.462
12	2.467
13	2.472
14	2.484

The United States and Canada use channels 1–11; the majority of Europe (except for France and Spain) uses channels 10–13; France uses channels 11 and 12; Spain uses channels 10 and 11; and Japan uses all 14 channels.

NOTE

The PMD can transmit the data at 11, 5.5, 2, or 1 Mbps. Recall that with dynamic rate selection, the transmission rate will adjust automatically from 1 Mbps to 2 Mbps, 5.5 Mbps, or 11 Mbps and down again depending on the signal strength and quality. For transmissions at 1 Mbps, two-level differential binary phase shift key (DBPSK) is specified as the modulation technique. The phase change for a DBPSK 0 bit is 0 degrees, while the phase change for a 1 bit is 180 degrees. Transmissions at 2, 5.5, and 11 Mbps use differential quadrature phase shift keying, similar to QPSK (covered in Chapter 2), which means a four-level phase/amplitude change is used. Instead of having only two variations in phases for 0 and 1, the four-level phase change has four variations in phases for the bits 00, 01, 10, and 11.

Recall that DSSS uses an expanded redundant code, called the Barker code, to transmit each data bit. The Barker code is used when 802.11b is transmitting at 1 Mbps or 2 Mbps. However, to transmit at rates above 2 Mbps, **Complementary Code Keying (CCK)**, a table containing 64 8-bit code words, is used instead. As a set, these code words have unique mathematical properties that allow them to be correctly distinguished from one another by a receiver. The 5.5 Mbps rate uses CCK to encode 4 bits per signal unit, while the 11 Mbps rate encodes 8 bits per signal unit.

Although the maximum transmission rate of 802.11 networks is 11 Mbps, since it uses a single frequency, 802.11 transmission is half-duplex. This means that the maximum throughput achievable in an 802.11b network is only between 5 and 6 Mbps.

NOTE

Media Access Control Layer

The 802.11b Data Link layer consists of two sublayers: Logical Link Control (LLC) and Media Access Control (MAC). The 802.11b standard specifies no changes to the LLC sublayer (the LLC remains the same as for wired networks). All of the changes for 802.11b WLANs are confined to the MAC layer.

On a WLAN, all of the devices share the same RF spectrum. For this sharing to succeed, some method of coordination must exist between the devices. The standard coordination protocol for 802.11b WLANs is known as distributed coordination function. The point coordination function is an optional function.

Distributed Coordination Function

Because devices in the same wireless network must share the medium by transmitting in the same frequency, if two computers start sending messages at the same time, a **collision** results and the data becomes scrambled, as seen in Figure 7-10. To prevent this, wireless network devices must use a variety of **channel access methods**. One way to prevent network collisions, for example, is for each device to listen to the medium first, to make sure no other device is transmitting.

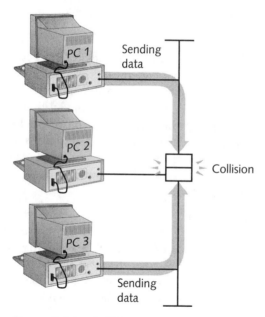

Figure 7-10   Collision

In Chapter 5, you learned about a channel access method called carrier sense multiple access with collision avoidance (CSMA/CA). CSMA/CA is based on a similar Ethernet technology. When Ethernet devices are connected using a shared medium, such as a coaxial cable, they use a contention access method called carrier sense multiple access with collision detection (CSMA/CD). CSMA/CD specifies that before a computer starts to send a message it should first listen on the cable to see if any other computer is transmitting. If it hears traffic, it should wait until that traffic is finished. If it hears no traffic, then the computer can send its message. However, what if two computers simultaneously listen and hear nothing on the cable and then both start to send at exactly the same time? A collision would still result. CSMA/CD also specifies that each computer must continue to listen while sending its message. If it hears a collision, each computer stops sending data and broadcasts a jam signal over the network, which tells all other computers not to send any messages temporarily. The two sending computers then pause a random amount of time (the backoff interval) before attempting to resend.

CSMA/CD cannot be used in a wireless system. Collision detection is virtually impossible with wireless transmissions, when the signals are transmitted and received in the same frequency. The RF signal from a transmitter is so strong when it gets to the antenna that it will overpower that same antenna's ability to receive a signal simultaneously. In short, while it is transmitting, a device drowns out its own ability to detect a collision.

The entire family of 802.11 standards uses an access method known as the **distributed coordination function (DCF)** to avoid collisions. The DCF specifies that a modified procedure—CSMA/CA—be used. Whereas CSMA/CD is designed to handle collisions when they occur, CSMA/CA attempts to avoid collisions altogether.

When using a contention-based channel access method, the time at which the most collisions occur is immediately after a device completes its transmission. This is because all other devices wanting to transmit have been waiting for the medium to clear so they can send their messages. Once the medium is clear, they may all try to transmit at the same time, resulting in collisions.

CSMA/CA handles the situation by making all devices wait a random amount of time (the backoff interval) after the medium is clear, which significantly reduces the occurrence of collisions. The amount of time that a device must wait after the medium is clear is measured in time slots. Each client must wait a random number of time slots as its backoff interval. The time slot for a DSSS 802.11b WLAN is 20 microseconds. If a wireless client's backoff interval is 3 time slots, then it must wait 60 microseconds (20 microseconds times 3 time slots) before attempting to transmit.

NOTE

The time slot for an 802.3 Ethernet 10 Mbps transmission is 51.2 microseconds; for 100 Mbps Ethernet it is 5.12 microseconds.

CSMA/CA also reduces collisions by using explicit **packet acknowledgment (ACK)**. An acknowledgment packet is sent by the receiving device back to the sending device to confirm that the data packet arrived intact. If the ACK frame is not received by the sending device, either the original data packet was not received or the ACK was not received intact. The sending device assumes that a problem has occurred and retransmits the data packet after waiting another random amount of time. This explicit ACK mechanism handles interference and other radio-related problems, such as one client device being able to hear the transmission from an AP but not being able to hear another client that is too far away. CSMA/CA and ACK are illustrated in Figure 7-11.

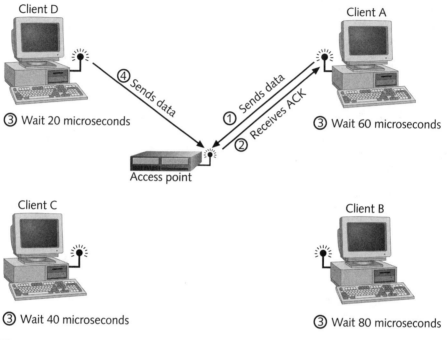

Figure 7-11   CSMA/CA

CSMA/CA reduces potential collisions, but it does not eliminate them altogether. The 802.11b standard provides two additional mechanisms to reduce collisions. The first is known as the **Request to Send/Clear to Send (RTS/CTS)** protocol (also called virtual carrier sensing). RTS/CTS is illustrated in Figure 7-12. A request-to-send (RTS) frame is transmitted by the wireless client, Client B, to the AP. This frame contains a duration field that defines the length of time needed for both the transmission and the returning ACK frame. The AP alerts all other wireless clients that Client B needs to reserve the medium for a specific period of time. The AP then responds back to the client with a clear-to-send (CTS) frame that also tells all clients that the medium is now being reserved and they should suspend any transmissions. Once the client receives the CTS frame, it can then proceed with transmitting its message.

The RTS/CTS protocol imposes additional overhead and is not used unless there is poor network performance due to excessive collisions.

The second option to reduce collisions is **fragmentation**. Fragmentation involves dividing the data to be transmitted from one large frame into several smaller ones. Sending many

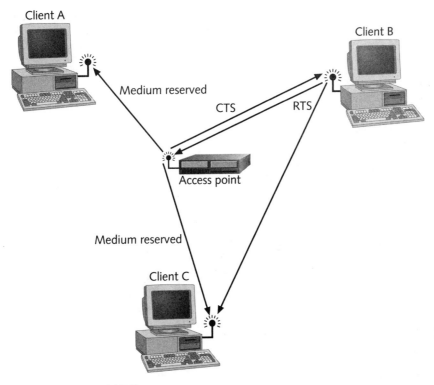

Figure 7-12   RTS/CTS

smaller frames instead of one large frame reduces the amount of time that the wireless medium is being used, and likewise reduces the probability of collisions.

In fragmentation, if the length of a data frame to be transmitted exceeds a specific value, the MAC layer will divide, or fragment, that frame into several smaller frames. Each fragmented frame is given a fragment number (the first fragmented frame is 0, the next frame is 1, and so on). The frames are then transmitted to the receiving client. The receiving client receives the frame, sends back an ACK, and then is ready to receive the next fragment. Upon receiving all of the fragments they are reassembled, based on their fragment numbers, back into the original frame at their destination.

Fragmentation can reduce the probability of collisions and is an alternative to RTS/CTS. However, fragmentation does have additional overhead associated with it for sending a separate ACK from the receiving client for each fragmented frame received. Fragmentation does not always have to be used separately from RTS/CTS. The 802.11b standard permits both to be used simultaneously.

Another type of channel access method is **polling**. With this method each computer is sequentially polled, or asked if it wants to transmit. If the answer is yes, then it is given permission to transmit while all other devices must wait. If the answer is no, then the next device in sequence is polled. It is a very orderly way of allowing each device to send a message when that device has its turn, as seen in Figure 7-13. Polling effectively eliminates collisions because every device must wait until it receives permission from the AP before it can transmit.

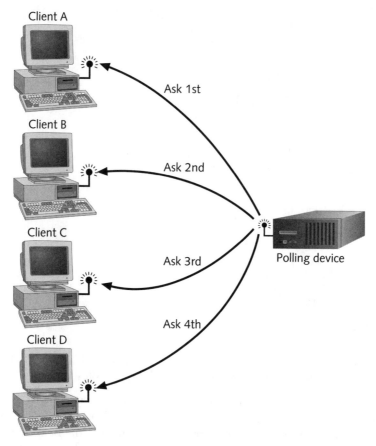

Figure 7-13   Polling

The 802.11b standard provides for an optional polling function known as **point coordination function (PCF)**. With PCF the AP serves as the polling device, or point coordinator and queries each client in an orderly fashion to determine if the client needs to transmit.

When using PCF, the point coordinator first listens for wireless traffic. If it hears no traffic, then it sends out a beacon to all clients. One field of this frame contains a value that indicates the length of time that PCF (polling) will be used instead of DCF (contention). After the clients receive this beacon frame they must cease transmitting for that length of time. The point coordinator then sends out another frame to a specific client, granting it permission to transmit one frame to any destination. If it has nothing to send, then that client returns a **null data frame** to the point coordinator.

PCF is most often used in WLANs that transmit time-sensitive frames. These types of transmissions—often audio or video—depend on each frame arriving in an orderly sequence very quickly one after the other. Delays in transmission can result in a video that freezes on the screen or a conversation that has gaps of dead space. Data transmissions, on the other hand, are not as sensitive to timely data delivery. DCF cannot distinguish between voice, video, and data frames. Using PCF or a combination of DCF and PCF allows for the smooth transmission of time-sensitive frames.

Association and Reassociation

The MAC layer of the 802.11b standard provides the functionality for a client to join a WLAN and stay connected. As you have already learned, the processes of joining and staying connected to a WLAN are known as association and reassociation. Recall that there are two different modes in RF WLANs, ad hoc and infrastructure. Regardless of which mode is being used, a client must first go through a process of communicating with the other wireless clients or the AP in order to become accepted as part of the network. This acceptance process is known as association.

The process of association begins with the client **scanning** the airwaves. The client that wants to connect to the wireless network must first scan the airwaves for the information that it needs to begin the association process. There are two types of scanning, passive and active. **Passive scanning** involves a client listening to each available channel for a set period of time (usually 10 seconds). The client listens for a beacon frame transmitted from all available APs. The information contained within the beacon frame includes the duration of the transmission, how often beacon frames are sent, the supported transmission rates of the network, and the AP's **Service Set Identifier (SSID)**. The SSID is an identifier unique to each AP. SSIDs are alphanumeric values.

TIP

SSIDs are case-sensitive. For example, if you set the SSID on an AP as "AP1" and set the SSID on the client devices as "ap1," the client devices will not be able to associate with the AP using this configuration. The same is true for ad hoc networks. All devices must use the same SSID.

The second type of scanning, **active scanning**, involves the client first sending out a special frame on each available channel, called a **probe** frame. It then waits for an answer, the **probe response** frame, from all available APs. Like the beacon frame, the probe response frame contains information the client needs to begin a dialogue with the AP.

Once the client scans and receives the connection information from the AP, it then begins to negotiate with one AP. The client sends an **associate request frame** to the AP that includes the client's own capabilities and supported rates. The AP then returns an **associate response frame**, containing a status code and client ID number for that client. At this point, the client becomes part of the network and can begin transmitting.

If the network includes multiple APs, the client may need to choose from many different APs. The decision can be based on several criteria. A client can be preconfigured to connect only to a specific AP. In this case, the client already contains the SSID of the AP with which it needs to connect. As it receives beacon frames or probe response frames from the different APs, it compares their SSID to the SSID of the preferred AP. The client will reject all APs until it finds a match, at which time it will then send an associate request frame to that AP. If a client has not been preconfigured to connect with a specific AP, it will connect with the AP from which it has received the strongest radio signal.

Connecting with one AP does not restrict a client from associating with other APs. Rather, a client may drop the connection with one AP and reestablish the connection with another. This is known as **reassociation**. Reassociation may be necessary when mobile clients roam beyond the coverage area of one AP and into the coverage area of another AP, in which case the client severs its association with the original AP and reassociates itself with the new AP. Reassociation also occurs when the signal weakens because of interference from another object.

When a client determines that the link to its current AP is poor, it begins scanning to find another AP. The client sends a **reassociation request frame** to the new AP. If the new AP accepts the reassociation request, it sends back a **reassociation response frame** to indicate its acceptance. The new AP then sends a **disassociation frame** to the old AP, through the wired network, terminating the old AP's association with the client. This process is illustrated in Figure 7-14.

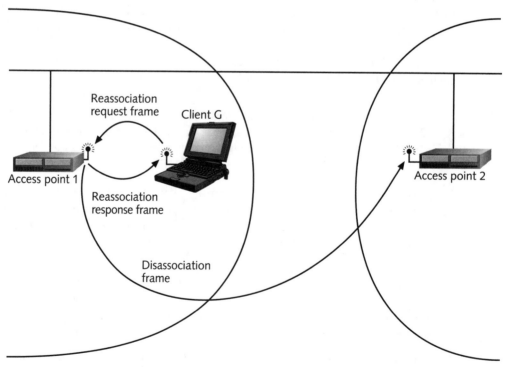

Figure 7-14   Reassociation process

NOTE

In the 802.11 and 802.11a/b/g standards, multiple APs can only communicate with each other over the network cabling. In other words, they cannot communicate over a wireless connection. As you will learn in the next chapter, there are two separate enhancements to the 802.11 standards that permit APs to communicate with each other over the wireless medium.

Power Management

Most clients in a WLAN are portable notebook computers or PDAs, giving the users the freedom to roam without being tethered to the network by wires. When these devices are mobile (and consequently not connected to a wall power socket), they depend on batteries as their primary power source. To conserve battery power they can go into **sleep mode** after a period of time, when particular functions (such as hard drive, display, and so on) are temporarily powered down by the computer's operating system.

CAUTION

Note that the Windows XP hibernation mode, which literally shuts down the computer, is not the same as the sleep mode previously discussed. Windows XP standby mode, however, is similar to sleep mode. As defined in 802.11, in sleep mode, the computer must remain powered up, although the hard drive and display may be temporarily shut down by the notebook's power save mode. In hibernate and standby modes, the NIC also shuts down completely.

When a client is part of a WLAN, it must remain fully powered up to receive network transmissions. Missing transmissions because it is in sleep mode may cause an application running on the device to lose connection with a server application running elsewhere on the network.

The answer to the preceding dilemma is known as power management. 802.11b standard **power management** allows the mobile client's NIC to be off as much as possible to conserve battery life but still not miss out on data transmissions. Power management in 802.11 is transparent to all protocols and applications so that it does not interfere with normal network functions. The 802.11b power management function can only be used when connecting in infrastructure mode.

The key to power management is synchronization. Every client on a WLAN has its own local timer. At regular intervals, the AP sends out a beacon signal that contains a timestamp to all clients. When the clients receive this frame from the AP, they synchronize their local timers with that of the AP.

When a mobile 802.11b client goes into sleep mode, the AP is informed of the change. The AP keeps a record of those clients that are awake and those that are sleeping (with the wireless NIC's receiver and transmitter powered down). As the AP receives transmissions, it first checks whether the client's NIC is in sleep mode. If it is sleeping, the AP temporarily stores the synchronized frames (this function is called **buffering**).

At predetermined times, the AP sends out a beacon frame to all clients. This frame contains a list, known as the **traffic indication map (TIM)**, of the clients that have buffered frames waiting at the AP. At that same set time, all clients that have been sleeping must awaken (by turning on their wireless NICs) and go into an active listening mode. If a client learns that it has buffered frames waiting, that client can send a request to the AP for those frames. If it has no buffered frames, it can return to sleep mode. This is illustrated in Figure 7-15.

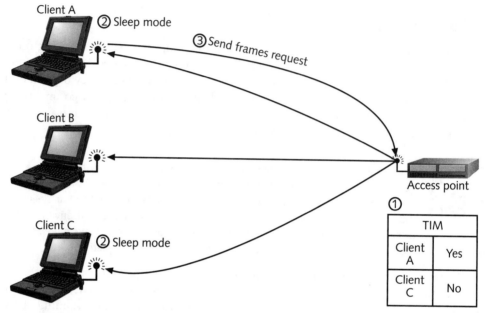

Figure 7-15   Power management

The maximum amount of sleep time for a mobile client is generally set to 100 milliseconds. This means that every client in sleep mode must awaken and listen for the TIM every 100 milliseconds.

NOTE

MAC Frame Formats

The 802.11b standard specifies three different types of MAC frame formats. The first are known as **management frames**. These are used to set up the initial communications between a client and the AP. The reassociation request frame, the reassociation response frame, and the disassociation frame are all types of management frames.

The format of a management frame is illustrated in Figure 7-16. The Frame control field indicates the current version number of the standard, and whether encryption is being used. The Duration field contains the number of microseconds needed to transmit. This value will differ depending on whether the point coordination function or distributed coordination function mode is being used. Sequence control is the sequence number for the packet and packet fragment number.

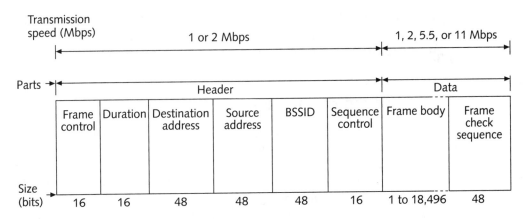

Figure 7-16   Structure of a management frame

Control frames are the second type of MAC frames. After association and authentication between the clients and the APs are established, the control frames provide assistance in delivering the frames that contain the data. A request-to-send (RTS) frame is a control frame and is illustrated in Figure 7–17.

Frame control	Duration	Receiver address	Transmitter address	Frame check sequence

Size (bits)   16   16   48   48   48

Figure 7-17   RTS frame

Data frames are the final type of MAC frames. They carry the information to be transmitted to the destination client. The format of a data frame is illustrated in Figure 7-18. The fields Address 1 through Address 4 contain the SSID, the destination address, the source address, and the transmitter address or the receiver address. Not all address fields are present in every type of MAC data frame. The content of the address fields varies depending on the type of frame transmitted.

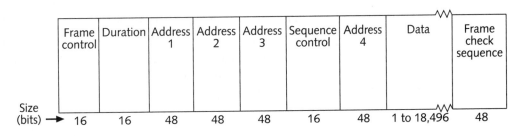

Figure 7-18   Data frame

NOTE For additional information regarding the content of the address fields, see sections 7.1.3 through 7.2.2 on pages 50 through 60 of the 802.11-1999 standard. You can find it at http://standards.ieee.org/getieee802/802.11.html.

Distributed Coordination Function Rules

To help you understand the message exchange process, which in turn will help you to understand the new standards outlined in the next chapter, it is essential to comprehend the collision avoidance mechanism in distributed coordination function (DCF) used by an AP and a client to communicate. For CSMA/CA to work properly in DCF, the 802.11 standard defines a number of **interframe spaces (IFS)** or time gaps. These interframe spaces are designed to handle the contention for the medium among several devices attempting to communicate.

To keep this explanation as simple as possible, we will only review the procedure and rules associated with using the DCF. We will not look at the procedure or rules associated with RTS/CTS or PCF. For additional information, you can download the 802.11-1999 standard from the address in the Note above.

Interframe spaces perform various functions, depending on their type:

- **Short interframe space (SIFS)** — A gap used for immediate response actions such as acknowledging a frame (ACK). All clients, except the one to which the last frame was addressed, must not transmit during the SIFS. This allows time for the receiving station to finish receiving and checking the frame, and then transmit the ACK.

- **Distributed coordination function interframe space (DIFS)** — The DIFS is a standard time interval during which all clients must wait between transmissions of data frames. The DIFS allows certain timing functions to reach their completion and is used for contention access to the network.

The times of these space intervals are measured in microseconds, as indicated in Table 7-5.

Table 7-5   Interframe spaces

DSSS Interframe Space	Duration in Microseconds
SIFS	10
DIFS	50

The basic rules of communication in an 802.11 network are as follows (see Figure 7-19):

- A device that wants to transmit begins listening for an RF signal (carrier sensing), which indicates the presence of frame traffic on the network, during the DIFS. If no signal is detected at the end of the DIFS, the device can begin transmitting a data or management frame.

- The size of a frame includes both the length of time necessary to send the data plus an SIFS. When the transmission is over, the sending device begins listening for an acknowledgement (ACK) from the receiving device. The receiving device must send the ACK within the SIFS.

- After receiving an ACK, the transmitting client begins to wait a random backoff interval.

- If the transmitting device does not receive an ACK within the SIFS, it is allowed to maintain control of the medium and begin retransmitting the frame that was not acknowledged immediately after the SIFS comes in.

- If the frame was acknowledged correctly, the transmitting device listens to the medium while waiting its backoff interval. Once the interval ends, the device checks for traffic at the end of the next DIFS and the process repeats itself from the first point above.

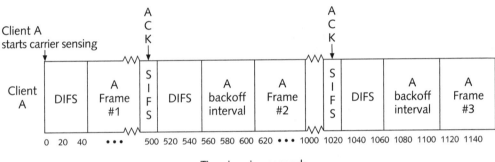

Figure 7-19   CSMA/CA with one client transmitting

In cases in which a device wants to transmit but detects traffic on the medium, the process works as follows (see Figure 7-20). Client A is using DSSS with a backoff interval of 3, while Client B has a backoff interval of only 2. Client A begins carrier sensing and, upon finding the medium free, transmits its first frame. Client B then begins carrier sensing while Client A's first frame is being sent. Because it detects traffic, Client B waits. Once Client A has received its ACK, both devices begin carrier sensing during the second DIFS. At the end of the second DIFS, Clients A and B begin their backoff interval. Because Client B's interval is only 2 (20 microseconds times 2), it will finish its backoff interval before Client A (20 microseconds times 3). Client B then begins transmitting its first packet.

Because each device continues to carrier sense at the end of each of its time slots, Client A detects that Client B is now transmitting. Client A remembers that it has already counted off two of its slot times. Client A must now wait until Client B's transmission and acknowledgement is complete and the next DIFS begins. After the DIFS, Client A and B both begin their backoff interval. However, this time Client A only has to wait one slot time. This is because Client A already waited for two of its time slots previously. If a device is bumped by

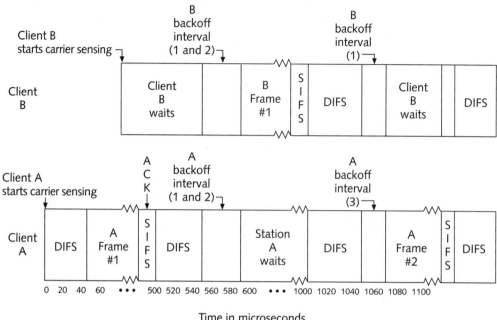

Figure 7-20   CSMA/CA with two clients transmitting

another device from transmitting, it only has to wait the remaining number of time slots and not start all over again. This increases the probability that those devices that are waiting will transmit sooner than a new device will. It also means that devices with a long backoff interval will get their chance to transmit and not have to remain waiting for long periods of time, even when collisions occur.

CHAPTER SUMMARY

- ❏ The wireless technology that attracts the most attention today is radio frequency (RF) wireless local area networks (WLANs). WLANs are unique in their ability to permit network access in a wide range of environments.

- ❏ A wireless NIC performs the same functions as a wired NIC. Instead of a port for a cable connection to the network, the wireless NIC uses an antenna to send and receive RF signals. Wireless NICs are usually a separate card that is inserted into one of the computer's expansion slots.

- ❏ An access point (AP) is a device that consists of three major parts: an antenna, a radio transmitter/receiver to send and receive signals, and an RJ-45 wired network interface that allows it to connect by cable to a standard wired network. It includes special bridging software. An AP acts as the base station for the wireless network and serves as a bridge between the wireless and wired networks.

□ Data can be sent and received in an RF WLAN either in ad hoc or infrastructure mode. In ad hoc (or peer-to-peer) mode, the wireless clients communicate directly between themselves without using an AP. Infrastructure mode, also known as the Basic Service Set (BSS), consists of wireless clients and an AP. If more users need to be added to the WLAN or the range of coverage needs to be increased, more APs can be added. This creates an Extended Service Set (ESS), which consists of two or more BSS wireless networks.

□ The IEEE 802.11 standard defines a local area network that provides cable-free data access for clients that are either mobile or in a fixed location at a rate up to 2 Mbps. The 802.11 standard also specifies that the features of a WLAN be transparent to the upper levels of the 802.11 standard. However, the slow bandwidth of only 2 Mbps for the 802.11 standard proved insufficient for most network applications.

□ The 802.11 standard uses an access method known as the distributed coordination function (DCF). The DCF specifies that a modified procedure known as carrier sense multiple access with collision avoidance (CSMA/CA) be used. CSMA/CA attempts to avoid collisions. Instead of making just the two clients responsible for the collision wait a random amount of time before attempting to resend after the collision, CSMA/CA has all clients wait a random number of time slots after the medium is clear. CSMA/CA also reduces collisions by using explicit packet acknowledgment (ACK). Although CSMA/CA dramatically reduces the potential for collisions, it does not eliminate them altogether. The 802.11 standard provides two options that may be used to reduce collisions. The first is known as Request to Send/Clear to Send (RTS/CTS) protocol. RTS/CTS reserves the medium for a single client to transmit. The second option to reduce collisions is fragmentation. Fragmentation involves dividing the data to be transmitted from one large frame into several smaller ones.

□ The 802.11 standard provides for an optional polling function known as point coordination function (PCF). With PCF, the AP serves as the polling device and queries each client to determine if the client needs to transmit. The MAC layer of the 802.11 standard provides the functionality for a client to join a WLAN and stay connected. This is known as association and reassociation. Association is the process of communicating with the other wireless clients or the AP in order to become accepted as part of the network. Association is accomplished by scanning. There are two types of scanning: passive scanning and active scanning. A client may drop the connection with one AP and reestablish the connection with another, which is known as reassociation.

□ Mobile WLAN devices often depend on batteries as their primary power source. To conserve battery power they can go into sleep mode after a period of time. Power management as defined by the 802.11 standard allows the mobile client to be off as much as possible to conserve battery life but still not miss out on data transmissions.

□ The 802.11 standard specifies three different types of MAC frame formats. The first are known as management frames that are used to set up the initial communications between a client and the AP. The second type, control frames, provide assistance in delivering the frames that contain the data. Data frames carry the information to be transmitted. The 802.11 standard also defines three different interframe spaces (IFS) or time gaps, which are standard spacing intervals between the transmissions of the data frames. Instead of being just dead space, these time gaps are used for special types of transmissions.

❑ In 1999, IEEE approved two new standards, 802.11b and 802.11a. The IEEE 802.11b standard added two higher speeds, 5.5 Mbps and 11 Mbps, to the original 802.11 standard. With the faster data rates, the 802.11b quickly became the standard for WLANs. The Physical Layer Convergence Procedure (PLCP) for 802.11b is based on direct sequence spread spectrum (DSSS). The PLCP must reformat the data received from the MAC layer (when transmitting) into a frame that the PMD sublayer can transmit. The frame is made up of three parts, which are the preamble, the header, and the data. The 802.11b standard uses the Industrial, Scientific, and Medical (ISM) band for its transmissions. The PMD can transmit the data at 11, 5.5, 2, or 1 Mbps.

KEY TERMS

4-pulse position modulation (4–PPM) — A modulation technique that translates two data bits into 4 light impulses.

16-pulse position modulation (16–PPM) — A modulation technique that translates four data bits into 16 light impulses.

802.11 standard — An IEEE standard released in 1990 that defines wireless local area networks at a rate of either 1 Mbps or 2 Mbps. All WLAN features are contained in the PHY and MAC layers.

802.11b standard — A 1999 addition to the IEEE 802.11 standard for WLANs that added two higher speeds, 5.5 Mbps and 11 Mbps. Also known as Wi-Fi.

active scanning — The process of sending frames to gather information.

ad hoc mode — A WLAN mode in which wireless clients communicate directly among themselves without using an AP.

associate request frame — A frame sent by a client to an AP that contains the client's capabilities and supported rates.

associate response frame — A frame returned to a client from the AP that contains a status code and client ID number.

Basic Service Set (BSS) — A WLAN mode that consists of wireless clients and one AP.

buffering — The process that the AP uses to temporarily store frames for clients that are in sleep mode.

channel access methods — The different ways of sharing resources in a network environment.

collision — The scrambling of data that occurs when two computers start sending messages at the same time in a shared frequency.

compact flash (CF) card — A small expansion card that is used with PDA devices.

Complementary Code Keying (CCK) — A table containing 64 8-bit code words used for transmitting at speeds above 2 Mbps. This table of codes is used instead of the process of adding a Barker code to the bit to be transmitted.

control frames — MAC frames that assist in delivering the frames that contain data.

data frames — MAC frames that carry the information to be transmitted to the destination clients.

disassociation frame — A frame sent by the new AP to the old AP to terminate the old AP's association with the client.

distributed coordination function (DCF) — The default access method for WLANs.

distributed coordination function interframe space (DIFS) — The standard interval between the transmission of data frames.

dynamic rate selection — A function of an AP that allows it to automatically select the highest transmission speed based on the strength and quality of the signal received from a client NIC.

Extended Service Set (ESS) — A WLAN mode that consists of wireless clients and multiple APs.

fragmentation — The division of data to be transmitted from one large frame into several smaller frames.

Independent Basic Service Set (IBSS) — A WLAN mode in which wireless clients communicate directly among themselves without using an AP.

infrastructure mode — A WLAN mode that consists of wireless clients and one AP.

interframe spaces (IFS) — Time gaps used for special types of transmissions.

management frames — MAC frames that are used to set up the initial communications between a client and the AP.

Mini PCI — A small card that is functionally equivalent to a standard PCI expansion card used for integrating communications peripherals onto a notebook computer.

null data frame — The response that a client sends back to the AP to indicate that the client has no transmissions to make.

packet acknowledgment (ACK) — A procedure for reducing collisions by requiring the receiving station to send an explicit packet back to the sending station.

passive scanning — The process of listening to each available channel for a set period of time.

peer-to-peer mode — A WLAN mode in which wireless clients communicate directly among themselves without using an AP.

point coordination function (PCF) — The 802.11 optional polling function.

polling — A channel access method in which each computer is asked in sequence whether it wants to transmit.

power management — An 802.11 standard that allows the mobile client to be off as much as possible to conserve battery life but still not miss out on data transmissions.

power over Ethernet (PoE) — A technology that provides power over an Ethernet cable.

probe — A frame sent by a client when performing active scanning.

probe response — A frame sent by an AP when responding to a client's active scanning probe.

reassociation — The process of a client dropping a connection with one AP and reestablishing the connection with another.

reassociation request frame — A frame sent from a client to a new AP asking whether it can associate with the AP.

reassociation response frame — A frame sent by an AP to a station indicating that it will accept its reassociation with that AP.

Request to Send/Clear to Send (RTS/CTS) — An 802.11 protocol option that allows a station to reserve the network for transmissions.

scanning — The process that a client uses to examine the airwaves for information that it needs in order to begin the association process.

secure digital (SD) card — A small expansion card that is used with PDA devices. SD cards are smaller than CF cards. See also compact flash (CF) cards.

Service Set Identifier (SSID) — A unique identifier assigned to an AP.

short interframe space (SIFS) — A time gap used for immediate response actions such as ACK.

sled — An external attachment for a PDA that permits external cards to attach to the device.

sleep mode — A power-conserving mode used by notebook computers.

subnets — A smaller unit of a network.

time slots — The measurement unit in a PLCP frame. The length of a time slot is predefined by the standard or specification for a particular system.

traffic indication map (TIM) — A list of the stations that have buffered frames waiting at the AP.

Wi-Fi — A trademark of the Wi-Fi Alliance, often used to refer to 802.11b WLANs that pass the organization's interoperability tests.

wireless residential gateway — A combination of several technologies that permit home users to have wireless capabilities and also allow Internet and printer sharing and provide better security than connecting a computer directly to the Internet.

Review Questions

1. A wireless NIC performs the same functions as a wired NIC except that
   _____ .

   a. it does not transmit the packet

   b. it uses an antenna instead of a wired connection

   c. it contains special memory

   d. it does not use parallel transmission

2. Wireless NICs are available in each of the following formats except
   _____ .

   a. PCI card

   b. PC Card Type I

   c. CF card

   d. Mini PCI

3. Some vendors have already integrated the components of a wireless NIC directly onto the notebook's _____ .

   a. motherboard

   b. floppy drive

   c. hard drive

   d. CD-ROM drive

4. Which of the following is not a function of an AP?

   a. Sends and receives signals

   b. Connects to the wired network

   c. Serves as a router

   d. Has special bridging software

5. The range of an AP acting as the base station is approximately _____ .

   a. 573 feet

   b. 375 feet

   c. 750 feet

   d. 735 feet

6. The highest data rate for an 802.11 diffused infrared WLAN is about _____ Mbps.

7. The IEEE 802.11 standards that outline the specifications for infrared WLANs are based on _____ transmissions.

8. Power over Ethernet delivers power to an AP through the unused wires in a standard unshielded twisted pair (UTP) Ethernet cable. True or False?

9. In ad hoc mode, the wireless clients communicate directly with the AP. True or False?

10. An Extended Service Set (ESS) is two or more BSS wireless networks. True or False?

11. On a regular basis, wireless clients will survey all the radio frequencies to determine if a different AP can provide better service. True or False?

12. Network managers like to subdivide networks into smaller units known as subnets because this makes it easier to manage the entire network. True or False?

13. The IEEE _____ standard defines a local area network that provides cable-free data access for clients that are either mobile or in a fixed location at a rate up to 2 Mbps.

14. Because all of the IEEE WLAN features are isolated in the PHY and _____ layers, any network operating system or LAN application will run on a WLAN without any modification necessary.

7

15. The Physical Layer Convergence Procedure standards (PLCP) for 802.11b are based on _____ spread spectrum (DSSS).

16. A PCLP frame is made up of three parts, which are the preamble, the header, and the _____ .

17. The PLCP frame preamble and header are always transmitted at 1 Mbps. What are the advantages and disadvantages of this?

18. Explain how carrier sense multiple access with collision avoidance (CSMA/CA) is different from carrier sense multiple access with collision detection (CSMA/CD).

19. Explain how packet acknowledgment works.

20. What is RTS/CTS? What are its advantages and how does it work?

21. What is polling? How does it differ from contention?

22. How can 4-PPM transmit at twice the speed of 16-PPM?

HANDS-ON PROJECTS

Project 7-1: Installing and Configuring a Wireless NIC

Although most notebook computers today already come equipped with a wireless NIC, there may be situations in which you need to install one in an older model notebook computer or install a second wireless NIC in a computer that already includes one. We will be using a Linksys WPC 54G, but note that this procedure is generic and keep in mind that manufacturers change setup software and instructions frequently. You should always follow the manufacturer's instructions to install the NIC. If the instructions provided here do not match the manufacturer's instructions for your adapter card, please follow the instructions that came with your NIC. If you do not have access to the documentation, use another network interface or another computer to access this information on the Internet by visiting the manufacturer's support or download page. All NIC manufacturers should allow you to download the user guide as well as the software from their sites. If you are installing a card on a desktop computer, please consult your instructor.

1. Ensure that you are using the latest version of Windows XP. If not, either install Service Pack 2 or higher or, if you are using Service Pack 1, search the Microsoft Web site at http://support.microsoft.com for the "wireless update rollup package," which updates the Windows client software to support the features available on some of the newer NICs.

2. Log in as administrator or to an account with administrator privileges. Windows will not allow you to complete any of the steps below unless you are the system administrator or your account has administrator privileges.

3. If your notebook computer already has a wireless NIC, you should disable it. If not, you may skip to step 5.

4. To disable your wireless NIC, click **Start** and then click **Control Panel**.

5. In Category View, click **Network and Internet Connection** and then click **Network Connections** to display all your network connections, as seen in Figure 7-21.

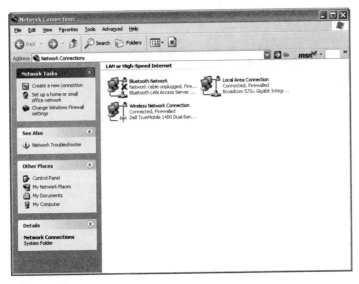

Figure 7-21   Windows Network Connections

6. Right-click **Wireless Network Connection**. You will see a pop-up context-based menu. Click **Disable**. Minimize this window.

7. Insert the CD containing the software for your wireless NIC. Once you see the Setup Wizard's Welcome Window, click **Install**.

8. At one point, the Setup Wizard will ask you to select **Infrastructure Mode** or **Ad Hoc Mode**. Select **Infrastructure Mode** and enter the SSID of the network. Follow these steps as instructed by the wizard. For the next project, you will use "WComm" as the SSID (note that the first two letters are in uppercase and the remaining three are in lowercase). Type the SSID in the text box provided and press **Next** to continue the Wizard.

9. If you follow the instructions carefully, you should be able to get the NIC installed and detecting wireless networks in the vicinity of your location.

Note that you can use the Windows Wireless Zero Configuration utility to connect to a wireless network. After installing your wireless NIC, an icon will appear in the Windows System Tray. A help bubble should quickly open if your computer has detected any wireless networks nearby. Clicking once on the bubble will take you to a screen similar to the one shown in Figure 7-22. From here you can select to which wireless network you want to be connected.

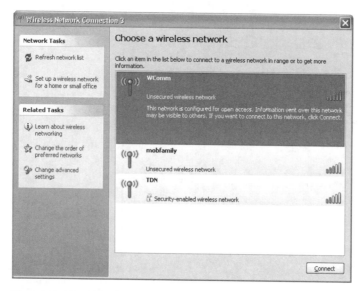

Figure 7-22 Windows Wireless Network Connection

Note also that there are usually two different ways to configure your wireless NIC to connect to a WLAN. One is using the Windows client software to configure the settings and the other is using the utility provided by your NIC manufacturer. The utility is installed by default and will execute automatically when you restart your PC. The two configuration modes are mutually exclusive and you must choose one or the other. In this book, you will be using the Windows configuration for most projects.

HANDS-ON
PROJECTS

Project 7-2: Installing and Configuring a Linksys AP or Broadband Router

In this project, you will manually install a Linksys WRT54G Broadband Router to create a WLAN. A broadband router includes an AP, a router and firewall, and a network switch. If you are installing only an AP or are installing a different manufacturer's device, the settings will be very similar, but you may have to adapt the instructions to your specific device.

1. Unpack the AP or broadband router.

2. Follow the instructions that came with the device to connect the antennas. Never install a wireless device without having the antenna connected first. The absence of a load at the output of the transmitter can damage the circuit. In addition, despite the very low power level of most WLAN devices, you are strongly advised never to touch the antennas when the device is turned on as this may represent a health risk.

3. Connect an RJ-45 Ethernet patch cable to one of the switch ports in the back of the device. Note that one port is separated from the others and is marked "WAN Port." If you are setting up a broadband router, make sure you do not connect the cable to the WAN port. Plug the other end of the cable to a wired Ethernet port on your notebook computer.

4. Plug in the power adapter and connect it to the back of your AP or broadband router.

5. Make sure that the Ethernet adapter on your computer is configured to obtain an IP address automatically. To do this, click **Start**, **Connect To**, then click **Show all connections**. When the Network Connections Window appears, right-click **Local Area Connection** and then click **Properties**. A dialog box like the one in Figure 7-23 will open. Under This connection uses the following items, scroll down if necessary and double-click **Internet Protocol (TCP/IP)**. Make sure the option button next to **Obtain an IP address automatically** is selected. Also select the option button next to **Obtain DNS server address automatically**. Click **OK**, then click **OK** again to close both dialog boxes.

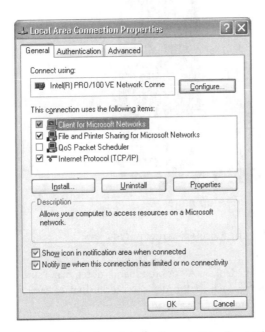

Figure 7-23   Local Area Connection Properties dialog box

6. Open a Web browser. In the address line, type **http://192.168.1.1** (in most current browser versions there is no need to type http:// first).

7. At the login prompt, leave the user name blank and type **admin** in the password field. The Linksys setup page will appear. For this project you will not use an Internet connection. You can leave all the fields in the main Setup page in their default settings. See Figure 7-24.

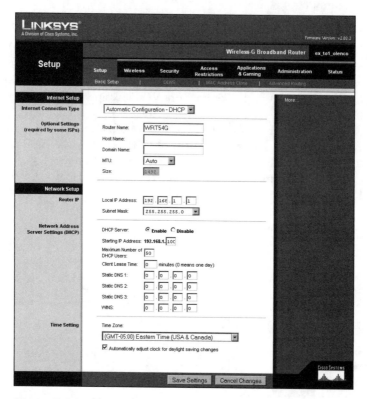

Figure 7-24 The Linksys WRT54G main setup page

8. Click the **Wireless** tab to display the wireless setup page.

If you are setting up more than one Linksys AP or broadband router, make sure you select a different channel for each of the devices. Recall that to avoid interference, you can only use channels 1, 5, and 11.

NOTE

9. Leave the mode as Mixed. Change the SSID to the one used in Step 8 in Project 7-1, **WComm**. Click **Save Settings**. A page should appear indicating that your settings are successful. Click **Continue** and you will be returned to the Wireless setup page. See Figure 7-25.

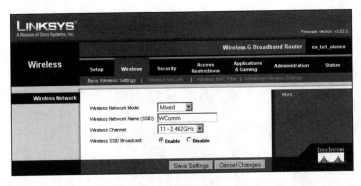

Figure 7-25 The Wireless setup page

10. On the notebook computer you set up in Project 7-1 (you may be using the same computer), right-click the **Wireless Network Connection icon** in the Windows System Tray and then click **View Available Wireless Networks**. A window will appear showing the wireless networks that your NIC is detecting, as shown in Figure 7-22.

NOTE If you see a warning stating that Windows cannot configure the wireless connection, you will need to do the following: 1. Click **Start**, click **Run**, type **%SystemRoot%\system32\services.msc /s**, and then click **OK**. 2. Double-click **Wireless Zero Configuration**. 3. In the Startup type list, click **Automatic**, and then click **Apply**. 4. In the Service status area, click **Start**, and then click **OK**.

11. In the right pane, click the **WComm network** to select it. Click the **Connect** button. Windows should display an information dialog box stating that you are connecting to an unsecured network. Click **Connect Anyway**. After a few seconds, Windows will redisplay the Wireless Network Connection window with a message telling you that Windows is acquiring a network address.

12. A few seconds later you should be connected to the Broadband Router. The word **Connected** followed by a star should appear at the top right-hand corner of the entry listing your WComm network.

Project 7-3: Testing the Wireless Connection

You will now test the connection by using a standard TCP/IP tool, Ping.

1. Open a Windows command prompt by clicking **Start**, **Run** and typing **cmd** in the text box of the Run dialog box.

2. Click **OK**.

3. A Windows command prompt window will appear. At the prompt, type **ping 192.168.1.1** and press **Enter**. Leave the command prompt window open.

7

4. If your connection is working, you should see a result almost exactly like that of Figure 7-26.

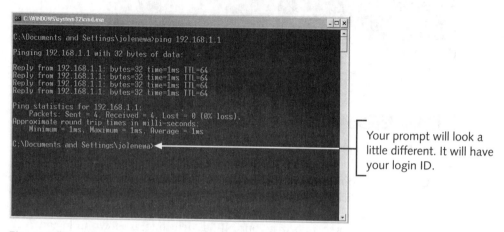

Your prompt will look a little different. It will have your login ID.

Figure 7-26   Pinging your AP or broadband router

5. If possible, set up a second notebook or desktop computer with a wireless connection to the same broadband router or AP. Follow the instructions in Project 7-1 again.

6. Once the second computer is connected to the Broadband Router or AP, again open a command prompt as outlined in Steps 1 through 3 above. At the prompt, type **ipconfig /all** and then press **Enter** (see Figure 7-27).

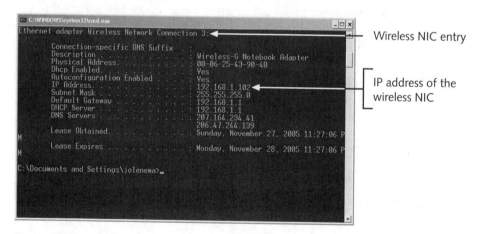

Wireless NIC entry

IP address of the wireless NIC

Figure 7-27   Finding the IP address automatically assigned to a computer

7. Locate the entry for your wireless NIC and then locate the line with the IP address below it. Record the IP address and return to the first computer where you set up a wireless connection.

8. At the command prompt, type **ping** followed by a space and the IP address of the second computer. Press **Enter**.

9. Assuming that both computers are connected, you should see a reply similar to the one shown in Step 4 above. If you do not see a reply, make sure you turn off the Windows Firewall on the second computer, and then try again.

CASE PROJECTS

CASE
PROJECTS

Project 7-1: Locating a Hotspot

A hotspot is a public place such as a train or bus station, coffee shop, or restaurant that offers (usually) free Internet access to its customers. Using the Internet, search for hotspots by accessing the Web sites for various nationwide cellular phone companies, such as Cingular or Sprint. Alternatively, you can search the local media Web sites and local Internet service provider (ISP) sites. If you have access to a notebook computer equipped with a wireless NIC, once you locate a hotspot, try to visit the site and get a connection to the Internet. If you do not have access to the Internet but you can either telephone the provider or visit the hotspot location, interview the staff at the location and write a one-page report describing how the wireless access is provided. What steps did you have to go through to get a connection? For how long was the connection available? Was there a cost associated with accessing the Internet? How many people use the service daily? Were there any limitations? Who provides technical support for the site?

CASE
PROJECTS

Project 7-2: Researching Unique WLAN Applications

Using the Internet, research wireless LAN applications. Compile a list of at least five applications that you had not imagined before for WLANs, and write a one-paragraph description below each one. The paragraph should mention the challenges that you might face if you were asked to provide support for each particular implementation. If possible, contact a user of the new application and ask him or her about their particular experiences with the WLAN implementation. Add this information to your report.

7

HIGH-SPEED WLANS AND WLAN SECURITY

After reading this chapter and completing the exercises, you will be able to:

♦ Describe how IEEE 802.11a networks function and how they differ from 802.11 networks

♦ Outline how 802.11g enhances 802.11b networks

♦ Discuss new and future standards and how they improve 802.11 networks

♦ Explain how the use of wireless bridges and wireless switches expands the functionality and management of WLANs

♦ List basic and expanded security features and issues of IEEE 802.11 networks

Higher data rates and lower prices have made WLANs competitive with wired networks. Large corporations are finally considering WLANs as an alternative to their wired networks.

WLANs have come a long way in a few short years, since the original IEEE 802.11 WLAN standard was established in 1997 and offered speeds of only 1 and 2 Mbps. Today's WLANs can operate at 54 Mbps, over 50 times the data transmission capacity of the original standard. New standards scheduled for publication within the next few years will double the data rates, and may achieve speeds of 2 Gbps and beyond.

In 1999, the IEEE approved the 802.11b standard that added two higher speeds, 5.5 Mbps and 11 Mbps, to the 802.11 standard. At that time, IEEE also issued the IEEE 802.11a standard with even higher speeds. **IEEE 802.11a**, also called Wi-Fi by the Wi-Fi Alliance, has a maximum rated standard speed of 54 Mbps and also supports 36, 24, 18, 12, 9, and 6 Mbps transmissions. 802.11a WLANs quickly became very attractive to users because the speed of transmission was a significant increase over 802.11b systems.

NOTE 802.11a, as well as the other standards discussed in this chapter, are enhancements to the original 802.11 standard. This means that an understanding of 802.11 and 802.11b is important to help you learn about the technologies discussed in this chapter.

IEEE 802.11A

This section introduces you to the 802.11a standard. Although the 802.11a and 802.11b specifications were published at the same time by the IEEE, 802.11b products started to appear almost immediately, while 802.11a products did not arrive until late 2001. 802.11a products came to the market later because of technical issues and the high cost of implementing them. As a result, devices based on the 802.11a use electronic components that cost more to design and produce.

The 802.11a standard maintains the same medium access control (MAC) layer functions as 802.11b WLANs. The differences are confined to the physical layer. 802.11a achieves its increase in speed and flexibility over 802.11b through a higher frequency band, more transmission channels, its multiplexing technique, and a more efficient error-correction scheme. These factors are detailed in the following sections.

U-NII Frequency Band

Recall that the 802.11b standard uses one part of the unlicensed Industrial, Scientific, and Medical (ISM) band for its transmissions and specifies 14 frequencies that can be used, beginning at 2.412 GHz and increasing by increments of .005 GHz. IEEE 802.11a uses another unlicensed band, the Unlicensed National Information Infrastructure (U-NII). The U-NII band is intended for devices that provide short-range, high-speed wireless digital communications. Table 8-1 compares ISM and U-NII.

Table 8-1   ISM vs. U-NII

Unlicensed Band	Frequency	WLAN Standard	Total Bandwidth
Industrial, Scientific, and Medical (ISM)	902–928 MHz 2.4–2.4835 GHz	N/A to WLANs 802.11b, 802.11g, 802.11n	26 MHz 83.5 MHz
Unlicensed National Information Infrastructure (U-NII)	5.15–5.25 GHz 5.25–5.35 GHz 5.47–5.725 GHz 5.725–5.825 GHz	802.11a 802.11a available to 802.11a 802.11a	100 MHz 100 MHz 255 MHz 100 MHz

The U.S. Federal Communications Commission (FCC) has segmented the total 555 MHz of the U-NII spectrum into four bands. Each band has a maximum power limit. These bands and their maximum power outputs are seen in Table 8-2.

Table 8-2   U-NII spectrum

U-NII Band	Frequency (GHz)	Maximum Power Output (mW)
U-NII Low Band	5.15-5.25	40
U-NII Middle Band	5.25-5.35	200
New unnamed band	5.47-5.725	200
U-NII High Band	5.725-5.825	800

NOTE   Although 802.11b wireless NICs can legally radiate as much as 1 watt in the ISM band, most only use 30 mW to help conserve battery life and minimize the level of heat generated.

NOTE   The U-NII High Band is only approved for outdoor use and is most often used for building-to-building wireless transmissions.

Outside the United States, however, the 5 GHz band is allocated to users and technologies other than WLANs, and the bands have different power limitations. For example, the High Band is available for WLAN use in the United States, but not in Europe or Japan, where it has already been reserved for outdoor applications (the 5.470-5.725 band is available in Europe for WLANs, but it has only been made available in the United States recently). In addition, the maximum power output for the Low Band is 200 mW in Europe and Japan but only 40 mW in the United States. This is not a problem for WLANs contained within a single country, but it is a problem for multinational companies and individuals who travel internationally and maintain different networks in different countries.

NOTE   Although other devices such as 2.4 GHz cordless phones, microwave ovens, and Bluetooth devices may cause interference problems with 802.11b networks in the 2.4 GHz ISM band, these devices do not interfere with 802.11a transmissions. This is because 802.11a operates in the 5 GHz frequency range and is not subject to interference from 2.4 GHz devices or networks. However, there is nothing prohibiting a cordless phone vendor from offering products that work in the same frequency as an 802.11a network.

802.11a devices can transmit at faster rates because of the higher frequencies and increased power levels at which they operate. And although it is segmented, the total bandwidth available for IEEE 802.11a WLANs using U-NII is almost four times that available for 802.11b networks using the ISM band. The ISM band offers only 83 MHz of spectrum in the 2.4 GHz range, while the U-NII band offers 300 MHz.

Channel Allocation

A second reason for the higher speed of an 802.11a WLAN is increased channel allocation. Recall that with 802.11b the available frequency spectrum (2.412 to 2.484 GHz) is divided into 11 channels in the United States. The center point of each channel (2.412, 2.417, 2.422, and so on) is where the transmission actually occurs. The standard requires a 25 MHz passband, so only three non-overlapping channels are available for simultaneous operation. This is illustrated in Figure 8-1.

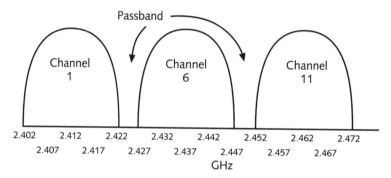

Approximate Frequency Domain representation of total bandwidth occupied by each 802.11 channel

Figure 8-1   802.11b channels

In 802.11a, however, eight frequency channels operate simultaneously in the Low Band (5.15 to 5.25 GHz) and Middle Band (5.25 to 5.35 GHz). Within each frequency channel there is a 20 MHz–wide channel that supports 52 carrier signals, with each signal 300 KHz wide. The center points for the eight channels are 5.18, 5.20, 5.22, 5.24, 5.26, 5.28, 5.30, and 5.32 GHz. This is illustrated in Figure 8-2.

NOTE   The 802.11a channel numbers are the result of a mathematical formula. For more information, see paragraph 17.3.8.3.2 in the IEEE 802.11a standard at http://standards.ieee.org/getieee802/download/802.11a-1999.pdf.

With an 802.11b WLAN, each access point (AP) can only use one of the three available channels. If more network bandwidth is required, a maximum of three APs can be installed in the same area and the number of users can be distributed among the three. However, even at 11 Mbps, this strategy only provides a maximum of 33 Mbps of bandwidth.

With an 802.11a WLAN, each AP can use one of eight available channels. Because there are eight available channels, additional APs can be added, providing up to 432 Mbps of aggregated bandwidth (8 × 54 Mbps) for wireless users in a single area; 802.11b can only provide 33 Mbps. This comparison is illustrated in Figure 8-3.

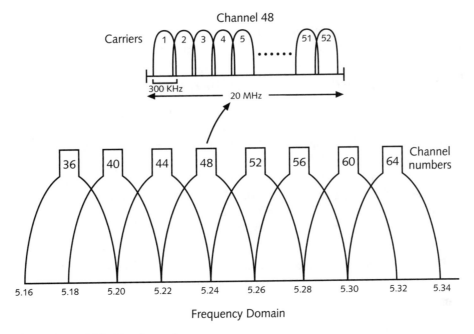

Figure 8-2   802.11a channels

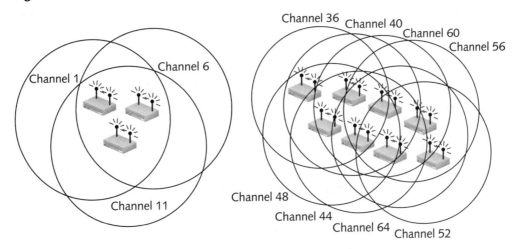

Figure 8-3   802.11b vs. 802.11a channels

There are additional advantages of having more channels. When multiple APs are used, more users can be supported by assigning specific channels to users associated with specific APs. Also, if a neighbor is using an 802.11a WLAN within range of the network, it can cause interference and bandwidth contention. With more channels available, you can set the AP to use a specific channel and eliminate the interference. New technologies such as wireless switches, discussed later, can offer load-balancing methods to automatically distribute clients across multiple channels, so one channel doesn't get overcrowded when others are available.

Orthogonal Frequency Division Multiplexing

Recall from Chapter 3 that with multipath distortion, the receiving device gets the signal from several different directions at different times. Even though the receiving device may have already received the complete transmission, it must still wait until all reflections are received. If the receiver does not wait until all reflections are received, then some of the signals that arrive later may spread into the next transmission, because the reflected signals traveled a longer path and were delayed. Increasing the speed of the WLAN only causes longer delays in waiting for reflections. The required waiting time effectively puts a limit on the overall speed of the WLAN. With current technology, this maximum is between 10 and 20 Mbps.

NOTE

A baseband processor, or equalizer, is required in 802.11b systems to unravel the delayed radio frequency signals as they are received.

The 802.11a standard solves this problem using a multiplexing technique called Orthogonal Frequency Division Multiplexing (OFDM). Its primary function is to split a high-speed digital signal into several slower signals running in parallel.

NOTE

OFDM is also the technology used for consumer-based Digital Subscriber Line (DSL) service, which provides home Internet access over standard telephone lines at speeds of 1 Mbps and above.

NOTE

You learned about multiband OFDM in Chapter 6. In MB-OFDM, a much wider frequency band is divided into multiple narrower bands that meet the 500 MHz minimum FCC requirement. Then OFDM is applied to the signals.

Instead of sending one long stream of data across a single channel, OFDM sends the transmission in parallel across several lower-speed channels. The sending device breaks the transmission down into pieces and then sends it over the channels in parallel. The receiving device combines the signals received from the individual channels to re-create the transmission. By using parallel transmission channels, OFDM can combine several lower-speed channels to send data at a higher speed. This is illustrated in Figure 8-4.

Although it may seem contradictory, OFDM breaks the 802.11b ceiling limit by sending the data at a slower bit rate than that of 802.11b. OFDM avoids problems caused by multipath distortion by sending the message slowly enough that any delayed copies (multipath

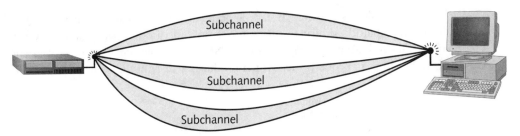

Figure 8-4 Transmitting on multiple subchannels simultaneously

reflections) are late by a much smaller amount of time than those sent in 802.11b transmissions. This means that the network does not have to wait long for the reflections. Because the transmissions are sent in parallel, the total throughput is actually increased. That is, in a given unit of time, the total amount of data sent in parallel is greater and the time spent waiting for reflections to arrive is less with OFDM than with a single channel transmission. This amounts to a higher throughput and a faster WLAN. A comparison between the two systems is shown in Figure 8-5.

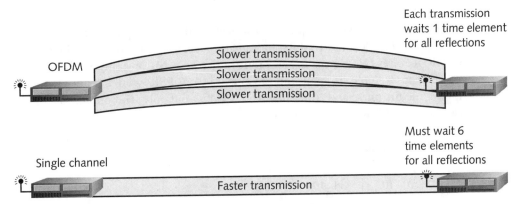

Figure 8-5 A comparison of OFDM and single channel transmission

In 802.11a, OFDM uses 48 of the 52 subchannels for data. The 48 data subchannels are also called subcarriers, since they are modulated to carry data. The remaining four subchannels are used for monitoring and correcting signal and timing errors during transmission.

The modulation techniques used to encode the data vary depending on the speed. At 6 Mbps, phase shift keying (PSK) is used (see Chapter 2). The change in the starting point of the cycle varies depending on whether a 0 or a 1 bit is being transmitted. PSK can encode 125 Kbps of data per each of the 48 subchannels, resulting in a 6,000 Kbps (125 Kbps x 48), or 6 Mbps, data rate. You may wish to review the waveform in Figure 2-29 in Chapter 2.

Whereas PSK only has a change in starting point, quadrature phase shift keying (QPSK) also has a change in amplitude, similar to quadrature amplitude modulation (again, see Chapter 2 for a review). This is illustrated in Figure 8-6. QPSK can double the amount of data encoded over PSK to 250 Kbps per subchannel, which produces a 12 Mbps (250 Kbps × 48) data rate.

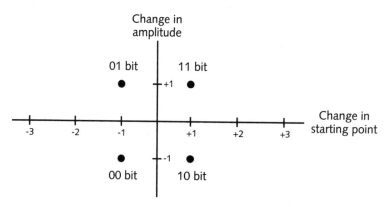

Figure 8-6   Quadrature amplitude modulation

Transmitting at 24 Mbps requires a 16-level quadrature amplitude modulation (16-QAM) technique. 16-QAM has 16 different signals that can be sent, as seen in Figure 8-7. Whereas QPSK requires two signals to send four bits, 16-QAM can transmit the same in only one signal. For example, to transmit the bits 1110, QPSK would send 11 and then 10 by modifying the phase and amplitude. 16-QAM would only send one signal (1110). 16-QAM can encode 500 Kbps per subchannel.

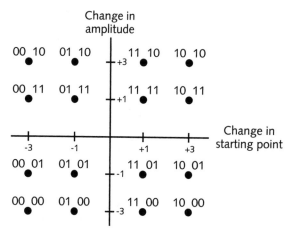

Figure 8-7   16-level quadrature amplitude modulation (16-QAM)

Data rates of 54 Mbps are achieved by using 64-level quadrature amplitude modulation (64-QAM). 64-QAM, illustrated in Figure 8-8, can transmit 1.125 Mbps over each of the 48 subcarriers.

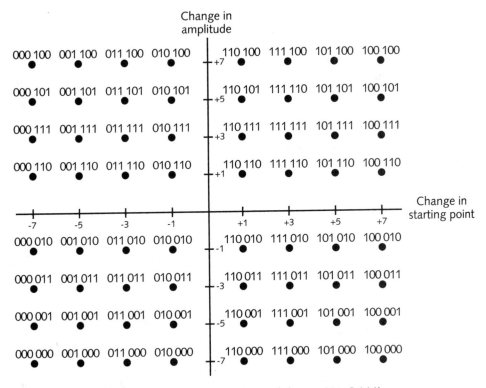

Figure 8-8 64-level quadrature amplitude modulation (64-QAM)

Although 54 Mbps is the official top speed of 802.11a, a few vendors have implemented higher speeds, known as turbo mode or 2X mode. 2X mode can be developed by each vendor and is not specified in the IEEE standard. Developers cannot further increase the complexity of the modulation on the subcarriers beyond the maximum 54 Mbps rate because of the amount of noise allowed. Instead, vendors can do such things as combine two frequency channels, resulting in 96 subchannels for speeds up to 108 Mbps. Other 2X mode techniques include increasing and reallocating the individual channels and using different coding rate schemes.

It is important to remember that 2X modes are proprietary. One vendor's AP running at 2X mode might not support a wireless NIC from another vendor.

NOTE

Error Correction in 802.11a

IEEE 802.11a also handles errors differently than 802.11b. The number of errors is significantly reduced due to the nature of 802.11a transmissions. Because transmissions are sent over parallel subcarriers, radio interference from outside sources is minimized. Instead of the interference impacting the entire data stream, it generally affects only one subchannel. Error correction in 802.11a is also enhanced. Forward Error Correction (FEC) transmits a secondary copy along with the primary information. If part of the primary transmission is lost, the secondary copy can be used to recover (through sophisticated algorithms) the lost data. This eliminates the need to retransmit if an error occurs, which saves time.

NOTE

Because of its high speed, 802.11a can accommodate the FEC overhead with a negligible impact on performance.

802.11a PHY Layer

The 802.11a standard made changes only to the physical layer (PHY layer) of the original 802.11 and 802.11b standards; the MAC layer remains the same. Recall that the basic purpose of the IEEE PHY layer is to send the signal to and receive the signal from the network.

The 802.11a PHY layer is divided into two parts. The Physical Medium Dependent (PMD) sublayer makes up the standards for the characteristics of the wireless medium (such as OFDM) and defines the method for transmitting and receiving data through that medium. The Physical Layer Convergence Procedure (PLCP) reformats the data received from the MAC layer (when transmitting) into a frame that the PMD sublayer can transmit and listens to the medium to determine when the data can be sent.

The PLCP for 802.11a is based on OFDM instead of direct sequence spread spectrum (DSSS). An example of a PLCP frame is illustrated in Figure 8-9.

The frame is made up of three parts: the preamble, the header, and the data. The preamble allows the receiving device to prepare for the rest of the frame. The header provides information about the frame itself. The data portion of the PLCP frame is the information that is to be actually transmitted. The fields in the PLCP frame are:

- Synchronization — Consists of 10 repetitions of a short training sequence signal and two repetitions of a long training sequence signal. The purpose of these signals is to establish timing and frequency with the receiver. The Synchronization field is transmitted in 16 microseconds.

- Rate — 4 bits long and specifies at which speed the Data field will be transmitted.

- Reserved — Kept available by the standard for future use.

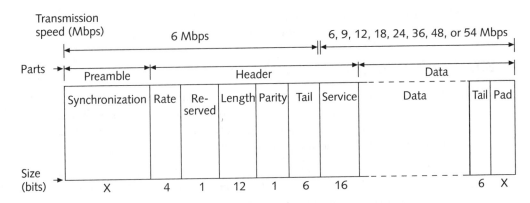

Figure 8-9 802.11a PLCP frame

- Length — Contains the value that indicates the length of the Data field, from 1 to 4095.

- Parity — Used for error checking.

- Tail (Header) — Indicates the end of the Header. All six bits are set to 0.

- Service — Synchronizes again with the receiver. The first seven bits are set to zero while the remaining nine bits are reserved for future use and are also set to 0. It is part of the Header, but is transmitted at the same rate as the Data field.

- Data — The actual data to be transmitted is contained in this field. The length of the Data field is from 1 to 4095 bits.

- Tail (Data) — Indicates the end of the data field. All six bits are set to 0.

- Pad — The IEEE standard specifies that the number of bits in the Data field must be a multiple of 48, 96, 192, or 288. If necessary, the length of the Data field may need to be *padded* with extra bits, which are found in this field.

802.11a WLANs are being deployed in areas that demand higher transmission speeds. The disadvantage of 802.11a networks is that they have a shorter range of coverage. An 802.11a WLAN has a range of approximately 225 feet, compared to 375 feet for an 802.11b WLAN. Of course, this depends upon a number of factors such as walls and other obstacles that can affect the RF transmission.

IEEE 802.11G

The tremendous success of the IEEE 802.11b standard shortly after its release prompted the IEEE to re-examine the 802.11b and 802.11a standards to determine if a third intermediate standard could be developed. This best of both worlds approach preserves the stable and widely accepted features of 802.11b but increases the data transfer rates to those similar to 802.11a. The **IEEE 802.11g** standard specifies that it operates in the same frequency band as 802.11b and not the higher frequency band used by 802.11a. The IEEE 802.11g standard, developed to meet these requirements, was published in June 2003.

802.11g PHY Layer

The PHY layer for 802.11g simply follows the same specifications for 802.11b with the changes outlined below for data rates between 1 and 11 Mbps. As with 802.11a, no changes were required to the MAC layer of the 802.11g standard. The standard outlines two mandatory transmission modes along with two optional modes.

The first mandatory transmission mode is the same mode used by 802.11b and must support the rates of 1, 2, 5.5, and 11 Mbps. The second mandatory mode uses the same OFDM mode used by 802.11a but in the same frequency band used by 802.11b. It uses the same 52 subcarriers (48 data subcarriers and 4 pilot subcarriers) to provide rates of 6, 9, 12, 18, 24, 36, 48, and 54 Mbps.

 NOTE   To be fully compliant with the 802.11g standard, a device must be able to transmit only at 1, 2, 5.5, 11, 6, 12, and 24 Mbps. 54 Mbps is not required by the standard.

However, the number of channels available with 802.11g is three, compared with eight channels for 802.11a. There are two optional transmission modes:

- The first uses PBCC (Packet Binary Convolutional Coding) and can transmit at 22 or 33 Mbps.

- The second optional mode is a combination known as DSSS-OFDM, which uses the standard DSSS preamble of 802.11b and transmits the data portion of the frame using OFDM.

One of these two optional modes is required to maintain backward compatibility with 802.11b. However, they are not required by the 802.11g standard. In other words, if an AP or a client can only work in 802.11g, then these optional modes are not required. In any situation combining 802.11b and 802.11g devices on the same network, one of the two optional transmission modes (PBCC or DSSS-OFDM) is usually incorporated into the AP.

There are two other important differences between 802.11g and the 802.11a and 802.11b standards related to signal timing. First, 802.11g specifies that any time a device is transmitting at a higher rate than 802.11b, a 6-microsecond quiet time of no transmission is included at the end of the data portion of every frame, to allow additional processing time for the receiver to decode the data. This requirement accommodates both 802.11b-only devices and devices that can transmit at higher data rates. Recall that this additional time is not required in 802.11a because the 802.11a hardware is built with faster technology and more expensive integrated circuit components. 802.11a also does not have to maintain backward compatibility with any other transmission method.

The other difference has to do with short interframe space (SIFS) timing. In Chapter 7, you learned that 802.11b time slots are 20 microseconds and the SIFS time is 10 microseconds. 802.11g maintains the same time slot; however, the SIFS time is affected by the addition of the quiet time. Therefore, when data is being transmitted at rates above 11 Mbps, the SIFS cannot begin until the quiet time is completed, effectively extending the SIFS to 16 microseconds. This change in the SIFS affects the performance of 802.11g, meaning that while it can also transmit at 54 Mbps, the overall performance is lower than that of 802.11a. Note that when the network is only supporting 802.11g devices, the standard allows the slot time to be optionally reduced to 9 microseconds, instead of 20 microseconds, which removes the performance difference between the 802.11a and 802.11g standards. Figure 8-10 shows the format of an 802.11g PLCP frame.

8

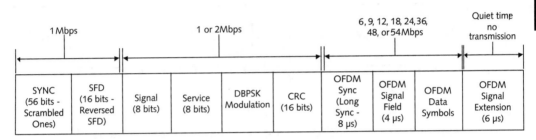

Figure 8-10   802.11g PLCP frame

The PLCP frame formats used in 802.11g are the same as for 802.11b. For transmission at 54 Mbps, the PHY layer follows the same general specifications for 802.11a. Note, however, that when both 802.11b and 802.11g devices share the same network, the standard defines how the frame header is transmitted at 1 or 2 Mbps using DSSS, for compatibility with 802.11b devices. If the device communicating is 802.11g-capable, the transmission changes to OFDM for the data portion of the frame. This is shown in Figure 8-11.

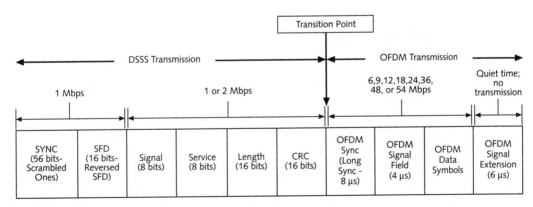

Figure 8-11   802.11g Single carrier to multi-carrier transition

The optional 22 Mbps rate is achieved by using the PBCC encoding method. PBCC uses a 256 state code (the spreading code) to send 8 bits per transmission symbol. To achieve the data rate of 33 Mbps using PBCC, the PHY layer specifications in the 802.11g standard define a change in the clock rate used to transmit the chips, from 11 MHz to 16.5 MHz. The preamble is transmitted with an 11 MHz clock (at 1 or 2 Mbps), and the change is accomplished in a 1 microsecond-long clock switch section of the PLCP frame, as illustrated in Figure 8-12.

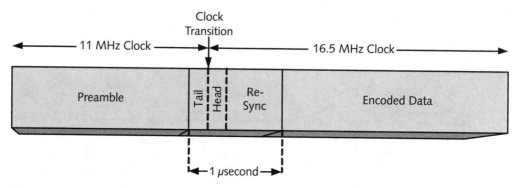

Figure 8-12   Clock switching during transition from 22 Mbps to 33 Mbps

The tail is 3 clock cycles at 11 Mchip/s, and the head is 3 clock cycles at 16.5 Msymbol/s (QPSK). The resync is 9 clock cycles at 16.5 Msymbol/s. The total clock switching time (tail, head, and resync) is 1 ms. The tail bits are equal to 1 1 1, the head bits are 0 0 0, and the resync bits are 1 0 0 0 1 1 1 0 1. The modulation is binary phase shift keying (BPSK), which is essentially the same modulation as PSK, which you learned about in Chapter 2. Only two phase changes are used to represent either a 1 or a 0. The phase is synchronized with the phase of the previous signal received.

OTHER WLAN STANDARDS

The future of WLANs will include some additional standards that are currently under development by the IEEE and some that are so new that they are just beginning to appear in new equipment.

IEEE 802.11e

The **IEEE 802.11e** standard was approved for publication in November 2005. It defines enhancements to the MAC layer of 802.11 to expand support for LAN applications that require Quality of Service (QoS) and provides for improvements in the capabilities and efficiency of the protocol. When combined with other recent enhancements (802.11g) to the 802.11a and 802.11b PHY layers, it promises to increase overall system performance and expand the application space for 802.11.

Unlike 802.11a and 802.11g standards, which require that each frame be acknowledged before a transmission can continue, 802.11e allows the receiving device to acknowledge after receiving a burst of frames, instead of acknowledging each frame. Figure 8-13 shows a logical diagram of the message exchange.

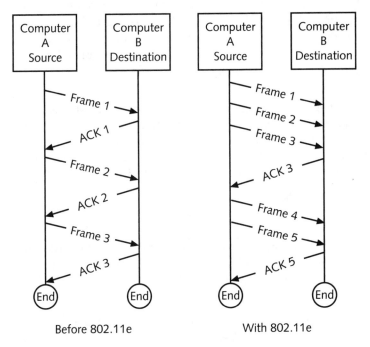

Before 802.11e   With 802.11e

Figure 8-13   802.11e frame acknowledgements

802.11e will enable prioritization of frames in distributed coordinated function (DCF) mode, taking advantage of the higher data rates of 802.11a and 802.11g. In addition to delayed or burst acknowledgements, 802.11e implements two new coordination functions: enhanced DCF (EDCF) and hybrid coordination function (HCF).

All APs that comply with the standard must implement both modes, although they may provide the users or network administrator with different levels of control over how these are configured. In addition, both modes include a traffic class (TC) definition. E-mails, for example, would be assigned a low priority TC, whereas voice communications would be assigned a higher priority TC. In EDCF, a station with higher priority traffic waits less to transmit, and therefore has a better chance of getting its traffic through.

HCF is a combination of DCF and point coordination function (PCF). The interval between beacon frames is divided into a contention-free period and a contention period. During the contention-free period, the hybrid coordinator (the AP) controls access to the medium and, based on information about the traffic received from a client, will allocate more time slots to the station with high-priority traffic. During the contention period, all stations work in EDCF mode.

This prioritization aspect is an important development of the 802.11 standards family. When implemented, it should enable voice, audio, and video to be transmitted reliably over WLANs, and allow a single home or business wireless network to handle all communications requirements. It should also enable streaming video and video conferencing, all with enhanced security for both mobile and nomadic applications. A **nomadic user** is one that moves frequently but does not use the equipment while in motion.

NOTE In addition to the Wi-Fi certification program, in which the Wi-Fi alliance ensures equipment compliance with the standards and interoperability, the Wi-Fi Alliance has also published a specification and certification program for wireless multimedia (WMM), which is a subset of the IEEE 802.11e standard. This specification is designed to compete with 802.15.3, which is covered in Chapter 6.

IEEE 802.11n

802.11n is a proposed standard aimed at providing data rates higher than 100 Mbps using the 2.4 GHz ISM band. It will likely continue to employ OFDM or a variation of this as a transmission technique. 802.11n is fully backward compatible with 802.11, 802.11b, and 802.11g.

Some manufacturers have already started to ship 802.11n products in anticipation of the standard's ratification. The proposed system bonds two 802.11 2.4 GHz ISM channels together and uses OFDM to send two data streams at 54 Mbps, yielding a maximum speed of 108 Mbps. It also implements **multiple-in, multiple-out (MIMO)** technology, which uses multiple antennas (usually three or four) and also uses the reflected signals (multipath) to extend the range of the WLAN by attempting to correctly decode a frame from multiple copies of it received at different times (multipath reflections).

NOTE The maximum theoretical data rate for 802.11 is 540 Mbps. However, transmitting at this speed would require much higher raw data rates at the PHY layer. This may be possible in the future, through the use of even more sophisticated coding schemes and faster electronic components.

One of the limitations of 802.11n is the fact that it uses more than one 2.4 GHz ISM channel. Depending on how many WLANs are installed in close proximity to one another, interference between them may mean that the actual data rate may not reach as high as 108 Mbps, or installation may be altogether impractical. For example, if two companies have offices next door to each other, and they both install 802.11n-compatible equipment, one of the three available ISM 2.4 GHz channels will suffer from severe interference. As a result, the two 802.11n systems will revert to 802.11g, on different channels and at a maximum of 54 Mbps.

IEEE 802.11r

The amount of time required by 802.11 devices to associate with one access point and disassociate with the other is in the order of hundreds of milliseconds. For 802.11 devices to be able to support cordless phones in the extended service set (ESS) of a large company, this time cannot exceed 50 milliseconds, which is the amount of time that can be detected by human ears. To support **voice over wireless LAN (VoWLAN)** in a business environment with multiple access points, the 802.11 standard needs a way to provide quicker handoffs. A **handoff** in a WLAN happens when a computer or a handset connects with a new access point and disconnects from the previous one. Another issue is that the current 802.11 MAC protocol does not allow a device to find out if the necessary QoS resources, such as the required number of time slots, are available at a new AP, until after the transition from one to the other is completed.

802.11r is designed to resolve these issues, in addition to security concerns regarding the handoff. It does so by refining the MAC protocol and providing a way for the client to communicate with other APs and establish all the necessary parameters while still connected to the original AP. Maintaining the original connection minimizes the impact on the data stream since the client device is not attempting to communicate with more than one AP on different channels. It also allows for secure associations to be set up prior to the handoff.

802.1r is expected to enhance the convergence of wireless voice, data, and video by improving functionality and performance and increasing the security of WLANs.

IEEE 802.11s

Imagine that you need to deploy a wireless network over the entire downtown area of a medium-sized city and provide seamless connectivity to all city employees for events and functions. Although this is possible, connecting each of the APs to the wired network would be a monumentally expensive undertaking. Installing network cabling outdoors is not an option, so the only way to address this would be to lease communications lines from the local telephone utility. Not only would this make the cost prohibitively high, but achieving high data rates may also be difficult, depending on the technology available.

The ideal solution would be to connect the wireless APs to each other over the wireless communications channels, passing data frames from one to the other until the frames reach a single wired network connection point. However, as you recall from the previous sections the 802.11 protocols do not currently provide a way for APs to communicate with each other, much less to forward wireless frame traffic, except over the wired interface.

802.11s will provide the solution when it is ratified by the IEEE, which is expected to happen in 2008. Figure 8-14 shows a wireless mesh network. In this figure, AP 5 provides the single connection to the Internet to keep the landline connection costs low. The notebook associated with AP3 and the PDA connected to AP7 would be able to access the wired network or the Internet because the APs can communicate with each other over the wireless interface and route the frames through AP5.

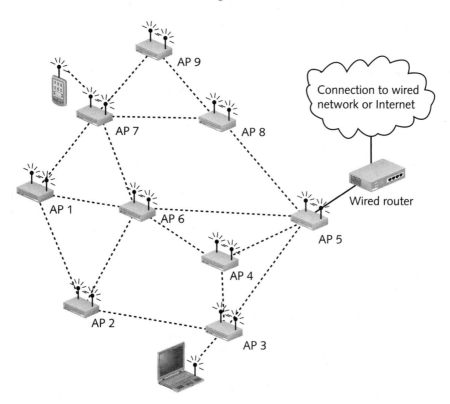

Figure 8-14   Wireless access points connected in a mesh network

NOTE   The proposals for the 802.11s standard have spawned a new organization called the Wi-Mesh Alliance. For more information, visit www.wi-mesh.org.

HiperLAN/2

HiperLAN/2 is a high-speed WLAN technology that is similar to the IEEE 802.11a standard. HiperLAN/2 was standardized in 2000 by the ETSI, the European Telecommunications Standards Institute. HiperLAN/2 and 802.11a share many characteristics, although the two standards remain very different in their implementation. In spite of having distinct advantages over 802.11a, and in spite of continued development by the ETSI, most manufacturers have ignored this standard, so far.

8

Whereas IEEE 802.11 networks can connect only to wired Ethernet networks, HiperLAN/2 offers high-speed wireless connectivity with up to 54 Mbps and seamless connectivity with other types of communications systems, such as cellular telephone systems and FireWire networks.

EXPANDING WLAN FUNCTIONALITY

Thus far, this book has focused on two primary WLAN hardware components: access points and network interface cards. In this section, you will learn about devices that expand the functionality of WLANs and improve the ability of IT managers to manage and support WLANs in large companies.

As you know, the signal range of a WLAN is limited to a few hundred feet. An optional component of a WLAN, **wireless bridges** are designed to connect two wired networks or to extend the range of a WLAN.

Wireless Bridges and Repeaters

Wireless bridges are the ideal solution for connecting sites such as satellite offices, remote campus settings, or temporary office locations when the sites are separated by obstacles such as bodies of water, freeways, or railroads that make using a wired connection impractical or very expensive. For 802.11b-based bridges, the distance between buildings can be up to 18 miles (29 kilometers) transmitting at 11 Mbps, or up to 25 miles (40 kilometers) when transmitting at 2 Mbps. 802.11a wireless bridges can connect at 54 Mbps at distances of up to 8.5 miles (13.5 kilometers) in point-to-point or 28 Mbps at up to 20 miles (30 kilometers). 802.11a wireless bridges operate in the U-NII High band, between 5.725 and 5.825 GHz, which is only approved for outdoor use.

NOTE

At 11 Mbps, remote wireless bridges are seven times faster than high-speed digital communications lines available from telephone carriers.

When used to connect two buildings, wireless bridges are used in a point-to-point configuration, as illustrated in Figure 8-15.

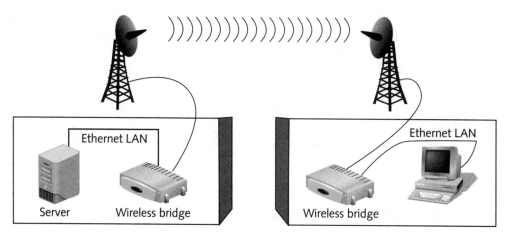

Figure 8-15 Wireless bridging of two LANs

For long-distance links, in which the signal may take longer to arrive at the receiver, transmitting wireless bridges can extend the SIFS time, thereby allowing the receiver enough time to acknowledge a frame (recall that the ACK is always sent during the SIFS).

NOTE

Extending the SIFS means that wireless bridges operate without fully conforming to the 802.11 standards. This is only possible in a point-to-point configuration.

WLAN Extension Using Wireless Bridges or Repeaters

Wireless bridges can also extend the range of a WLAN by allowing the wireless bridge to connect to an AP as a repeater in point-to-multipoint mode. Client devices that are out of the range of the access point can associate with the bridge, which will receive and acknowledge each frame sent by the AP or by the client, store the frame for a short period of time, then forward the frame by communicating with either the AP or client, depending on the direction of the transmission.

TIP

Some manufacturers' APs can also be connected as a repeater or as a bridge. Before purchasing an access point for this purpose, you should carefully check the user manual to make sure that it will meet your requirements.

One thing that a network designer must keep in mind is the amount of extra delay introduced in WLAN extension applications. Because the wireless bridge must receive each frame correctly, acknowledge it, then wait the appropriate number of back-off time slots for its next turn to communicate, certain kinds of applications running on the client may not be able to tolerate the resulting additional transmission delay.

Wireless Switching

8

When a large number of APs are deployed throughout a building or campus, managing these devices remotely can become very difficult. Most configuration settings can be distributed and administered remotely, but physical problems such as antenna and network connections, antenna placement and orientation, and hardware failures demand that a technician be sent to the location—an expensive way to provide support.

In addition, the fact that APs may have to be installed in different subnets can also present challenges. Complex configurations using multiple expensive network devices and software must be implemented and managed to allow users to roam beyond their local subnets and maintain a seamless connection to the network. The number and variety of networking devices that must be managed rapidly adds up. Furthermore, the more features an AP has, the more complex it can be to configure and maintain.

A few manufacturers have come up with a clever solution to this dilemma. By moving most of the features and functions of an AP into a single device and deploying less expensive, multiple *dumb radios* for handling the wireless communications, the management of wireless network devices is effectively centralized. This approach is called **wireless switching**. Wireless switching devices can help, for example, prevent the failure of a single AP from crippling wireless access in an entire area by automatically increasing the transmit power in one of the dumb radios to compensate for another radio failure.

Quality of Service (QoS) features incorporated into the wireless switches can make it easier to deploy voice over wireless LAN (VoWLAN), which allows users to make telephone calls while roaming across several subnets of a large network, using the same WLAN connection as their computers. Wireless switches can greatly simplify the deployment of large wireless networks and incorporate many additional features that also assist in maintaining and securing the WLAN.

NOTE

For more information on wireless switches, see www.arubanetworks.com, www.cisco.com (search for airespace), www.trapezenetworks.com, and www.3com.com.

Other WLAN Expansion Hardware

The explosive growth in the WLAN market has spawned an entirely new range of devices for the wireless home and office. Some of these are:

- Wireless presentation gateway — Devices that facilitate business presentations by allowing one or more computers to connect wirelessly to any display projector. Most presentation gateways do not require an existing wireless network and can connect a computer with a wireless NIC directly with the projector.

- Wireless media gateway — A variety of devices that allow you to use an existing wireless or wired network to stream music and video files from your computer or from the Internet directly to your TV or stereo system. They also support the display of digital still pictures to the TV set from a computer.

- Wireless VoIP gateway — Devices that are typically configured and secured by Internet phone service providers, who then sell or provide them to their customers as part of the service (these gateways are rarely sold directly to consumers). Most allow a regular cordless phone to be connected directly to a telephone port on the device, but an 802.11 wireless handset can sometimes be used instead (see Chapter 12 for VoWLAN).

- Wireless gaming adapter — Devices designed for multiplayer, network-based computer games. They are compatible with existing wireless residential gateways but can also be used standalone to connect two or more computers equipped with wireless NICs.

WLAN SECURITY

No discussion of WLANs is complete without looking at the topic of security. Broadcasting network traffic over the airwaves has created an entirely new set of issues for keeping data transmissions secure. These issues have been underscored by studies that reveal that some of the security provisions in the original IEEE 802.11 are flawed. This section examines the various types of network attacks, the basic security in WLANs (802.11b, 802.11a, and 802.11g), and additional measures to improve WLAN security.

Before you learn about the techniques and enhancements, it is important to keep in mind that these security measures apply equally to wireless networks, regardless of the standard they use. Because the standards define how data is transmitted at the PHY layer, the security implementations are analogous to those in an Ethernet network. However, because the transmissions occur over a free-space medium, a wireless network is far more exposed to intrusion, jamming, and hijacking of the information.

No security setup can prevent 100% of potential breaches. Security must always be viewed as a work in progress. Network administrators must check systems and logs regularly to ensure that the security features have not been compromised. For example, a user who travels often with a laptop computer may have temporarily reconfigured his system to solve an immediate problem. This change could expose the corporate or the wireless network, unless this computer's original configuration is restored and tech support applies a more permanent solution to the user's problem.

Attacks Against WLANs

A variety of attacks can be generated against WLANs. Some of the more dangerous include hardware theft, AP impersonation, passive monitoring, and denial of service (DoS) attacks.

Hardware theft is a threat to a wireless network because a wireless device may contain information that can assist someone in breaking into the network. For example, if the Service Set Identifier (SSID) or security key and passwords can be recovered from a device, they can be used to attempt to gain access to the network.

A drawback of IEEE WLANs is that clients authenticate themselves to APs, but APs do not authenticate themselves to clients. A rogue AP can impersonate a valid device, tricking clients into associating with it. Information from the wireless clients can be obtained and form the basis for other types of security attacks. This type of attack is called a man-in-the-middle attack.

In passive monitoring, data transmissions can be monitored to acquire information such as the addresses of APs and wireless clients or time of association and disassociation with the network. Over time, a hacker can build a profile of the network, based on statistical analysis, that he can use to break into the network. In other cases it is possible to determine the contents of the transmission itself. An attacker can use a utility to capture enough frames to decode the security key. Although this requires capturing several hundred thousand to several million packets, as well as a huge amount of computer processing—a massive job—it can be done, especially if an attacker is targeting a particular company.

Because the messages to associate or disassociate from the WLAN are not encrypted, they can be intercepted and data can be gleaned from them. An unauthorized user can use this information to flood the network with transmissions and deny others access to the AP in a DoS attack.

Attacks such as DoS and using a rogue AP can be easily avoided through the acquisition of special equipment and software such as AirMagnet Enterprise (see www.airmagnet.com). Although the equipment and software can cost upward of $5,000 for a large wireless network, it can prove a worthwhile investment if the company is subject to an attack—which may end up costing a lot more. Another way to prevent these types of attacks is to deploy an external authentication mechanism such as those outlined in 802.1X and 802.11i, described later in this chapter.

802.11 Security

The IEEE 802.11 standard incorporates some basic security measures. Authentication and privacy processes inherent in 802.11 provide a basic level of user authorization.

Authentication

Authentication is a process that verifies that the client device has permission to access the network. Although authentication is important in wired local area networks, it is even more important in WLANs because of the open nature of a wireless network.

IEEE 802.11 WLANs provide a very basic means of authenticating potential client devices. Each WLAN client can be given the SSID of the network. This value is transmitted to the AP when the client is negotiating with it for permission to connect to the network. Only those clients that know the SSID are then authenticated as valid users and are allowed to connect to the network.

A wireless client can be given an SSID in one of two ways. First, the SSID can be manually entered into the wireless client device. Once it is entered, anyone who has access to that wireless device can see the SSID and freely distribute it. The second way is even less secure. APs can freely advertise the SSID to any mobile device that comes into the range of the AP. The default setting on most APs is to freely broadcast SSIDs. You should always configure an AP not to broadcast the SSID, even when you set up more sophisticated security measures to protect your network. However, keep in mind that when a client transmits a probe frame, the AP will usually send a response that includes the SSID of the network. Turning off SSID broadcast can only protect your network against someone finding it unintentionally. An attacker using a sniffing tool will still be able to obtain the SSID of the access point.

NOTE   SSIDs provide only a rudimentary level of security because they apply only to devices, not individual users, and because SSIDs themselves are not well secured. IEEE WLAN authentication is therefore only an auxiliary method to the user authentication mechanisms used by the network's operating system, such as Microsoft Windows or Linux. These network operating systems use standard user authentication measures such as login names and passwords.

Privacy

Privacy is different from authentication. Authentication ensures that the user (or device) has permission to be part of the network. Privacy standards attempt to ensure that transmissions are not read by unauthorized users, even if those transmissions fall into the wrong hands. This is accomplished with data encryption, which scrambles the data in a way that it cannot be read and can only be decoded by the intended recipient, who has access to the encryption key and can decode the message. The strength of encryption rests not only on keeping the keys secret but also on the length of the key itself. The longer the key is, the stronger the encryption, because longer keys are more difficult to break.

Wired Equivalent Privacy

The 802.11 standard provides an optional **Wired Equivalent Privacy (WEP)** specification for data encryption between wireless devices to prevent eavesdropping. WEP encryption comes in two versions: 64-bit encryption is actually made up of a 40-bit key (5 bytes or 10 hexadecimal digits) plus a 24-bit initialization vector (IV), which is a part of the encryption key that is sent in clear text, before the encrypted data. Likewise, 128-bit encryption is made up of a 104-bit key plus a 24-bit IV. Some vendors offered 256-bit encryption in their equipment; however, this equipment also uses the same 24-bit IV. 256-bit encryption may not be compatible between equipment from different manufacturers.

In late 2000, it was revealed that the IV used to encrypt transmissions with WEP is reused about once every five hours. In theory, a person who could capture these packets over the airwaves could see the pattern in reuse and be able to break the WEP encryption. In 2001, researchers at various universities around the country outlined how an attacker could collect the necessary data for breaking WEP encryption. By late 2001, researchers were able to decrypt the 128-bit WEP key used in a WLAN transmission in less than two hours.

WEP has five major characteristics:

8

- Authentication — In the 802.11 standard, an AP authenticates the client device but the device does not authenticate the AP. This allows an attacker with an unauthorized access point to impersonate an approved AP.

- Encryption — WEP uses a weak implementation of the RC4 encryption algorithm. The RC4 algorithm was developed by Ron Rivest for RSA Data Security, Inc. The algorithm itself has never been officially made public, but a description of it was once published to an Internet newsgroup. Since then, data encrypted with RC4 has been decrypted many times. The WEP key must be entered in hexadecimal on some systems, and users tend to create keys based on a simple sequence of the digits 0-9 and characters A-F, which further simplifies the task of breaking the key.

- Static keys — Because the implementation uses static keys (keys that do not change) once the encryption is broken, an attacker can decrypt all subsequent messages.

- Single set of keys — Because WEP uses a single pair of keys for the entire network, if the keys are compromised, then the entire wireless network is also compromised.

- 24-bit initialization vector (IV) — Each packet encrypted with WEP uses a different 24-bit IV. However, precisely because the IV is only 24 bits, there are only a limited number of them available. Since each packet gets its own IV, all the possible combinations are quickly used. This permits a hacker to capture a series of packets, from the millions sent in a few hours, and then use easily obtainable tools from the Internet to break the keys and decrypt the packets.

Wi-Fi Protected Access

Wi-Fi protected access (WPA) is a standard for network authentication and encryption introduced by the Wi-Fi Alliance, in response to the weaknesses in WEP described in the previous section. One of the primary motivations for using WPA is that it usually can be implemented with a simple software upgrade on the AP or residential wireless gateway.

WPA uses a 128-bit **pre-shared key (PSK)**, which is also called personal mode. WPA-PSK uses a different encryption key for each client device, for each packet, and for each session, unlike WEP, which only varies the 24-bit IV. PSK is not suitable for larger companies with many client devices, because the passphrase has to be created by the user and manually input on both the AP and clients. Strong passphrases should be longer than 8 bytes and should include a mixture of letters, numbers, and non-alphanumeric characters. The key in personal mode is rotated, based on a user-configurable timer. This mode does not offer the same level of protection as enterprise class systems that rely on an authentication server installed somewhere else on the network.

WPA employs the **temporal key integrity protocol (TKIP)**, which provides per-packet key-mixing. In addition, TKIP also provides **message integrity check (MIC)**, which uses a combination of variable and static data items, such as the current network uptime (not based on current clock time) or the value of a continually incrementing variable, and other data items to ensure that the encrypted data has not been tampered with. With WEP it was possible to tamper with the encrypted data without possibility of detection. Message integrity verifies that the data was sent by the intended source device and that it has not been modified by an attacker.

TKIP uses a 48-bit hashed initialization vector, and also changes the key after a user-specified amount of time. WPA includes the mechanism necessary for the AP to change the keys and transmit the new key to all client devices.

WPA2 is the version of WPA that has been certified by the IEEE to be compatible with IEEE 802.11i, described in the next section. It adds support for the advanced encryption standard (AES), which meets U.S. government security requirements. However, because AES requires additional processing power, it may not be supported by older hardware.

NOTE   The Wi-Fi Alliance also has certification programs for WPA and WPA2. Vendors use these certification programs to verify that their equipment complies with the standard and to ensure that it will interoperate with equipment from other vendors. Vendors pay the Wi-Fi Alliance and supply equipment for the interoperability tests. In exchange, if the equipment passes all tests, vendors are allowed to add special Wi-Fi Alliance logos to their equipment, packaging, brochures, and other promotional material.

IEEE 802.11i and IEEE 802.1X

The 802.11i standard enhancement to 802.11 is the final result of a series of efforts to deal with the security weaknesses of the original WLAN standard. It was ratified in June 2004. In combination with **IEEE 802.1X**, **IEEE 802.11i** defines a **robust security network association (RSNA)**, which is a grouping of several security functions that protects data frames by providing mutual authentication between client devices and access points, controlled access to the network, establishment of security keys, and key management. Although full coverage of 802.11i and 802.1X is beyond the scope of this text, you can obtain more information by downloading the 802.1X and 802.11i standards documents from http://standards.ieee.org/getieee802/index.html.

NOTE   802.1X is part of the IEEE 802.1 group of network standards and applies to wired as well as wireless networks.

In 802.11i, a client device must be authenticated on the network by an external authentication server, such as a Remote Authentication Dial In User Service (RADIUS), a popular method of authenticating users on a network, before associating with an AP. Another option is for the client to be authenticated by an authentication server provided by the AP itself. All communication between the client device and the AP is blocked until the authentication process is completed. After the authentication process is completed, data protection through encryption and MIC are enabled. Only then is the client association with the AP allowed and communication unblocked. Figure 8-16 is a diagram of a typical network employing an authentication server.

8

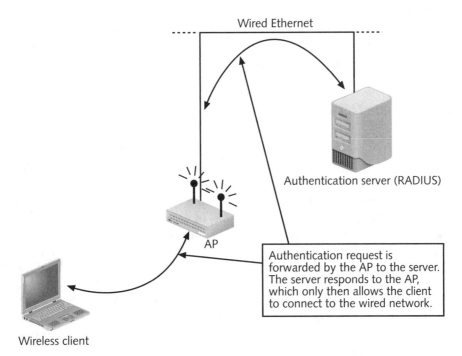

Figure 8-16   Securing a wireless network using an authentication server

NOTE   RADIUS software is available from many different vendors and also in a free version called FreeRADIUS. The *dial in* portion of the RADIUS acronym is a holdover from the old telephone-line modem days. RADIUS is applicable to wired as well as wireless networks. FreeRADIUS is available for download from many Internet sites and is supported by a variety of networking devices, including APs, routers, and so on.

802.1X uses the **Extensible Authentication Protocol (EAP)** for relaying access requests between a wireless device, the AP, and the RADIUS server. There are several variations of

EAP, each supporting a different authentication method and its associated network security policy. For EAP to work, all three devices must support the same authentication method. When EAP is used, the network administrator does not need to configure a WPA passphrase or WEP key in each computer. The key is provided to the wireless device and AP by the RADIUS server. This saves configuration effort and time initially and also when the key has to be changed for any reason.

Push-Button Wireless Security

Since many home users who install wireless networks fail to set up proper security, leaving their networks exposed to potential attack by hackers, a few vendors joined forces to create a new method of configuring wireless residential gateways, as well as a number of other devices. While each vendor has a different name or acronym for their particular method, virtually all of them provide an additional button on the front panel of the wireless gateway or in the configuration software that automatically configures the security settings. Keep in mind that to take advantage of push-button wireless security, both the wireless NIC and the AP or gateway must support the feature. The button needs to be activated once on both devices, for each client, one at a time. The feature transfers the security key to the wireless NIC, then automatically establishes a connection with the wireless device. If you are using wireless NICs and gateways from different vendors, check first to make sure this feature is compatible.

Virtual Private Networks

Virtual private networks (VPNs) use an encrypted connection to create a virtual tunnel between two points, across a public or corporate network. VPNs using strong encryption algorithms, such as AES, are the most secure method of implementing a wireless network. Due to the encryption requirements, VPNs consume a large amount of processing resources and thus some time-sensitive applications, such as client-server communications, may not perform acceptably in a VPN environment. In these cases, wireless networks should be secured using one of the techniques described previously in this chapter. However, wireless-equipped portable computers that are used to access a company network through the Internet from locations such as airports and coffee shops should only do so through a VPN. Most public wireless networks are not secure, which can expose corporate data, such as e-mails and even customer names and addresses, to an attacker. In fact, if VPNs are not implemented properly, the entire corporate network can be exposed to attacks from the Internet. Disabling access to the Internet when users log in to the corporate network through a VPN avoids this problem, so most VPNs are set up in this way.

Additional WLAN Security Strategies

In addition to the security strategies discussed in the previous section, you can increase WLAN security by reducing WLAN transmission power. However, keep in mind that an attacker equipped with a high-gain directional antenna would still be able to detect the RF signal. Changing the default security settings on the APs is probably the most important first step. Don't forget antivirus and antispyware software. Mobile wireless clients are exposed to more of these threats when operating outside company offices and can introduce those threats into your wired network.

For highly secure WLANs, you may need to separate WLAN transmissions from wired network traffic by placing a firewall between the WLAN and the wired LAN, although this means that you will need to implement virtual local area networks (VLANs) in order to allow authorized users to access the wired network. This is especially important if you allow guest wireless devices to connect to your WLAN.

CHAPTER SUMMARY

- Operating in the 2.4 GHz ISM frequency range, 802.11b has a maximum data rate of 11 Mbps, and has been widely accepted. However, the ISM band is crowded and subject to interference from other networking technologies, cordless phones, and Bluetooth. Another drawback of 802.11b is that it provides no means of prioritizing transmissions (QoS).

- The 802.11a standard has a maximum rated speed of 54 Mbps and also supports 48, 36, 24, 18, 12, 9, and 6 Mbps. 802.11a achieves its increase in speed and flexibility over 802.11b through a higher frequency, more transmission channels, and a new multiplexing technique.

- IEEE 802.11a networks use the Unlicensed National Information Infrastructure (U–NII) band. The total bandwidth available for IEEE 802.11a WLANs using U–NII is almost four times that available for 802.11b networks using the ISM band.

- In 802.11a, eight frequency channels can operate simultaneously. Within each frequency channel there is a channel 20 MHz wide that supports 52 carrier signals, with each signal 300 KHz wide. Because there are an increased number of available channels, more users can access more bandwidth in an 802.11a WLAN when managed correctly.

- IEEE 802.11b WLAN reception is slowed down by multipath distortion. The 802.11a standard solves this problem through a new multiplexing technique called Orthogonal Frequency Division Multiplexing (OFDM), which sends transmissions in parallel across several channels instead of one long stream of data sent across a single channel, and sends the message slowly enough so that any delayed copies (reflections) are late by only a fraction of time.

- OFDM uses 48 of the 52 subchannels for data, while the remaining four are used for error correction. The modulation techniques used to encode the data vary depending upon the speed.

- The number of errors in an 802.11a transmission is significantly reduced compared to 802.11b. Because transmissions are sent over parallel subchannels, interference is minimized. Error correction is also enhanced using Forward Error Correction (FEC), which transmits a secondary copy along with the primary information.

- The 802.11a standard made changes only to the physical layer (PHY layer) of the original 802.11 and 802.11b standard; the MAC layer remains the same. The 802.11a PHY layer is divided into two parts. The Physical Medium Dependent (PMD) sublayer makes up the standards for both the characteristics of the wireless medium (such as OFDM) and defines the method for transmitting and receiving data through that medium. The Physical Layer Convergence Procedure (PLCP) reformats the data received from the MAC layer (when transmitting) into a frame that the PMD sublayer can transmit and listens to the medium to determine when the data can be sent.

8

❑ 802.11g preserves the features of 802.11b but increases the data transfer rates to those of 802.11a. The 802.11g standard specifies that it operates entirely in the 2.4 GHz ISM frequency and not the U–NII band used by 802.11a.

❑ The 802.11e standard adds QoS to the original 802.11 standards through both burst acknowledgements and two new coordination functions: enhanced DCF (EDCF) and hybrid coordination function (HCF).

❑ 802.11n is a proposed standard that will increase the speed of WLANs to 108 Mbps using the 2.4 GHz ISM band. This is accomplished by bonding two 2.4 GHz ISM channels and using OFDM to transmit two data streams at 54 Mbps. MIMO is also used in 802.11n.

❑ 802.11r is a proposed standard for fast roaming that will reduce the time for the process of association and disassociation from hundreds of milliseconds to less than 50 milliseconds, allowing WLANs to support VoWLAN in ESS environments. It will also allow a wireless device to securely connect with another AP using the current wireless connection.

❑ The 802.11s proposed standard will enable APs to communicate and pass traffic from one to the other, over a wireless connection, supporting cost-effective deployment of extensive WLANs over larger geographical areas.

❑ HiperLAN/2 is a high-speed WLAN specification that is similar to the IEEE 802.11a standard. It offers high-speed wireless connectivity at up to 54 Mbps and seamless connectivity to cellular telephone systems, ATM, and FireWire.

❑ WLANs can suffer a range of security attacks. IEEE WLANs require enhanced security measures. WLAN security has been greatly enhanced through the introduction of Wi-Fi protected access (WPA and WPA2).

❑ WLANs can be protected through the use of VPNs, 802.11i authentication, and 802.1X measures to ensure privacy. Authentication verifies that the user or device has permission to access the network. Privacy makes certain that transmissions themselves are not read by unauthorized persons.

KEY TERMS

authentication — A process that verifies that the client device has permission to access the network.

Extensible Authentication Protocol (EAP) — A collection of protocols used by IEEE 802.1x for network authentication between a wireless device, an AP, and a RADIUS server.

handoff — The transition that occurs when a client device connects with a new access point and disconnects from the previous one.

HiperLAN/2 — A proposed high-speed WLAN that is similar to the IEEE 802.11a standard.

IEEE 802.11a — A standard for WLAN transmissions developed in 1999 for networks with speeds up to 54 Mbps and beyond.

IEEE 802.11e — A standard for WLAN applications that requires QoS and provides for improvements in the capabilities and efficiency of the protocol.

IEEE 802.11g — A standard for WLAN transmissions for networks with speeds up to 54 Mbps using the ISM band.

IEEE 802.11i — An enhancement to 802.11 that deals with security weaknesses of the original standard.

IEEE 802.1X — A standard to increase the security of IEEE 802 WLANs.

message integrity check — A combination of variable and static data items that ensure that encrypted data has not been altered.

multiple in, multiple out (MIMO) — A technology that uses multiple antennas (usually three or four) and also uses reflected signals (multipath) to extend the range of the WLAN by attempting to correctly decode a frame from multiple copies of it received at different times (multipath reflections).

nomadic user — A user that moves frequently but does not use the equipment while in motion.

pre-shared key — A 128-bit key used by WPA.

privacy — Standards that ensure that transmissions are not read by unauthorized users.

robust security network association (RSNA) — A grouping of several security functions to protect data frames by providing mutual authentication between client devices and access points, controlled access to the network, establishment of security keys, and key management.

temporal key integrity protocol — A security protocol used in WPA that provides per-packet key-mixing

virtual private network (VPN) — A secure, encrypted connection between two points.

voice over wireless LAN (VoWLAN) — In WLANs that support QoS, it is possible to support telephone calls over the same wireless connection.

Wi-Fi Protected Access (WPA) and **WPA2** — A security enhancement introduced by the Wi-Fi Alliance, in advance of the 802.11i standard, to deal with the security flaws in WEP.

Wired Equivalent Privacy (WEP) — The IEEE specification for data encryption between wireless devices that prevents eavesdropping.

wireless bridge — A networking component that connects two wired networks or extends the range of a WLAN.

wireless switching — Construction of a wireless network with devices that incorporate all of the functions of an AP and can control multiple dumb 802.11 radios.

REVIEW QUESTIONS

1. The original IEEE 802.11 standard established in 1999 was for WLANs operating at what maximum speed?

   a. 1 Mbps

   b. 2 Mbps

   c. 3 Mbps

   d. 4 Mbps

2. The maximum mandatory speed of an IEEE 802.11a WLAN, according to the standard, is _____ .

    a. 11 Mbps

    b. 33 Mbps

    c. 54 Mbps

    d. 108 Mbps

3. The most important change made to the MAC layer of 802.11a was _____ .

    a. to make the frames shorter

    b. to increase security

    c. to make the frames longer for efficiency

    d. None of the above

4. IEEE 802.11a achieves its increase in speed and flexibility over 802.11b by each of the following except _____ .

    a. higher frequency

    b. lower bandwidth

    c. more transmission channels

    d. a new multiplexing technique

5. The Unlicensed National Information Infrastructure (U-NII) band operates at the _____ frequency.

    a. 2.4 GHz

    b. 33 GHz

    c. 5 GHz

    d. 16 KHz

6. The Federal Communications Commission (FCC) has segmented the 300 MHz of the original U-NII spectrum into three segments or bands and each band has a maximum power limit. True or False?

7. The 5 GHz bands are available to WLANs worldwide. True or False?

8. Although other devices such as 2.4 GHz cordless phones, microwave ovens, and Bluetooth devices may cause interference problems with 802.11b networks in the 2.4 GHz ISM band, these devices are not a problem with 802.11a. True or False?

9. Within each frequency channel in an 802.11a WLAN, there is a channel 20 MHz wide that supports 52 carrier signals. True or False?

10. A problem with 802.11a WLANs is the multipath distortion of the radio frequency signals that bounce off walls and furniture and are delayed reaching the receiver. True or False?

11. OFDM uses _____ subchannels for data, and four are used as pilot carriers.

12. Although 54 Mbps is the official top speed of 802.11a, some vendors have implemented higher speeds known as turbo or _____ .

13. The IEEE _____ standard incorporates the stable and widely accepted features of 802.11b with the increased data transfer rates to those similar to 802.11a.

14. Using eight channels in a single area, 802.11a allows a maximum data bandwidth of _____ .

15. Explain the benefit of 802.11e for WLANs.

16. What are the types of systems with which HiperLAN/2 can connect?

17. What are some advantages and disadvantages of IEEE 802.11a WLANs?

18. What are the maximum transmitter power specifications for each of the three original U-NII frequency bands?

19. What is authentication? What is the disadvantage of the authentication included in the 802.11 standards, and what kind of authentication should be considered for WLANs?

20. List three shortcomings of WEP.

8

HANDS-ON PROJECTS

**HANDS-ON
PROJECTS**

Project 8-1: Setting Up an Access Point or Broadband Router MAC Filter

Since you already set up a broadband router and one or two client notebooks in Chapter 7, in this chapter's projects we focus on setting and tightening security. A MAC filter does not prevent a security attack, since the MAC address is easy to spoof or fake, but when added to other security measures, MAC filters make it harder for the attacker to penetrate your network. They also make it much harder for your network to be unintentionally detected, since the router or access point will not allow anyone that does not have a permitted MAC address to simply find your network. The following steps use a Linksys broadband router model WRT54G version 2.0; however, they can be easily adapted to most other manufacturers' equipment. Most of the terminology should follow the specifications from the Wi-Fi Alliance but may appear on different configuration pages. To work on this project, you will need to have the following items already configured (refer to Chapter 7):

◻ A Linksys WRT54G broadband router/residential gateway or Linksys WAP54G access point (the settings are very similar), or a similar AP or residential router. A connection to the Internet is not required. For the WRT54G, ensure that you are using firmware version 4.20.7 or higher.

◻ One or two laptop or desktop PCs with a Linksys wireless G adapter card (most other manufacturer cards that support WPA security will work as well).

◻ An RJ-45 Ethernet patch cable.

If you have more than one AP or router in your classroom or lab, consult your instructor to select different channels to minimize interference between the devices. Channel selection appears in the Basic Wireless Settings tab.

NOTE

The settings below refer to the wireless configuration only. There are many other settings on the router that relate to the security of the Internet connection. These will not be reviewed here. For detailed information and suggestions on securing a Linksys wireless network, you can check document no. 759 "Setting up Wireless Security," under Easy Answers, on the Technical Support page at www.linksys.com.

1. Connect and power up your broadband router or AP. Also, turn on your computers and confirm that they can connect to the router or AP. Plug one end of the RJ-45 Ethernet patch cable into one of the switch ports on the router or the Ethernet port on the AP. Plug the other end of the RJ-45 Ethernet patch cable to the wired Ethernet port of your PC.

TIP

Whenever possible, you should use a wired connection to change settings on a router or access point. Some of the settings, such as security, will cause your computer to disconnect until you reconfigure it to use the new settings.

2. On the same PC, browse to the router and open the main configuration page by typing the address of the router in the address line of the browser. Login to the router with the default password *admin* or the password set up by your instructor.

3. Open a command window by clicking **START**, **Run** and typing **cmd**. Press **Enter**. At the command prompt, type **ipconfig /all**, then press **Enter**. Scroll up if required and locate your wireless NIC to obtain the MAC address (Physical Address). Leave the Command window open. In the router configuration browser window, click the **Wireless** tab, then click **Wireless MAC Filter** in the menu line just below the tabs. Click the radio button next to Enable to enable the Wireless MAC Filter. You should see a screen like the one in Figure 8-17. This screen allows you to select computers to access the router through the wireless interface.

4. Click the radio button next to **Permit only** PCs listed to access the wireless network, then click the **Edit MAC Filter List** button. A second browser window, like the one shown in Figure 8-18 should open. Enter the MAC address of your computer in the first line (**MAC 01**). Note that all zeroes on the left side are significant and that your MAC address should have 12 hexadecimal digits. Scroll down to the bottom of the screen and press the **Save Settings** button. When the Settings are successful page appears, click the **Continue** button. Close the MAC Address Filter List page and click the **Save Settings** button for the Wireless MAC Filter page. The page should change to display the statement Settings are successful. Click the **Continue** button to return to the Wireless MAC Filter page.

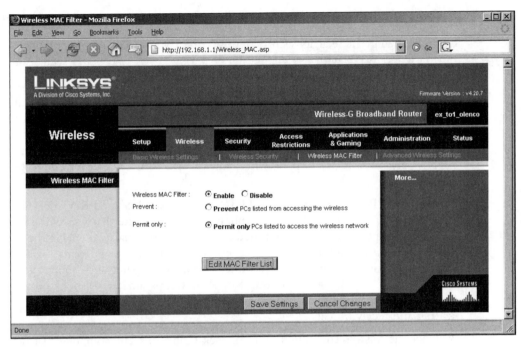

Figure 8-17   The Wireless MAC Filter main configuration screen

Figure 8-18   Editing the MAC filter list

5. Your computer should remain connected to the router, but the second computer will no longer be able to access the router. The MAC Filter List window should still be open. Obtain the MAC address of the second computer and enter it in the list as in Step 4 above. Once you click Save Settings, the second computer should soon automatically reconnect to the router. Close the second browser window and leave the Wireless MAC Filter page open.

6. Before you go on to the next project, you should also disable broadcast of the network SSID. To accomplish this, click the **Basic Wireless Settings** tab and then click **Disable** next to Wireless SSID Broadcast. If both your computers have the correct SSID entered in the profile, they should remain connected to the network. When the SSID is not being broadcast, you will not be able to see the network in the Windows Zero Configuration window. You must manually create a profile under Advanced settings that includes the SSID for the network.

Project 8-2: Setting Up WPA Security on the Router and PC

As you learned in the security section of this chapter, you should not rely on WEP to protect your network. WPA, with its dynamically changing key, is a far better security method. In this project, you will set up your AP or router to use WPA.

1. Select the **Wireless Security** menu item under the Wireless tab of the router configuration in the browser. Next to Security Mode use the drop-down box to select WPA-PSK or WPA Personal (depending on the firmware version of your router or access point). WPA-PSK stands for Wi-Fi Protected Access – Pre-Shared Key. You can only use WPA Enterprise when you have an RADIUS server connected to your network.

2. Next to WPA Algorithms select **TKIP**. Next to WPA Shared Key enter a passphrase such as WirelessComm2. This passphrase is the same one that you will enter in the client computers and it will be used as the initial key that will enable the computers and router to establish communications. WPA will change or rotate this key based on the amount of time specified under Group Key Renewal or about every 60 minutes. If you change the Group Key Renewal parameter, try not to make it too short or your computers will spend a lot of time changing keys instead of transmitting and receiving data.

3. Click the **Save Settings** button. Then click **Continue**. The computer that is connected to the router via its wireless interface will be disconnected from the wireless network. Modify the profile and enter the same password that you entered in the router.

4. To connect the wireless computer to the router, open **Network Connections**, right-click the wireless network connection, and click **Properties**. Click the **Wireless Networks** tab. If you have more than one profile showing in the lower box, select the WComm connection you created in Project 7-1. Click the **Properties** button. Next to Network Authentication, select **WPA-PSK** and next to Data encryption, select **TKIP**.

5. Enter the passphrase you used in Step 2 under Network key and enter it again under Confirm network key. Click **OK** to close the WComm properties dialog box, then click **OK** again on the Wireless Network Connection Properties dialog box. Within about 10 seconds, your wireless PC should connect to the router.

6. Repeat the above procedure to connect the computer that is wired to the router through the wireless interface. You may disconnect the Ethernet cable, if you wish. Once the computer connects to the wireless router or access point, refer back to Chapter 7 and use the procedure in Project 7-3 to test the connection.

Project 8-3: Limiting the Number of Computers that can Connect to the Wireless Network

One of the other ways you can secure a wireless network is to limit the number of computers that can connect to a wireless broadband router. This measure will not prevent an attack, but it can prevent too many computers from associating with an AP that is using simple security settings such as WPA-PSK. In a small company using a broadband router for

Internet connectivity, this can make it harder for an attacker to receive an IP address from the DHCP server and connect to the network. Although it is a limited capability defense, it represents an added barrier against attacks.

However, make sure this configuration is well documented so that if anyone else needs access to add another computer to the wireless network, they will realize you have limited the total number of connections. Documenting your steps is also helpful in case you forget the details of how you changed the settings. This configuration revision will affect the wired connections to the router as well. You must include any servers or other devices that are using a wired connection to the router.

1. From a computer that is using a wired connection to the router, open the browser and connect to the router. Select the **Setup** tab, if necessary. Under the section Network Address Server Settings, locate the heading Maximum Number of DHCP Users. Enter the total number of computers that are allowed to connect to the router, including the ones that are using a wired connection. Scroll down to the bottom of the page and click the **Save Settings** button.

8

Case Project

Project 8-1: Mobile Users and Enterprise Security

The Baypoint Group (TBG) needs your help with a presentation for Academic Computing Services (ACS), a nationwide organization that assists colleges and universities with technology issues. ACS needs more information about the differences between the IEEE 802.11a and IEEE 802.11g standards so that their salespeople will be better equipped to sell this wireless technology to schools.

1. Prepare a PowerPoint presentation that compares how 802.11a works and lists the advantages and disadvantages of 802.11a over 802.11g. Because ACS is a technical group, the presentation should have a high level of technical detail. Your presentation should last 15–20 minutes.

2. ACS is pleased with your presentation, but its management is concerned about security with WLANs. Prepare another presentation that outlines the security strengths and weaknesses of WLANs and makes recommendations about the level of security that they should implement for their customers in a variety of situations, such as when equipment is used in office applications and when wireless notebook computers are used by students. Your presentation should consist of at least 15–20 slides.

To assist you in preparing your second presentation, read a white paper called "What Hackers Don't Want You To Know About Securing Your WLAN" from the AirMagnet Web site at www.airmagnet.com/products/wp-index.htm.

TIP

OPTIONAL TEAM CASE PROJECT

Imagine that you work for a college or university. Your institution is considering the deployment of a wireless network to provide mobile access to the students. Since the students download and upload a lot of training material, a decision on whether to implement full security or to allow students free access to the network is still pending. At issue is the performance of the network with full WPA security, compared with performance without WPA.

One of the best ways to perform this test is to use a utility that checks network throughput. The Qcheck utility is available free of charge from Ixia; download it from http://www. ixiacom.com/CD/IxChariot/qcheck.html. Set up your AP and two computers as described in the Hands-on Projects for this chapter. One of the computers should be wired to the network or to the AP directly. The other computer should be connected using a wireless 802.11b or g interface. Set up the AP as outlined in Chapter 7 and connect the client PC with no security. Download and install Qcheck on both computers. Ensure that the Windows XP SP2 firewall is turned off.

Test the throughput of the network and record your findings. Next, set up security as outlined in the Hands-on Projects. Run your tests again and record your findings. Ensure that you are using a channel with little or no interference. Check the strength of the signal, and perform all your tests only when the signal indicates "Excellent."

NOTE
Although Qcheck is a fairly small program, on some computers the installation may stop for more than five minutes and appear to be "hung." Be patient. The program will eventually continue the installation.

Produce a one-page report that answers the questions below:

1. What was the throughput of the network without security?

2. What was the throughput of the network with WPA security?

3. Was there a significant difference in performance—enough to be noticeable by the users when downloading or uploading large files?

4. What is your recommendation to your training organization? Back up your recommendation with the data you collected, along with your suggestions regarding using security in a training environment.

9

WIRELESS METROPOLITAN AREA NETWORKS

> ## After reading this chapter and completing the exercises, you will be able to:
>
> ♦ Explain why wireless metropolitan area networks (WMANs) are needed
> ♦ Describe the components and modes of operation of a WMAN
> ♦ List the range of WMAN technologies, including FSO, LMDS, MMDS, and 802.16 (WiMAX)
> ♦ Explain how WMANs function
> ♦ Outline the security features of WMANs

By now, you understand the tremendous impact that wireless communications has and will continue to have on the world around us. Wireless networks allow users to be connected as they move about, freeing them from cables and phone lines. However, the WPANs and WLANs you have learned about thus far have restricted both connections and mobility, letting users roam only a few hundred feet from the source of the RF signal. Users have also been limited to staying within line-of-sight of antennas. Therefore, except for voice communications and low-speed data over cellular networks, user mobility has remained largely confined to homes, offices, and hotspots offering wireless access, such as coffee shops and airports, as well as some public locations in larger cities.

Limits on the strength of RF signals—to prevent interference in unlicensed bands—have also restricted user mobility in Wi-Fi networks. In small towns and remote areas, the relatively small number of wireless network users may not make it economically viable to implement hotspots and mobile access. In fact, in areas with low user density, the cost of installing wired high-speed communications channels over long distances often prevents telephone companies or small ISPs from offering high-speed Internet access at all.

In this chapter, you will learn about existing and future technologies and standards that can offer practical solutions for these challenges. The chapter begins with coverage of existing infrared (IR)-based short- and medium-distance technologies and concludes with recently approved and upcoming standards for medium- and long-distance RF-based WMAN technologies.

WHAT IS A WMAN?

Wireless metropolitan area networks (WMANs) are a group of technologies that provide wireless connectivity across a substantial geographical area such as a large city. WMANs have two primary goals. One is to extend the reach of wired networks beyond a single location without the expense of high-speed cable-based connections. The second goal is to extend user mobility throughout a metropolitan area. An important additional benefit of a WMAN is that it can provide high-speed connections, including Internet, to areas not serviced by any other method of connectivity. Such connectivity can encompass metropolitan areas, surrounding small towns, and remote locations not usually serviced by high-speed communications lines.

Last Mile Wired Connections

The **last mile connection** is the link between a customer and ISP. Even today, most last mile connections are based on copper wiring. Less than 25% of U.S. office buildings use fiber optics for last mile connections, and only a very small number of U.S. office buildings are wired for cable TV. Installing fiber optics is slow, inconvenient, and expensive. Figure 9-1 illustrates an example of a last mile connection.

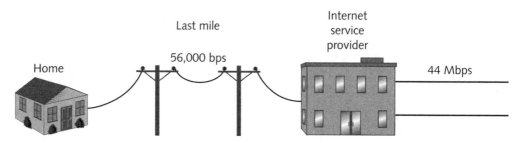

Figure 9-1   Last mile connection

Home users can usually take advantage of both DSL and cable TV connections at up to 5 Mbps. However, these types of connections are usually not available in small, remote communities. Business users do have a few other options beyond basic copper wiring. As you have learned, ISDN, T1, and DSL technologies offer higher data rates, are widely available, and are wire-based. Similar to T1 is T3, which is a faster but more expensive digital line. Table 9-1 summarizes the connection options and speeds for homes and office buildings.

Table 9-1 Connection options

Connection type	Speed	Typical use	Approximate cost per month	Approximate time to transmit contents of one full 680 MB CD-ROM (hours:minutes)
Dial-up modem	56 Kbps	Home	Free and up	26:53
ISDN (1 or 2 ch.)	64 or 128 Kbps	Home or office	$100 plus usage fees	24:10/12:50
Cable modem	5 Mbps	Home	$45 and up	0:18
DSL	5 Mbps	Home	$30 and up	0:18
T1	1.544 Mbps	Office	$400 and up	0:58
T3	44.736 Mbps	Office, ISP	$2,500 and up	0:02
OC-3 (optical fiber)	155 Mbps	ISP	$20,000 to $45,000	32 seconds
OC-12 (optical fiber)	622.08 Mbps	ISP	Varies greatly	8 seconds
OC-192 (optical fiber)	9.6 Gbps	Large ISP	Varies greatly	½ second

9

For long-distance connections between cities and states, copper-based digital communications lines, such as T1, require the signal to be regenerated every 6,000 feet (1.8 kilometers). In addition to the challenges of cable installation and maintenance, regenerating the signal also requires electrical power at each repeater location. Maintenance costs for this type of connection are extremely high, especially in areas where the geography is challenging, such as in the Rocky Mountains in the western part of North America.

Last mile delivery of telephone and data lines has long been a problem for the **carrier**, who must be able to justify the cost of installing wired connections to remote areas. Note that previously in this book, the term carrier referred to the RF signal that carries data. The term carrier also refers to telephone, cable TV, and other communications providers who own the wires and transmission towers that carry voice and data traffic.

Since the early 1980s, fiber-optic technology has largely replaced all other technologies for connections between major metropolitan centers, mainly because it has a higher capacity for carrying voice and data transmissions, lower maintenance requirements, and is much more reliable than copper wiring. However, the higher costs of the fiber-optic medium and in-ground installation often preclude its use in remote and less-populated areas.

Last Mile Wireless Connections

Microwave links were introduced in the early 1950s by AT&T, bringing about a new era in communications. **Microwaves** are higher frequency RF waves. Microwave transmissions take place in the 3 to 30 GHz range of the electromagnetic spectrum known as the **super high frequency (SHF)** band. Microwaves were originally used to transmit data in a point-to-point fashion, using the lower and middle part of the SHF band. The conventional thinking was that the lower frequency, high-powered approach was the only way in which microwaves could be used for communication. High frequency microwave transmissions were ignored for many years, and the section of the RF spectrum between 27.5 and 29.5 GHz went virtually unused.

Microwave towers are installed roughly 35 miles (56 kilometers) apart from each other, and a link operating at 4 GHz carries about 1,800 voice calls simultaneously. In comparison, a T1 link can carry only 24 simultaneous voice calls. Improvements in microwave technology have reduced the cost of the equipment and have made telephone and data communications services available in many additional remote locations across the United States that were previously out of range of high-capacity connections.

NOTE   The first transcontinental microwave link was completed in 1951, connecting New York and San Francisco. It used 107 towers spaced about 30 miles (48 kilometers), covering a distance of about 3,200 miles (5,140 kilometers). The same link with T1 digital copper-based lines requires over 2,850 repeaters to regenerate the signal.

As an alternative to last mile wired connections, many users have turned to wireless options. These options include free space optics, RF-based local multipoint distribution service and multichannel multipoint distribution service, as well as WiMAX technologies, and are outlined in the remainder of this chapter. The advantages of these last mile wireless connections are that they can cost less, can be installed faster, offer greater flexibility, and have better long-term reliability. Using wireless as the last mile connection for buildings is called **fixed wireless** because buildings are fixed in one location.

Fixed wireless networks have been used for several years for both voice and data communications, generally in backhaul networks operated by telephone companies, cable TV companies, utilities, railways, paging companies, and government agencies. A **backhaul** connection is a company's internal infrastructure connection. For example, a phone company's backhaul network may be a connection from one telephone company central office to another.

Fixed wireless systems can be used to transmit the same type of data that is sent over a wired cable system. However, point-to-point long-distance microwave links, such as those employed by telephone carriers, use high-power signals that are not suitable or safe for use in crowded city skylines. In addition, microwaves require licensed frequencies, which, as you know, carry a high cost and are very limited in terms of availability.

In Chapter 8, you learned that WLAN equipment such as 802.11 wireless bridges can be set up to interconnect two buildings, provided that the installation does not interfere with other wireless links using the same unlicensed RF bands. Longer-distance connections with this technology—beyond the range of Wi-Fi (375 feet)—can be a lot more complicated. Connections requiring multiple bridges to repeat the signal are extremely challenging. Such setups are needed when achieving line-of-sight between the two antennas is difficult or not possible. Additionally, the digital bandwidth of 802.11 bridges is typically only enough to carry a limited amount of data, such as e-mail, Web browsing, and moderate file transfers, mainly due to the half-duplex characteristic of wireless bridges. While using multiple bridges to increase bandwidth can alleviate the problem, it tends to make antenna installation far more complicated.

Baseband vs. Broadband

There are two ways in which digital signals can be transmitted. The first technique is called broadband. A **broadband** transmission sends multiple signals at different frequencies. This allows many different signals to be sent simultaneously. The second technique is called baseband. A **baseband** transmission treats the entire transmission medium as if it were only one channel. The signals are transmitted at one set frequency, allowing only one signal to be sent at a time. This is illustrated in Figure 9-2. By using broadband technology, fixed wireless systems can send and receive multiple signals simultaneously.

9

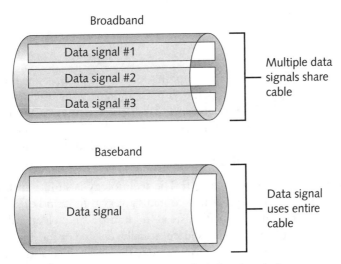

Figure 9-2   Baseband vs. broadband transmissions

NOTE

Computer local area networks use baseband transmission. The names of some networks use the word "base," which stands for baseband. An example is Ethernet 100BaseT, which means 100 Mbps, baseband signaling with twisted pair cabling.

LAND-BASED FIXED BROADBAND WIRELESS

The communications industry has developed a few different solutions for last mile connections over the past few decades. Some have proven too costly and were hard to justify. Others have proved to be less than 100% reliable for implementation in all locations, as you will see below. Most are proprietary solutions or RF-based equipment that require licensed frequency bands. Until 2001, RF-based fixed broadband systems operated at frequencies and with modulation techniques that limited implementation to line-of-sight only. In addition, most fixed broadband systems could only send from one device to one other device at a time. By comparison, in cellular telephone systems, a single base station can communicate with several mobile devices simultaneously. However, cellular technology is not designed for high-capacity data transmissions.

Faced with having to rely on land-based lines from telephone and cable TV carriers, many companies have adopted the kinds of connectivity solutions discussed below. This section begins with an IR-based solution called free space optics, then looks at two types of proprietary last mile connection technologies—local multipoint distribution service and multichannel multipoint distribution service. Later in the chapter, you will learn about the IEEE 802.16 group of wireless standards, which is already in use in many fixed business wireless network and Internet connectivity applications. Recent enhancements to the 802.16 standards also promise to help solve the challenges of user mobility and can compete with DSL, cable TV, and even local telephone carriers.

Free Space Optics

Free space optics (FSO) is an optical, wireless, point-to-point, line-of-sight broadband technology. Although it was originally developed over 30 years ago by the military, FSO has become an excellent alternative to high-speed fiber-optic cable. Currently, FSO can transmit at speeds comparable to fiber-optic transmissions, reaching up to 1.25 Gbps at a distance of 4 miles (6.4 kilometers) in full-duplex mode. Future improvements in the technology will likely push the top speed to hundreds of Gbps.

FSO uses infrared (IR) transmission instead of RF. The technology is similar to that used with a fiber-optic cable system. A fiber-optic cable contains a very thin strand of glass called the core, which is as thick as a human hair. Instead of transmitting electrical signals, fiber-optic cables use light impulses. A light source, usually created by a laser or light emitting diodes (LEDs), flashes a light at one end of the cable that is detected at the receiving end. Light travels at 186,000 miles (300,000 kilometers) per second, so fiber-optic cable systems can transmit large amounts of data at high speeds. In addition, these transmissions are immune to electromagnetic interference and cannot be easily intercepted.

FSO is an alternative to fiber-optic cables. Sometimes called fiberless optical, FSO does not use a medium, like a fiber-optic cable, to send and receive signals. Instead, transmissions are sent by low-powered invisible infrared beams through the open air. These beams, which do not harm the human eye, are transmitted by transceivers, as illustrated in Figure 9-3. Because FSO is a line-of-sight technology, the transceivers are mounted in the middle or upper floors of office buildings to provide a clear transmission path. However, unlike other technologies that require the units to be located on an open roof (which sometimes requires leasing roof space from the building's owner), FSO transceivers can be mounted behind a window in an existing office.

Figure 9-3   FSO transceiver (transmitter/receiver)

 Under perfect conditions, such as environments free of fog, dust, and high heat and humidity, FSO can transmit at distances of up to 6.2 miles (10 kilometers).

NOTE

Recall that the lower-frequency portion of the electromagnetic spectrum is the area in which RF waves travel. The spectrum above 300 GHz is the area in which IR waves move. FSO also uses this part of the spectrum. This higher frequency is unlicensed worldwide, so it can be freely used. The only limitation on its use is that the radiated power must not exceed specific limits in order to avoid harming the human eye.

 FSO equipment works at either of two wavelengths. A single worldwide wavelength will likely be standardized for these devices.

NOTE

Advantages of FSO

The advantages of FSO include cost, speed of installation, transmission rate, and security.

FSO installations cost significantly less than installing new fiber-optic cables or even leasing lines from a local carrier. One recent project compared the costs of installing fiber-optic cables to FSO in three buildings. The cost to install the fiber-optic cables was almost $400,000, vs. less than $60,000 for FSO.

FSO can be installed in days or weeks, compared to months—or sometimes years—for fiber-optic cables. In some instances, installers can set up FSO systems over a weekend without disrupting the users.

The transmission speed can be scaled to meet users' needs, anywhere from 10 Mbps to 1.25 Gbps. If high speeds are not required, the user does not have to pay a premium for unused capacity.

Security is a key advantage in an FSO system. IR transmissions cannot be as easily intercepted and decoded as some RF transmissions.

Disadvantages of FSO

The primary disadvantage of FSO is that atmospheric conditions can have an impact on FSO transmissions. **Scintillation** is defined as the temporal and spatial variations in light intensity caused by atmospheric turbulence. Turbulence caused by wind and temperature variations can create pockets of air with rapidly changing densities. These air pockets can act like prisms and lenses that distort an FSO signal. Inclement weather is also a threat. Although rain and snow can distort a signal, fog does the most damage to transmissions. Fog is composed of extremely small moisture particles that act like prisms on the light beam, scattering and breaking up the signal.

Scintillation is readily observed in the twinkling of stars in the night sky and the shimmering of the horizon on a hot day.

NOTE

FSO overcomes scintillation by sending the data in parallel streams from several separate laser transmitters. These transmitters are all mounted in the same transceiver but are separated from one another by distances of about 7.8 inches (200 mm). It is unlikely that while traveling to the receiver, all the parallel beams will encounter the same pocket of turbulence, since scintillation pockets are usually quite small. At least one of the beams will arrive at the target node with adequate strength to be properly received. This solution is called **spatial diversity**, because it exploits multiple regions of space. Spatial diversity is illustrated in Figure 9-4.

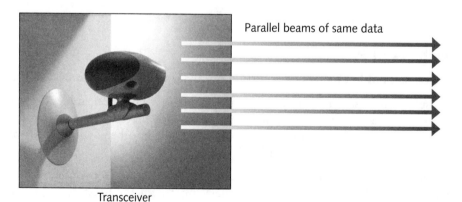

Parallel beams of same data

Transceiver

Figure 9-4   Spatial diversity

In dealing with fog, there are several potential solutions. One solution is simply to increase the transmit power of the signal (the intensity of the light). In regions of heavy and frequent fogs, it may be necessary to choose FSO systems that transmit at the highest available frequency because these devices can send at higher power levels. Several vendors also claim they customize their distance and product recommendations based on weather statistics for particular cities. Other FSO vendors use a backup (wired) connection along with FSO to ensure that transmissions can go through in foggy weather.

NOTE In order to prove that FSO can send transmissions through fog, one vendor ran trials in some of the foggiest cities in the United States. In San Francisco, one of the worst cities in the country for fog, one vendor has proven that FSO can maintain carrier-class transmission speeds (T1) over 90% of the time.

NOTE Some experts recommend that the distance between FSO transceivers in regions of heavy and frequent fogs should be limited to 650 to 1,640 feet (200 to 500 meters).

Signal interference can also be a potential problem for FSO, such as birds flying through the IR beam and blocking it. If the signal is temporarily blocked, the beam automatically reduces its power, then raises itself to full power when the obstruction clears the beam's path.

Another problem is that tall buildings or towers can sway due to wind or seismic activity. Storms and earthquakes can cause buildings to move enough to affect the aim of the beam. This problem can be handled in two ways. In the first method, *beam divergence*, the transmitted beam is purposely allowed to spread, or diverge, so that by the time it arrives at the receiving device it forms a fairly large optical cone. If the receiver is initially positioned at the center of the beam, divergence can compensate for any movement of the buildings. The second method is through *active tracking*. Active tracking is based on movable mirrors that control the direction in which the beams are sent. A feedback mechanism continuously adjusts the mirrors so that the beams stay on target.

FSO Applications

There are a variety of applications for FSO. Some of the more common include:

- Last mile connection — FSO can be used in high-speed links that connect end-users with Internet service providers or other networks.

- LAN connections — FSO devices are easily installed, making them a natural solution for interconnecting LAN segments that are housed in buildings separated by public streets or other obstacles, such as in a university campus spanning several city blocks.

- Fiber-optic backup — FSO can be deployed in redundant links to back up fiber-optic cables in case of a break in the cable.

- Backhaul — FSO can be used to carry cellular telephone traffic from antenna towers back to facilities wired into the public switched telephone network.

Most experts agree that FSO holds great potential for fixed wireless communications as well as for other wireless applications. In spite of all the other technology developments, FSO has remained a stable player in the wireless field.

Local Multipoint Distribution Service (LMDS)

Local multipoint distribution service (LMDS) is a fixed broadband technology that can provide a wide variety of wireless services. These services include high-speed Internet access, real-time multimedia file transfer, remote access to local area networks, interactive video, video-on-demand, video conferencing, and telephone service. LMDS can transmit from 51 to 155 Mbps downstream and 1.54 Mbps upstream over a distance of up to about 5 miles (8 kilometers).

One of the best ways to describe LMDS is by examining each of the words that make up its name:

- Local (L) refers to the area of coverage of LMDS systems. Because it uses high frequency low-powered RF waves, these systems have a limited range. The coverage area for LMDS is only 2 to 5 miles (3.2 kilometers to 8 kilometers).

NOTE

The U.S. Federal Communications Commission (FCC) grants LMDS licenses to carriers for a specific area.

- Multipoint (M) indicates that signals are transmitted out to the remote stations in a point-to-multipoint fashion, from a base station omnidirectional antenna. The signals that are transmitted back from the remote stations to the base station are point-to-point transmissions from directional antennas. This is illustrated in Figure 9-5.

- Distribution (D) refers to the distribution of the various types of information that can be transmitted. These include voice, data, Internet, and video traffic.

- Service (S) means that there are a variety of services available. However, the local carrier determines which services will be offered. All of the services that can be offered—voice, data, Internet, and video traffic—may not be available to the local LMDS users. The services offered through an LMDS network are entirely dependent on the carrier.

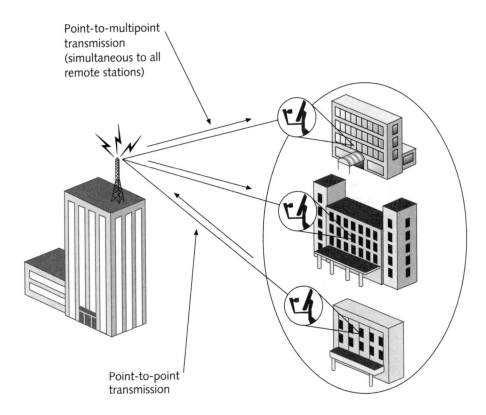

Point-to-multipoint transmission (simultaneous to all remote stations)

Point-to-point transmission

Figure 9-5 LMDS transmissions

NOTE

LMDS is popular around the world. In Canada it is known as Local Multipoint Communication Systems (LMCS). Canada already has 3 GHz of spectrum set aside for LMDS and is actively setting up systems around the country. Many developing countries began to use this technology as a way to bypass the expense of installing fiber-optic cables.

Frequency

For many years, communication technologies were focused on the lower part of the RF spectrum, roughly below 300 MHz, because low frequency RF signals, when transmitted with enough power, reach long distances and penetrate buildings. Television and radio signals are examples of low frequency, high-power signals.

In the 1980s, research shifted from low frequency, high-powered microwaves to high frequency, low-powered signals over short distances. Engineers were interested in creating a point-to-multipoint video network in the high frequency band. This eventually became the technology behind LMDS, which uses high frequency, low-powered waves to send and receive signals over a shorter distance.

One of the early problems with the LMDS frequency spectrum was that this was the same spectrum used by certain satellite systems. In 1996, the FCC made initial spectrum allocations for LMDS. The spectrum between 27.5 MHz and 28.35 MHz (a total of 850 MHz worth of frequency) was allocated to LMDS systems on a primary basis. In addition, another 150 MHz of frequency, between 29.1 MHz and 29.25 MHz, was allocated to LMDS on a co-primary (shared) basis, along with 30 GHz, 31.075 GHz, and 31.225 GHz.

Architecture

Because an LMDS signal can only travel up to 5 miles (8 kilometers), an LMDS network is composed of cells much like a cellular telephone system. A transmitter sends out signals to the fixed buildings within the cell, as seen in Figure 9-5. However, there are several differences between LMDS cells and a cellular telephone system. First, a cellular telephone system is intended for mobile users; LMDS is a fixed wireless technology for buildings. Also, in a cellular telephone system, the size of each cell is approximately the same and is based on the distance the RF signal can travel from the tower to the user. That is not the case with LMDS. There are a variety of factors that can affect the size of the LMDS cell. Most of these are based on the fact that LMDS requires a direct line of sight. The main factors that determine the cell size are line-of-sight, antenna height, overlapping cells, and rainfall.

- Line of sight — A direct line of sight between the transmitter and receiver is essential. In areas where there are tall buildings or other high obstructions, the cell size may need to be smaller to reach more customers. In Figure 9-6, a tall building obstructs the signal to other buildings. One solution is to divide the area into smaller cells, as seen in Figure 9-7.

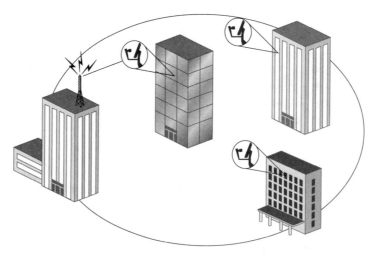

Figure 9-6   Tall building obstructs signal

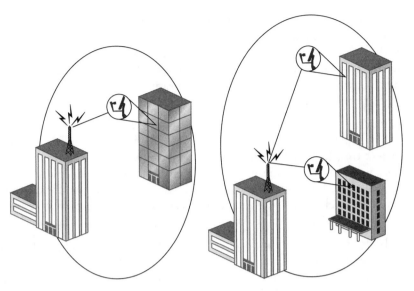

Figure 9-7   Divide into smaller cells

- Antenna height — Another factor to be considered is the height of the transmission and reception antennas. If the transmitting and receiving antennas can be placed on the rooftops of tall buildings, particularly those buildings that are farthest away from each other, then cells can typically be larger because the number of obstructions is reduced. This is seen in Figure 9-8.

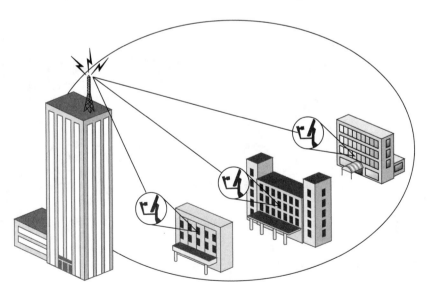

Figure 9-8   Antenna height

- Overlapping cells — Because LMDS is a line-of-sight technology, a signal sent from one tower may not reach all of the recipients. In one study, a single LMDS transmitter reached only slightly more than 60% of the buildings in an LMDS cell. With overlapping cells, however, that number increased to almost 85% of the buildings. The improvement resulted from the second transmitter being able to reach buildings that the first one could not because the second had better line of sight.

- Rainfall — Cell size is also determined by the amount of local rainfall. Because LMDS signals are microwaves, these signals react with water and lose strength. To correct this, LMDS can either increase the power of the transmissions when it rains, in an attempt to ensure a strong signal that reaches its destination, or reduce the cell size. Most LMDS cells are sized based on the average local annual rainfall. An LMDS cell, under ideal conditions, can be up to 5 miles (8 kilometers) across. However, most cells are between 2 to 5 miles (3.2 to 8 kilometers).

LMDS signals are broadcast from radio hubs (transmitters) that are deployed throughout the carrier's market, which is the area in which the LMDS provider has a license to use a certain frequency. This area is usually limited to a city or part of a city. Each hub broadcasts signals to buildings within its cell. The hub connects to the service provider's central office, which in turn can connect to other networks such as the Internet. This is seen in Figure 9-9.

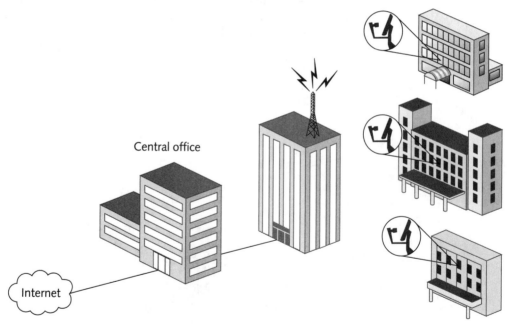

Figure 9-9   LMDS infrastructure

At the receiving site there are three pieces of equipment: a 12- to 15-inch diameter directional antenna, a digital radio modem, and a network interface unit. The antenna, which transmits and receives signals in a restricted direction, is usually installed on the roof of the building and must have a direct line of sight to a hub. The digital radio modem performs digital-to-analog and analog-to-digital conversions. The **network interface unit (NIU)** connects to other services, such as a local area network or telephone system. Rarely are individual telephones, computers, and video equipment connected directly to the NIU. This is illustrated in Figure 9-10.

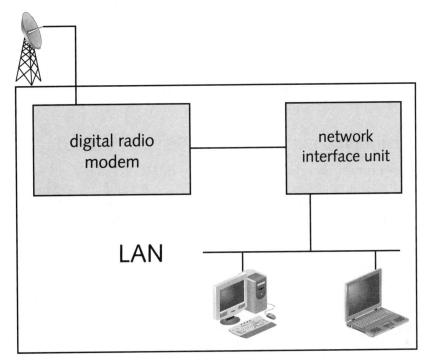

Figure 9-10   LMDS receiving equipment

LMDS systems can use either time division multiple access (TDMA) or frequency division multiple access (FDMA) to share the frequency spectrum among users. The modulation techniques can also vary among carriers. Most use a form of quadrature phase shift keying (QPSK) or quadrature amplitude modulation (QAM).

Advantages and Disadvantages of LMDS

The advantages of LMDS include cost, service area, and data capacity.

LMDS costs less to implement than fiber-optic cables. These costs are low for both the user and the carrier. For the user, the cost is minimal to install the antenna, modem, and NIU, compared to the cost of installing fiber-optic cable. For the carrier, LMDS is an attractive last mile solution because it allows large numbers of concentrated customers to access the carrier's network at a lower cost than wired alternatives.

The service area of an LMDS network can be expanded one cell at a time. This means that an LMDS network can be installed selectively to cover the most profitable users first and later expanded as the customer base increases.

LMDS carriers can have as much as 1,300 MHz of spectrum in a local market. This spectrum can simultaneously support 16,000 telephone calls and 200 video channels.

The disadvantages of LMDS have to do with physical restrictions. LMDS requires a direct line of sight between buildings. Obstructions such as buildings, trees, branches, and even leaves can block an LMDS signal. This means that the layout of an LMDS network can be limited by surrounding objects.

LMDS signals are susceptible to interference from rain and fog. High frequency microwaves are absorbed by water, reducing the strength of the signal during rain. LMDS systems may be better suited for regions with minimal rainfall, although carriers can use a variety of techniques to minimize the impact of rain on an LMDS signal.

Multichannel Multipoint Distribution Service (MMDS)

Multichannel multipoint distribution service (MMDS) is a fixed broadband wireless technology that has many similarities to LMDS. One significant difference relates to transmission capabilities. MMDS can transmit video, voice, or data signals at 1.5 to 2 Mbps downstream and 320 Kbps upstream at distances of up to 35 miles (56 kilometers), compared to 155 Mbps downstream and 1.54 Mbps upstream transmissions of up to 5 miles for LMDS.

Note that there is only one difference between the acronym of the two systems, the first letter (M for multichannel vs. L for local). The word multichannel goes back to the original use of this technology. MMDS was designed in the 1960s to provide transmission for 33 one-way analog television channels (simplex transmission). This multiple-channel technology (hence the word multichannel) was designed for educational institutions to provide long-distance learning. The FCC allocated part of the frequency spectrum, from 2.5 GHz through 2.7 GHz, for MMDS.

NOTE MMDS is sometimes expanded to Multipoint Microwave Distribution System or Multi-channel Multi-point Distribution System. All three terms refer to the same technology.

However, the original vision for MMDS never fully materialized. Private companies later purchased part of this spectrum to compete against wired cable television companies (MMDS is sometimes called wireless cable). Using MMDS, television signals could be wirelessly beamed to homes instead of delivered over a cable system. In the 1980s, new digital technology allowed service providers to increase their capacity from 33 analog channels to 99 digital channels. Later improvements in compression and modulation techniques increased the capacity of MMDS to broadcast 300 channels.

A major change to MMDS came about in 1998. The FCC allowed service providers to use the 200 MHz of bandwidth in the MMDS frequency bands to provide two-way services such as wireless Internet access at the same time as voice and video transmissions. In the home, Internet access using MMDS is an alternative to cable modems and DSL service, particularly in rural areas where cabling is scarce. For businesses, MMDS is an alternative to T1 or expensive fiber-optic connections. MMDS uses the 2.1 GHz and 2.5 GHz through 2.7 GHz bands to offer two-way service at speeds of up to 1.5 Mbps downstream and 300 Kbps upstream.

NOTE MMDS operates in many international markets at 3.5 GHz.

NOTE For Internet access, most of the traffic is downstream. For example, when you are browsing the Web, fewer packets are sent upstream to request the pages from the servers. The amount of data transmitted from the Web servers to the user's computer (downstream), which may include graphics, is much larger. Most home Internet users download far more data than they upload. This is why services such as DSL, cable Internet, MMDS, and others have a higher bandwidth downstream and a lower bandwidth upstream. Business users that run their own Web servers require a different type of connection with higher upstream speeds.

Layout

An MMDS hub (transmitter) is typically located on a high point such as a mountain, tower, or building. The hub uses a point-to-multipoint architecture that multiplexes communications to multiple users. The tower has a backhaul connection to the carrier's network, and the carrier network connects with the Internet.

Because they operate at a lower frequency than LMDS signals, MMDS signals can travel longer distances. This means that MMDS can provide service to an entire area with only a few radio transmitters. LMDS signals require more transmitters to travel the same distance. MMDS uses cells like LMDS does. However, an MMDS cell size can have a radius of up to 35 miles (56 kilometers), which covers 3,800 square miles (9,482 square kilometers) in area. A similar area would require over 100 LMDS cells.

At the receiving location, a directional antenna approximately 13 by 13 inches (33 cm) is aimed at the hub to receive the MMDS signal, as seen in Figure 9-11. This antenna, sometimes called a **pizza box antenna** for obvious reasons, is usually installed on the roof of a building so that it has a direct line of sight to a radio transmitter. A cable runs from the antenna to an MMDS wireless modem, which converts the transmitted analog signal to digital. The modem then can connect to a single computer or a LAN, as seen in Figure 9-12.

Figure 9-11   Pizza box antenna

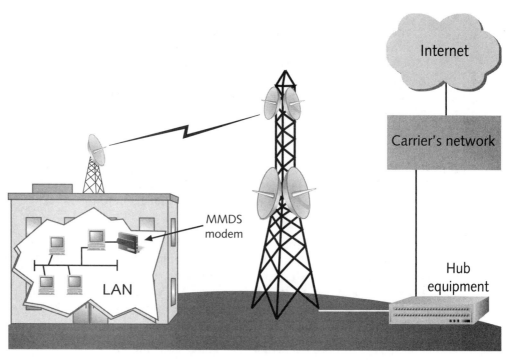

Figure 9-12   MMDS infrastructure

Advantages and Disadvantages of MMDS

Advantages of MMDS include signal strength, cell size, and cost. Low frequency MMDS RF signals can travel farther, generally are less susceptible to interference from rain or fog, and are better able to penetrate buildings than high frequency LMDS RF signals. These character-istics permit MMDS transmitters to cover areas seven times larger than LMDS transmitters. Finally, the cost of electronic equipment is typically linked to the frequency used to transmit: the higher the frequency, the higher the cost of the equipment. Because MMDS uses a lower frequency in comparison to LMDS, MMDS equipment is less expensive.

The disadvantages of MMDS include physical limitations, frequency sharing, security, and availability of the technology.

Current generation MMDS still requires a direct line of sight between the tower and the buildings. This makes installation more difficult and prevents MMDS from being used in a large number of buildings in a given cell because they are blocked by taller obstructions. Also, a single MMDS cell might be servicing a larger number of users within its 35 mile (56 kilometer) radius. These users all share the same radio channels. As a result, data throughputs and speed are decreased as more users are added. Providers of MMDS technology sometimes quote transmission rates of up to 10 Mbps, but because the channels are shared, the actual speed may be closer to 1.5 Mbps.

Carriers do not encrypt the wireless MMDS transmissions. Although only a highly sophisticated user could intercept and read the transmissions, business users should add security enhancements to their transmissions to keep them safe. Finally, MMDS is available in only a limited number of areas across the United States at the present time, and is not expected to experience much future growth, due to competition from WiMAX technolo-gies, which are covered in the next section.

9

IEEE 802.16 (WiMAX)

IEEE 802.16 is the standard for wireless broadband metropolitan area networks. The IEEE introduced 802.16 in 2000, with the goal of standardizing fixed broadband wireless con-nections as an alternative to wired access networks such as fiber-optic links, cable TV modems, and DSL. Although LMDS and MMDS systems had been used for several years, 802.16 supports enhancements and extensions to the MAC protocols so that it is possible for a **base station (BS)** (the transmitter connected to the carrier network or to the Internet) to communicate with another BS and also directly with **subscriber stations (SS)**, which can be either a laptop computer or device that attaches to a LAN. LMDS and MMDS do not provide connectivity with mobile devices. FSO also cannot support mobile communica-tions because of its directional requirements.

In January 2006, Samsung introduced a notebook computer and mobile telephone handset that were both 802.16-compliant.

Neither FSO, LMDS, or MMDS is based on an open standard, which means that equipment from different manufacturers may not interoperate. This shortcoming forces customers to purchase all of their equipment from a single manufacturer or, in cases where they may be using an outside provider for their wireless connection, to purchase all the equipment from the provider.

A group of large manufacturers formed the **WiMAX Forum** to address this problem. The organization is dedicated to promoting the implementation of 802.16 by testing and certifying equipment for compatibility and interoperability. Currently, the forum Web site lists over 330 member companies. The term **WiMAX** stands for worldwide interoperability for microwave access.

Many standards become loosely known by the more popular name of the industry organizations, such as WiMAX. You can find out more about WiMAX by visiting the forum Web site at www.wimaxforum.org.

The IEEE 802.16 family of standards offers multiple RF interfaces (PHY layers), depending on the frequencies used and associated regulations for different countries, but they are all based on a common MAC protocol. Next, you will learn about the applications and situations in which WiMAX can be employed.

South Korea was one of the first countries in the world to implement wireless broadband networks based on the nation's WiBro standard. The IEEE subse-
quently made the 802.16 standard fully compatible with the Korean standard.

WiMAX Applications

With data rates ranging up to 70 Mbps in the 2 to 11 GHz bands, and up to 120 Mbps at short distances (within a large office environment) in the 10 to 66 GHz bands, WiMAX is suitable for backhaul applications for business, and last mile delivery applications replacing T1, DSL, and cable TV modems for Internet connectivity. WiMAX can also support simultaneous voice, video, and data transmission. Quality of service (QoS) support makes WiMAX particularly suitable for voice-over-IP (VoIP) connections, which may enable more small companies to enter the telecommunications market and compete with major telephone companies for providing telephone services.

WiMAX enables vendors to create many different types of products, including various configurations of base stations and **customer premises equipment (CPE)**, the devices that are installed in a customer's office or home. In addition to supporting the point-to-multipoint applications mentioned above, WiMAX can also be deployed as a point-to-point network to provide broadband access to rural and remote areas.

To see examples of CPE and base station devices, antennas, and other WiMAX hardware, visit www.redlinecommunications.com and browse the RedMAX product line.

Manufacturers can design and build standards-based equipment that can be employed by wireless operators using licensed frequencies, business users using both licensed and unlicensed frequencies, and individuals using unlicensed frequencies. Compared to MMDS and LMDS, the cost for the equipment and service has dropped significantly already. Whereas an LMDS network can cost upward of $60,000, an 802.16 network can be put together for under $10,000. In 2003, service providers were looking forward to getting the price for the customer premises equipment for MMDS down to the $200 level. Since 2004, 802.16 manufacturers and providers have anticipated that CPE devices will continue to drop in price—possibly even below $50. These WiMAX CPE devices will support TV (video), telephone (voice), and data on the same network. This type of transmission convergence is called **triple-play**.

The WiMAX MAC layer includes features designed to make it easy for carriers to deploy the network. Once the BSs are in place, an end-user can connect to a WiMAX network by simply taking the CPE device out of the box, placing the antenna near a window or mounting it on an outside wall, roughly in the direction of the BS, and turning it on. Little or no configuration should be required. This process also has the effect of dramatically reducing the installation costs for the service provider, who will no longer have to send a technician to the customer's site. By remotely managing the device, the provider will also reduce maintenance costs.

In December 2005, Nortel announced that it would deploy a WiMAX network covering 8,000 square miles (20,720 square kilometers) in the southeast region of Alberta, Canada, in 2006. The network will operate in the 3.5 GHz band and provide Internet access at speeds between 1 and 3 Mbps to this large rural area, serving both the public and the provincial government. Nortel also said that the network is easily upgradeable to 802.16e mobile WiMAX, once the standard is published and equipment becomes available.

The range of a WiMAX network is measured in miles, unlike Wi-Fi, which is measured in feet. With low costs and interfaces becoming available for laptop computers and other hand-held devices, even at slightly lower speeds, WiMAX can offer serious competition to 802.11 networks and hotspots.

Cellular phone operators can easily incorporate WiMAX networks for data applications over their existing transmission tower infrastructure. Since cellular networks were originally designed for circuit-switched connections and not for packet-switched data, one of the advantages of this approach is that cellular handsets equipped with WiMAX chipsets could connect to both networks simultaneously and carry far more data than is possible with cellular technology, at a much lower cost.

NOTE   In October 2005, Nokia announced that it completed a data call from a cellular telephone handset using WiMAX. Nokia is conducting WiMAX trials in 2006. Intel expects to ship integrated WiMAX chips for laptop computers in 2007 and for cellular handsets in 2008.

Standards Family Overview

802.16 covers a wide range of functionality and has variations that address specific functions. Most of the variations of the 802.16 standard are extensions of the original standard. In this section, you will learn about 802.16-2001, 802.16-2004, 802.16a, 802.16c, and 802.16e.

Both 802.16-2001 and 802.16-2004 standards define the interface specification for fixed, point-to-multipoint broadband wireless metropolitan area networks. The initial 802.16-2001 standard includes a PHY layer specification for systems operating between 10 GHz and 66 GHz and forms the basis for all the other standards in the family. 802.16-2004 is a revised version of the initial standard and consolidates the initial standard with two amendments published later: 802.16a, which adds support for systems operating in the 2 GHz to 11 GHz band, and 802.16c, which mostly provided clarifications related to performance evaluation and testing.

802.16.2-2004 is also a revision of the 802.16.2-2001 standard. It addresses the recommended practices for implementation of 802.16 networks to enable coexistence with other 802.16 networks and minimize interference problems.

The 802.16e standard, which was ratified in December 2005, is an amendment to the 802.16-2004 standard that defines the specifications for a *mobile* version of WiMAX. This enhancement can enable data rates of up to 2 Mbps for portable devices that are slow moving or stationary, and speeds of up to 320 Kbps can be achieved in fast-moving vehicles.

Except where otherwise noted, all subsequent mentions of 802.16 in the remainder of the chapter refer to the 802.16-2004 standard.

WiMAX Protocol Stack

Like many of the technologies you have learned about in this book, the only layers that change between different networking standards are the PHY and MAC layers. WiMAX is unique in that, in addition to the PHY layer supporting multiple frequency bands, it also supports several modulation techniques that adapt to the requirements of the network, the amount of interference, and the distance between transmitters. It also provides different mechanisms for multiple access. Furthermore, the modulation techniques and access mechanisms can change dynamically in WiMAX, depending on with which device the BS is communicating with at the moment, the existence of any interference, or the requirements of the particular device itself.

Unlike Ethernet and other protocols, the WiMAX MAC layer is *connection oriented* and includes service-specific convergence sublayers that interface to the upper OSI layers. The convergence sublayers can map a service to a connection, which allows WiMAX to offer multiple simultaneous services through the same link and carry a mix of protocols, such as asynchronous transfer mode (ATM), IPv4, IPv6, Ethernet, and VLAN, all in the same network. The privacy sublayer is used in securing the link (discussed later, in the security section of this chapter). The protocol stack is shown in Figure 9-13. In the next sections, you will learn about some of the specific functionality of the PHY and MAC layers.

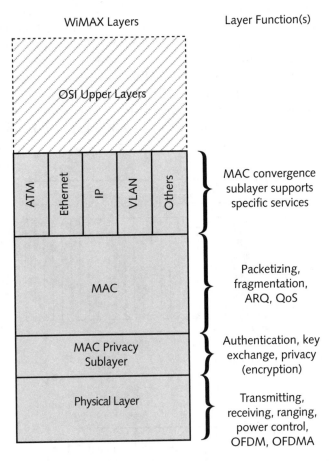

Figure 9-13 802.16 protocol stack

PHY Layer

There are five variations of the PHY layer in 802.16. Determining which variation to use for a particular implementation depends on the frequency range and whether it is a point-to-point or point-to-multipoint setup. The first two are based on the modulation of a single carrier signal. Recall that when transmitting on a single frequency, all transmitters have to work in half-duplex mode because they cannot transmit and receive at the same time. In this case, each transmission is divided into fixed duration frames that are 0.5 ms, 1 ms, or 2 ms long. Each frame is subdivided into one uplink subframe and one downlink subframe. The BS transmits to the SSs during the downlink subframe and the SSs transmit to the BS during the uplink subframe.

The subframes are further divided into a series of time slots. The number of time slots in the uplink and downlink subframe varies, which helps the BS allocate more time slots for the uplink or downlink. The number of uplink or downlink time slots allocated depends on the amount of data being transmitted in either direction. A data transmission to or from a single device is called a **burst** in the 802.16 standard. A burst can also be a broadcast transmission from the BS to all SSs. A transmission also contains commands or network management information that is sent prior to the transmission of the frame's data portion. The BS allocates time slots for specific SSs in both the downlink frame and the uplink frame. The amount of data contained in a burst depends on the number and length of the time slot, and on the modulation and coding used for that particular burst. This mechanism, called **time division duplexing (TDD)**, is illustrated in Figure 9-14.

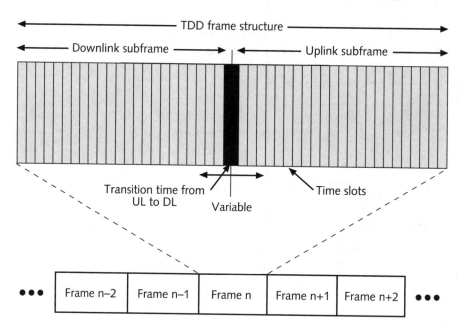

Figure 9-14 WiMAX TDD frame

WiMAX also allows the use of two different frequency channels, in which case one is used for downlink and another for uplink. This mechanism is called **frequency division duplexing (FDD)**. The structure of the frame in FDD is similar to TDD, except that one frequency is used exclusively for the downlink and the other is used exclusively for the uplink.

WiMAX can support both less expensive half-duplex equipment that does not transmit and receive simultaneously, as well as higher performance full-duplex stations that can transmit and receive simultaneously, using different frequencies on the same network and at the same time. The adaptive characteristic of the uplink and downlink, coupled with support of both TDD and FDD, allows 802.16 to use the frequency spectrum more efficiently.

A WiMAX FDD network can support a mixture of full-duplex and half-duplex devices. When half-duplex transmitters are connected to an FDD network, the BS needs to make sure that it does not schedule time for those devices to transmit and receive simultaneously.

In a point-to-multipoint architecture, the BS transmits using time division multiplexing (TDM). SSs are each allocated a time slot, in sequence. Note that since only the BS transmits in the downlink direction, it does not have to be concerned with contention and can simply address information in different time slots, to different SSs.

Access in the uplink direction from the SS to the BS uses time division multiple access (TDMA), in which one or more time slots are allocated to each SS depending on the requirements of the type of data being transmitted. Some of the time slots are also allocated for contention access, which enables SSs that are not currently members of the network to communicate with the BS for the purpose of establishing a connection to the network.

There are two variations of the PHY layer specified in the standard. **WirelessMAN-SC (single carrier)** is used for point-to-point connections in the 10 to 66 GHz bands. The other variation, **WirelessMAN-SCa (single-carrier access)**, is more complex and is also used in point-to-point applications, but in the 2 to 11 GHz bands.

At the higher frequencies of 10 to 66 GHz, line of sight to the transmitter and directional antennas are a requirement. In the 2 to 11 GHz bands, which include unlicensed frequencies, the 802.16 standard also provides support for non-line-of-sight applications. **Non-line-of-sight (NLOS)**, as the term implies, is when the transmitter antenna cannot be seen from the receiver end or vice-versa, because of the geography of the area or because of obstructions such as buildings and trees that block the direct path of the signal. Outdoor, tower-mounted antennas for homes can be very expensive to purchase and even more expensive to install, especially in areas subject to high winds or ice accumulation. Significant multipath distortion is likely to occur in such installations. Recall that when using directional antennas in line-of-sight applications, multipath distortion is negligible and can be ignored; however, in point-to-multipoint, the BS will typically use an omnidirectional antenna. This is illustrated in Figure 9-15.

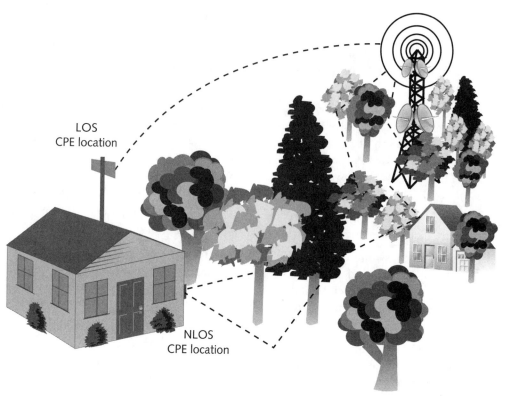

LOS
CPE location

NLOS
CPE location

Figure 9-15   Non-line-of-sight

To support NLOS applications, 802.16 also introduced two additional Physical layer transmission mechanisms:

- WirelessMAN-OFDM, which uses TDMA. This mechanism is mandatory for unlicensed bands and divides the frequency band into up to 192 data subcarriers to make it resistant to multipath problems. It is intended for fixed wireless implementations.

- WirelessMAN-OFDMA, which uses **orthogonal frequency division multiple access (OFDMA)**, a technique based on OFDM that divides the available channel into a large number of orthogonal subcarriers. These subcarriers are then grouped into subchannels. Each SS can be allocated a subchannel, allowing multiple stations to communicate with the BS simultaneously. OFDMA subdivides the frequency channel into 1,536 data subcarriers and is extremely resistant to multipath problems.

A third transmission mechanism, **wireless high–speed unlicensed metro area network (WirelessHUMAN)**, is also based on OFDM and is specifically designed for use in the 5 GHz U-NII band.

Both OFDM and OFDMA in 802.16 are also scalable, meaning that the number of subcarriers allocated to an SS for the uplink can vary, depending on the QoS requirements of the transmission, the signal quality, or the distance between the SS and the BS.

Another key characteristic of the 802.16 PHY is that it supports adaptive modulation. In simple terms, this means that for each transmission, 802.16 can dynamically change the modulation, increasing or decreasing the data rate based on signal quality. In addition, in order to meet the regulatory requirements in different countries as well as to optimize the use of the spectrum, the 802.16 standard allows transmitters to use frequency bandwidths of a minimum of 1.25 MHz up to a maximum of 20 MHz. Table 9-2 summarizes the WiMAX specification's nomenclature, frequencies used, applications, and duplexing alternatives.

Table 9-2   WiMAX specifications summary

Designation	Frequencies	Application	Duplexing
WirelessMAN-SC	10-66 GHz licensed bands	Fixed only	TDD, FDD
WirelessMAN-SCa	Below 11 GHz licensed bands	Fixed or mobile (802.16e)	TDD, FDD
WirelessMAN-OFDM	Below 11 GHz licensed bands	Fixed, mobile, or mesh	TDD, FDD
WirelessMAN-OFDMA	Below 11 GHz licensed bands	Fixed or mobile	TDD, FDD
WirelessHUMAN	Below 11 GHz	Fixed or mesh	TDD only

Modulation and Error Correction

In 802.16, modulation and error correction are directly linked to each other. Recall that forward error correction (FEC) is a technique that either repeats the same bits several times or inserts additional bits in the data stream to enable the receiver to detect multiple bit errors and to correct single bit errors. In addition to FEC, 802.16 also uses automatic repeat requests (ARQ) to ensure the reliability of the transmissions. 802.16 was designed to achieve 99.999% reliability. FEC improves the chances of receiving the data correctly and thus reduces the number of retransmissions, which consequently increases the performance of the link. However, the additional bits add overhead to the transmissions, increasing the total amount of data and therefore reducing the overall performance of the link. By dynamically changing the modulation, 802.16 achieves an optimum balance of speed and transmission success for a given signal quality.

Table 9-3 lists the types of modulation supported in 802.16 and the associated mandatory FEC coding. The coding rates are listed here for informational purposes only. A full explanation of the FEC coding requires complex mathematical formulas and is beyond the scope of this book. However, it is important to know that the different FEC coding rates are used for increasing the reliability of the transmission.

Table 9-3 802.16 modulations and mandatory FEC coding

Modulation	FEC Coding Rates
BPSK	1/2, 3/4
QPSK	1/2, 2/3, 3/4, 5/6, 7/8
16-QAM	1/2, 3/4
64-QAM	2/3, 5/6
256-QAM (optional)	3/4, 7/8

The ability of 802.16 to dynamically change modulations is also one of the key elements in the ability of WiMAX to reduce latency and improve QoS. **Latency** is the amount of time delay that it takes a packet to travel from source to destination device. Figure 9-16 illustrates how WiMAX uses different modulations. Adaptive modulation also helps WiMAX use the channel bandwidth more efficiently. QoS will help it reach a broader customer base, especially those with demanding business customers.

The BS sends information to the SSs about which modulations it will use for a particular burst and for a particular SS in a downlink map (DL-MAP) in the first few data frames at the beginning of the transmission. The SSs respond by sending an uplink map (UL-MAP) at the beginning of their assigned bursts. The DL-MAP and UL-MAP are parts of the frame that describe the method of transmission as well as the contents of the bursts, time allocations, and other information.

The 802.16 standard defines several transmission **profiles**, which are sets of predefined connection parameters that include the frequency channel, bandwidth of the channel, and transmission mechanism (OFDM, OFDMA, etc.). The implementation of these profiles by the manufacturer of the WiMAX equipment simplifies deployment in the field and eliminates the need for a large number of separate configuration items. These profiles are also intended to reduce or eliminate the need for **truck-rolls**, which are support technician visits to the site. WiMAX also specifies basic profiles: point-to-multipoint (P2MP), point-to-point (PTP), as well as an optional mesh networking profile, which is also included in the standard. A WiMAX **system profile** is a combination of the basic profile and one of the transmission profiles and is preset on the equipment before it is shipped to an end-user site.

NOTE

Each truck-roll to install a single broadband network device at a customer site can cost an operator up to $400.

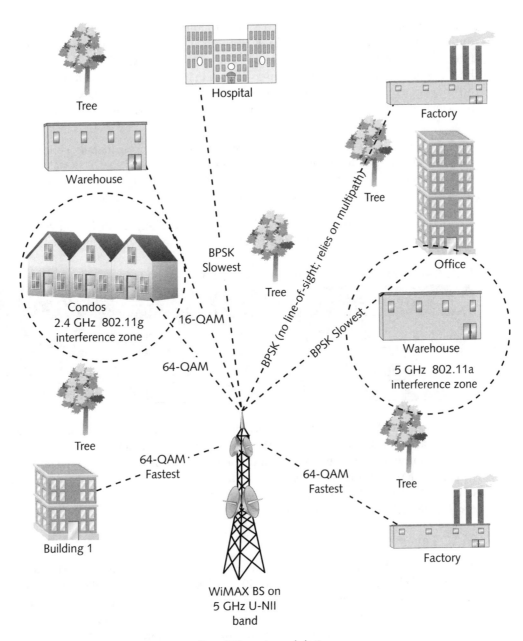

Figure 9-16 How WiMAX applies different modulations

Range and Throughput

The maximum distances achievable in a WiMAX network depend on the frequency band used. Recall that the higher the frequency, the shorter the range of the signal at a given power setting. Conversely, higher frequency signals allow for higher data rates.

In general, higher frequencies are used for metropolitan area line-of-sight, point-to-point, or multipoint applications at very high data rates for carrier networks using licensed frequencies. Lower licensed frequencies—below 11 GHz—will likely be used for private, line-of-sight network connections up to 10 miles (16 kilometers) as well as for long distance links of up to 35 miles (56 kilometers). Frequencies below 11 GHz will also be used for non-line-of-sight networks with a maximum range of up to 5 miles (8 kilometers).

NOTE WiMAX base stations and subscriber stations perform ranging (distance) calculations based on signal quality. This process occurs when a subscriber station initially joins the network and periodically thereafter, and helps the equipment establish the modulation and FEC coding to use for data transmissions.

Maximum achievable data rates depend on the modulation, channel bandwidth, and FEC coding used. Table 9-4 summarizes these combinations for the most typical implementations.

Table 9-4   Maximum WiMAX data rates (Mbps)

	Modulation/ FEC Coding	QPSK 1/2	QPSK 3/4	16 QAM 1/2	16 QAM 3/4	64 QAM 2/3	64 QAM 3/4
Channel Bandwidth	1.75 MHz	1.04	2.18	2.91	4.36	5.94	6.55
	3.5 MHz	2.08	4.37	5.82	8.73	11.88	13.09
	7.0 MHz	4.15	8.73	11.64	17.45	23.75	26.18
	10.0 MHz	8.31	12.47	16.63	24.94	33.25	37.40
	20.0 MHz	16.62	24.94	33.25	49.87	66.49	74.81

Note that a wider channel bandwidth also means that more data can be sent per signal unit, as you learned in Chapter 2, hence the higher data rates achievable with wider channels. Realistic throughput will be lower than the rates shown in Table 9-4. One reason for this is that the WiMAX channel bandwidth is shared, and therefore it is impacted by the number of users. Another is that some additional transmission overhead, such as MAC layer framing, is not included in the rate calculations above.

MAC Layer

Most wireless MAN implementations function in a point-to-multipoint basis with one BS and potentially hundreds of SSs. The 802.16 MAC dynamically allocates bandwidth to individual SSs for the uplink—this is the key to the high data rates possible in WiMAX networks. In addition to supporting a large number of SSs, the MAC convergence sublayers allow WiMAX to be implemented as an efficient transport in point-to-point systems for backhaul applications, and supports protocols such as ATM and T1, among others.

A point-to-multipoint WiMAX network usually operates with a central BS that can be equipped with a smart, sectorized antenna, also called an **advanced antenna system (AAS)**, which can transmit multiple simultaneous signals in different directions to stations that fall within the range of each of the antennas. All stations in the range of each antenna receive the transmission. Recall that for the uplink, the only stations sending signals are the ones that were scheduled by the BS to transmit. WiMAX can also take advantage of multiple in multiple out (MIMO) antenna systems to reduce interference with other systems (see WiMAX coexistence below) and the impact of multipath distortion.

To address a burst to a particular SS, the BS uses a 16-bit number called a connection identifier (CID), which is used to identify both the device and the connection, after it connects to the WiMAX network (recall that the WiMAX MAC is connection oriented). Each station also has a 48-bit MAC address, which is only used during connection establishment. When the stations receive a transmission from the BS, they check the CID and keep only the MAC frames that contain data addressed to them.

Stations can request additional dedicated bandwidth (for QoS) if this is required to support a particular service, such as the transmission of telephone calls or a video stream. The BS polls the SSs periodically to identify their bandwidth needs and grants bandwidth as required. Except in the case of connections that require a guaranteed bit rate, such as T1, most data connections cannot tolerate errors but can tolerate latency and **jitter**, which is the maximum delay variation between two consecutive packets over a period of time. Web browsing, transmitting e-mail messages, and downloading files are latency- and jitter-tolerant activities. Video and voice, on the other hand, can tolerate a certain amount of errors, but not latency or jitter.

The WiMAX MAC protocol maintains a consistent bandwidth by using a self-correcting mechanism for granting more bandwidth to SSs. This creates less traffic on the network, since there is no need for SSs to acknowledge the grant. Instead, if an SS does not receive the bandwidth grant or the BS does not receive the request, the SS will simply request it again. The requests from the SSs are cumulative, but they will also periodically inform the BS of their total bandwidth needs. This mechanism is far more efficient than those used by other networking standards.

NOTE The scheduling services in WiMAX that map the connections in the uplink direction for allocating channel bandwidth to the SSs are based on the scheduling services defined for cable modems in the data over cable service interface specification (DOCSIS) standard. See www.cablemodem.com/specifications/.

A MAC frame includes a fixed-length header, an optional and variable-length payload (data), and an optional cyclic redundancy check (CRC). Header-only MAC frames are used to send commands and requests between the BS and the SSs. The generic MAC frame format is shown in Figure 9-17.

Most
significant
byte

Least
significant
byte

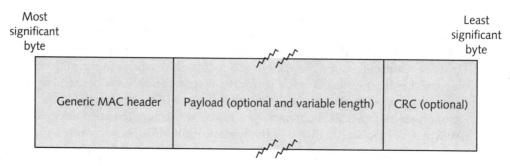

| Generic MAC header | Payload (optional and variable length) | CRC (optional) |

Figure 9-17   802.16 (WiMAX) MAC frame

WiMAX Coexistence

One of the concerns of end-users and carriers when considering wireless data transmission in the unlicensed bands is that as the number of transmitters grows, so does interference. Eventually, interference can make the technology and, consequently, the user's investment, unusable. This concern is of particular importance considering the distances achievable with 802.16.

WiMAX is different from technologies such as 802.11 in that it is not limited to the 2.4 GHz or the 5 GHz bands. While business users are encouraged to develop a sharing agreement when operating in the unlicensed bands (see IEEE 802.16.2-2004 at standards. ieee.org/getieee802/index.html), service providers that expect to sell wireless connectivity to customers should consider a low-cost purchase or lease of a small amount of spectrum in the 2 to 11 GHz band. FCC policies allow spectrum holders to resell unused spectrum to other operators.

The ISM band offers approximately 80 MHz of bandwidth; however, the U-NII band offers 12 channels and about 300 MHz of bandwidth, which users and operators can share. Depending on the distance between transmitters, interference may not be a serious problem, since WiMAX signals are limited to between 30 and 35 miles (approximately 48 to 56 Kilometers) under ideal, line-of-sight conditions. When adaptive modulations, variable data rates, and FEC are taken into account, any remaining concerns can be easily dispelled by testing the performance of a link. Most vendors, eager to sell their equipment, would usually be happy to assist in this process. Power levels can also be adjusted, as long as adjustments do not create interference with licensed frequencies, which is highly unlikely. Smart antenna systems are also another potential solution to this type of problem.

NOTE

The European Telecommunications Standards Institute (ETSI), which you learned about in Chapter 3, published a standard called high-performance metropolitan area network (HIPERMAN). HIPERMAN is based on 802.16 and specifies systems that are based on OFDM and work at frequencies below 11 GHz only.

WMAN Security

As with other types of networks, security in WMANs is a major concern. Despite using multiple beam technology (which could allow an attacker to attempt to capture information by interrupting a single beam), FSO systems are generally considered secure. Anyone trying to *sniff* information from FSO systems would have difficulty accessing the equipment and blocking only a portion of an invisible beam. In addition, such interference would affect the performance of the network, immediately alerting the user or operator. In LMDS and MMDS systems, RF signals can be captured by a receiver without blocking the radio signal. Since most of these systems are proprietary and expensive, system manufacturers or operators are typically responsible for designing custom security measures into their equipment. Because most WMAN installations will likely be based on WiMAX technology, this section will focus on WiMAX security measures.

WiMAX Security

As you learned in the section on the WiMAX protocol stack, the MAC layer includes a privacy sublayer. Unlike 802.11 and Bluetooth, the WiMAX standard was initially designed to include very powerful security measures. These features make it extremely difficult—if not impossible—for a would-be hacker to steal information from WiMAX transmissions.

The privacy sublayer provides a client/server authentication and key management protocol with the BS controlling the distribution of security keys to the SSs. In addition, the standard also encrypts all of the data transmitted between the BS and SSs and makes use of **digital certificates**, which are messages digitally signed by a certification authority, as well as public-key infrastructure embedded in the BS, to ensure privacy and protection against information theft. Manufacturers install a unique digital certificate, which includes a serial number in every device. The digital certificates can be verified with the manufacturer as being valid and unique by sending a copy of the certificate encrypted with the manufacturer's public key over the Internet if a connection is available. This is a requirement of the 802.16 standard.

There are two separate protocol components in the privacy sublayer:

- An encapsulation protocol for encrypting packet data that includes a set of cryptographic suites (the encryption and authentication mechanisms) used to apply encryption to the transmitted data.

- A privacy key management protocol that provides secure key distribution from the BS to the SSs. This protocol is used for synchronizing the security keys between the BS and SSs as well as to prevent unauthorized stations from associating with a WiMAX network.

Once a device is authenticated with the BS using the digital certificate, a **traffic encryption key (TEK)**, the security key used to encrypt the data, is exchanged between the BS and SS for each different service connection being carried over the wireless interface. Recall that the 802.16 MAC is connection oriented and can carry multiple types of service. TEKs expire, and the SS must renew the keys periodically with the BS. The default TEK lifetime is 12 hours. The minimum value is 30 minutes, and the maximum value is seven days.

Only the headers are not encrypted in WiMAX, to allow SSs to associate with the network. Although data can be sent unencrypted, most users use encryption. All data sent across the wireless medium is then encrypted using one of the following algorithms:

- 3-DES (Triple-DES) — Data is encrypted three times with a 128-bit key, using the United States **Data Encryption Standard (DES)**.

- RSA with 1024-bit key — **RSA** is an algorithm developed in 1977 by Ron Rivest, Adi Shamir, and Leonard Adleman. The algorithm is owned by RSA Security, and the company licenses the technology and sells development kits.

- AES with a 128-bit key — The **Advanced Encryption Standard (AES)**, the latest encryption standard, was developed by the National Institute of Standards and Technology (NIST) to replace DES. AES is considered unbreakable and is used to encrypt unclassified U.S. government material.

The security mechanisms designed into WiMAX should help ensure the wide and quick adoption of this standard in the marketplace.

NOTE The high reliability and high security of WiMAX, together with its long-distance and NLOS characteristics, make it an excellent candidate for use by security companies providing burglar alarms for homes and businesses. WiMAX makes it viable to secure a building or home using a live video link and IP-based security cameras.

CHAPTER SUMMARY

- WMANs are a group of technologies that provide wireless connectivity throughout an area such as a city without cable infrastructure. WMANs also extend user mobility throughout a metropolitan area.

- Last mile wired connections are the link between the customer's premises and an ISP. Most last mile connections today are still based on copper wiring.

- Long-distance telephone and data connections between cities today have mostly migrated to fiber-optic cable due to its high speed, reliability, and channel capacity.

- There are two ways in which a signal can be sent. The first technique is called broadband, which sends multiple signals at different frequencies. This allows many different signals to be sent simultaneously. The second technique is called baseband, which treats the entire transmission medium as if it were only one channel. Until 2001, RF-based fixed broadband systems were limited to connecting with only one other device at a time and could only transmit using a line-of-sight link.

- Free space optics (FSO) has been an excellent alternative to costly high-speed fiber-optic connections. FSO transmissions are sent by low-powered infrared beams through the open air. Because FSO is a line-of-sight technology, the transceivers must be mounted in high locations to provide a clear transmission path.

- Local multipoint distribution service (LMDS) is a fixed broadband technology that can provide a wide variety of wireless services, including high-speed Internet access, real-time multimedia file transfer, remote access to LANs, interactive video, video-on-demand, video conferencing, and telephone service. LMDS can transmit from 51 to 155 Mbps downstream and 1.54 Mbps upstream over a distance of up to about 5 miles (8 kilometers).

- Because an LMDS signal can only travel up to 5 miles, an LMDS network is composed of cells much like a cellular telephone system. A transmitter sends signals to the fixed buildings within the cell. LMDS is a fixed technology for buildings. The main factors that determine the LMDS cell size are line-of-sight, antenna height, overlapping cells, and rainfall.

- Multichannel multipoint distribution service (MMDS) is a fixed broadband wireless technology. MMDS can transmit video, voice, or data signals at distances of up to 35 miles (56 kilometers). Because it operates at a lower frequency, MMDS signals can travel longer distances. These longer distances mean that MMDS requires fewer radio transmitters compared to the equipment required by LMDS to send the same signal. MMDS is used as an option in both home and business settings. MMDS uses the 2.1 GHz and 2.5 GHz through 2.7 GHz bands to offer two-way service at speeds of up to 1.5 Mbps upstream and 300 Kbps downstream. LMDS and MMDS technology is not based on standards.

- The IEEE 802.16 (WiMAX) standard was introduced in 2000 with the goal of standardizing fixed broadband wireless services as an alternative to wired access networks. A single WiMAX base station (BS) can communicate with hundreds of subscriber stations (SSs) simultaneously in point-to-multipoint mode or with another BS, in point-to-point. 802.16 equipment can either transmit in the 10 to 66 GHz range or in the 2 to 11 GHz range and can also use unlicensed frequency bands. A BS can also connect directly with a laptop computer. All 802.16 systems are based on a common MAC protocol.

- WiMAX can transmit at speeds up to 70 Mbps in the 2 to 11 GHz bands and can also achieve 120 Mbps at short distances in the 10 to 66 GHz bands. QoS support makes WiMAX suitable to carry simultaneous voice, video, and data (triple-play) at a much lower cost than LMDS and MMDS networks. WiMAX equipment is relatively easy and inexpensive to install and maintain.

- WiMAX range is measured in miles. Cellular phone operators can overlay WiMAX networks on their existing networks, which will reduce the cost of sending data from handheld cellular phones.

- The 802.16e standard will bring full support of mobile devices to WiMAX technology. Mobile WiMAX can achieve data rates of up to 2 Mbps for portable devices that are slow moving or stationary and up to 320 Kbps in fast-moving vehicles.

9

❏ The WiMAX MAC layer is connection oriented and includes convergence sublayers that allow WiMAX to support ATM, T1, Ethernet, and VLANs, in addition to other services, directly. There are five variations of the 802.16 PHY layer. The first two are based on the modulation of a single carrier signal. All devices work in half-duplex. The PHY frames can be 0.5 ms, 1 ms, or 2 ms long and are divided into a variable uplink subframe and downlink subframe. The subframe is divided into time slots that carry the payload. A single or multiple time slots can be allocated to a specific station. The mechanism is called time division duplexing. WiMAX also supports the use of two frequency channels, one for the uplink and another for the downlink. This is called frequency division duplexing.

❏ The BS can support both half-duplex and full-duplex devices simultaneously on the network and is the only device transmitting on the downlink. The BS transmits using time division multiplexing. The stations transmit using time division multiple access. A contention period is allocated by the BS in the uplink subframe to allow stations that are not members of the network to establish a connection and join the network.

❏ There are two variations of the WiMAX PHY layers for point-to-point connections: WirelessMAN-SC for the 10 to 66 GHz bands and WirelessMAN-SCa for the 2 to 11 GHz bands. The standard also provides three other layers for non–line-of-sight applications in the 2 to 11 GHz bands. WirelessMAN-OFDM is mandatory for the unlicensed bands and uses OFDM technology with up to 192 subcarriers. WirelessMAN-OFDMA uses orthogonal frequency division multiple access with 1,536 data subcarriers. Both variations are extremely resistant to multipath problems. The third variation, WirelessHU-MAN, is based on OFDM and is specific to the 5 GHz band.

❏ OFDM and OFDMA in 802.16 are scalable. The number of subcarriers allocated to an SS for the uplink can vary depending on the QoS requirements of the SS, the distance between the SS and BS, and the signal quality. The WiMAX PHY layer uses adaptive modulation. It can dynamically change modulation techniques depending on the distance and signal quality. WiMAX transmitters can transmit using signal bandwidths from 1.25 MHz up to 20 MHz. Through the use of error correction techniques and adaptive modulation, WiMAX makes efficient use of the spectrum and achieves high-performance.

❏ A WiMAX transmission profile specifies the frequency channel, bandwidth and transmission mechanism. A basic profile specifies whether the network is point-to-point or point-to-multipoint. A system profile is the combination of a basic profile and transmission profile. The use of profiles helps make WiMAX installations simpler and reduce the cost to the operator.

❏ The MAC layer is the key to the intelligence and security behind WiMAX networks. Efficient bandwidth-saving protocols and QoS help WiMAX reduce latency and jitter and maintain a consistent bandwidth. WiMAX includes a number of features that help operators and end-users reduce interference problems.

❏ The security features of WiMAX were designed to offer operators and end-users the peace of mind that other wireless technologies have failed to provide so far. The use of verifiable digital certificates, the most advanced encryption mechanisms (3-DES, RSA, and AES), as well as secure key exchange protocols should promote the quick and wide adoption of WiMAX technology.

KEY TERMS

advanced antenna system (AAS) — An antenna that can transmit multiple simultaneous signals in different directions to stations that fall within the range of each of the antennas.

Advanced Encryption Standard (AES) — The latest encryption standard, developed by the National Institute of Standards and Technology (NIST) to replace the United States data encryption standard (see DES).

backhaul — A company's internal infrastructure connection.

baseband — A transmission technique that treats the entire transmission medium as only one channel.

base station (BS) — The transmitter connected to the carrier network or to the Internet.

broadband — A transmission technique that sends multiple signals at different frequencies.

burst — A transmission containing data to or from a single SS or a broadcast transmission from the BS.

carriers — Telephone, cable TV, and other communication providers who own the wires and transmission towers that carry voice and data traffic.

customer premises equipment (CPE) — The WiMAX devices that are installed in a customer's office or home.

Data Encryption Standard (DES) — The encryption standard used in the United States until the adoption of AES (see AES).

digital certificates — A special message signed by a certification authority, used for security and authentication.

fixed wireless — A wireless last mile connection.

free space optics (FSO) — An optical, wireless, point-to-point, line-of-sight broadband technology.

frequency division duplexing (FDD) — A mechanism that uses one frequency for uplink and another for downlink (see also TDD).

IEEE 802.16 — The IEEE standard for wireless broadband metropolitan area networks.

jitter — The maximum delay variation between two consecutive packets over a period of time.

last mile connection — The link between the customer's premises and the telephone company, cable TV company, or an ISP.

latency — The amount of time delay that it takes a packet to travel from source to destination device.

local multipoint distribution service (LMDS) — A fixed broadband technology that can provide a wide variety of wireless services.

microwaves — Part of the spectrum from 3 to 30 GHz.

multichannel multipoint distribution service (MMDS) — A fixed broadband wireless technology that transmits at 1.5 Mbps over distances of 35 miles (56 kilometers).

network interface unit (NIU) — A device that connects an LMDS modem to a LAN or telephone system.

9

non-line-of-sight (NLOS) — When the transmitter antenna cannot be seen from the receiver end, or vice-versa.

orthogonal frequency division multiple access (OFDMA) — A multiple access technique, based on OFDM, that divides the frequency channel into 1,536 data subcarriers.

pizza box antenna — A small antenna used for MMDS systems.

profiles — Sets of predefined WiMAX connection parameters that include the frequency channel, bandwidth of the channel, and transmission mechanism (OFDM, OFDMA, etc.).

RSA — An encryption algorithm developed in 1977 by Ron Rivest, Adi Shamir, and Leonard Adleman.

scintillation — The temporal and spatial variations in light intensity caused by atmospheric turbulence.

spatial diversity — The sending of parallel beams during free space optical transmissions.

subscriber station (SS) — In a WiMAX network, either a CPE device that attaches to a LAN or a laptop computer.

super high frequency (SHF) — Part of the frequency spectrum from 3 to 30 GHz.

system profile — A combination of the basic WiMAX profile and one of the transmission profiles.

time division duplexing (TDD) — A mechanism that divides a single transmission into two parts, an uplink part and a downlink part (see also FDD).

traffic encryption key (TEK) — The security key used to encrypt the data in a WiMAX network.

triple-play — The support of transmission of video, voice, and data on the same network.

truck-rolls — Support technician visits to a site.

WiMAX — Worldwide interoperability for microwave access.

WiMAX Forum — An industry organization dedicated to promoting the implementation of 802.16 by testing and certifying equipment for compatibility and interoperability.

wireless high-speed unlicensed metro area network (WirelessHUMAN) — A WiMAX specification based on OFDM, specifically designed for use in the 5 GHz U–NII band.

WirelessMAN-SC (single carrier) — A WiMAX specification that uses a single carrier and is intended for point-to-point connections in the 10 to 66 GHz bands.

WirelessMAN-SCa (single-carrier access) — A WiMAX specification that uses a single carrier and is intended for point-to-point connections in the 2 to 11 GHz bands.

wireless metropolitan area networks (WMANs) — A group of technologies that provide wireless connectivity across a substantial geographical area such as a large city.

Review Questions

1. The term fixed wireless is generally used to refer to _____ .
    a. buildings
    b. cars
    c. satellites
    d. cell phones

2. What is the connection that begins at a fast service provider, goes through the local neighborhood, and ends at the home or office?

a. 1 mile

b. Last mile

c. ISP

d. Link

3. All of the following are last mile connections for home users except

_____ .

a. satellite

b. dial-up modem

c. DSL

d. baseband

9

4. A leased special high-speed connection from the local telephone carrier for business users that transmits at 1.544 Mbps is _____ .

a. T1

b. T3

c. DSL

d. Ethernet

5. The transmission that treats the entire transmission medium as if it were only one channel is _____ .

a. broadband

b. analog

c. baseband

d. line

6. WiMAX can communicate at speeds of up to _____ in the 10 to 66 GHz bands, over short distances.

a. 100 Mbps

b. 70 Mbps

c. 120 Mbps

d. 30 Mbps

7. The convergence sublayers in the WiMAX MAC protocol allow it to support

_____ .

a. T1

b. ATM

c. voice and video

d. all of the above

8. In the uplink direction, 802.16 transmits using _____ .

    a. TDMA

    b. half-duplex only

    c. TDM

    d. the downlink frame

9. LMDS has an advantage over MMDS in that the signals can travel up to 35 miles from the transmitter. True or False?

10. One of the limitations of LMDS and MMDS is that these systems operate at frequencies that require line of sight. True or False?

11. Devices in a WiMAX network must transmit in half-duplex only. True or False?

12. The WiMAX base station controls all transmissions in a WiMAX network. True or False?

13. Non-line-of-sight transmissions in the 802.16 standard are only supported in the 2 to 11 GHz bands. True or False?

14. Sometimes called fiberless optical, _____ uses no medium like a fiber-optic cable to send and receive signals; instead, transmissions are sent by low-powered infrared beams through the open air.

15. The maximum coverage area for a local multipoint distribution service (LMDS) network is _____ miles.

16. A single WiMAX base station can communicate with _____ terminals simultaneously.

17. WirelessHUMAN stands for _____ . This transmission mechanism is specific to the _____ band(s).

18. What is the significance of the fact that the distances in a WiMAX network are measured in miles (or kilometers)?

19. What is the purpose of adaptive modulation in WiMAX?

20. List three modulation techniques used in 802.16.

21. How does the BS send information to the SSs about which modulations will be used for a particular burst or transmission?

22. What is the difference between the 48-bit MAC address and the CID? What is the purpose of the CID?

HANDS-ON PROJECTS

Project 9-1: Identifying WiMAX Equipment Vendors

Identify at least two manufacturers of WiMAX equipment. Prepare a report on what type of equipment they supply (such as base stations, CPEs, or adapter cards for laptop computers). Ensure that the manufacturer can supply at least two of the different classes of products noted. List the operating frequencies and one other important feature of the equipment.

Project 9-2: Identifying WiMAX Deployments

Research news media Web sites and locate one or two places in North America that are not mentioned in the chapter where the local government, a vendor, or a business association is planning to deploy a WiMAX network. Outline the purpose and the extent of the deployment, as well as the expectations of the project.

9

CASE PROJECT

Project 9-1: Connecting Sites Using WiMAX Technology

Wheeler University's campus is spread over a remote area about the size of three city blocks to the south of Buffalo, New York. Wheeler administrators have contacted The Baypoint Group (TBG) and asked for a proposal to connect their three student residence buildings to the university's network. The buildings are wired for Ethernet, but students currently do not have access to either the university's network or the Internet because the dorms are in a remote area without DSL or cable TV service. The university considered implementing a satellite-based system or installing fiber optics, but the cost of each option proved prohibitive. The university has access to the Internet through a backhaul MMDS connection to an ISP, but the cost of installing a private MMDS network also was too high. TBG has asked you to become involved, since you are its wireless networking expert. The residence buildings have line-of-sight access to each other and to the computer center building.

Based on the research you did for Hands-on Project 9-1, prepare a two-page recommendation, including a 10-minute PowerPoint presentation, for a specific WiMAX implementation that also outlines the features of WiMAX and how it can provide long-term benefits for the university. Pay particular attention to whether the equipment you have chosen is WiMAX certified or is in the process of being certified. Include photos and specifications of the equipment in your presentation.

10

WIRELESS WIDE AREA NETWORKS

> **After reading this chapter and completing the exercises, you will be able to:**
>
> ♦ Describe wireless wide area networks (WWANs) and how they are used
>
> ♦ Describe the applications that can be used on a digital cellular telephone
>
> ♦ Explain how cellular telephony functions
>
> ♦ List features of the various generations of cellular telephony
>
> ♦ Discuss how satellite transmissions work

A wireless wide area network (WWAN) spans a geographical area as large as an entire country or even the entire world. WWANs use cellular telephone and satellite technology to connect users to a voice or data network through e-mail and Internet connections. WWAN users also can connect to a corporate network and run business applications from virtually any location around the planet using Smartphones, PDAs, and PCMCIA cellular adapter cards plugged into notebook computers. The BlackBerry from RIM (www.blackberry.com) is just one example of a wireless device in use in business and government.

From the user's perspective, digital cellular technology is ubiquitous. No matter where you go around the world, everyone seems to be using digital cellular phones to make and receive calls, send and receive short text and e-mail messages, access the Web, send faxes, and even watch TV and movies. Using a digital cellular telephone today is as simple as using a traditional wired telephone. In many parts of the world, especially where the telephone cable infrastructure is either outdated or nonexistent, cellular phones are making telephone service available to users who never before had access to a private telephone line. In fact, the cellular telephone is replacing the traditional land-based telephone line in many instances.

Cellular technology has changed lives as well. By the time fishermen tie their boats to the dock, the catch is already sold to the highest bidder. Farmers in remote communities sell their products while on their way to the market. Often this remote marketplace enables fishermen, farmers, and other small manufacturers to bypass the middlemen and enjoy increased profits, something that ultimately benefits everyone, all the way to the consumer.

From a technological point of view, there is nothing simple about digital cellular telephony. It is one of the most fiercely competitive and complex of all wireless communication technologies. First, there is no single underlying digital cellular technology used worldwide. There are a variety of technologies battling for the users' desire for speed and quality of connection, with such strange acronyms as GSM, EDGE, UMTS, and CDMA2000 1xEVDO. Second, not only are there competing technologies, there are also dozens of competing carriers in many countries, some of them among the largest corporations on the planet, each pushing a specific technology. Even governments have gotten in on the boom, auctioning off parts of the wireless spectrum to the highest bidders, earning billions of dollars in the process.

For many years, satellites have provided service for global positioning systems, communications for the remotest of areas, as well as TV and radio signals that can be watched or listened to by virtually anyone, anywhere on the planet, in real-time. In this chapter, you will also learn about the role of satellites in WWANs. Satellites can deliver signals to any point on the vast oceans that cover most of the surface of our planet, to the Arctic and Antarctic continents, and to remote mountainous areas where electricity and radio frequency (RF) transmission tower infrastructure does not yet exist. Because of the complexity of launching them into space and placing them in the correct orbit, satellites are one of the most expensive wireless communications technologies.

This chapter explores how cellular telephones work and looks at the complex technology behind digital cellular networks. We will also examine what tasks can be achieved using digital cellular devices, the various platforms and software that make these enhanced features work, and issues surrounding implementation of digital cellular technology. Finally, we will take a look at how satellites are deployed, some of the issues surrounding the use of satellites for data transmission, and how satellites complement cellular telephony to help provide a truly global wireless wide area network.

CELLULAR TELEPHONE APPLICATIONS

New and expanded applications and features that digital cellular networks provide to mobile users are the main incentive for the growth of these technologies. The list of these features is impressive. Because the networks are based on digital instead of analog technology, and can transmit at much higher speeds, they are not limited to voice communications. Digital cellular telephones can be used to:

- Browse the Internet
- Send and receive short messages and e-mails

- Participate in videoconferencing

- Receive travel, entertainment, news reports, and other types of information

- Run a variety of business applications

- Connect to corporate networks

- Watch television or on-demand movies

- Take and transmit pictures and short movies

- Locate family members and employees using GPS

One of the most widely used applications today is **Short Message Services (SMS)**. SMS allows for the delivery of short, text-based messages between wireless devices such as cellular telephones and pagers. SMS is not like two-way paging, which allows users to send many lines of text over data networks. SMS messages are brief, limited to about 160 characters in length (or 70 characters for non–Latin Arabic and Chinese characters). In addition, SMS is not like text-message services that send messages over the Internet from a central site, such as an answering service sending a message to a physician. Instead, SMS lets users send messages directly from one device to another device without using the Internet or some other server-based application, such as e-mail or instant messaging on the Internet (although the cellular telephone equipment will store a message if the other user's telephone is out of range or powered off).

NOTE Pagers work in a similar fashion to SMS. A user dials a phone number that is actually calling a device known as a paging terminal. Once the page is entered, the paging terminal converts it into a code and relays the code to transmitters, which send the code out as a radio signal throughout the coverage area.

SMS is used in several applications. These include:

- Person-to-person: This is the most common use of SMS, namely one user sending a text message to another user. It has been called the digital cellular equivalent of instant messaging.

- Agent-to-person: Automated agents can send notifications whenever an event occurs. These events are configured by the user. For example, an automated agent can send out an SMS message when a stock reaches a certain price or the user has received a voice mail message.

- Information broadcast services: These include news, weather, and sports scores sent on a regular basis or when a breaking story occurs.

- Software configuration: Changes to the software running on the cellular device can be performed by SMS.

- Advertising: Messages containing advertising can be sent to users over SMS.

NOTE Unsolicited advertising, or spam, over SMS is becoming a major problem for users. Although guidelines have been recommended for SMS advertising, such as limiting the message to 100 characters, users still complain of receiving numerous unsolicited advertising messages daily on their mobile devices.

Although SMS is very popular in many countries, it has been slow to catch on in North America. Many industry experts attribute this to differences in culture and technology. For example, most people in the United States who have wireless digital cellular technology also have Internet access at home or work and send messages by e-mail. In Japan and Europe, where Internet access is much more limited because of its high cost, SMS has become a viable alternative to e-mail.

Another reason for the slow growth in the United States is that the cost of making a wireless cellular telephone call is so inexpensive that it often makes more sense to pick up the phone and call someone than to type a text message. Overseas customers, on the other hand, pay much higher rates for wireless digital cellular telephone calls. Many of these users opt for using SMS, which is a cheaper way to communicate. In addition, U.S. consumers have a variety of alternatives to SMS, such as e-mail and two-way paging services.

Cultural differences also have an impact. In many nations, small technological devices are viewed as being very popular and trendy, whereas in the United States, the overall emphasis is not focused on the device that sends the message but on the content of that message.

Despite its slow start in North America, SMS, or text messaging, has become one of the major applications used on digital cellular telephones, especially among young people. With the average number of SMS messages sent annually worldwide in excess of 200 billion, it is probably just a matter of time before SMS becomes popular in the United States.

HOW CELLULAR TELEPHONY WORKS

Cellular telephones work in a manner that is unlike wired telephones. There are two keys to cellular telephone networks. The first is that the coverage area is divided into smaller individual sections, called **cells**, as seen in Figure 10-1. In a typical city, the cells measure approximately 10 square miles (26 square kilometers). At the center of each cell is a cell transmitter (and a receiver, of course) with which the mobile devices in that cell communicate, sending and receiving RF signals. These transmitters are connected to a base station, and each base station is connected to a **mobile telecommunications switching office (MTSO)**. The MTSO is the link between the cellular network and the wired telephone world and controls all transmitters and base stations in the cellular network. A large city may have multiple MTSOs.

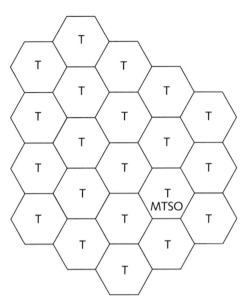

T = Transmitter

MTSO= Mobile telecommunications switching office

Figure 10-1 Cellular network

Cells are always drawn as hexagons, simply because it makes it easier to show adjacent cells without overlapping lines. In reality, the cell shape is closer to a circle, but the shape may be affected by buildings and other geographic features.

NOTE

Projections for global cell phone use predict an estimated 2.5 billion cellular telephone subscribers worldwide by the end of 2006, with growth to 3.5 billion subscribers by 2010.

NOTE

The second key to cellular telephone networks is that all of the transmitters and cell phones operate at a low power level. This enables the signal to stay confined to the cell and not interfere with any other cells. Because the signal at a specific frequency does not go far beyond the cell area, that same frequency can be used in other cells at the same time, except in adjacent cells. This is illustrated in Figure 10-2.

Because of frequency reuse, a typical cellular telephone network in one city uses only 830 frequencies to handle all callers.

NOTE

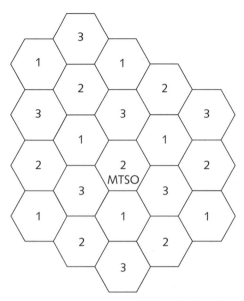

MTSO= Mobile telecommunications
switching office

Figure 10-2   Frequency reuse with three frequencies

All cell phones have special codes associated with them. These codes are used to identify the phone, the phone's owner, and the carrier or service provider (such as AT&T, Sprint, and many others). The codes that are used are summarized in Table 10-1.

Table 10-1   Cellular telephone codes

Code Name	Size	Purpose
System Identification Code (SID)	5 digits	The carrier's unique identification number
Electronic Serial Number (ESN)	32 bits	The cellular phone's unique serial number
Mobile Identification Number (MIN)	10 digits	A unique number generated from the phone's telephone number

NOTE

The ESN is permanently assigned to a specific cellular phone when it is manufactured. The MIN and SID codes are programmed into the phone when it is activated.

When a cellular telephone user moves around within the same cell, the transmitter and base station for that cell handle all of the transmissions. As the user moves toward the next cell, the cellular telephone will automatically associate with the base station of that cell in a handoff. However, what happens if a cellular user moves beyond the coverage area of the entire cellular network, for example, from Nashville to Boston? In this case, the cellular telephone would automatically connect with whatever cellular network is in place in the remote area. The cellular network in the remote area (Boston) would communicate with the cellular network in the home area (Nashville), verifying that the user can make calls, and would also charge for the calls. This remote connection is known as **roaming**. Handoff and roaming are illustrated in Figure 10-3.

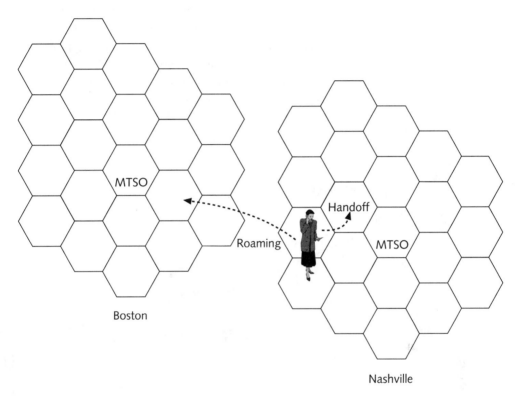

Figure 10-3 Handoff and roaming

A cellular user's home area is the location where she lives or works and where she has an account with the cellular carrier. When connected to the home area, the user pays local, per-minute call rates. When roaming, the per-minute rates tend to be much higher. Per-minute rates and roaming rates depend on the carrier with which the user has an account.

The steps that a cellular telephone uses to receive a call are as follows:

1. When the cell phone is turned on, it listens for the SID being transmitted by the base station on the **control channel**, which is a special frequency that the phone and base station use for setup. If the phone cannot detect a control channel, it is out of range and displays a message to the user such as "No Service."

2. If the cell phone receives an SID, it compares it with the SID that was programmed into the phone. If they match, the cell phone is in a network owned by its carrier. The cell phone transmits a registration request number to the base station that the MTSO uses for tracking the cell(s) in which the phone is located.

3. If the SIDs do not match, then the cellular phone is roaming. The MTSO of the remote network contacts the MTSO of the home network, which confirms that the SID of the phone is valid. The MTSO of the remote network then tracks the phone and sends the call information (including length of call and the call's status as a roaming connection) back to the home MTSO.

4. When a call comes in, the MTSO locates the phone through the registration request and then selects a frequency that will be used for communication. The MTSO sends the frequency information to the phone over the control channel. Both the phone and the transmitter switch to that frequency, and the connection is then completed. This is illustrated in Figure 10-4.

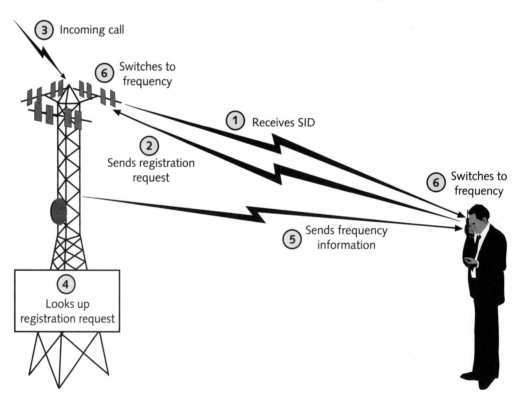

Figure 10-4   Receiving a call on a cell phone

5. As the user moves toward the edge of a cell, the base station notes that the phone's signal strength is decreasing while the base station in the next cell determines that the phone's signal strength is increasing. The two base stations coordinate with each other through the MTSO. The cellular phone then gets a message on the control channel to change frequencies as it is handed off into another cell.

6. The phone and transmitter change frequencies as required.

NOTE Although the Telecommunications Act of 1996 makes it illegal to intercept cellular transmissions, callers should remember that their conversations are being broadcast across the public airwaves and may not be as private as calls using the wired telephone network.

DIGITAL CELLULAR TECHNOLOGY

10

Cellular telephones have been available since the early 1980s in the United States. Since that time, cell phone technology has changed dramatically. Most industry experts outline several generations of cellular telephony.

First Generation Cellular Telephony

The first generation of wireless cellular technology is known, appropriately enough, as **First Generation (1G)**. 1G uses analog signals, which are radio frequency (RF) transmissions in which the caller's voice is modulated using basic frequency modulation (FM).

1G technology is based on the **Advanced Mobile Phone Service (AMPS)**. AMPS operates in the 800-900 MHz frequency spectrum. Each channel is 30 KHz wide with a 45 KHz passband. There are 832 frequencies available for transmission. 790 frequencies are used for voice traffic and the remaining 42 are used for the control channel. However, because two frequencies are used for a cellular telephone conversation (one to transmit and one to receive), there are actually 395 voice channels and 21 used for control channel functions.

NOTE Channels that are 30 KHz wide provide voice quality comparable to a standard wired telephone transmission, which is why AMPS channels are 30 KHz.

AMPS uses Frequency Division Multiple Access (FDMA), which you learned about in Chapter 3. Recall that for RF systems there are two resources, frequency and time. Division by frequency, so that each caller is allocated part of the spectrum for all of the time, is the basis of FDMA. This is illustrated in Figure 10-5. FDMA allocates a single cellular channel with two frequencies to one user at a time. If the channel deteriorates due to interference from other frequencies, the user is switched to another channel.

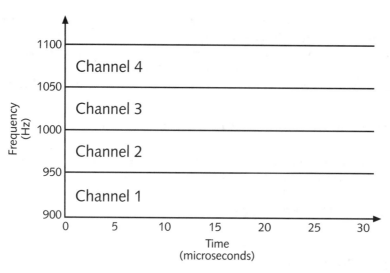

Figure 10-5   FDMA

AMPS was one of the first wireless communications systems to use FDMA. Today AMPS is not commonly used; however, tri-mode mobile phones still support the AMPS system.

1G networks use circuit-switching technology. When a telephone call is made, a dedicated and direct physical connection is made between the caller and the recipient of the call through the telephone company's switch. While the telephone conversation is taking place, the connection remains open between only these two users. No other calls can be made from that phone while the first conversation is going on, and anyone who calls that phone will receive a busy signal. This direct connection lasts for the duration of the call. At the end of the call, the switch drops the connection and the frequencies are released, so that they can be used by another caller.

Analog signals, the basis for 1G cellular telephony, are prone to interference and do not have the same quality as digital signals. In addition, sending data over an analog signal requires a modem or similar device to convert the signals from digital to analog and then back again. A 1G analog cellular telephone can be realistically used only for voice communications. For these reasons, 1G was soon replaced with improved digital technology.

Second Generation Cellular Telephony

The next generation of cellular telephony is known as **Second Generation (2G)**, which started in the early 1990s and continues to the present. 2G networks transmit data between 9.6 Kbps and 14.4 Kbps in the 800 MHz and 1.9 GHz frequencies. The only major feature that 2G systems share with 1G is that they are circuit-switched networks.

2G systems use digital instead of analog transmissions. Digital transmissions provide several improvements over analog transmissions:

- Digital transmission uses the frequency spectrum more efficiently.

- Over long distances, the quality of the voice transmission does not degrade as with analog.

- Digital transmissions are difficult to decode and offer better security.

- On average, digital transmissions use less transmitter power.

- Digital transmission enables smaller and less expensive individual receivers and transmitters.

Another difference between 1G and 2G systems is that the carriers of 2G cellular networks build their cellular networks around different multiple access technologies. Three different technologies are used with 2G: Time Division Multiple Access (TDMA), CDMA, and GSM. Whereas Frequency Division Multiple Access (FDMA), used with AMPS, divides by frequency, so that each caller is allocated part of the spectrum for all of the time, TDMA divides by time, so that each caller is allocated the entire spectrum for part of the time, as seen in Figure 10-6. TDMA divides a single 30 KHz radio frequency channel into six unique time slots, and each caller uses two time slots (one for transmitting and one for receiving). TDMA can send three times as many calls over a single channel as FDMA.

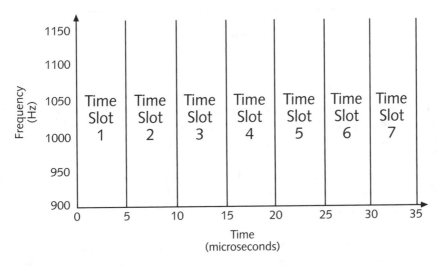

Figure 10-6   TDMA

Another multiple access technology is Code Division Multiple Access (CDMA; introduced in Chapter 3). With CDMA, every caller is allocated the entire spectrum all of the time, as seen in Figure 10-7. CDMA uses direct sequence spread spectrum (DSSS) and unique digital codes, rather than separate RF frequencies, to differentiate between the different transmissions. A CDMA transmission is spread across the frequency and the digital codes are applied to the individual transmissions. When the signal is received, the codes are removed from the signal.

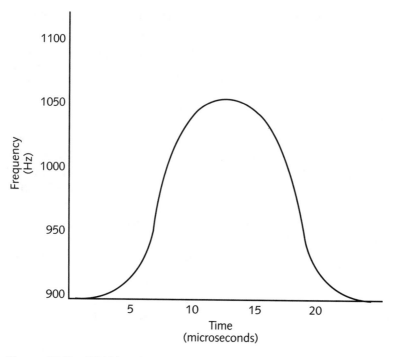

Figure 10-7 CDMA

The third multiple access technology used in 2G systems is **GSM (Global System for Mobile communications)**. GSM was developed in Europe as a standard for public mobile communications in the 1980s. GSM uses a combination of FDMA and TDMA technologies. GSM divides a 25 MHz channel into 124 frequencies of 200 KHz each. Each 200 KHz channel is then divided into eight time slots using TDMA. The modulation employed is a variation of FSK called Gaussian minimum shift keying (GMSK), which uses filters to help reduce interference between adjacent channels. GSM systems can transmit at speeds up to 9.6 Kbps.

NOTE   In 1989, the Cellular Telecommunications Industry Association (CTIA) chose TDMA over FDMA as the technology of choice for digital cellular networks. However, with the growing technology competition of CDMA and the fact that Europe was using GSM for mobile communications, the CTIA reconsidered and decided to let carriers make their own technology choices.

These three technologies—TDMA, CDMA, and GSM—make up the backbone of 2G digital cellular telephony.

2.5 Generation Cellular Telephony

Current digital cellular telephony has far surpassed the characteristics of 2G. The industry's transition to third generation is proceeding at an accelerated pace. Carriers are making major changes to the network infrastructures and a completely new generation of mobile cellular devices is on its way. Until the migration to third generation technology is completed, an interim step known as **2.5 Generation (2.5G)** has been widely deployed throughout North America. 2.5G networks operate at a maximum speed of 384 Kbps. 2.5G networks are also widely deployed in many nations, such as China, Japan, and Korea, along with a few cities in the United States and Europe.

The primary difference between 2G and 2.5G networks is that 2.5G networks are packet-switched instead of circuit-switched. Although circuit switching is ideal for voice communications, it is not efficient for transmitting data, because data transmissions normally occur in bursts with periods of delay in between when nothing is being transmitted. The delays result in time wasted while a channel is tied up, dedicated to one user.

Packet switching has two major advantages over circuit switching. First, packet switching is much more efficient because it can handle more transmissions over a given channel. Packet switching can handle three to five times more traffic than circuit switching. The second advantage is that packet switching permits an always-on connection. With a circuit-switched network, a connection between two devices ties up an entire channel that is dedicated only to those devices; it is not practical to keep that connection open when there is little or no traffic. This would be like calling a friend on the telephone and then laying the telephone down but not hanging up just in case you want to talk later. Doing so prevents any other calls from coming in or going out. With packet switching, it becomes practical to keep the connection up all the time. Each packet is transmitted independently through the network, to the destination, and only uses the channel for a small amount of time.

NOTE The always-on feature, along with higher transmission speeds, has made cable modems and DSL connections more popular than dial-up connections for home use. With a cable or DSL connection, the computer can always be connected to the network and there is never a wait for a connection to be established.

There are three 2.5G network technologies. The migration (upgrade) of the carrier's networks from 2G to 2.5G depends on which 2G network technology is being used. For TDMA or GSM 2G networks, the upgrade path is a 2.5G technology known as **General Packet Radio Service (GPRS)**. GPRS uses eight time slots in a 200 KHz spectrum and four different coding techniques, in addition to the modulation used by GSM, to transmit at a top speed of up to 114 Kbps. The next step beyond GPRS is **Enhanced Data rates for GSM Evolution (EDGE)**.

10

EDGE is considered a booster for GPRS systems and can transmit up to 384 Kbps. EDGE is based on a modulation technique called **8–PSK**, in which the phase of the carrier is shifted in 45-degree increments and 4 bits can be transmitted per phase change. EDGE-based networks can coexist with standard GSM networks.

If the network transition is from a 2G CDMA network, instead of migrating to GPRS, the transition to 2.5G is to CDMA2000 1xRTT. **CDMA2000 1xRTT** (1xRTT stands for 1–times Radio Transmission Technology) operates on a pair of 1.25 MHz-wide frequency channels and is designed to support 144 Kbps packet data transmission and to double the voice capacity of CDMA networks. The 1xRTT acronym comes from a similar technology called 3xRTT, which used a pair of 3.75 MHz-wide channels (or three times 1.25 MHz). 3xRTT, which was also known as multi-carrier CDMA2000, is not currently under development.

Third Generation Cellular Telephony

Imagine using your cellular telephone to videoconference with a friend in the United States while you are traveling on a train to Tokyo. That's the vision of **Third Generation (3G)**. 3G is intended to be a uniform and global standard for cellular wireless communication. The International Telecommunications Union (ITU) has outlined the standard data rates for a wireless cellular digital network. These rates are:

- 144 Kbps for a mobile user
- 386 Kbps for a slowly moving user
- 2 Mbps for a stationary user

As with 2.5G digital cellular networks, converting a 2.5G network to 3G depends on the 2.5G technology being converted. If the transition is being made from CDMA2000 1xRTT, the next step would be to **CDMA2000 1xEVDO** (for **Ev**olution **D**ata **O**ptimized). This technology can transmit at 2.4 Mbps. However, EVDO can only send data and must be coupled with 1xRTT to process both voice and data. EVDO transmissions are very similar to those of 1xRTT, but EVDO uses a pair of separate dedicated channels for data, often in new frequency bands being added to the bands available for use with CDMA2000 technologies, and measures the signal-to-noise ratio (SNR) in each channel pair every 1.667 milliseconds to determine which cellular phone device to service next. By using dedicated data channels and continually optimizing transmissions to the devices that have the best signal at any given time, EVDO can achieve its higher data rates. The successor to CDMA2000 1xEVDO will be **CDMA2000 1xEVDV** (for **Ev**olution **D**ata and **V**oice), which can send both data and voice transmissions simultaneously. EVDV is the next upgrade path for this technology. It can reach data transfer speeds of up to 3.09 Mbps. Release D of EVDV supports up to 1.0 Mbps upstream.

NOTE   In 2005, Verizon Wireless and Sprint Nextel Corporation in the United States, and Bell Canada and TELUS in Canada initiated nationwide deployment of 1xEVDO in North America. Alaska Communications Systems (ACS) is deploying 1xEVDO in the main population centers of Alaska. EVDO is currently operational in South America, Indonesia, Taiwan, and North America.

If a network is transitioning from EDGE 2.5G technology, **Wideband CDMA (W-CDMA)** is the 3G next-step technology. W-CDMA adds a packet-switched data channel to a circuit-switched voice channel. W-CDMA can send at up to 2 Mbps in a fixed position and 384 Kbps when mobile.

Beyond W-CDMA, the upgrade path is to High-Speed Downlink Packet Access (HSDPA), which can transmit at 8 to 10 Mbps downstream. HSDPA uses a 5 MHz W-CDMA channel, together with a variety of adaptive modulation, multiple in multiple out (MIMO) antennas, and hybrid automatic repeat request (HARQ) techniques grouped together to achieve very high data rates. Several carriers in North America are currently testing HSDPA technology for a future deployment.

As competition increases, networks are being rapidly upgraded to 3G digital cellular technology. These technologies are currently available worldwide, but the cost of upgrading is prohibitive for many carriers, as you will learn later in this chapter. Figure 10-8 summarizes the technology paths to 3G.

10

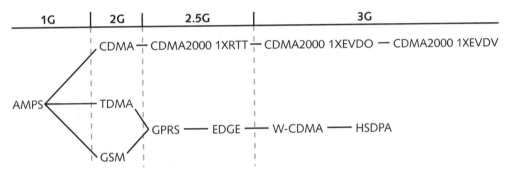

Figure 10-8 Digital cellular migration path

Table 10-2 summarizes digital cellular technologies.

Table 10-2 Digital cellular technologies

Name	Generation	Technology	Maximum Data Rate
AMPS	1G	Analog circuit-switched	9.6 Kbps
GSM	2G	Digital circuit-switched	9.6 Kbps
TDMA	2G	Digital circuit-switched	14.4 Kbps
CDMA	2G	Digital circuit-switched	14.4 Kbps
GPRS	2.5G	Digital packet-switched	114 Kbps
CDMA2000 1xRTT	2.5G	Digital packet-switched	144 Kbps

Table 10-2   Digital cellular technologies (continued)

Name	Generation	Technology	Maximum Data Rate
EDGE	2.5G	Digital packet-switched	384 Kbps
CDMA2000 1xEVDO	3G	Digital packet-switched	2 Mbps
W-CDMA	3G	Digital packet-switched	2 Mbps
CDMA 1xEVDV	3G	Digital packet switched	3.09 Mbps
HSDPA	3G	Digital packet switched	8 to 10 Mbps

Figure 10-9 summarizes the speed of data transmission of several cellular technologies.

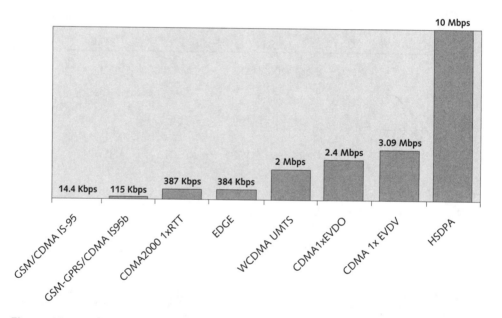

Figure 10-9   A comparison of data rates between cellular technologies

NOTE

In December 2005, Ericsson, one of the major global suppliers of 3G cellular base station equipment and handsets, announced that its HSDPA equipment is now operational in 15 countries in Asia, the Middle East, Africa, Europe, and North America.

CLIENT SOFTWARE

Features such as Internet surfing or videoconferencing require client software to operate on a wireless digital cellular device. The software provides the functions and interfaces that allow users to display or manipulate the data. Some client software is unique to cellular telephones, while other software is used in a variety of different applications. This section introduces the most common types of digital cellular client software: WAP, i-mode, Java, and BREW. These technologies will enable business applications to be used in virtually any location; this flexibility will provide businesses with remote processing capabilities that were previously unachievable.

Wireless Application Protocol (WAP and WAP Version 2)

As you learned in Chapter 1, the Wireless Application Protocol (WAP) and WAP2 provide a standard way to transmit, format, and display Internet data for devices such as cell phones. Developed in 1997 for Internet-enabled digital cellular phones, pagers, and other handheld devices, WAP enables these devices to send and receive Internet text-only data. The slow transmission speed and smaller viewing areas of 2G cellular telephones prevents these devices from supporting video and graphical data. An example of a WAP display is seen in Figure 10-10.

10

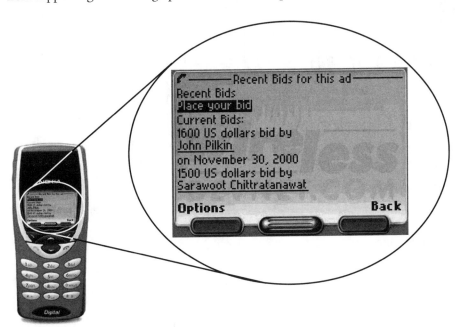

Figure 10-10   WAP display

A WAP cell phone runs a tiny browser program called a microbrowser that uses Wireless Markup Language (WML) instead of HTML. WML displays text-based Web content on the small screen of a cell phone. A WAP gateway (sometimes called a WAP proxy), which is a computer running special conversion software, must be used to translate between WML and HTML. Many features of HTML are not supported in WML, such as font types and sizes.

WML is case sensitive; all tags must be in lowercase.

NOTE

WML is based on the **Extensible Markup Language (XML)**. Defined by the World Wide Web Consortium (W3C), XML is similar to HTML, which uses tags to describe how an item should be displayed on the screen. A WML document is called a **deck** that contains one or more blocks, known as **cards**. Most documents are too large to fit into the space of a cell phone display screen. To accommodate the small display, a document is divided into smaller pieces (cards) and displayed one at a time. Each card has text content and navigation controls. Although only one card can be displayed at a time on the cell phone, navigation between the cards is very fast because the entire deck is stored by the microbrowser. This concept is illustrated in Figure 10-11.

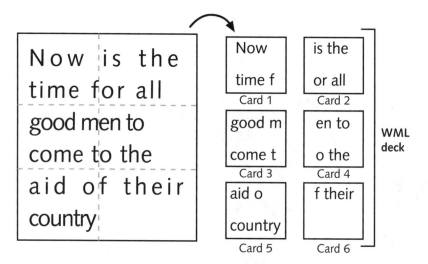

Figure 10-11   WML deck

Because most cellular devices have limited storage space (1.4 Kb is typical), the number of cards in a deck should also be limited. Usually five or six cards per deck is optimum.

NOTE

WAP2 is based on XHTML, which is an extension of HTML version 4. Because WAP2 supports HTML version 4, it can display graphics and multiple font styles on color screen-equipped mobile devices such as cell phones, PDAs, and Smartphones. WAP2 also includes a protocol stack that allows it to support TCP/IP directly. The WAP2 specification embraces Internet standards directly, unlike the original WAP standard, by adopting XHTML. WAP2 defines a new **profile**, an extension of XML, specifically to support mobile devices. WAP2 is backward compatible with WAP version 1, so WAP2-compatible mobile devices can still access Web sites designed for the original WAP version.

NOTE

The specifications and definition of XHTML, including its relationship to HTML version 4 and XML, can be found at www.w3.org/TR/xhtml1/#xhtml.

i-Mode

Another technology similar to WAP is **i-mode**. i-mode is an Internet access system owned by the Japanese corporation NTT DoCoMo, and is based on **compact HTML** (cHTML), a subset of HTML designed for mobile devices. cHTML has its own set of tags and attributes.

NOTE

In addition to cHTML tags, i-mode has its own tags, such as a tag to set up a link that dials a telephone number when pressed.

Although i-mode is similar to WAP in terms of its functionality, it differs in several ways. i-mode uses cHTML instead of WML. Also, i-mode users pay for the service by the amount of information downloaded plus a service charge, while WAP services are charged by the connection time.

Java

The **Java** programming language was developed by Sun Microsystems as an object-oriented language used for general-purpose business programming as well as interactive Web sites. Java can run on almost any hardware platform. A subset of Java, **Java 2 Micro Edition (J2ME)**, was specifically developed for programming wireless devices.

J2ME-enabled cellular telephones have more intelligence than basic digital cellular telephones that run a WAP microbrowser or i-mode. J2ME enables a cellular phone to access remote applications and e-mail, as well as run programs on the cellular phone itself. These programs include voice-activated dialing, calendars, and voice recorders. The cellular phone can handle specific tasks, such as automatically turning off the phone's ringer and forwarding calls to voicemail when the user is in a meeting that has been entered into the phone's calendar.

10

Binary Runtime Environment for Wireless (BREW)

WAP, WAP2, and i-mode are specifications for Web browsers, while J2ME is a programming language that requires a specific software interpreter on the mobile device to decode its instructions and interact with the user. Unlike these technologies, the **Binary Runtime Environment for Wireless (BREW)** is a thin software environment, a very small program that resides on a wireless device and is capable of running applications that can be downloaded by the device on demand. BREW is compatible with the Java, C, and C++ programming languages.

BREW efficiently uses the limited amount of memory available on cellular phones. BREW occupies only a small amount of flash memory, and it dynamically allocates RAM for applications when they are running. BREW can also be used in combination with other applications and software elements that may reside on the device. For example, BREW can be installed on a device that already has an operating system installed. And any type of browser (HTML, WAP, cHTML, and so on) can run on BREW as an application.

Although WAP and i-mode do allow users remote access to the Internet, their lack of support for a rich set of graphics limits their popularity. Both J2ME and BREW are the major platforms today for a variety of wireless devices that includes PDAs in addition to digital cellular telephones and Smartphones.

DIGITAL CELLULAR CHALLENGES AND OUTLOOK

Despite strong public skepticism in the late 1990s and early 2000s, cellular telephony did sweep the world, and significantly changed the way people work and communicate. However, there are still multiple cellular communications standards used worldwide, and competition continues to be fierce among providers in certain parts of the world, such as North and South America. With other options competing for users, such as WiMAX, and with globalization of markets continuing, users will benefit the most from digital cellular telephony once the industry settles on a single cellular standard. Having one standard available worldwide will force carriers to deliver more competitive pricing and services, and will also enable consumers to use their phones regardless of where they are.

Competing Technologies

There is no single road to 3G digital telephony. In Europe, it appears that W-CDMA, and HSDPA will become the standards, whereas in China and South Korea, CDMA2000 1xEVDO seems to be the standard of choice. Japan is leaning toward W-CDMA. In the United States, 3G technologies HSDPA and CDMA2000 1xEVDO are contenders.

Because these competing technologies are incompatible with each other, the goal of creating one global digital cellular network seems out of reach. The competition between the different technologies is confusing to consumers and is a major hindrance to the acceptance of the next generation of digital cellular telephony.

Limited Spectrum

The single largest factor limiting the development of 3G is spectrum. This problem is especially apparent in the United States, where a shortage of frequencies may seriously undermine 3G implementation. Although 3G can operate at almost any spectrum, the various 3G industry associations and forums have endeavored to designate the same part of the spectrum for 3G communications around the world, which would permit use of 3G from anywhere on the planet. Currently, 1.710 to 1.855 GHz and 2.520 to 2.670 GHz are designated as the worldwide spectrum to be used for 3G.

NOTE The FCC has started opening up other parts of the spectrum for 3G use. In late 2001, it determined that frequencies used by instructional television fixed services (ITFS) could also be used by 3G wireless carriers.

The U.S. Department of Defense currently uses the 1.7 GHz band for satellite control and military purposes. It will cost the U.S. government $935 million to move all of its users out of the 1.710 to 1.755 GHz band, opening up this portion of the spectrum for wireless operators. The government can easily recover this cost through auctioning the frequency allocations to various carriers.

10

NOTE For additional information on 3G cellular technologies, visit the following Web sites: www.evdoinfo.com, www.3gpp.org, and www.umts-forum.org. There are also many other organizations with Web sites dedicated to providing information on 3G cellular technologies.

Both cellular equipment manufacturers and carriers are continually looking for ways to maximize the use of the available frequency bands. Overlaying a WiMAX network on a cellular network for handling data is one potential way to free up more bandwidth for voice calls and allow for a higher user load for data as well.

Costs

The costs for 3G technology are also a drawback to its acceptance. The monthly service fees for data transmission can run as high as $90 per month for only a few megabytes of e-mail. Compared with the very reasonable costs of 2.5G digital cellular service and devices today, many people are questioning whether the high price is worth the additional functionality that 3G provides.

However, the user cost for 3G pales in comparison to the billions of dollars in costs for the carriers to build entire 3G networks. Just the cost of buying the necessary spectrum is astronomical. In early 2001, carriers in Germany paid over $46 billion for licenses to use the spectrum. Carriers in other nations face similar costs, and that's just one element in building a 3G network. New base stations and transmitters must all be factored into the equation as well. So far, only business users have been able to afford the service in large scale.

Other Wireless Options

Like Bluetooth and IrDA, 3G networks are faced with competition from other wireless technologies. The top speed for a 3G user is 10 Mbps downstream, when the user is standing still. In comparison, 802.11g WLANs offer speeds of over 54 Mbps even when the user is mobile. Although the coverage area of a single WLAN is far less than a digital cellular network, deploying multiple access points can create large areas of coverage with high bandwidth and mobility—at a fraction of the cost of building a 3G network. The higher power consumption and the large number of electronic components of 802.11g are factors that have kept this technology from being implemented in cellular phone handsets, especially with users looking for ever smaller devices.

NOTE Recent developments in chipsets have enabled cellular phone manufacturers to begin introducing handsets that can also connect with 802.11 networks. These devices can automatically detect and connect to 802.11 networks when in range and use VoIP services for telephone calls. When out of range of an 802.11 network, they automatically connect to the cellular network. See www.nokia.com and www.utstar.com.

The variety of wireless connection options has led several carriers to install less-expensive WLANs in high-traffic hot spots in selected cities, instead of investing in 3G. This permits carriers to provide mobile services to users requiring data access from notebook computers using a relatively inexpensive yet stable technology.

Impact of WiMAX

With the introduction of WiMAX technology, there are two distinct kinds of WWAN set-up that have widely different implications for users. As you learned in Chapter 9, 802.16-2004 is intended mostly for fixed wireless and some nomadic deployment, whereas 802.16e is designed specifically for mobile and nomadic users.

An 802.16e WiMAX network can be overlaid on an existing cellular tower infrastructure spanning the continent, and be employed to provide mobile users with lower cost access to data at speeds equivalent to EVDO, approximately 3 Mbps. It can also potentially be deployed by companies offering voice and data services to compete with the major carriers, using either licensed or unlicensed frequencies. The carrier cost-per-user of a cellular network is approximately five cents per minute, while on a WiMAX network it is less than one cent per minute. The implementation of WiMAX can benefit both the carriers and the end-users. The cost of each WiMAX base station is only about $5,000 to $10,000 per cell, whereas a single cellular base station can cost upwards of $300,000. WiMAX chipsets for cellular phones are expected in 2008. Until then, industry experts predict that 3G technologies will likely continue to dominate the market.

802.16-2004 WiMAX, on the other hand, is currently being deployed by carriers who leased the licensed frequencies at government auctions. The technology is used to provide Internet and cable TV access to rural areas and remote cities where these classes of service are not yet available. Until WiMAX is more widely deployed, tested, and proven in real-life situations, EVDO and HSDPA will be the only choices in locations where other broadband technologies are not yet available (see evdo-coverage.com and hsdpa-coverage.com).

NOTE In Ontario, Canada, two large, fierce competitors teamed up in 2005 to build a WiMAX infrastructure across the country. Rogers Communications, which provides cable TV, cellular, and VoIP, and Bell Canada, the local telephone carrier, which also provides satellite TV, cellular, and VoIP, currently own the leases for most WiMAX licensed frequency bands. The two companies struck an agreement in 2005 to share the cost of the towers and some equipment, but intend to continue to compete openly in the new markets. Service in some locations was available in March 2006.

SATELLITE BROADBAND WIRELESS

Although the use of satellites for personal wireless communication is fairly recent, satellites themselves have been used for worldwide communications for over 40 years. Satellite use falls into three broad categories. First, some satellites are used to acquire scientific data and perform research in space, such as those that measure radiation from the sun. The second category of satellites looks at Earth from space. These include weather and mapping satellites, as well as military satellites. The third category of satellites includes devices that are simply *reflectors*; that is, they bounce or relay signals from one point on Earth to another point. These satellites include communications satellites that reflect telephone and data transmissions, broadcast satellites that reflect television signals, and navigational satellites. These are illustrated in Figure 10-12. Wireless communications uses the third category of satellites, as objects to bounce signals from one point on Earth to another.

Satellite Transmissions

Satellites generally send and receive on one of four frequency bands, known as the L band, C band, Ku band, and Ka band. These are summarized in Table 10-3.

Table 10-3 Satellite frequencies

Band	Frequency
L band	1.53–2.7 GHz
C band	3.6–7 GHz
Ku band	11.7–12.7 GHz downlink; 14–17.8 GHz uplink
Ka band	17.3–31 GHz

10

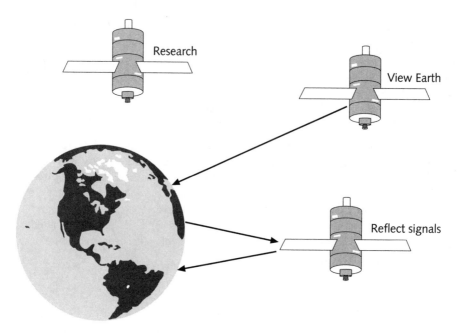

Figure 10-12   Three types of satellites

As you already know, frequency band affects the size of the antenna. Figure 10-13 illustrates the different sizes of antennas used for the four bands.

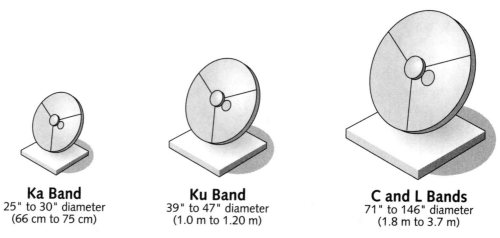

Ka Band
25" to 30" diameter
(66 cm to 75 cm)

Ku Band
39" to 47" diameter
(1.0 m to 1.20 m)

C and L Bands
71" to 146" diameter
(1.8 m to 3.7 m)

Figure 10-13   Satellite antenna sizes

Class and Type of Service

Satellites can provide two classes of service: consumer class service shares the available bandwidth between the users; business class service offers dedicated channels with dedicated bandwidth and is the more expensive of the two classes. In addition, satellites can provide point-to-point, point-to-multipoint, or even multipoint-to-multipoint connectivity. This is ilustrat illustrated in Figure 10-14.

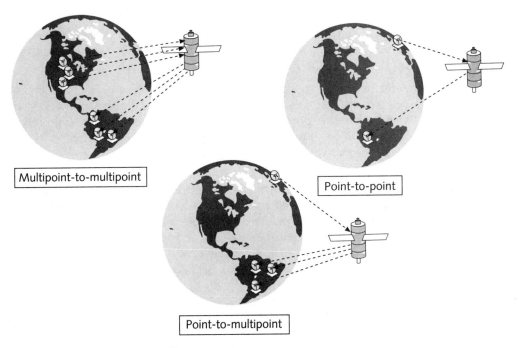

Figure 10-14   Types of satellite service

Modulation Techniques

Satellites use a variety of common modulation techniques (most of these were introduced in Chapter 3). These are listed below:

- Binary phase shift keying (BPSK), in which the phase of the carrier wave is shifted by 180 degrees, depending on whether a 1 or a 0 is being transmitted.

- Quadrature phase shift keying (QPSK), in which the phase of the RF signal is shifted by 90 degrees and two bits can be transmitted per phase change.

- Eight-phase shift keying (8-PSK), defined in the 2.5G cellular technology section of this chapter.

- Quadrature amplitude modulation (QAM), explained in Chapter 2, is primarily used for sending data downstream. QAM is considered very efficient but it is also susceptible to interference so it is not generally used for upstream transmissions.

Multiplexing Techniques

Satellite systems employ two common multiplexing techniques, FDMA and TDMA, along with some specialized techniques designed to maximize utilization of these very expensive communications channels. Detailed coverage of these specialized techniques is beyond the scope of this book, but they are listed here for your information:

- Permanently assigned multiple access (PAMA) — One of the oldest techniques, in which a frequency channel is permanently assigned to a user.

- Multi-channel per carrier (MCPC) — Uses multiplexers or routers to statistically consolidate traffic from different users. It is typically used in point-to-multipoint applications in the European digital video broadcasting standard.

- Demand assigned multiple access (DAMA) —Allocates bandwidth on a per-call or per-transmission session between two or more Earth stations. DAMA can efficiently share the pool of frequency and time resources available and permits full mesh routing, similar to how a telephone company's switch works. However, it requires more complex and costly hardware.

NOTE

For TV broadcasting directly to the user (satellite TV), the set-top box at the user's home or office includes a utility that enables the installation technician to align the dish antenna with the satellite antenna. The antenna needs to be initially positioned in a certain direction and at a certain angle, then the technician uses the TV set and set-top box to move the antenna slightly until the strongest possible signal is achieved.

Low Earth Orbit (LEO)

Satellite systems are classified according to the type of orbit that they use. The three orbits are low earth orbit (LEO), medium earth orbit (MEO), and geosynchronous earth orbit (GEO).

Low earth orbit (LEO) satellites circle the Earth at an altitude of 200 to 900 miles (321 to 1,448 kilometers). Because they orbit so close to Earth, LEO satellites must travel at high speeds so that the Earth's gravity will not pull them back into the atmosphere. Satellites in LEO travel at 17,000 miles (27,359 kilometers) per hour, circling the Earth in about 90 minutes.

Because LEOs are in such a low orbit, their area of Earth coverage (called the footprint) is small, as seen in Figure 10-15. This means that more LEO satellites are needed to provide coverage, compared to MEO and GEO satellites. One LEO system calls for over 225 satellites for total coverage of the Earth.

LEO systems have a low latency (delays caused by signals that must travel over a long distance) and use low-powered terrestrial devices (RF transmitters). It takes about 20 to 40 milliseconds for a signal to bounce from an Earth-bound station to a LEO, then back to an Earth station.

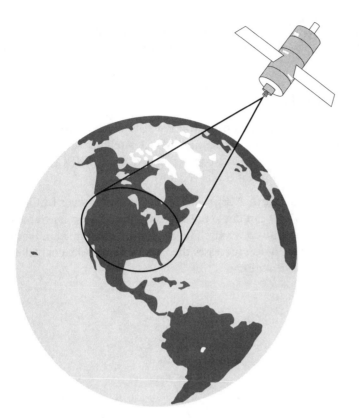

Figure 10-15   LEO footprint

LEO satellites can be divided into *Big LEO* and *Little LEO* groups. Little LEOs provide pager, satellite telephone, and location services. Using a Little LEO satellite, a user can make a phone call from anywhere on Earth. In contrast, cellular telephone services require the user to be within RF range of a transmission tower. Big LEOs carry voice and data broadband services, such as wireless Internet access. Some satellite Internet services provide shared downstream data rates of up to 400 Kbps but require a telephone connection for upstream data to an ISP. Another LEO wireless Internet service provides two-way data services with speeds of up to 500 Kbps. Two-way satellite Internet users need a two-foot by three-foot dish antenna and two modems (one each for uplink and downlink).

NOTE   When using LEO for wireless Internet access, the user must have a clear view in the direction of the equator. This is because LEO satellites orbit over the equator area. Foliage from trees and heavy rains can affect reception of signals.

In the future, LEOs are expected to be in demand for three markets: rural conventional telephone service, global mobile digital cellular service, and international broadband service. The speeds for wireless access are expected to exceed 100 Mbps.

Many companies today use satellite technology to reduce line costs. Drugstore and super-market chains in particular, which usually have stores located in remote towns, link these stores with their head office using LEO satellites.

Medium Earth Orbit (MEO)

Medium earth orbit (MEO) satellites orbit the Earth at altitudes between 1,500 and 10,000 miles (2,413 to 16,090 kilometers). Some MEO satellites orbit in near-perfect circles, have a constant altitude, and travel at a constant speed. Other MEO satellites revolve in elongated orbits called highly elliptical orbits (HEOs).

Because they are farther from the Earth, MEOs have two advantages over LEOs. First, they do not have to travel as fast; a MEO can circle the Earth in up to 12 hours. Second, MEOs have a bigger Earth footprint and thus fewer satellites are needed, illustrated in Figure 10-16. On the other hand, the higher orbit also increases the latency. A MEO signal takes from 50 to 150 milliseconds to make the round trip.

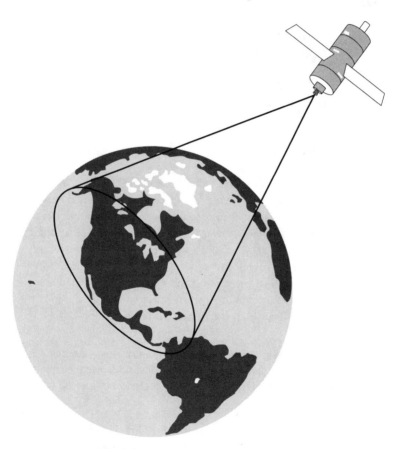

Figure 10-16 MEO footprint

The average orbit characteristics of a HEO satellite are about the same as a MEO. HEO satellites have a high apogee (maximum altitude) and a low perigee (minimum altitude). In addition, HEO orbits can provide good coverage in extreme latitudes. The orbits also typically have a 24-hour period, which means the satellites dwell for a long time at a fixed point over the Earth. This means that with just two satellites in the same orbit, one is always visible from any point on the ground. The Sirius digital satellite radio service is an example of the use of HEO satellites.

Geosynchronous Earth Orbit (GEO)

Geosynchronous earth orbit (GEO) satellites are stationed at an altitude of 22,282 miles (35,860 kilometers). A GEO satellite orbit matches the rotation of the Earth and moves as the Earth moves. This means that it remains "fixed" over a given location on the Earth and seems to hang motionless in space. Because of its great distance from the Earth, a GEO satellite can provide continuous service to a very large footprint. In fact, only three GEO satellites are needed to cover the entire Earth except for the polar regions. Their high altitude causes GEO satellites to have high latencies of about 250 milliseconds and require high-powered terrestrial sending devices. GEO satellites are used for world-wide communications and typically not for fixed broadband wireless.

Although it is much more expensive to launch a GEO satellite, such a device has a lifespan of 12 to 15 years. The average lifespan of a LEO satellite is only five years. Because the footprint of a GEO is so large, GEO satellites are much more efficient compared to LEO satellites. LEO satellites spend a portion of their orbit over sparsely populated areas where continuous coverage may not be needed.

NOTE

The International Telecommunications Union (ITU) regulates GEO usage.

Table 10-4 summarizes some of the satellites in use today, their purpose, and the companies that operate them.

Table 10-4   Satellites and operators

Operator	Number and Type of Satellites	Launch Date	Types of Services
Inmarsat	9 GEOs	1982	Voice, data, IP
Eutelsat	18 GEOs	1983	Radio, TV, and IP
PanAmSAT	21 GEOs	1983	Voice, data, and broadcast
Intelsat	19 GEOs	1984	Internet, voice, TV, and radio
Orion	3 GEOs	1994	IP multicast
Iridium	66 LEOs	1999	Mobile telephony
Globalstar	48 LEOs	1999	Mobile telephony
Ellipso	2 GEOs	2001	Global Mobile Personal Communications via Satellite (GMPCS)

Table 10-4   Satellites and operators (continued)

Operator	Number and Type of Satellites	Launch Date	Types of Services
Thuraya	2 GEOS	2001	Mobile telephony and GPS
Europ Star	2 GEOs	2001	Broadcast, data, voice
Hughes Spaceway	2 GEOs	2002	IP and Broadcast
Astra	7 MEOs	2002	GMPCS
ICO-Teledisc	10 MEOs	2003	Mobile telephony
Astrolink	4 GEOs	2003	2-way broadcast
Teledisc	290 LEOs	2004	IP
Skybridge	80 LEOs	2004	IP

NOTE

An interesting exercise is to connect to NASA's J-Track 3D Web site, which lets you see the orbits of all the satellites around Earth, in real-time, and get information on each satellite, such as its purpose, who owns the satellite, the orbital altitude, and current location around the planet. Make sure you have Java installed on your computer and visit science.nasa.gov/RealTime/JTrack/3d/JTrack3D.html. Note that you can also click the picture, hold the left mouse button, and rotate the planet to view it from any angle.

Table 10-5 provides a summary of satellite orbits, advantages, and disadvantages.

Table 10-5   Satellite technology

Satellite Orbit	Pros	Cons
LEO	• Low-latency (20-40 milliseconds) • Low-power • High-speed communications (500 Kbps or higher, depending on application)	• Very high orbital speed • Average of 225 satellites to cover the entire Earth • Small footprint • Short life span (average 5 years)
MEO	• Medium latency (50-150 milliseconds) • Larger footprint than LEO; 24 satellites required to cover the Earth • Slower orbital speed; dwells over an area longer; 12-hour orbit • Longer life span than LEO (10+ years)	• Higher latency than LEO • More expensive to replace than LEO
HEO	• Similar speed and latency characteristics to MEO; can dwell over an area longer • Footprint similar to MEO • Can provide good coverage at extreme latitudes (North and South poles)	• More satellites required to cover the Earth than MEO • At apogee (high point of orbit), latency increases • Highly elliptical orbit requires great accuracy; increases cost

Table 10-5 Satellite technology (continued)

Satellite Orbit	Pros	Cons
GEO	• Very large footprint; only three satellites required to cover entire Earth • Synchronized with Earth's rotation allowing for permanent, fixed antennas • Very high speeds used for broadcasting • Long life span (15+ years)	• Very high latency (250 milliseconds); not efficient for two-way IP comm • Very expensive to replace • Distance from Earth requires high power; more subject to interference • Does not provide good coverage at very high latitudes

Experimental Technologies

The U.S. National Aeronautics and Space Administration (NASA) has been experimenting with ultra-lightweight, solar-powered, high-flying aircraft since the 1990s. The idea behind developing these vehicles is that an aircraft powered by solar cells and using fuel cells as a backup, flying at approximately 100,000 feet, could carry cellular telephone-switching equipment and circle the same area for several days. These aircraft could be used in place of a satellite or ground-based antenna tower infrastructure and would be significantly less expensive to launch and operate than a LEO satellite. The aircraft could also be repaired, which is extremely difficult and expensive to do with a satellite.

Satellite Technology Outlook

The fact that satellites can provide wireless communication service in areas not covered by cellular or WiMAX means that end-users and companies will continue to rely on this technology, indefinitely. Satellites today are enabling carriers—in combination with airlines, merchant shipping, and tourism operators—to offer Internet access and voice calls to passengers and crews across large oceans as well as in high latitudes and remote corners of the Earth. As communications and reliance on data connectivity continue to increase, these companies will continue to look for ways of providing uninterrupted, faster, and lower cost access for end-users. In addition, satellites can also make these services available in many other unpopulated areas of the planet such as deserts, large forests, and mountainous regions, where it is not economically viable for any carrier or operator to deploy the required infrastructure.

CHAPTER SUMMARY

❑ In cellular telephone networks, the coverage area is divided into sections called cells. Each cell includes a transmitter with which the mobile devices communicate. All of the transmitters and cell phones operate at a low power level, which enables the signals to stay confined to the cell and not interfere with any other cells. This enables the same frequency to be used in other, non-adjacent cells at the same time. Cell phones have special codes associated with them that identify the phone, the phone's owner, and the carrier or service provider.

❑ When a cellular telephone user moves between adjacent cells, the cellular telephone will automatically associate with the base station of that cell. This is known as a handoff. If a cellular user moves beyond the coverage area of his cellular network, the cellular telephone automatically connects with whatever cellular network is in place in the remote area. The cellular network in the remote area communicates with the one in the home area and verifies that the user can make calls and that it can also charge for the calls. This is known as roaming.

❑ First generation cellular technology, or 1G, uses analog signals, is based on the AMPS standard, operates in the 800-900 MHz frequency spectrum, and uses FDMA. 1G networks use circuit-switching technology and can transmit data at a maximum speed of 9.6 Kbps.

❑ The 2G generation of cellular telephony can transmit data between 9.6 Kbps and 14.4 Kbps in the 800 MHz and 1.9 GHz frequencies and uses circuit-switched networks. 2G systems use digital instead of analog transmissions. 2G systems use three different multiple access technologies: TDMA, CDMA, and GSM. GSM was developed and is most popular in Europe. GSM uses a combination of FDMA and TDMA technologies.

❑ 2.5G networks operate at a maximum speed of 384 Kbps and are the most common current cellular telephony technology. The primary difference between 2G and 2.5G networks is that 2.5G networks are packet-switched instead of circuit-switched. Circuit switching is ideal for voice communications, but is not efficient for transmitting data.

❑ 3G networks will provide new or expanded applications and features to mobile users. Because the networks are based on digital rather than analog technology and can transmit at much higher speeds, they will not be limited to voice communications. Transitioning from 2.5G to 3G cellular technology requires specific steps and technologies based on the original 2.5 technology being used.

❑ One of the most widely used applications in Europe and Japan is Short Message Services (SMS). SMS allows for the delivery of short, text-based messages between wireless devices such as cellular telephones and pagers.

❑ 2.5G WAP-enabled cell phones run a tiny browser program called a microbrowser that uses Wireless Markup Language (WML) instead of HTML to display text-based Web content on the small screen of a cell phone. A WAP Gateway must translate between WML and HTML.

❑ 3G cell phones allow Internet surfing or videoconferencing using WAP2. WAP2 is HTML compatible and permits cellular phones equipped with color screens to display rich content. WAP2 also includes support for the TCP/IP protocols. i-mode is another browser based on compact HTML (cHTML), which is a subset of HTML designed for mobile devices that is used in Japan. i-mode is similar to WAP in terms of its functionality.

- Java 2 Micro Edition (J2ME) is a subset of Java specifically developed for programming wireless devices. J2ME enables a cellular phone to access remote applications and e-mail and run programs on the cellular phone itself.

- BREW is a runtime environment that resides on a wireless device. It allows users to download programs and run them on BREW-enabled devices.

- The issues preventing the rapid acceptance of advanced generations of digital cellular telephony include competing cellular technologies and lack of standards, spectrum limitations, and the high costs of implementing 3G technology. Nevertheless, many carriers worldwide are upgrading their networks to 3G at an accelerated pace.

- The introduction of WiMAX technologies may have a significant impact on how 3G technologies are eventually employed. There are two kinds of WWAN setups that have different implications for the future of this technology. 802.16-2004 fixed wireless may eventually replace cellular and other technologies for providing cable TV and Internet service to rural and remote areas. 802.16e can also provide data and possibly VoIP access to nomadic and mobile users across the continent.

- Satellites used for wireless data connectivity employ common modulation and multiplexing techniques, as well as some that are unique. Satellite systems can transmit point-to-point, point-to-multipoint, and multipoint-to-multipoint.

- LEO satellites orbit the Earth at a low altitude and at high speeds. LEO satellites have a limited footprint and low latency and use low-powered terrestrial devices.

- MEO satellites orbit the Earth at higher altitudes than LEOs but do not travel as fast and have a bigger Earth footprint, requiring fewer satellites. MEOs have higher latency than LEOs.

- GEO satellites orbit at much higher altitudes than MEOs, and their orbits match the rotation of the Earth and move as the Earth move. GEO satellites have high latencies and require high-powered terrestrial sending devices. GEO satellites are used for world-wide communications and typically not for fixed broadband wireless.

10

Key Terms

2.5 Generation (2.5G) — An interim step between 2G and 3G digital cellular networks.

8-PSK — A modulation technique in which the phase of the carrier is shifted in 45 degree increments and 4 bits can be transmitted per phase change.

Advanced Mobile Phone Service (AMPS) — The standard used for 1G analog cellular transmissions based on FDMA.

Binary Runtime Environment for Wireless (BREW) — A thin software interface layer that resides on a wireless device and creates a runtime environment.

cards — A small block of a WML document.

CDMA2000 1xEVDO — The 3G digital cellular technology that is a migration from CDMA2000 1xRTT.

CDMA2000 1xEVDV — The 3G digital cellular technology that is a migration from CDMA2000 1xEVDO.

CDMA2000 1xRTT — A 2.5G digital cellular network technology that is a migration from CDMA (1xRTT stands for 1-times Radio Transmission Technology).

cell — A smaller area of a mobile network.

compact HTML (cHTML) — A subset of HTML that is designed for mobile devices.

control channel — A special frequency that cellular phones use for communication with a base station.

deck — A WML document.

Enhanced Data rates for GSM Evolution (EDGE) — A 2.5G digital cellular network technology that boosts GPRS transmissions.

Extensible Markup Language (XML) — A definition language that uses tags to describe the data.

First Generation (1G) — The first generation of wireless cellular telephony that transmitted at 9.6 Kbps using analog circuit-switched technology.

General Packet Radio Service (GPRS) — A 2.5G network technology that can transmit up to 114 Kbps.

geosynchronous earth orbit (GEO) satellites — Satellites that are stationed at an altitude of 22,282 miles (35,860 kilometers).

GSM (Global Systems for Mobile communications) — One of three multiple access technologies that make up the 2G digital cellular system that uses a combination of FDMA and TDMA.

i-mode — An Internet access system for digital cellular telephones.

Java — An object-oriented programming language used for general-purpose business programming and interactive Web sites.

Java 2 Micro Edition (J2ME) — A subset of Java specifically developed for programming wireless devices.

latency — Delays caused by signals that must travel over a long distance.

low earth orbit (LEO) satellites — Satellites that orbit the Earth at an altitude of 200 to 900 miles (321 to 1,448 kilometers).

medium earth orbit (MEO) satellites — Satellites that orbit the Earth at altitudes between 1,500 and 10,000 miles (2,413 to 16,090 kilometers).

mobile telecommunications switching office (MTSO) — The connection between a cellular network and wired telephones.

profile — An extension of the XML language.

roaming — The automatic transfer of the RF signal when moving from one cellular network to another network.

Second Generation (2G) — The second generation of cellular telephony that uses circuit-switched digital networks.

Short Message Services (SMS) — A delivery system for short, text-based messages sent between wireless devices such as cellular telephones and pagers.

Third Generation (3G) — Digital cellular wireless generation of cellular telephony with speeds up to 2 Mbps.

Wideband CDMA (W-CDMA) — The 3G digital cellular technology that is a migration from EDGE.

wireless wide area network (WWAN) — A network that spans a geographical area as large as an entire country or even the entire world.

REVIEW QUESTIONS

1. The area of a cell is approximately how many square miles?

   a. 5

   b. 10

   c. 30

   d. 40

2. The device that connects a base station with a wired telephone network is the _____ .

   a. transmitter

   b. cell phone

   c. MTSO

   d. CDMA

3. Each of the following is a valid cellular telephone code except _____ .

   a. System Identification Code (SID)

   b. Electronic Serial Number (ESN)

   c. Digital Serial Code (DSC)

   d. Mobile Identification Number (MIN)

4. _____ occurs when a user begins moving toward another cell and the phone automatically associates with the base station of that cell.

   a. Roaming

   b. Handoff

   c. Hunting

   d. Multiplexing

5. The special frequency that a cellular phone and base station use for exchanging setup information is called the _____ .

   a. W-CDMA

   b. cell tunnel

   c. control channel

   d. GB line

10

6. First Generation (1G) networks use analog signals, and the maximum transmission speed is 9.6 Kbps. True or False?

7. 1G technology is based on Advanced Mobile Phone Service (AMPS). True or False?

8. Division by frequency, so that each caller is allocated part of the spectrum for all of the time, is the basis of TDMA. True or False?

9. 2G systems use digital instead of analog transmissions. True or False?

10. There are two different technologies that are used with 2G—W-CDMA and CDMA2000. True or False?

11. The primary difference between 2G and 2.5G networks is that 2.5G networks are _____ instead of circuit-switched networks.

12. When migrating from a TDMA or GSM network, the next step would be to a _____ .

13. _____ is considered a booster for GPRS systems and can transmit up to 384 Kbps.

14. _____ Generation is intended to be a uniform and global worldwide standard for cellular wireless communication.

15. What is Short Message Services (SMS)?

16. Explain how WAP works.

17. What are WML decks and cards?

18. What are some differences between WAP and i-mode?

19. What are some advantages of Java 2 Micro Edition (J2ME)?

20. What is BREW? How is it different from other client software?

21. List the three major ways in which satellites are used. Which is used for fixed broadband wireless?

22. Describe low earth orbit (LEO) satellites.

23. How can the geosynchronous earth orbit (GEO) satellite system cover the Earth with only three satellites?

HANDS-ON PROJECTS

HANDS-ON PROJECTS

Project 10-1: Researching Deployment of 3G Cellular Technology

Conduct research to determine where 3G cellular technology has been deployed. Include information on what types of technology have been deployed in Japan and South America, in addition to the United States and Canada. Write a one-page report on your findings.

Project 10-2: Writing Applications for Cellular Phones

Writing an application in XHTML is not as difficult as it may seem. Using the Internet, find information about this new language for WAP2-enabled devices. There are also several WAP emulators available on the Internet that support XML for mobile devices. Some can even be used online. Using one of these, write a short application that displays your name and today's date using XML. What problems did you encounter? How is XHTML similar to other languages with which you may be familiar? Write a one-page paper on your research and include your XHTML application.

Project 10-3: Researching XML

Extensible Hypertext Markup Language (XML) has become a key component in computers today. Even this textbook was produced in XML format from a standard Windows application. Using the Internet, research XML. What are its origins? How exactly does it differ from other descriptive languages? What are its strengths and weaknesses? Write a one-page paper on your findings. List five applications in which it is being used.

10

Project 10-4: Researching 2.5G and 3G Data Rates

Just as the industry is divided regarding what digital cellular technologies will be found in the future, there is also concern about listed data rates. Studies reveal that there is a wide gap between the advertised data rate, such as 2 Mbps for a stationary user using 3G technology, and the actual rate, which may be much less. Using the Internet and other sources, find the real speeds of the 2.5G and 3G technologies. Re-create Table 10-2 and add another column entitled "Actual Speed." Include a paragraph that explains why these speeds may actually be slower than the advertised speed. In your opinion, which figures should be used when comparing these technologies?

Project 10-5: Researching Satellite Transmission Speeds

There are several new techniques being promoted to increase data transmission speed in satellite technology. Using the Internet and other sources, locate information on these new techniques. Outline their strengths, weaknesses, and in which applications they are most often found. How are they implemented if we cannot retrieve the satellites and modify their radios? Write a one-page paper on your findings.

CASE PROJECTS

The Baypoint Group (TBG), a company of 50 consultants who assist organizations and businesses with issues involving network planning and design, has again requested your services as a consultant. Telecom Argentina is a company that is licensed to provide wired services in the northern part of the country. The company has contracted TBG to assist it with the selection and implementation of a new field service system. The goal is to provide service technicians with wireless access to the corporate network and a vast electronic library of technical manuals and schematic diagrams, which would reduce or eliminate the need for staff to carry a large number of books and drawings, especially while servicing equipment underground or when climbing on transmission towers. In addition, this means that the technicians would also be able to read and update the records for all of the equipment immediately, avoiding massive amounts of paperwork, as well as potential errors and omissions. However, the company is having trouble deciding on which technology to adopt—handheld cellular or notebooks equipped with cellular cards. TBG has asked you to help.

CASE PROJECTS

Project 10-1: Advantages of Cellular Technologies

Create a presentation outlining the advantages of using digital cellular handsets or cellular wireless cards for Telecom Argentina. Research the ability of the smaller cellular handsets, as opposed to notebook computers—which may be difficult to carry everywhere—to display standard PC documents such as Word, Excel, and PDF files, and evaluate how this could help the company. Because the group you will be presenting to is composed of non-technical managers, be sure that your presentation is not too technical. Limit yourself to a maximum of 15 PowerPoint slides.

CASE PROJECTS

Project 10-2: Purchasing 3G Equipment

Jose Riveras, one of the senior executives of Telecom Argentina, was convinced by your presentation. However, Jose recently heard about 3G and wants to know how this technology will affect the company's plans to purchase equipment now. TBG has asked you to create another presentation for Jose that explains the different generations of cellular technology. Create a PowerPoint presentation of 15-18 slides.

OPTIONAL TEAM CASE PROJECT

Telecom Argentina is unsure about investing in cell phones. The company is considering alternatives, including using Wi-Fi and notebook computers. Working with three other students, form two teams of two people, with each team selecting one of these technologies. Research in depth the advantages and disadvantages of these respective technologies and how they work. Hold a friendly debate in which each two-person team presents a five minute talk about the advantages of their technology. After the talk, allow time for the others to ask questions. Be prepared to defend your technology, knowing that the other individuals will be aware of its disadvantages.

11

RADIO FREQUENCY IDENTIFICATION

> **After reading this chapter and completing the exercises, you will be able to:**
>
> ◆ Define Radio Frequency Identification (RFID)
>
> ◆ Explain the need for RFID and how RFID works
>
> ◆ List the components of an RFID system
>
> ◆ Outline the challenges of RFID

Imagine that you are just making a quick stop at a local supermarket to pick up a few grocery items you need at home. As you enter the store, you pick up a bag near the door. Then you walk through the aisles and load the bag with the products you need. When you are finished, you simply walk through an arch-like structure and exit the store. There's no need to stop at a cash register to pay for your products or even to show anyone which products you purchased. You reach for your Smartphone, check the receipt, and connect to your bank, instantly verifying that the correct total was deducted from your account.

Arriving home, you put your purchases in the refrigerator. A display screen on the refrigerator door is automatically updated with the contents, the expiration date of each individual product, and the quantity.

While this example may sound like a futuristic dream, the standards and technology that will allow it to happen—radio frequency identification—are already in use. In fact, there is practically no end to the potential applications of this technology. In this chapter, you will learn about how radio frequency identification works, how it is being used and will be applied in the future, as well as some of the challenges posed by its implementation.

What Is RFID?

Radio frequency identification (RFID) is a technology similar to the barcode labels used in almost every single product available off-the-shelf today around the world, except that RFID uses radio frequency waves instead of laser light to read the product code. RFID stores product information in electronic **tags** that contain an antenna and a chip. RFID can store significantly more information about items than the barcode system. This data, held in read-write or read-only memory, can include the date, time, and location where the product was manufactured, the manufacturer name, product serial number, and so on. In comparison, barcode labels typically include only an item's stock-keeping unit (product code).

RFID technology is not new; it has been in use around the world, in one form or another, for many years. In the late 1930s, the U.S. Army and Navy introduced a system designated IFF (Identification Friend-or-Foe) that distinguished Allied aircraft from enemy aircraft by use of special codes that could be read by a friendly aircraft at a distance. Likewise, for many years, microchips and antennas inside tiny capsules have been implanted under the skin of household pets. These tags contain a numeric code that gets registered by the company that supplies the tags in a centralized database. The tags can be read by a special device available at veterinary and animal control offices, helping reunite lost animals with their owners. You are also probably familiar with a simpler form of RFID that has been used in retail stores to prevent theft. After you pay for an item, the small tags that are attached to clothing and other items are run through a powerful magnet at the checkout; the magnet disables the tag, preventing it from activating the alarm at the door.

What is new about RFID has to do with the standardization efforts of the International Organization for Standardization (ISO) and **EPCglobal Inc**. EPCglobal is an organization entrusted by industries worldwide to establish RFID standards and services for real-time, automatic identification of information in the supply chain of any company, anywhere in the world. By publishing a single worldwide set of standards, it will be possible for RFID to be implemented and utilized in a global context. EPCglobal adopts the ISO standards for communications, including the frequencies, and PHY and MAC layer specifications, and concentrates on defining services and higher layer functions of the standards. In this section, you will learn about the hardware, software, and services that are required to implement RFID.

NOTE

For more information about EPCglobal, visit www.EPCglobalinc.org.

RFID System Components

Several components are required to implement an RFID system, connect it with a corporate network, enable integration with existing business software, and ultimately connect with the services that enable worldwide integration of a company's suppliers, manufacturers, distributors, and transportation providers. This section describes the most common components required to implement an RFID system—the tags, antennas, readers, software, and the EPCglobal Network services.

Electronic Product Code (EPC)

RFID systems utilize product codes and data formats standardized by EPCglobal Inc. The mission of EPCglobal is to make organizations more efficient by making information about any kind of product available at any time and anywhere. The standards published by EPCglobal enable users to track products from manufacturing through to the end-user and beyond—potentially all the way to the recycling depot or garbage heap. The **electronic product code (EPC)** is a standardized numbering scheme that can be programmed in a tag and attached to any physical product. Think of EPC as the evolution of the barcode or Universal Product Code (UPC), which you can find today in most products.

EPC allows a unique number or code to be associated with each item so that it can be identified electronically. EPCs are usually represented in hexadecimal notation. A sample code is shown in Figure 11-1.

11

01 • 0001B6F • 0000F3 • 00002A9C3

| Header | Domain Manager | Object Class | Serial Number |

Figure 11-1   96-bit electronic product code (EPC)

The EPC is either 64 or 96 bits long and includes the following fields:

- Header — Identifies the EPC version number.

- EPC Domain Manager — Identifies the company using the EPC number. At 96 bits, this field can accommodate 268 million different companies.

- Object Class — The stock keeping unit (SKU) of a product, used to identify each type of product that a company manufactures or sells. At 96 bits, this field can represent up to 16 million unique types of products for each company.

- Serial Number — A unique instance of the product. At 96 bits, for each object class there can be 68 billion unique serial numbers.

NOTE   A 256-bit version of the EPC may be defined in the future. All the EPCglobal specifications for the physical layer allow for the EPC to be expanded without any changes in the protocol.

The structure of some of the 64- and 96-bit electronic product codes is shown in Figure 11-2.

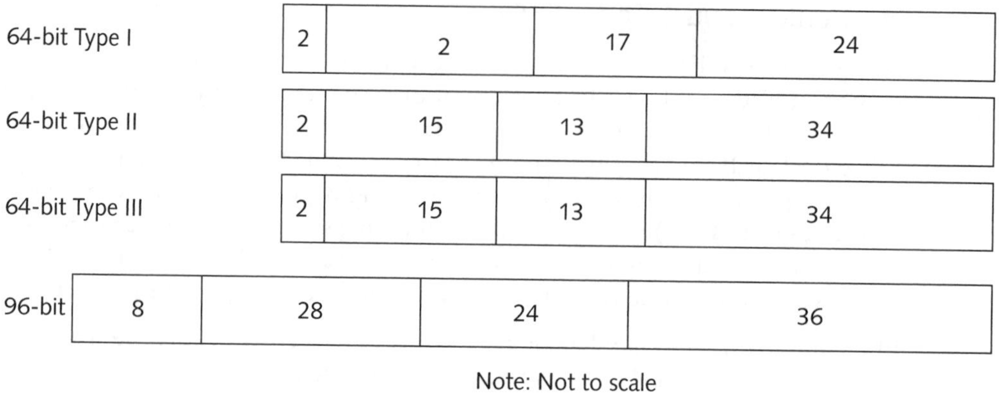

64-bit Type I	2	2	17	24

64-bit Type II	2	15	13	34

64-bit Type III	2	15	13	34

96-bit	8	28	24	36

Note: Not to scale

Figure 11-2   Structure of EPC

RFID Tags

RFID tags are also commonly known as **transponders**; the word is a combination of *transmitter* and *responder*. A typical RFID tag includes an integrated circuit that contains some non-volatile memory and a simple microprocessor. These tags can store data that is transmitted in response to an interrogation (a transmission) from a **reader**, the device that captures and processes the data received from the tags.

There are two basic types of tags: passive and active. **Passive tags** are the most common type; they are small, can be produced in large quantities at low cost, and do not require battery power. Passive tags use the electromagnetic energy in the RF waves transmitted by the reader's antenna to power the built-in chip and transmit the information stored in its internal memory. Animal tracking microchip implants, asset management, and access management (access cards for security controlled doors and parking lots) are examples of passive tag applications. Figure 11-3 shows an example of a passive tag.

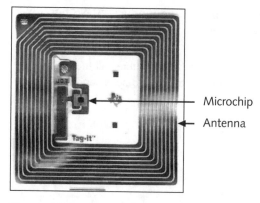

   Microchip

   Antenna

Figure 11-3   A typical RFID passive tag (Courtesy of R. Moroz Ltd.)

NOTE To see how passive RFID tags are used to speed up international customs processing, watch this video clip about the Nexus system at the following link: http://www.intermec.com/eps_files/eps_misc/Nexus_768k.wmv.

Active tags are equipped with a battery to power the microprocessor chip and memory. Having their own power source means that these tags can transmit the signal farther away than passive tags can; however, active tags have a limited life due to the battery. They are also far more expensive ($20 and higher) than passive tags and therefore are used to track only high-value items such as an entire pallet or container. An example of the application of active tags is to track military supplies shipped around the world, but they can also be used for commercial applications. One class of active tags is called **beacons** because they transmit on a periodic basis, without receiving an interrogation from a reader.

A third type of tag is the **semi-active tag**. This type of tag uses a built-in battery to power the circuit only when a reader first energizes (powers) the tag. The energy transmitted by the reader activates the tag, which then uses the internal battery to power its circuits and respond to the reader. The best example of this type of tag is the devices used for electronic toll collection along highways. The battery in semi-active tags usually lasts several years since it is only used occasionally, when the tag is activated by the reader's electromagnetic field.

11

The size of the memory in a tag varies with the manufacturer and application, but is usually between 16 bits (for storing temporary operation parameters) and hundreds of kilobits. The tags are initially programmed with a unique identification code obtained from EPCglobal. The additional memory can be used to record historical information about the product to which the tag is attached, such as the health and vaccination records of cattle, the temperatures that a product has been exposed to during shipping (using a sensor attached to the tag), manufacturing and testing dates, calibration records for test equipment, and so on.

All three types of tags can be produced in flexible packages, also called **smart labels**. Flexible tags include an adhesive backing and can be attached to a box, the underside of a product casing, or a pallet. These types of tags can also be used to track luggage in airplanes and trains, for example. Because they use RF, the tags are not limited to being placed in a visible area or on the outside packaging of a product. They can be read regardless of their position or orientation. This flexibility avoids the difficulty that store clerks sometimes have, getting the equipment at the counter to read the barcode labels on products.

1-bit tags are passive devices used in retail stores. They do not contain a unique identification code, a chip, or any memory. They are simply used to activate an alarm to prevent theft. An emerging form of RFID is **chipless tags**, also known as RF fibers. The details of the technology behind chipless tags are beyond the scope of this book. Simply put, they do not make use of any integrated circuit technology to store information; instead, these tags use fibers or materials that reflect a portion of the reader's signal back; the unique return signal can be used as an identifier. The fibers are thin threads, fine wires, or even labels or laminates. Chipless tags are used in applications that might not work well with other types of RFID tags.

Chipless tags can be used to identify paper-based documents uniquely and inconspicuously. They tend to perform far better than other types when the tag is attached to a metal surface or to a liquid container. Both cans and bottles present significant problems for most RFID systems because metal surfaces can affect the propagation of RF waves and most liquids attenuate the signal. Chipless tags can also be read at greater distances than 1-bit or passive tags.

Sensory tags, as their name indicates, can be equipped with thermal, gas, smoke, pressure, and a variety of other kinds of sensors to monitor and record environmental conditions, liquid volume levels, or attempts to tamper with a product. They can be produced as passive tags; however, the sensors are not powered until a reader interrogates the tag. Most sensory tags are considerably more expensive than other types of passive tags, come in larger packages, and may be equipped with replaceable batteries that allow them to be used for longer periods of time.

NOTE   You can learn more about sensory tags by watching the video clip at www.symbol.com/video/RFID_VNR_Only_1.wmv.

The cost of a tag can vary greatly, depending on the type and the number of tags purchased over a period of time. In general, passive tag prices vary between $0.05 and $0.25 each. As the technology develops and the volumes increase, RFID manufacturers and users expect the cost to fall well below $0.05 per tag.

There are two classes of tags:

- **Class 0** tags are read-only and contain only an EPC that is written to the tag at manufacturing time.

- **Class 1** tags are read/write. Some tags are WORM (write once, read many), while others may be equipped with flash memory, which allows information to be recorded on the tag at any time during the life of the product or of the tag itself.

Tags and readers are further classified according to the standards developed by EPCglobal, as outlined in Table 11-1.

Table 11-1   EPCglobal tag and reader specifications

Standard	Class	Characteristics
Generation 1	Class 0 (900 MHz HF) Class 1 (13.56. MHz UHF) Class 1 (860 to 930 MHz HF)	In the 860 to 930 MHz range, tags and readers can interoperate with those from another manufacturer only if they transmit at the exact same frequency.

Table 11-1 EPCglobal tag and reader specifications (continued)

Standard	Class	Characteristics
Generation 2	Class 0 Class 1	Tags and readers can interoperate with those from other manufacturers across the entire EPC spectrum of frequencies. (See Table 11-2.) Improved Class 1 read/write capabilities Improved tag performance in environments with many readers The first true global standard for RFID

Reader

In addition to interfacing with the tags, readers, also called interrogators, are also the devices that connect with the company's network and transfer the data obtained from the tags to a computer. Some readers can also write data onto tags, but the device is still called a reader. Readers that work with passive tags also provide the energy that activates the tags. The read distance is determined by the size and location of the tag and the reader antennas, as well as the amount of power transmitted. These specifications are generally limited by national regulations that specify how much power can be transmitted in each frequency. Variations in regulations can result in incompatibilities between equipment manufactured and licensed for use in different countries.

NOTE It is important to keep international standards and regulations in mind when designing and implementing an RFID system that will be used to identify products worldwide. All standards and regulations are generally available from the ISO and EPCglobal.

The frequency ranges and common applications used in RFID systems are outlined in Table 11-2.

Table 11-2 RFID frequencies and common applications

Frequency Band	Common Applications
Low Frequency (LF) – 135 KHz	Animal identification Access control Industrial automation
High Frequency (HF) – 13.56 MHz	Smart cards Books, clothing, luggage, and various other individual item tracking applications
Ultra High Frequency (UHF) – 433 MHz and 860 to 930 MHz	Asset tracking Inventory control Warehouse management
Microwaves – 2.45 and 5.8 GHz (ISM band)	Electronic toll collection Industrial automation Access control

11

Antennas

Recall from Chapter 4 that antennas are responsible for converting the RF energy from the transmitter into electromagnetic waves. Also, the design and location of an antenna can significantly affect the range of the signal and the reliability of the communication. RFID antennas used in tags may be limited in size due to the dimensions of the tag itself. Most tags are small, to allow them to be placed in a variety of different products and packaging.

There are two main types of tag antennas: linear and circular. Linear antennas offer greater range but less accurate reads. Circular antennas have greater read accuracy, especially in applications where the orientation of the antenna varies due to positioning of the products, but have a more limited range. Some older-style RFID tags sported a large circular antenna that spiraled outward from the center of the tag, where the chip was located. These types of tags are not often used today.

Larger antennas allow the tags to be read at greater distances than smaller antennas. However, recall that as the frequency increases, the wavelength gets smaller, and, consequently, so does the antenna. Higher frequency antennas can be made relatively small and still allow the tags to be read at greater distances than lower frequency tags with the same antenna size. Conversely, to detect a higher frequency signal and minimize attenuation, the antenna needs to be approximately between 10 and 20 microns thick (1 micron = 0.0003937 inches or 1/1000 of a millimeter). Lower frequency antennas can be two microns thick. RFID tag design can be quite complex, due to antenna size and thickness, which can significantly affect read performance. In certain kinds of tags, the antenna itself acts as the energy storage device, which supplies electricity to the tag and allows it to respond to a reader.

Figure 11-4 shows additional examples of RFID tags and the different antenna types.

Reader antennas also have to be designed for the specific type of application. Whether the antenna will be located at a retail store entrance for security reasons, near a warehouse shelf, or on a refrigerator door, the type, size, shape and location of the antenna is critically important to ensure good readability and accuracy. No "typical" style of antenna exists; the variety is huge. You can search the World Wide Web for antenna images and information. To see examples of different RFID reader antenna types, visit the following sites:

- www.ti.com/rfid/docs/products/antennas/antennas.shtml
- www.symbol.com/products/rfid/rfid.html (select Antennas from the menu on the left)
- www.intermec.com (select Products, RFID, and Antennas)

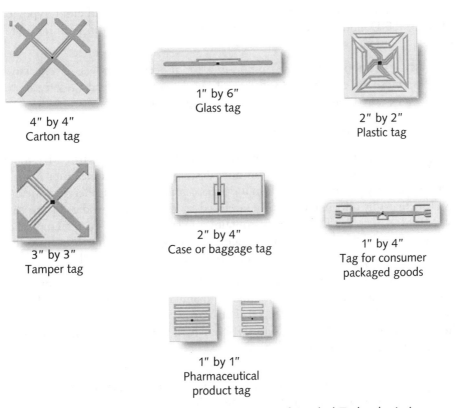

4" by 4"
Carton tag

1" by 6"
Glass tag

2" by 2"
Plastic tag

3" by 3"
Tamper tag

2" by 4"
Case or baggage tag

1" by 4"
Tag for consumer
packaged goods

1" by 1"
Pharmaceutical
product tag

Figure 11-4   RFID tags and antennas (courtesy of Symbol Technologies)

Software

The type of software used in an RFID implementation depends on the specific RFID application. Nevertheless, there are three basic categories of software components present in every RFID system:

- System software
- Middleware
- Business application software

System software is usually stored in read-only memory (ROM) or flash memory and is present in both the tag and the reader. System software is executed by the microprocessor in each device and is used to control hardware functions, implement communication protocols (including collision control, error detection and correction, authorization, authentication, and encryption), and control the flow of data between tags and readers.

Middleware is responsible for reformatting the data from the readers to comply with the formats required by the business applications. It usually runs on a computer that is implemented as a gateway between the readers and the other data-processing equipment at the end-user company. Since each company will likely use different types of business software, RFID middleware allows users to ensure that they can communicate with the RFID equipment.

Business application software is responsible for processing orders, inventory, shipments, invoices, and so on. This type of software also usually relies on database software to store and manage all of the transaction records in a typical business period.

EPCglobal Network Services

Using barcodes, a business would have to record the item's UPC (barcode), the company's internal product number (SKU), a product description, the manufacturer name, the price, and the quantity of items in stock in a database, and then cross-reference the barcode and SKU so that this information can be accessed by the barcode readers at the cash register. With RFID, since the EPC already contains a reference to the manufacturer along with a product code, the need for cross-referencing is reduced; the potential for introducing errors when entering this information into the database is lessened as well.

The manufacturer name is used to reorder products when the stock is low or depleted. With EPCs, companies will be able to acquire the manufacturer's name over the Internet using a service from EPCglobal Inc. called **Object Name Service (ONS)**. ONS is modeled after the Internet's Domain Name System (DNS), which translates a Web site address or URL to its corresponding IP address.

For more information on the Domain Name System (DNS), read information at http://computer.howstuffworks.com/dns.htm.

NOTE

Eventually trillions of products from thousands of companies will likely be included in the ONS database. Like DNS, ONS will be a worldwide distributed database that will allow EPCglobal network users to identify and get additional information about the products by simply issuing a query to the ONS service, over the Internet.

An additional component that will enable companies around the world to exchange information regarding their trade transactions is EPC Information Services (EPCIS). Similar to the electronic data interchange specifications that many large companies use to complete paperless transactions today, EPCIS will eventually enable large organizations to purchase, invoice, and track product orders over the Internet, eliminating the need to send paper documents by mail or fax. Figure 11-5 shows the five fundamental components of an EPCglobal RFID system: tags, readers, middleware, business applications, and EPCglobal services, as well as how they are logically connected.

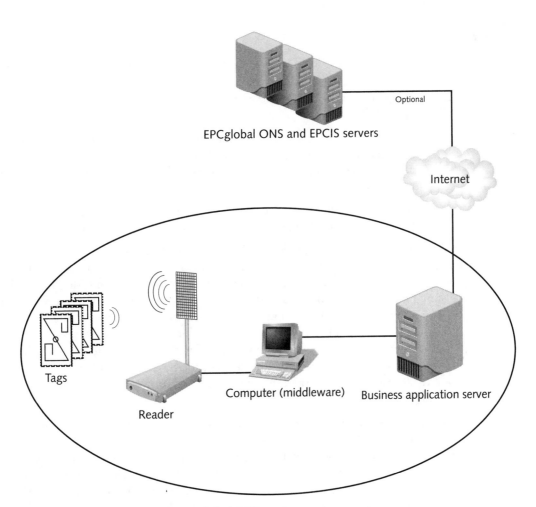

Figure 11-5   Fundamental EPCglobal RFID system components

How RFID Works

The subject of how the different RFID tags and readers work could fill an entire book by itself. Tags and readers use different transmission mechanisms in each frequency band. In this section, you will get an introduction to the technical details of how two of the most common types of passive tags and readers transmit and communicate with each other: UHF (400 to 900 MHz) and HF (13.56 MHz).

PHY Layer

A passive tag, the most common type, only transmits when it receives a signal from the reader, which is also called an interrogator. The connection between the tag and reader is called a **coupling**. RFID uses two types of coupling, depending on the devices and application:

- *Inductive coupling systems* are designed for tags that either touch the surface of the antenna or are inserted in a slot, such as smartcards. In these systems, the tags are typically used at a maximum distance of half an inch (just over 1 centimeter) from the antenna.

- *Backscatter coupling* is designed for tags that can be read at distances greater than 3.3 feet (one meter), up to 330 feet (100 meters) in some cases.

Backscatter is a reflection of radiation. Recall that passive tags are powered by an RF signal sent by the reader. After the reader transmits data (the reader transmission itself supplies power to the tag, so it can receive and decode the reader's transmission), it then begins to transmit a clean, **continuous wave (CW)**, which is an unmodulated sine wave. The CW is captured by the tag's antenna, and the tag uses it to supply power to the chip so that the tag can respond to the interrogator. The tag essentially reproduces (reflects) the same wave it receives from the reader, but it modulates this signal with the data by changing the electrical properties and consequently the reflection coefficient of its own antenna. This means that the antenna will transmit with more or less power, affecting the amplitude of the signal reflected.

Backscatter modulation is based on variations of amplitude shift keying (ASK) or a combination of ASK and phase shift keying (PSK), both of which you learned about in Chapter 2. The data is also digitally encoded to ensure that there will be enough transitions between 0 and 1 and vice-versa to assist the devices in maintaining synchronization during transmission (refer to the section in Chapter 2 titled Binary Signals, under Digital Modulation).

The reader has separate transmitter and receiver circuits and antennas and, since it is a powered device, it transmits a much stronger (higher amplitude) signal than the tags. When the reader is not transmitting commands or data to the tag, it sends out a CW. In order to detect the modulation of the signal from the tag, the receiver in the reader compares its own strong CW signal with the backscatter. The difference between the two is the data sent by the tag.

Both reader and tag modulate the signal in amplitude by as much as 100% or by as little as 10%. 10% modulation is more sensitive to interference and noise, but the signal can travel farther. 100% modulation is easier for the reader to detect; but during the periods without a CW, the tags are not being powered, so the distance between tag and reader must be significantly reduced. Figure 11-6 illustrates both modulations. The signals in the figure are not drawn to scale, neither in amplitude nor in frequency, but the figure is included here to illustrate the concept.

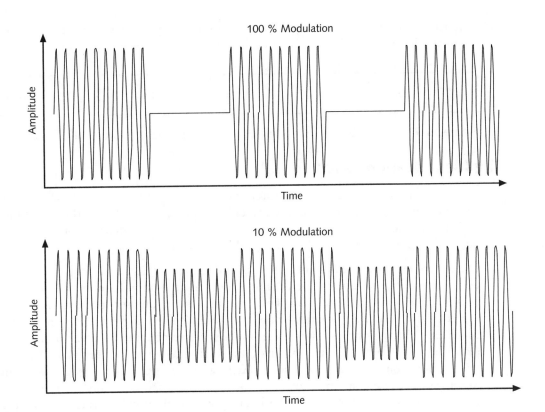

Figure 11-6 Backscatter modulation

Communications between tag and reader are always half-duplex. Interrogators and tags do not transmit and receive data simultaneously. To prevent interference issues from affecting the reliability of RFID systems, and to allow for environments where multiple readers are installed in the same area (also called dense interrogator environments), the EPCglobal standards also specify the use of frequency hopping spread spectrum (FHSS) and direct sequence spread spectrum (DSSS) transmission.

HF Tag Communication

HF RFID transmission uses a protocol called **slotted terminating adaptive protocol (STAC),** in which the tags reply within randomly selected positions or time intervals, referred to as slots. The interrogator transmits signals to mark the beginning and end of each slot, depending on the amount of data requested from each tag. Figure 11-7 illustrates the concept of slots. Note that the slots are not equal in size (the figure is not to scale). The number of slots is regulated by the interrogator and is always a power of two. Some shorter slots may exist when there is no reply from any tags, in which case the interrogator terminates the slot. The mechanism is described further in the next section. Note that slot

F signals the beginning of the reply intervals. It is the only slot with a fixed size. It also ends automatically, meaning that the interrogator does not signal the end of slot F.

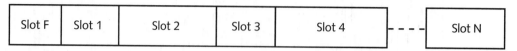

Figure 11-7   Reply intervals in the slotted terminating adaptive protocol (STAC)

Tag Identification Layer

When an interrogator initiates communication in an RFID system, there must be a way to prevent every tag within range of the reader's signal from responding at the same time. The tag identification layer defines three methods that allow an interrogator to manage the population of tags within reach of its signal: select, inventory, and access.

In *select*, an interrogator can send a series of commands to select a particular segment of the population of tags within its reach. This is done in preparation for an inventory or for the purpose of accessing a specific tag. The selection is based on user-specified criteria such as a particular category of products from one manufacturer. Tags do not respond to these commands. They simply set internal flags (bits) for responding to later transmissions. To perform an *inventory* in UHF, an interrogator sends out a series of query commands to get information from one tag at a time. As each tag receives an acknowledgement from the interrogator, it resets the inventory flag and does not respond to further inventory commands in the same round. In HF, the interrogator simply waits for each tag to reply in a different slot.

In the *access* approach, the interrogator can send one or more commands to multiple tags or exchange data with a single tag at a time, after uniquely identifying the tag with a command.

The minimum amount of information contained in a tag's memory is the EPC, a 16-bit cyclic redundancy check (CRC), and a destroy password. The **destroy password** is a code programmed into the tag during manufacturing. After the destroy password is transmitted by the reader, the tag is permanently disabled and can never be read or written to again. This structure is shown in Figure 11-8.

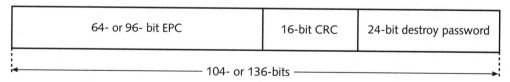

Figure 11-8   Structure of tag information

Tag Collision Handling in UHF

Since the reader initially may not know which tags are present within the range of its signal, and because new tags may enter the reader's signal field from time to time, the reader may send a VerifyID command. However, if you consider how shelves in a store or warehouse are typically organized, the tags within a certain reader's field belong to certain groups of products. All tags within the reader's field that are the intended recipients of the verification command will reply with their EPC, CRC, and destroy password. If the reader can identify at least one of these tags, it can proceed to select a range of tags by sending a series of commands that instruct the tags about an upcoming inventory. The process repeats until the reader has identified every group of tags within range of its signal. The reader can also tell a tag or a group of tags to be quiet, by sending a special command.

This selection process can be compared to a teacher that meets her class for the first time at the beginning of a semester and does not have a list with the names of all the students. To identify each student, the teacher might begin by asking all students to call out their full names. Initially several students may reply at the same time. The teacher can then ask the students whose last names begin with the letter A to call out their names. Again, she may get more than one reply and not be able to single out a student. Next, she can request that only those students whose last names begin with the letters AA, call out their names. This time, the chances of getting multiple simultaneous replies will be much smaller.

Eventually the reader will have enough information to be able to communicate with all the tags within a group. It then sends a command to an entire group to set an inventory flag. The next command instructs the tags that the reader will begin an inventory round. During the inventory round, the reader sends an inquiry to each individual tag. Once a tag has replied to an inventory query, it resets its inventory flag and does not reply again until the next inventory round is announced by the reader.

Tag Collision Handling in HF

In HF systems, the reader selects tags based on a process that is similar to the one used in UHF systems. Each tag uses its EPC, CRC, and destroy password to calculate a number that becomes the slot number in which each particular tag will reply. The calculation is based on parameters sent by the reader that depend on the total number of tags belonging to a particular group and also uses a random number generator in each tag. The reader can then begin an inventory round and wait for each tag to reply in its own slot, which prevents collisions. The standard makes the assumption that the number of potential collisions in these cases will be less than 0.1%.

Reader Collisions

Reader collisions may also happen in dense reader environments. If a reader does not receive any replies, it assumes a collision has occurred and backs off for a random period of time before listening for network traffic and attempting to transmit again.

MAC Layer

The RFID MAC layer is responsible for establishing and communicating the transmission parameters, such as transmission bit rate, modulation type, operating frequency range, and frequency hop channel sequence that are used for communications at the PHY layer. The reader sends commands to the tags establishing the communication parameters for each communications session. The MAC layer parameters for different types of tags—HF, UHF, and others—differ. These variances usually don't pose a problem because it is unlikely that a company will use multiple types of tags in a single environment or application.

Data Rates

As you learned earlier, the amount of data stored in a typical passive RFID tag is relatively small. The lack of a power supply and low processing power, which helps keep the tag costs low, means that the resulting data transmission rates for the tags are also low. Some EPCglobal standards specify a minimum number of tags per second that a reader should be able to access, instead of a specific data rate.

The specifications for HF tags call for readers to be capable of reading 200 tags per second. For tags containing just an EPC, the actual rates will likely be between 500 and 800 tags per second.

The UHF specifications define the tag-to-reader data rate as twice that of the reader-to-tag. In North America, the allowed tag-to-reader data rate can be up to 140.35 Kbps. In Europe, due to the RF signal power limitations, the maximum data rate is only 30 Kbps. Conversely, reader-to-tag data rates are respectively 70.18 Kbps in North America and 15 Kbps in Europe.

RFID APPLICATIONS

RFID is used in a vast array of ways. This section outlines just a few interesting applications for RFID. These examples are only the tip of the iceberg, however. The potential uses for RFID are practically unlimited.

NOTE   One of the recent applications of RFID is a wireless mouse that doesn't require batteries. The RFID reader is built into a special mouse pad, and the mouse is essentially a passive RFID tag. See the information located at www.a4tech.com under Battery Free Wireless Mouse.

Automobile Security

Many new cars are equipped with an antitheft device called an immobilizer. The vehicle's ignition key head contains a tiny Class 1 RFID chip that transmits in the 135 KHz frequency band. A hardware store copy of the key can be inserted in the ignition, but it cannot start the engine. When the original key is inserted in the ignition, a small reader device in the steering column transmits a signal to the key to activate it. The computer that controls the engine only allows the engine to start upon receiving a response from the tag chip in the key.

If you lose your key and obtain a replacement from the dealer, you must program the new key following the detailed instructions in the owner's manual.

Health Care

In hospitals, RFID tags in a patient's identification bracelet can provide vital information that cannot be easily misplaced. The tag can contain the patient's admission history, blood type, medications, prescribed dosages, and so on, and can be read by handheld devices carried by staff. In addition, the EPC on the tag can instantly link the hospital staff with the patient's record in the hospital's database. This feature can prevent errors and also enhance patient comfort and safety.

For elderly and very young patients, the system can sound an alarm if the patient leaves a designated area. Newborn babies and their mothers can wear bracelets that contain matching information, ensuring that the right baby goes to the right mother. Such tags could also prevent babies from being taken out of the hospital by an unauthorized person.

11

Transportation and Military

RFID tags embedded in standard courier packages and other small boxes can speed up and help automate sorting, in addition to preventing errors. The wide variety of shapes and sizes of packages today make it almost impossible to completely automate the process. Humans must still handle the packages and barcode readers by hand.

During the recent wars in the Middle East and Bosnia, materials officers were faced with having to transport millions of pieces of equipment, ammunition, and replacement parts, often on short notice. With many of these items stored in sealed containers at very large military warehouses all over the United States, coordinating and tracking these shipments is a challenge. Missing or incorrectly stored spare parts and ammunition can put the lives of large factions of the military at serious risk. The U.S. Department of Defense (DoD)'s material goods inventory is valued at over $700 billion, and part of it is composed of perishable or sensitive items that must be protected from extreme environmental conditions.

NOTE During Operation Desert Storm, over 40,000 containers were shipped to the Persian Gulf. Because these shipments could not be adequately tracked while in transit, "iron mountains" accumulated in ports and airfields, which, in many instances, contained redundant materials and supplies. At least two-thirds of these containers had to be opened so that personnel could see what was inside.

The DoD currently handles approximately 100,000 ground combat and tactical vehicles, 250,000 wheeled vehicles, 1,000 strategic missiles, 300 ships, and 15,000 aircraft and helicopters. These items are involved in approximately 300,000 shipments per year. The DoD RFID system comprises more than 800 locations with over 1,300 read/write stations used to manage the flow of supplies through the military's In-Transit Visibility (ITV) network.

Sports and Entertainment

RFID tags are used for monitoring tire pressure in race cars. The tiny tags with a built-in sensor and battery are installed right on the tire valve and can be read automatically or manually from inside the car. This technology can also be used in transport trucks and interstate buses; on these vehicles, the tags help save money by controlling tire wear and prevent accidents related to tire condition. Tire pressure monitors are beginning to appear in luxury automobiles as well, and can provide an added measure of safety. Monitoring participants in marathons and triathlons is another common use for RFID tags.

RFID usage is not limited to exotic sports. Common sports such as golf can also benefit from RFID technology. The cost of a high-quality golf ball today can be quite staggering. Passive tags can be installed inside the balls so that if they are lost during a game, a pocket reader can help the owner locate the ball in tall grass fields, among trees or fallen leaves, and even under water, depending on the technology employed.

In 2004, the Golden Globe awards used an inconspicuously placed RFID tag in the event invitations to prevent unwelcome paparazzi and other members of the public from entering the event.

People Monitoring, Crowds, and Access

In large amusement parks, parents of children wearing special bracelets containing RFID tags can instantly locate the kids if they become separated. Readers installed throughout the park track the location of the youngsters, and parents can go to a kiosk that instructs them how to locate their children, based on information the reader gets from the parent's own RFID tags.

In an application similar to the Golden Globe awards, RFID-tagged concert and sports event tickets can simplify the jobs of security personnel. Even with extensive use of barcodes today, some fans attempt to gain access to a stadium with fake tickets, sometimes trying to take advantage of the volumes of people, to bypass the gate security. RFID tags embedded in the tickets can make this much more difficult, if not impossible.

NOTE   Many gas companies, including Shell, Mobil, and Esso, implemented loyalty systems in the 1990s that allow customers to pay for gas at the pump, by simply swiping a tiny RFID transponder that can be mounted on the key chain in a certain area at the front of the pump. Customers sign up for the service, and the charges are automatically made on the customer's bank account or credit card every time they stop at a gas station to fuel their vehicles.

Pharmaceuticals

The pharmaceutical industry is vulnerable to counterfeit drugs that cause monetary damage and can also pose a health hazard to consumers. Individual drug packages use specialized tags that store the date of manufacture and detailed tracking information generated as the packages move through the supply chain. This tracking can also help isolate the exact location of counterfeiting activity by monitoring events at every stop in the supply chain.

Tags in over-the-counter and prescription medication allow vision-impaired people using a special device to listen to a description of their drugs and dosages. This system can be used at home or in a pharmacy.

RFID CHALLENGES

It is not hard to think of a thousand other applications for RFID that have the potential for making life and business easier, safer, and simpler. However, the technology does face some challenges, as you will learn in this section.

Impact on Corporate Networks

One of the major challenges for the implementation of RFID systems is the impact of the volume of data on a company's network. With manual or barcode-based inventory control systems, the amount of data that is collected and transmitted across a company's network is usually limited to the on-hand quantities of particular products, along with the UPC code for each product. However, RFID systems are usually implemented so that inventory can be counted by simply activating the tags. To ensure that the shelves are always fully stocked with products in a large retail store, for example, the system can direct the readers to interrogate *all* of the RFID tags every five minutes or so. This scanning can add a lot of traffic to an organization's network.

To get a perspective of the amount of increased traffic on a company's network, consider a scenario in which a large national retailer tags each of the 10,000 individual items on its shelves, in every one of its 1,000 stores, and interrogates all of the readers from a central head office location every 15 minutes. At 17 bytes per product (recall that with the 96-bit EPC, the minimum information from a tag is about 136 bytes), this would generate 170 MB of data for a single read. It would fill a CD-ROM in one hour and create 5.44 GB of network traffic in a typical eight-hour business day. In only one month, the total volume of traffic would swell to 1.632 terabytes of data. In comparison, the entire collection of 17 million books in the U.S. Library of Congress equals 136 terabytes of data. It would only take seven years for this company to process that much data through its network. Although most of this data will be processed and the duplicate data discarded, we are still talking about a significant increase in the volume of data on the network.

Network Availability

Assume that such a system is eventually implemented, and that the company relies on it to replenish inventory automatically. In this case, network availability becomes a serious factor in the store's ability to serve its customers. As retailers become dependent on RFID systems to increase service and reduce costs, greater network bandwidth must be available and the network must be reliable, that is, it must remain functional (99% availability means that the network can be expected to be down for approximately 80 hours per year). Any downtime that occurs during business hours can quickly become a serious problem. For most companies, these demands will translate to expanding and adding redundant equipment and communications capabilities to their existing networks, a costly undertaking at best.

Products are out of stock in grocery stores and large retail establishments for 7% of the time, and some popular items are not available 17% of the time. This inventory shortfall can represent significant losses for retailers. To combat this problem, many retailers order more product than they need or can sell out of one location. Supermarkets often are forced to discard perishable products, which leads to higher costs for all consumers. Item-level tagging is a means to reduce or eliminate these problems.

Storage Requirements

Large banks and corporations already are saddled with archiving tremendous amounts of historical data—potentially tens or in some cases hundreds of terabytes of data for each company. In addition, new laws designed to protect investors and consumers, such as the Sarbanes-Oxley Act, require companies to accumulate and securely store even more information. The huge volume of data that can be generated by RFID systems significantly increases the need to store information accurately and reliably.

NOTE   Cattle producers in Canada and Europe have been using RFID to track the history of animals since 2003. As of January 1, 2005, each head of cattle in Canada must have an RFID tag. The tags store all of the information required on every animal in the herd, including health issues, vaccinations, movement (locally or to a new herd), and production of milk and offspring throughout its life. Records must be kept on slaughtered cattle for many years afterwards.

Device Management

Even without RFID in place, businesses are already finding it a challenge to manage the huge numbers of devices on their networks. Network management software does not come at a low price. Even for small networks with less than 1,000 devices, the cost of network management software can easily escalate to well over half a million dollars. As networks expand, the need to remotely monitor and manage servers, routers, switches, and RFID readers from a central location becomes a critical factor in a company's ability to ensure greater network availability. Add to this the task of managing and tracking hundreds, thousands, or even millions of RFID tags. Then consider security related to wireless RFID transmissions. You can see how managing RFID systems can quickly become a very complex and costly job.

Security Considerations

Development of worldwide standards for RFID and growth of RFID for everyday use have given rise to a large number of security and privacy concerns. There are solutions for RFID-related security issues, but these solutions are not perfect fixes.

In the United States, in particular, the concerns are centered on privacy. Tag data used for products after they are purchased could be linked to the consumer and used for targeted marketing. Such data could be collected by governments and the companies with which the individuals conduct business. This idea is not much different from data that can be captured from the use of debit and credit cards, but the difference is that RFID-generated data can be captured without the user being aware of it.

Security related to RFID readers falls under the wired network security policy. Reader-to-tag and tag-to-reader communications have the same vulnerabilities as any wireless network, the only exception being that capturing the tag-to-reader communications may be very difficult. Tag transmissions occur at very low power levels; readers are also transmitting a CW during tag-to-reader communications. Once a tag is installed on a product or packaging, it usually cannot be removed without permanently damaging the tag; however, it is still possible to tamper with the *data* in a Class 1 (read/write) tag by recording over the existing tag data or by adding new data.

Passive tags do not employ authorization or encryption security methods because they do not have their own power supply, have chips with low processing power, and are low in cost. Shielding stores and warehouses to prevent RF signals from coming in or going out may solve some of the problems associated with unauthorized access from outside the building, but is a very expensive proposition. In addition, once consumers take the products to their home or workplace, they may still be exposed to privacy violations by someone using an interrogator nearby.

Data in tags can be locked and require a password for the tag to be used again. By using a combination of the EPC, CRC, and built-in destroy password, tags can also be permanently disabled. Locking the tags would make it very difficult to use the information from the tag throughout the distribution channels. Permanently destroying the tag, either by issuing a *kill* command or by physically damaging it, would prevent a retailer from using the tag again if the customer returned the product, limiting the functionality of the RFID system. Physically destroying tags would also prevent the consumer from taking advantage of features like the smart refrigerator application described at the beginning of this chapter.

A **blocker tag** is a device that can be used to simulate the presence of a virtually infinite number of tags. Blocker tags can be used to disable unauthorized readers from accessing the information from a selective group of tags by sending so many responses that an unauthorized reader cannot differentiate between the blocker tag and a legitimate tag. This device offers an alternative solution that minimizes some of the issues described above at a much

11

lower cost. After getting her purchase home, the consumer may optionally destroy the blocker tag so she can continue to use the legitimate tags. Blocker tags require the use of Class 1 writable tags, which can be exposed to tampering.

Security for RFID systems is a complex topic, and there is no single solution that addresses all possible situations. Applications of RFID far outweigh the potential problems, however. RFID usage will continue to expand, and eventually RFID will be present in nearly every aspect of our lives. Educating users and implementing legislation related to data collection and privacy will play a big part in raising consumers' comfort level with the technology, just as it has with the Internet.

CHAPTER SUMMARY

- ❏ Radio frequency identification (RFID) stores information about an item's manufacturer and the date and location of production in electronic tags that include an antenna and a chip.

- ❏ Standards being published by EPCglobal Inc. will allow RFID to be used worldwide.

- ❏ RFID systems are composed of electronic tags, readers, antennas, software and the EPCglobal network services. The format of the Electronic Product Code (EPC) is defined by the EPCglobal standards. The EPC is either 64 or 96 bits long and includes a code that refers to the manufacturer, a stock keeping unit number and a serial number.

- ❏ RFID tags are also known as transponders. Typical tags include a microprocessor and memory. Tags are accessed by a reader device that captures and processes the data. There are two basic types of tags, passive and active. Passive tags are the most common type. They do not have a power source and rely on the electromagnetic energy in the RF waves transmitted by the reader to power their microprocessor. Active tags are equipped with a battery and can cost upward of $20. The life span of active tags is usually limited by the battery. Semi-active tags also include a battery. However, it is only used when the tag is activated by a transmission, which helps the battery last many years.

- ❏ Tags can be produced in flexible packages called smart labels with an adhesive backing. They can be affixed to product packaging, pallets, or to the product itself. They are also used to track passenger baggage. Tags are not limited to being placed in a visible are and can be read in virtually any position.

- ❏ 1-bit tags are passive devices used in retail stores to prevent theft. They do not include a unique identification, a chip, or any memory and are only used to activate an alarm. Chipless tags use fibers or materials that reflect a portion of the reader's signal with a unique pattern that can be used as an identifier.

- ❏ Sensory tags are equipped with thermal, smoke, or other type of sensors used to monitor environmental conditions to which a product may have been exposed during shipping and storage. The cost of a tag can vary depending on the type. Most passive tags cost between $0.25 and $0.05. Class 0 tags are read-only. Class 1 tags are read/write. Some tags are of the WORM (write once read many) type. Tags are also classified as Generation 1 and Generation 2.

❏ A reader or interrogator communicates with both the tags and the corporate network. Some readers have the ability to write data to the tags. Readers also provide the energy to activate and power the tags. Readers and tags operate in one of four frequency bands, 135 KHz (LF), 13.56 MHz (HF), 433 MHz and 860 to 930 MHz (UHF), and 2.5 GHz and 5.8 GHz (ISM).

❏ There are two types of tag antennas, linear and circular. Linear antennas have a better range, but circular antennas achieve more reliable reads.

❏ RFID software includes system software that controls the functions of the tag and reader hardware, middleware that is responsible for reformatting the data to meet the requirements of the business applications, and the programs that companies use to process business transactions. EPCglobal standards also specify an object naming service that is modeled after DNS.

❏ RFID has a multitude of uses ranging from healthcare to entertainment-related applications. The systems are also being used in pharmaceuticals to prevent drug fraud and assist patients.

❏ The connection between a reader and a tag is called a coupling. Inductive coupling tags need to be placed within ½-inch of the antenna. Backscatter coupling allows tags to be read at distances from three to 300 feet. Backscatter is a reflection of the reader's signal modulated with the tag data. In order to power the tags, when the reader is not transmitting, it sends out a continuous wave. Backscatter modulation is based on variations of ASK and PSK. Communications between tags and readers are always half-duplex.

❏ In HF, the tags use time slots to communicate with the reader. The number of slots is always a power of two, and the communication is always controlled by the reader. Tags never initiate communications with the reader.

❏ RFID has the potential for significantly increasing the amount of traffic and storage requirements in the corporate network. With the implementation of RFID systems, network availability and device management become even more critical.

❏ There are many concerns regarding security and privacy vulnerabilities linked with the implementation of another wireless technology such as RFID. A tag can be locked or destroyed (electronically or physically), but doing so can limit its functionality. Blocker tags may offer an alternative solution. User and consumer education, along with legislation by governments, should help raise the comfort level and allow RFID usage to expand.

11

KEY TERMS

1-bit tags — RFID devices that do not include a chip or memory and cannot store an EPC. 1-bit tags are only used to activate an alarm at retail store entrances as a means of preventing theft.

active tags — RFID tags that include a battery.

backscatter — The type of modulation used by passive RFID tags. Backscatter is a reflection of radiation in which the tag reflects the signal sent by an interrogator while modulating it with the data to be transmitted.

beacons — RFID tags that are battery powered and transmit on a periodic basis.

blocker tag — A type of Class 1 passive tag that can be used to disable unauthorized readers from accessing the information from a selective group of tags by sending so many responses that a reader cannot differentiate between the blocker tag and a legitimate tag.

chipless tags — RFID devices that use embedded fibers to reflect a portion of the RF waves emitted by a reader. The reflected portion of the RF waves is unique and can be used as an identifier.

continuous wave (CW) — An unmodulated sine wave sent by the reader to power the passive tag so that it can transmit a response.

Class 0 — A class of RFID tags that are read-only.

Class 1 — A class of RFID tags that are read/write.

coupling — A connection between a reader and a tag.

destroy password — A code programmed into the tag during manufacturing that can be used to permanently disable the tag.

Electronic Product Code (EPC) — A standardized numbering scheme that can be programmed in a tag and attached to any physical product.

EPCglobal Inc. — An organization entrusted by industry worldwide to establish RFID standards and services for real-time, automatic identification of information in the supply chain of any company, anywhere in the world.

Object Name Service (ONS) — An EPCglobal Inc. service, modeled after DNS, that can assist in locating information about a product, over the Internet.

passive tags — The most common type of RFID tag. They do not include a battery and are powered by the electromagnetic energy in the RF waves transmitted by the reader. Passive tags never initiate a transmission and must wait for a reader to interrogate them.

radio frequency identification (RFID) — A technology that uses electronic, flexible tags, equipped with microprocessor chips and memory, to identify products. RFID tags can store significantly more information than the current barcode system.

reader — The RFID device that captures and processes the data received from the tags.

semi-active tag — RFID tags that include a battery that is only used when the tag is interrogated. The batteries in semi-active tags usually last for several years.

sensory tags — RFID devices that include a thermal or other kind of sensor and can record information about the environmental conditions to which a product has been exposed during transportation or storage.

slotted terminating adaptive protocol (STAC) — The communications protocol used by passive RFID tags that work in the 13.56 MHz HF band.

smart labels — Another name for flexible RFID tags that include a microprocessor chip and memory.

tags — Devices that include an antenna and a chip containing memory and can store information about products, such as the manufacturer, product category, and serial number, along with date and time of manufacturing.

transponders — Another name for RFID tags.

REVIEW QUESTIONS

1. _____ tags are read-only.
   a. STAC
   b. Class 1
   c. Class 0
   d. Blocker

2. 1-bit tags _____ .
   a. store a unique identification code
   b. can only be read by a passive reader
   c. do not carry any information about the product
   d. are also known as RF fibers

3. One of the main characteristics of sensory tags is that _____ .
   a. they can sense the presence of other tags
   b. they can block the signal from other tags
   c. they only respond to the reader if a password is sent first
   d. they can capture information about environmental conditions

4. What is the purpose of an interrogator?
   a. To read information from the tags
   b. To prevent unauthorized access to the tags
   c. To increase the read distance
   d. To store a charge that powers passive tags

5. RFID middleware is used to _____ .
   a. store information about the types of tags used
   b. convert the data read from the tags into a format that is compatible with that of the business application
   c. control the functions of the reader hardware
   d. control the functions of the tag hardware

6. Reader antennas are designed for the specific application. True or False?

7. The orientation of the tag's antenna usually does not affect readability. True or False?

8. RFID is not expected to have a major impact on network traffic. True or False?

9. UHF passive tags use a variation of amplitude and phase modulation. True or False?

10. A reader uses a method called coupling to connect with the corporate network. True or False?

11. To power passive tags, the reader transmits_____ .

11

12. To modulate a response signal using backscatter, a tag has to _____ .

13. Interrogators and tags _____ simultaneously. This is known as _____ communications.

14. The minimum amount of information stored in a smart label is _____ .

15. In a(n) _____ an interrogator will assume that there was a collision when_____ .

16. Which transmission techniques are included in the EPCglobal standards?

17. List three specific challenges associated with RFID system implementation.

18. Which methods can be used to temporarily or permanently disable a tag?

19. Explain the mechanism for handling tag collisions in HF.

20. List several potential applications for RFID that were not discussed in the chapter's text.

HANDS-ON PROJECTS

Project 11-1: Researching RFID Tags

Using the Internet, locate suppliers of tags that can be used to track animals. What types and classes of tags are available? What kinds of animals are the tags being used on and for what purposes other than tracking herds of cattle? Write a one-page report on your findings.

Project 11-2: Issues Surrounding RFID Security

As you know, security is an extremely important aspect of any wireless communications. There are still many issues surrounding RFID security, especially now with the U.S. government promoting the use of RFID in passports. Using the Internet, research some of these issues and the organizations involved in creating possible solutions, as well as what is being done about increasing security and privacy protection. Write a one-page report on your findings, focused on one of the issues you identify.

Project 11-3: Identifying Tags and Reader Antennas

Inquire with large local businesses as to whether they are currently using or are required to use RFID tags on any products they ship to their customers. Be conscious of some of the security issues with RFID and identify yourself as a wireless communications student before you ask any questions regarding their use of RFID. Keep in mind that some job opportunities may be available through contacts that you initiate through this project, therefore be sure to present yourself in a professional and serious manner. If possible, visit the company or retailer and make a list of the types and classes of tags used. Write a one-page report on your findings.

Due to concerns regarding theft, it is not advisable that you attempt this at a retail establishment. Concentrate your efforts on manufacturing or warehousing facilities, if possible.

NOTE

CASE PROJECTS

CASE PROJECTS

Project 11-1: Instrument Rentals Inc.

Instrument Rentals Inc. (IRI) rents electronic test equipment to a variety of heavy industries. Equipment is usually rented for a period of one week to one year. IRI offers a guarantee to its customers that the equipment will be available when they need it and that the instruments will have been calibrated to factory specifications. With 120 locations across the country, IRI will ship instruments wherever they are needed, check the calibration upon arrival, and recalibrate when needed. Every piece of equipment returned at the end of a rental period must also be checked by a technician. IRI will often service the equipment at the customer's site, which can be in the middle of an oil field or inside a mine, to maintain it in top working condition.

To prevent delays, minimize errors with lost or misplaced paperwork, and avoid Internet access problems that can prevent access to a database of records, IRI would like to keep each instrument's calibration records, technicians' names, rental/travel log, and other information stored with the instrument. The service call software that the technicians have in their notebook computers should be able to read a record, display it on the screen, and update the record on the instrument record storage device automatically. All of the instruments are leased for a period of three years. When the lease expires, IRI will look at the records for a particular instrument and make a decision either to replace it with a new model or to extend the lease to prevent interruption of service to their customers. As a well-known RFID expert, you have been asked to make a recommendation to IRI on whether this technology would be the right solution for its needs.

You should prepare a 10- to 15-slide PowerPoint presentation listing the advantages and disadvantages of RFID for this type of application, and specifying the type of tag and reader that IRI should acquire, should it decide to go ahead with this project.

Project 11-2: Instrument Rentals Inc. Decides to Go with RFID

CASE PROJECTS

IRI has decided to go ahead with the project and has asked you to provide a proposal (five pages maximum) including all of the equipment required to add this technology to 1,000 of

11

their most expensive test instruments. There are two technicians per location, but only one will be equipped to service the equipment in the field. The other technician will be servicing equipment in the office.

Your proposal should include pricing for the tags, including about 100 replacement tags, a portable reader, a fixed reader, middleware, and other equipment. If required, IRI's IT staff will be in charge of reprogramming the middleware to interface with the company's in-house database. Keep in mind that if the project is successful, it may be expanded within six months to one year to cover IRI's entire instrument asset base consisting of more than 10,000 instruments.

OPTIONAL TEAM CASE PROJECT

The trade union to which the technicians at IRI belong has sent a letter to the company expressing concerns about the privacy of its members. IRI plans to include the name of the technician who last serviced the instruments in the RFID tag, and the company has asked you to become involved. A team of three people from IRI will research the union's concern, including checking state regulations, and organize a meeting between all the parties to discuss the matter.

You and five other classmates should form two teams: one representing the union and another representing IRI. Research the issues outlined above and engage in a friendly debate in which you will first listen to and then satisfy the union's concerns. The union team should also do research and be prepared to argue and defend their members' rights.

CHAPTER 12

WIRELESS COMMUNICATIONS IN BUSINESS

After reading this chapter and completing the exercises, you will be able to:

◆ List the advantages of wireless communications for businesses

◆ Discuss the challenges of wireless communications

◆ Explain the steps needed to build a wireless infrastructure

In the early 1930s, a mathematician developed a formula that could be used to make accurate weather forecasts, something that was unheard of at that time. However, because there were no computers or calculators at that time, it took almost three months of hand calculations to come up with the next day's forecast. This obviously was far from useful, and many individuals scoffed at such a preposterous solution to weather forecasting. However, with the introduction of computers by the late 1940s, the amount of time needed for the calculations was dramatically decreased. Suddenly, this model became very popular, and today it forms the basis for all weather forecasting.

The point here is that it sometimes requires vision to see how an idea or technology could be used. This vision also applies to new technologies like wireless communications. Some users question why we should consider wireless technology when the existing wired system seems to work just fine.

In this chapter, you will learn what it takes to convert the potential of wireless technology into a successful business reality. We'll look at the steps needed to incorporate wireless technology into a business, and at the advantages and challenges that face business users who consider adopting this new technology.

ADVANTAGES OF WIRELESS TECHNOLOGY

The advantages of incorporating wireless technology into a business are far-reaching and can positively impact an organization in many ways. In addition to the advantages already discussed in this book—mobility of data access, easier network installation, increased reliability, and better disaster recovery—wireless technology provides business-specific advantages, including universal access to corporate data, increased productivity, ability for customers to access their own data, data availability around the clock, and improved information technology (IT) support.

NOTE In a survey prepared by the Wireless LAN Association in 2001 (WLANA—see www.wlana.org), 92% of companies that deployed wireless LANs found definite, measurable economic and business benefits. In another survey commissioned by Cisco in 2002, 87% of end-users responded that they believe WLANs improved their quality of life by increasing flexibility, productivity, and time savings. Forty-three percent of these believed this improvement was significant.

Universal Access to Corporate Data

The first advantage of wireless technology is that it provides access to corporate data from almost any location. This universal access can help a business generate more revenue. For example, a traveling sales representative calling on a customer needs the most current information at his fingertips before he walks in the door. He could review printouts in his hotel room the night before, but these are only as recent as the day they were printed. He could access the company's corporate database from his hotel room that morning, but changes in inventory and sales will occur before his 2:00 P.M. appointment.

With wireless technology, the sales representative can use a WiMAX network—or his digital cellular telephone connected to his notebook—to access live data, such as the status of the customer's most recent order, buying history, current inventory, and an up-to-the-minute competitor price list. This information is accessible before he steps out of his car for his appointment, or even while he is meeting with the customer. By having universal access to the latest data, the sales representative will be well prepared to make the sale.

Traveling sales representatives are not the only users who can benefit from universal access to corporate data. Anyone who needs to be mobile but needs access to data can benefit from it. Physicians who move around a hospital can have current data at their fingertips to make decisions that result in lower costs and improved care for patients. Factory managers likewise can access data as they check available warehouse storage space for arriving inventory. Wireless technology can also be useful when all parties are in one location. For example, during an intense negotiation session, attorneys, bankers, and clients can all use wireless notebooks to access data or receive SMS messages on their cellular phones that would help them make the best decision.

NOTE

In 2004, The Baycrest Center for Geriatric Care in Toronto, Ontario, was one of the first hospitals in North America to implement a computerized physician order entry system. The system lets doctors order tests, exams, and medications directly from a patient's bedside using a WLAN. Physicians can also check the patient's records and charts in the hospital's health information system.

Industry experts agree that access to corporate data from almost anywhere is the greatest advantage of wireless technology. This access allows decisions to be made quickly from any location with the most up-to-date information. For a business, these factors translate into increased revenues.

Increased Productivity

Having universal access to corporate data leads to increased productivity by employees. In a survey by Cisco in 2001, users reported that when using a WLAN they could access data almost two additional hours each day than if they were only using a wired network. This increase occurred when users were away from the computer in their offices but still connected to the WLAN during meetings, conferences, and sales calls. If the additional two hours of connection time translated into 70 minutes of increased productivity (a standard ratio), this means the average user could be 22% more productive. For a worker with a salary of $64,000, this means that the annual productivity improvement per wireless user could be worth as much as $7,000 each year to the business. In addition, almost two-thirds of WLAN users reported that the wireless connection improved the accuracy of their everyday tasks.

Increased Access to the Customer's Own Data

A key factor in reducing business costs is to shift the burden of accessing a customer's data from the business to the customer. If customers can see data about themselves on the business' computer system, they can make better and more informed decisions. This self-service decreases the use of the business' human resources, which in turn reduces costs and increases revenue for the business.

An example of customer access to their own data can be seen in the airline industry. Most airlines have Web sites where customers can view schedules, make reservations, print boarding passes, and check on the current status of their frequent flier miles. These sites generate cost savings for the airlines because they can hire fewer telephone reservation clerks. Some airlines are adding wireless technology in the airports themselves. Customers can use the WLAN to check their flight information once they enter the terminal, learning their gate number and check-in time. Personal check-in is available for those who have a wireless PDA, which allows customers to print their own boarding passes and check in their baggage at curbside (though they still must pass through the standard security procedures). This helps the airline make better use of their staff or even reduce staffing. In addition, customer satisfaction is increased because travelers spend less time waiting in lines. Increased satisfaction means a repeat customer. All of these benefits result from wireless technology that makes the customer's data available from more locations, which reduces the burden on the business and thus increases revenue.

12

Data Availability Around the Clock

Leaving work at 5:00 P.M.—and leaving the work behind—is a thing of the past. Business professionals regularly work evenings, nights, weekends, and holidays to catch up and stay ahead. This means that business users need access to corporate data 24 hours a day, 7 days a week. In the past this required a trip back to the office on weekends or staying late at night to finish that report. Wireless technology, however, can help make data available from almost anywhere at any time. This means that a business user can still catch her son's soccer match or daughter's music performance without sacrificing productivity.

NOTE   The introduction of RIM's BlackBerry device—especially with the current models that are both a cellular phone and data device—represented a paradigm shift in accessibility to e-mail and corporate data. Many business applications have been developed for the BlackBerry, including software that allows a field technician to update trouble tickets and applications that allow construction foremen to enter payroll work-hour records while on-site. See https://www.blackberry.com/ThirdParty/search.jsp.

Improved IT Support

Wireless technology can help improve the support that information technology (IT) departments provide to users. Two of the most significant advantages for IT departments are easier system setup and decreased cabling costs compared to wired systems. Troubleshooting a wireless network is often simpler than troubleshooting cabling problems, especially for businesses that have large offices with many connection points and hidden cabling infrastructure. Cabling infrastructure issues are frequently overlooked as a potential source of serious network connectivity issues, and can be very labor-intensive and time consuming (which, of course, means expensive) to troubleshoot and repair.

Other improvements include easier and faster moves of equipment, more efficient use of office space, and lower support and maintenance costs. These benefits can lead to lower costs for the business and more availability for the IT staff to provide improved support to the users.

Voice over Wireless LAN (VoWLAN)

Consider the cordless telephone you have probably grown to rely on at home. Until 2003, there were few options for businesses that wanted to enable their staff to move around the office while remaining available at their extension numbers. VoWLAN is about to change this, without the high cost of cellular telephone calls.

NOTE
As of June 2004, there were approximately 1,600 hospitals in the United States using VoWLAN. See www.spectralink.com, www.vocera.com, www.nortel. com, and www.alcatel.com. Also, check vowlan.wifinetnews.com/ for the latest industry news and information.

In many kinds of workplaces, such as hospitals, sports facilities, construction sites, and manufacturing plants, some of the staff must remain mobile within the confines of a building or site at all times, which can limit voice communications, since these people are not always near a phone. Cellular telephones have largely solved this problem, albeit at a high cost. Although cordless phones are common in homes, business telephone systems offered few mobility options. WLAN technology allows businesses to go beyond data access and transform the way staff communicates while performing their daily tasks. The new WLAN standards discussed in Chapter 8, along with 802.11-enabled telephone handsets manufactured by a growing number of companies, means that businesses today can benefit from the full potential of mobile communications.

VoWLAN takes advantage of Voice over IP (VoIP) technology but instead of using the wired network to carry voice calls, VoWLAN uses the wireless infrastructure to carry both voice and data. **Wireless VoIP phones**, the telephone handsets that connect to a WLAN's access point (AP), enable you to use the WLAN for regular telephone calls. Depending on what type of connection a location has with the telephone carrier—either traditional land-based telephone lines or over the Internet—additional equipment may be required to interconnect the wireless network with the phone lines. As more manufacturers and telephone carriers enter the VoIP market, and more customers sign up for these services, the wireless VoIP handsets will likely become commonplace, eventually replacing cordless phones and enabling both data and voice connectivity without wires through a single, common interface.

VoIP carriers such as Vonage (see www.vonage.com) and others also offer **wireless VoIP SOHO routers** that can be connected to a DSL or cable modem and provide both a WLAN and telephone services through the user's Internet connection. SOHO is an acronym for small office/home office. These devices may be optimized to ensure the best quality voice connections while still maintaining reasonable throughput for the data connection using quality of service (QoS). Wireless VoIP SOHO routers are essentially the same device as a wireless residential gateway but are preconfigured by the service provider to connect to its network and allow regular telephone calls to be made over the Internet. This configuration is password secured by the VoIP provider so that users cannot tamper with it, which usually results in poor call quality or problems with simultaneous voice and data transmissions. Making telephone calls using VoIP can save a substantial amount of money in long-distance calls. In addition, most VoIP providers allow a business to have a telephone number that has an area code belonging to a different part of the country, or even the world. This can also generate significant savings when most of a company's business comes from a different region.

12

CHALLENGES OF USING WIRELESS TECHNOLOGY

Just as there are distinct advantages for a business to use wireless technology, there are challenges as well. These challenges include competing technologies, data security and privacy, user reluctance, and a shortage of qualified staff.

Competing Technologies

Some wireless technologies are clearly based on approved industry standards, such as WLANs following the IEEE 802.11b and 802.11a standards. A business that uses an IEEE standard WLAN is assured that it is investing in a technology that will be the standard for several years to come and can be upgraded, in most cases, by simply loading a new version of the software on the APs and client devices.

Yet with other wireless technologies, such as digital cellular telephony, there is no clear indication of which one will become the standard and which ones will fade away. This uncertainty poses a critical decision for businesses. Selecting the wrong technology may mean investing hundreds of thousands of dollars in a technology that may be orphaned in a few years, with dwindling users and support.

As long as technologies continue to compete before one becomes the standard, companies face a certain amount of risk in selecting the right wireless technology. An organization must not only determine which technology is best for it, but also which technology will be viable into the future, a task that can be made much easier by having trained staff on board or hiring the right reseller or consulting organization to provide guidance on which is the right technology for the company's current and future needs.

Table 12-1 provides a summary of the wireless technologies discussed in this book, along with some of their applications, pros, and cons.

Table 12-1 Wireless technologies

Wireless Technology	Primary Applications	Pros	Cons
Bluetooth (IEEE 802.15.1)	Cable replacement	Wide availability	Low speed, limited range
ZigBee (IEEE 802.15.4)	Residential and industrial controls	Low-cost, low-power, mesh networking	Limited security (encryption), low speed
WiMedia (IEEE 802.15.3)	Multimedia distribution, interconnecting consumer entertainment equipment, telephones, and even data	Low-cost, low-power, high-speed (22 Mbps) and even higher possible with UWB (IEEE 802.15.3a) and mesh networking with IEEE 802.15.5, QoS	Some devices may have limited processing power and consequently limited security; limited range without mesh networking

Table 12-1 Wireless technologies (continued)

Wireless Technology	Primary Applications	Pros	Cons
WLANs—802.11a/b/g/n	Mostly data networking	Established technology; new enhancements to the standards allow it to support voice, QoS, mesh networking, faster handoffs, multimedia; good security with RADIUS or VPN; LOS required; up to 108 Mbps	Currently has limited ability to handle voice and multimedia; 802.11b/g/n has limited spectrum and range without mesh networking; 802.11a has limited range
WiMAX (IEEE 802.16)	Data, voice, video; fixed or mobile	40 to 75 Mbps fixed wireless shared-bandwidth with range of up to 35 miles; high-security; 2 Mbps+ for mobile applications; can be overlaid on cellular network; LOS or NLOS	Complex technology
Cellular	Voice and data	EVDO network deployed; up to 2 Mbps nomadic, 300+ Mbps mobileHSDPA network deployed; up to 10 Mbps nomadic	High-cost per-minute/per-user
Satellite	Voice, data, video	Covers remote areas not available with other technologies; can achieve 1 Gbps in dedicated connections	Very high cost of deployment; requires high-gain directional antennas for most applications
RFID	Data for product identification only	Worldwide standard for product identification	Short range, low-security due to low processing power of tags

12

Data Security and Privacy

Wireless technology's greatest strength—allowing users to roam freely without being connected to the network by wires—can also be its greatest weakness if not addressed properly. Just as a roaming user can receive radio frequency (RF) signals anywhere within a building, so too can an unauthorized user outside the building. Broadcasting network traffic over the airwaves has created a concern for keeping that data secure. Most industry experts agree that opening up a corporate network by adding a wireless component without considering security is simply asking for serious problems.

User Reluctance

In technology, changes are nearly constant because as standards and technology advance, established vendors continue to improve their products and to make it easier, simpler, and more transparent for users to adapt. Change can be painful for users because it takes time and energy to learn a new system. Unless users can see an immediate benefit to abandoning their comfortable old ways of doing things, they will be reluctant to do so. The human factor in implementing wireless technology is sometimes a significant obstacle.

Shortage of Qualified Staff

Wireless communications technology has touched almost every business in one way or another, including manufacturing, health care, telecommunications, retail, and many others, and is poised to continue growing, as you have learned in this book. As the use of wireless technology continues to expand, the need for information technology (IT) professionals to develop and implement wireless applications and provide support is skyrocketing. However, many schools and training facilities have not yet caught up with the demand for wireless IT workers. Consequently, there is a shortage of qualified IT professionals trained to install, support, and maintain wireless systems.

As technology improves and becomes ever easier to use, the life of a network administrator or a reseller can get more complicated. Users who begin to feel more comfortable with the technology may feel empowered to modify settings, occasionally creating connectivity issues or perhaps exposing the network to security risks. In companies that implement WLANs, network support staff and administrators must not only be aware of these issues, continually monitoring them, but also must ensure that their knowledge and training keeps pace with the advances in the IT industry, something that is even more critical when dealing with wireless technologies.

The advantages and challenges of wireless technology are summarized in Table 12-2. Before embarking on building a wireless infrastructure in a business, it is critical that the advantages and challenges be considered carefully to identify the needs, solutions, and threats, and to determine the best compromise of these factors.

Table 12-2 Wireless advantages and challenges

Advantages	Challenges
Universal access to corporate data	New technology
Increased productivity	Competing technologies
Increased access by customers to their own data	Data security and privacy
Data availability 24/7	User reluctance

BUILDING A WIRELESS INFRASTRUCTURE

Once a business has decided to invest in wireless technology, it faces the task of building a new wireless infrastructure. This is much like adding a new network to the organization. In fact, several of the steps necessary to build this new infrastructure are similar to those needed when adding a new wired network.

Needs Assessment

"Do we really need it?" is a question that must be asked first when adding a wireless infrastructure to a business. Sadly, this question is often asked too late in the process. Sometimes a change in a procedure or additional personnel may meet a perceived need instead of investing in wireless technology that might not be fully justified.

12

Evaluating the need for wireless technology is a time-consuming process, but it is the essential first step. Evaluating needs involves looking at the organization and the current network, gathering basic information, and determining costs.

Look at the Organization

The first step in assessing the need is to step back and examine the organization or business as a whole. Sometimes users fall into the trap of viewing only their department or unit instead of seeing the big picture of the entire organization. There are a series of basic yet vital questions that need to be asked, including:

- What is the current size of the organization?

- How much growth is anticipated?

- How do employees in different positions and departments perform their daily activities; meaning, do they need to move around the office and work from different locations?

- How frequently does the company move staff to other offices and need to reconfigure the wiring setup?

Employees that work primarily with one computer at their desks, such as call center/customer service operators, may not require wireless access. If the room configuration is static, a wired network will provide performance that is more consistent, in the long run.

Although these questions may seem very basic, they can help to refocus the thinking back onto the organization as a whole and away from one part of it. In addition, questions like these can often reveal a great deal in terms of assessing needs and identifying priorities; a company's employees themselves may not be aware of all the implications of implementing a wireless network, such as the need for new security policies and continuous monitoring, as well as potential interference problems that can affect user and application performance and offset the advantages of a WLAN.

Assess the Current Network

The next step is to look at how the organization or business actually uses its current network. For example:

- How does the current network support the organization's mission?
- What are the strengths and weaknesses of the current network?
- How many users does it support?
- What essential applications run on the network?

Different industries often have different network requirements. The banking industry must have networks offering a very high degree of security. The manufacturing industry may have networks that must be completely fault-tolerant and cannot afford any downtime. Educational institutions may be able to tolerate a small amount of downtime but are faced with authenticating thousands of new users every few months. Each segment is unique and has different network requirements. These factors should be taken into consideration when viewing the current network.

Assessing the current network can help to identify why a new technology may be needed. If the current network can be upgraded or adapted to meet the current needs, then wireless technology may not be necessary at this time. However, if the current network cannot support the anticipated future growth of the business or there is a clear indication that wireless technology can help the business grow, then the investment may be worthwhile.

The task of assessing the current network can be helped by documenting the current network in detail. Networks tend to grow in an unplanned fashion as new users or equipment are suddenly needed, so documenting the network is necessary to gain a view of the system as a whole.

A table like Table 12-3 that summarizes the network can be helpful. If the network is complex, a diagram or layout of the network can also help. An example of a diagram is seen in Figure 12-1.

Table 12-3   Sample current network table

Description	Data
Number of clients	55
Types of clients	35 – Windows XP 20 – Windows 2000
Number of servers	1 – Windows 2000
Type of network	Ethernet 100BaseT switched
Type of cable (medium)	Category 5e
Types of devices	5 – Laser printers1 – scanner

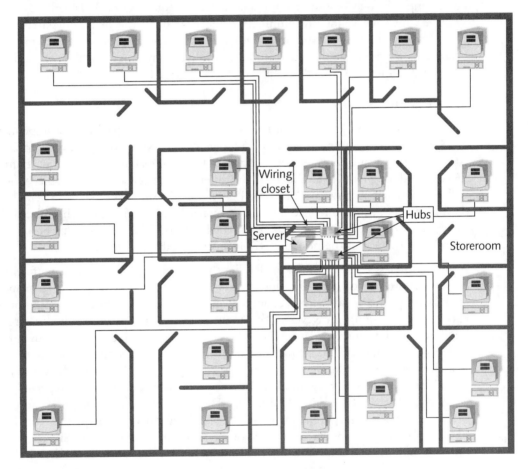

Figure 12-1

Gather Information

After the organization and the current network have been evaluated and it is determined that wireless technology can fit into the current business strategy, the next step is to gather information. With all of the different wireless technologies available and the constant changes taking place in this area, the expertise to gather the information may be beyond that of the current IT staff. Many organizations turn to outside consultants and vendors to help provide information at this point. Some organizations may send out a **request for information (RFI)**. An RFI is a document that seeks information about what vendors may have to offer. RFIs are general in scope. For example, a broad statement such as, "The vendor will install a wireless network on the second floor of the building to accommodate 45 users" may be enough to start things rolling. Several different vendors are encouraged to respond with information about the particular products that they sell that will meet those needs.

Once all of the RFIs have been returned, the organization can examine each of them in detail. Generally, a pattern will emerge from the RFIs that come in from the various vendors. For example, if four vendors recommend a radio frequency (RF) IEEE 802.11a wireless WLAN while one vendor recommends using Bluetooth, the direction starts to become clear. Evaluate RFIs with caution. Vendors want to sell a product or service, and may overemphasize the strength of their product while minimizing its weaknesses. Independent research is still needed after the RFIs have been received.

Wireless Site Survey

The information you gather about the current network in preparation for implementing a WLAN will not be complete without a proper **wireless site survey**. A wireless site survey consists of measuring the strength and quality of the signal and the resulting transmission speeds and throughput achievable in all the different locations around the office where users will need wireless access to the network. In addition, the site survey will also help determine the existence of interference sources, both internal and external, which will establish the susceptibility of the WLAN to environmental factors. The survey helps ensure that the actual performance of the network will meet the needs of all the users.

A simple wireless site survey for a small office/home office (SOHO) can be performed using an AP, a wireless adapter card, and the client software provided by the adapter card manufacturer (the Windows XP client software is far too simplistic and does not provide enough information). However, a comprehensive site survey, especially for large office buildings, manufacturing plants, multiple floors of a building, or any other complex environments, should be performed using more sophisticated software tools and by people who have a level of training and experience that may not be currently available in the organization. The site survey should ideally be performed using the same type and model of equipment that will be eventually installed. The cost of tools and equipment to perform a site survey is fairly high; purchasing them can only be justified if you will be using these tools on a regular basis. There are many prerequisites and steps involved in a site survey. One of the most important and time-saving items to include in the survey is a building floor plan, preferably one that includes the location of office furniture items and large machinery. Floor plans will assist in the site survey and yield more detailed and complete reports.

TIP

A variety of site survey guides and white papers is available on the Internet, from different organizations. The best approach to find more information is to do a search for *Wireless Site Survey Guide*.

A wireless site survey will identify a number of additional factors regarding the potential implementation of a WLAN, such as:

- Security features and policies required
- Radio signal range (distance requirements)
- Number of channels required (based on user/application load)
- Throughput required
- Location of AP radios and antennas
- Location of client devices
- Type of client adapters (WNICs) and whether external antennas may be required
- Power (electricity) requirements (Power over Ethernet or line?)
- Growth (expansion) requirements and impact on current design
- Potential interference sources and their location, as well as the effect on all of these answers
- Standards and frequencies to be implemented (802.11a or g)
- Requirements for integration with the company's wired network (additional equipment such as switches, firewalls, authentication servers)

The answers to all of these questions will help determine the type and range of equipment that will need to be purchased for implementing the WLAN and will assist in creation of a request for proposal (RFP; discussed later in this chapter). The wireless site survey may be performed by the company's own technical staff, by a potential vendor, or by a consulting organization but should always be done before a vendor provides you with a final proposal.

Return on Investment

After the company has collected potential solutions from vendor RFIs and conducted independent research, it must make a determination of the costs of the project. The cost by itself cannot be the sole basis of the decision. Rather, the company must consider the cost in light of the benefit that the project will provide. It may cost $50,000 to implement wireless technology, which might seem like a high cost. However, if the new technology will increase revenue by $250,000, then that cost may seem very reasonable.

Determining the cost in relationship to the benefits is known as calculating **return on investment (ROI)**. In strict accounting terms, ROI is the profit divided by the investment. ROI projections are useful when considering the purchase of products or services needed for a business. ROI is best expressed over a specific period of time. For example, you might project that a $50,000 wireless network will save a total of $75,000 in 18 months. The trick with ROIs is to determine all of the costs as well as all of the projected savings.

When determining costs, it is important to consider all costs involved. **Upfront costs** are costs that are necessary to start a project, such as installing the wireless technology in order to start using it. For example, upfront costs for a WLAN include purchasing APs and wireless

NICs for all devices and computers. The number of APs depends on the coverage area, number of users, and types of services needed. Hardware costs may vary depending on such factors as performance requirements, coverage requirements, and bandwidth.

Upfront costs are not the only costs to be considered. **Recurring costs** are often overlooked when determining final costs. A recurring cost is a cost that a user may continue to pay over an extended period of time. For example, if the company leases a free space optics transceiver or a wireless bridge from a local carrier, the annual lease cost is recurring and should be considered as part of the total cost for the technology, over its useful life. The initial cost of equipment is usually amortized (reduced) by a certain percentage every year, but lease and maintenance costs either remain the same or may increase over time. The representing installation, projected maintenance, hardware or software maintenance contracts, IT staff training, and user training should all be factored into the total cost of implementation.

A much more difficult task is to determine the savings that can be accumulated. Because the system is not already in place, it may be very difficult to calculate the savings or increased revenue that can accrue. The key here is to be as conservative as possible. Gathering information from other users of the technology can be very helpful.

NOTE   A study conducted by Cisco in 2001 concluded that wireless technology would save the average college almost $57,000 per year, and the average hospital $130,000.

NOTE   Although ROI studies are considered very important, they still are not conducted as frequently as they should be. In a recent survey, only 26% of those responding said that they conducted an ROI analysis prior to installing a WLAN system. Almost 25% indicated there was "simply no need to," while 16% said that cost was simply not an issue.

Develop a Plan

Once it has been determined that a real need exists that can be solved by implementing wireless technology, and the ROI is positive, the next step is to create a plan. The adage that "those who fail to plan, plan to fail" is never more true than when considering a new technology. The landscape is littered with projects that were poorly planned at the beginning and abandoned after cost overruns escalated astronomically. Developing a sensible, workable plan is perhaps the most critical piece of the entire process. Planning should never be done in a vacuum; instead, the IT staff, users, and consultants may all be asked for their input. Once the plan has been completed, a **request for proposal (RFP)** is sent out to vendors, who will respond with a formal cost for the project or equipment. A request for proposal is a detailed planning document that is sent to potential vendors with precise specifications for the products and services that the organization intends to buy.

Another type of document that is often sent to vendors is a request for quotation (RFQ). The difference between an RFP and an RFQ is that RFPs ask the vendor to submit a proposal for the entire project, whereas in an RFQ the company has usually preselected the equipment and is simply asking different vendors to provide their most competitive pricing. RFQs are generally used when the project will be entirely designed and implemented by the company's internal staff.

NOTE

Whom to Involve

Making an investment in wireless technology involves the efforts of many people. One of the most important groups is the organization's IT team. The purpose of using the IT staff is twofold. First, they have a broad background in technology and can contribute much to the dialog regarding their experiences and knowledge base. They are the most trained technologists for the organization, and they need to be treated as such. Nothing alienates an IT staff more quickly than to hire an outside consultant without first tapping the expertise in house.

The most important reason for involving the IT staff at this point is to make them aware of the proposed project, since they will be the ones who will provide technical support and training. This group will be the strongest promoters of the new technology to the users. If the IT staff is alienated from the planning process, the project will likely be slow to take off or even fail.

12

Another important group to involve in planning is the users themselves, since they will be the ones who are actually using the new wireless technology. Generally, it is not practical to involve all users at this stage. Instead, a representative group can be selected to participate. However, the group should represent a true cross-section of the user base. Too often the most technological users who are enthusiastic about any new technology are the only ones chosen to participate. These users will enthusiastically support any new technology project, especially if they get to be among the first to test it. The representative group should not just include these types of users. Instead, it should also include the average user, as well as those who have a reputation of being opposed to change and new technology. This approach will allow for impartial input to the planning process, and it may also serve to get a better cross-section of users on board when the new technology rolls out.

Because they work with customers on a daily basis, the IT staff may be able to provide names of positive, negative, and neutral users to help in the planning process.

TIP

External consultants are generally the third group that participates in the planning process. They have the advantage of being outside the organization and can view the organization and its needs from an unbiased perspective.

A common mistake is to turn an entire project over to consultants and allow them to create the plan. This approach results in a plan that does not benefit from the expertise of the local users and IT staff, and may in fact antagonize them. Instead, consultants should be used as one source of input, but not the sole source. It is important to schedule regular meetings with consultants and ask them for detailed explanations as the project moves forward. Consultants should provide in the plan a schedule of activities, a list of proposed technology, and a phased implementation plan—a complete project management plan. This plan prioritizes and allocates time required for the responses from the other participants in the process and also ensures that the planning phase stays on target.

Request for Proposal

Once a plan for wireless technology has been designed, the next step is for the organization to submit a request for proposal (RFP). RFPs are much more detailed than RFIs. An RFP may start with, "The vendor will install an 802.11b WLAN network for 45 users in an area in which users are no more than 275 feet from the access point," and should include more detailed information such as a proposed schedule, known issues (such as a building that contains certain types of hazardous materials like asbestos or chemicals), and any other information that would assist the vendor in creating its response. Some of the key elements to be contained in an RFP include:

- Statement of values — A statement of values helps the vendors understand the philosophy of the business and identify its priorities. For example, is network performance more important than the average response time that it takes the vendor to respond to a problem, or is the immediate availability of the hardware and software more important than price? A statement of values assists the vendor in developing their response RFP.

- Description of operations — A description of the business itself is also helpful for the vendors. This would include any future business plans that might affect the RFP, such as a planned expansion in a branch office building.

- Current network and applications — The RFP should describe the current network, such as the number of sites, the current configuration, the applications that are currently being used, and the planned additions.

- Timetable — The RFP should include a timetable that lists specific dates. An example is shown in Table 12-4.

Table 12-4   Sample RFP timetable

Proposed Date	Activity
May 1	Date RFP is issued
May 15	Last date that written questions must be submitted by vendors
May 30	Date RFP responses are due
June 15	The week that initial cuts will be made
July 1	The week that presentations will be made by the finalists
July 15	Date the contract will be awarded
August 15	Date the contract will be finalized
September 10	Date work is to begin
February 12	Date work is to be completed

Vendors will respond to the RFP with their proposal for the project. The vendor's response should contain detailed information regarding what will be installed, suggested timelines, and how much it will cost. If a site survey has not been performed, it should be included as a mandatory requirement in the RFP. Once all of the RFPs have been received and analyzed, the company can make a final decision regarding which vendor to select. Choosing a vendor should be done carefully by checking the vendor's background and references. Selecting a vendor who submits the lowest-cost RFP can often turn out to be a very costly decision.

If the technology to be implemented is based on other types of handheld devices, instead of 802.11, one of the responses that may appear in the RFPs could be from a **wireless application service provider (WASP)**. A WASP can design and create a wireless application to run on a specific range of devices such as cellular phones, PDAs, and other handhelds, and can often deliver the software, hardware, security, and networks as one complete package. Because many of the wireless devices, languages, and applications are so new and diverse, a WASP may have the expertise needed to get the project up and running quickly. Many WASPs will host the application on their own wireless network, in which case the services are subscribed to rather than purchased. WASPs may become more common and important if a company's planned wireless technology setup includes WiMAX (802.16).

Perform a Limited Trial

After the RFPs have been received and the vendor has been selected, it is important to perform a limited trial, also known in the industry as a *pilot project*. It is usually possible to borrow sample hardware and software from the vendor who won the bid. The IT staff should be thoroughly involved in the trial, along with a select group of users. Those users who were involved in the planning process are good candidates.

The new wireless technology should be thoroughly tested. Devices should be connected and then taken offline, the base stations should be disconnected, and other similar activities should be performed to see how the technology reacts under both normal and unusual circumstances. Throughput and applications should be tested. This is a time in which the IT department can be introduced to the technology and start learning troubleshooting techniques while dealing with the trial group of users. The security of the new technology should also be thoroughly tested at this point. It is also an opportunity for managers to see the technology in action so that they can begin to understand how it will impact the business.

Begin Training

After the technology has been tested thoroughly, the next step is to begin training. Do not underestimate this step. Training provides all users as well as support specialists with the knowledge to effectively operate and support the new wireless technology, and can save time and costs during the transition. Users need to know how to use the new hardware and software, and the support staff needs to know how to manage the network and diagnose problems. Training will increase the effectiveness of the new technology once it is installed because users will have less of a learning curve. This, in turn, will minimize the temporary drop in productivity that is normally associated with the installation of a new system. Also, well-trained users will have fewer questions and require less IT support after they start using the new system.

The IT staff must be trained first. This may include on-site training from the vendor, if it was included as part of the RFP, or attending workshops or specialized classes that cover the technology. Once the staff has been trained, they in turn can train the users. Because all users learn differently, a variety of training sessions should be offered to accommodate them. The different types of training include:

- Small group sessions
- Detailed written instructions explaining how to connect to the network and describing potential issues and how to solve them
- Web-based training
- One-on-one sessions

Rollout to All Users

As the training moves toward completion, the final rollout of the wireless solution to all users can begin. The most efficient way to do a widespread rollout of a wireless technology is to do it in phases. If possible, start with introducing the wireless technology to just one department or unit of the business. The IT staff will be able to deal with problems more easily if they only have to deal with one department or unit at a time. This also limits the effect of any rollout problems to one department instead of the entire community of users.

On occasion, a project may need to go live before it is entirely debugged and before every feature is added. If this is the case, it is important that the key users understand this, feel comfortable with the temporary state of the new technology, and are aware of the full scale of the project. The key users' leadership among the other users can determine the success of the project.

Once the system is installed and running in a unit, it is a good idea for the vendor and the IT staff to confer and identify any problems that may have arisen before additional units are brought on. IT staff members can also compare notes to determine if the training sessions meet the needs of the users based on the type and number of questions they received. The training can then be tweaked as the remaining users are trained.

Provide Support

Whereas training is primarily done before the new system is turned on, support is the continued follow-up for answering questions and assisting users. User support functions can be organized in a variety of different ways. These include:

- Establish informal peer-to-peer support groups
- Create formal user support groups

- Maintain a help desk center
- Assign support to the IT department

Each of these has its own set of strengths and weaknesses. However, establishing and staffing an internal help desk is one of the most effective means of support. A **help desk** is a central point of contact for users who need assistance using technology. The help desk manages customer problems and requests, and also provides support services to solve the problem. The help desk can provide basic information to users, such as why an FSO connection is slower in the rain. The help desk can also be a good source of identifying areas, based on user responses, where improved technology can save the company money. Some suggestions regarding a help desk include:

- Have one telephone number for the help desk.
- Plan for temporarily increased call volume after the new network is installed.
- Create a method to track problems effectively.
- Use surveys to determine user satisfaction and to identify any remaining issues.
- Periodically rotate network personnel into the help desk.
- Use information from the help desk to organize follow-up training.

12

CHAPTER SUMMARY

- Wireless technology can positively impact an organization in many ways. WLANs allow current data to be accessed quickly from any location. Universal access to corporate data can also lead to increased mobility, productivity, and accuracy by employees.

- VoWLAN uses IP phones and VoIP on the same network the company uses for data. VoWLAN can help to enhance employee availability and customer service. Implementing VoIP may increase the load on the network and require the replacement of some wired network devices, such as switches and routers.

- Wireless technology challenges include investing in the correct technology. Unauthorized users outside a building can receive RF signals from an inside WLAN. Some users are reluctant to change to a new technology. The need for information technology (IT) professionals to develop and implement wireless applications and provide support is skyrocketing.

- Once a business has decided to invest in wireless technology, it faces the task of building a new wireless infrastructure. The first step is to evaluate the need for wireless technology by examining the entire organization. Another important step is to look at how the organization or business actually uses its current network. If the current network cannot support the anticipated future growth of the business or there is a clear indication that wireless technology can help the business grow, then investing in it may be the answer. After the organization and the current network have been evaluated and it is determined that wireless technology can fit into the current business strategy, the organization must gather information, then perform a wireless site survey, which can answer critical questions, such as the number of APs required, types of antennas, interference, and security needs.

❏ Security needs may increase the cost of the project significantly, since many other devices such as additional switches and authentication servers may be required. Security is always a work-in-progress and must be continually reviewed. New security policies may have to be created and implemented as the result of adding a wireless network.

❏ Some organizations may send out a request for information (RFI). After evaluating potential solutions suggested by vendor RFIs and independent research, the business determines the costs of the project. The business should balance total cost of implementing a wireless network against the benefit that the project will provide. Determining the cost in relationship to the benefits is the return on investment (ROI).

❏ Once it has been determined that a real need exists that can be solved by implementing wireless technology and the ROI is positive, the next step is to create an implementation plan. Planning should include the IT staff, users, and consultants. Once a plan has been designed, the organization submits a request for proposal (RFP).

❏ After the RFPs have been received and the vendor has been selected, the company performs a limited trial or pilot project involving a range of users and circumstances. It is usually possible to borrow sample hardware and software from the vendor who won the bid. The IT staff should be thoroughly involved in the trial, along with a select group of users.

❏ Once the technology has been tested thoroughly, the next step is to begin training. Training provides all users as well as support specialists the knowledge to operate and support the new wireless technology effectively.

❏ As the training nears completion, the business rolls out the technology to all users in phases.

❏ Support is continued follow-up and consists of answering questions and assisting users. User support functions can be organized in a variety of ways, with an internal help desk being one of the most effective support systems.

KEY TERMS

help desk — A central point of contact for users who need assistance using technology.

recurring costs — Costs that continue to be paid over a period of time.

request for information (RFI) — A document sent to a vendor to gain general information about a vendor's products or solutions to a problem.

request for proposal (RFP) — A detailed planning document with precise specifications for the products and services.

return on investment (ROI) — The profit or advantage of an action.

upfront costs — Costs that are necessary to start a project.

wireless application service provider (WASP) — An organization that can design, create, and deliver a complete wireless application.

wireless site survey — The task of measuring the signal strength and quality in several locations around the office to determine how many APs will be required, how many and which channels will be used, as well as identifying interference sources and security needs.

wireless VoIP phones — The telephone handsets that connect to a WLAN's AP, permitting use of the WLAN for telephone calls.

wireless VoIP SOHO routers — Devices that can be connected to a DSL or cable modem and provide both a WLAN and telephone services through the user's Internet connection.

REVIEW QUESTIONS

1. The principal advantage of wireless technology is _____ .

   a. universal access to corporate data

   b. lower cost

   c. newer technology

   d. reduced bandwidth

2. A help desk can provide service to users by performing all of the following tasks, except for _____ .

   a. having one telephone number

   b. creating a method to track problems effectively

   c. reporting users' questions to their supervisor

   d. using surveys to determine user satisfaction

3. Using VoWLAN instead of a traditional business telephone system means that the company has _____ .

   a. 802.11a technology

   b. 802.11g technology

   c. cordless IP phones

   d. a VoIP router

4. If customers can see data about themselves on the business' computer system, it will enable them to _____ .

   a. gain access to secret corporate data

   b. sell this data to other people

   c. reduce the amount of bandwidth needed for their home computer

   d. make better and more informed decisions

5. _____ is not an advantage to the IT department for adopting wireless technology.

   a. Easier setup

   b. Less time-consuming moves of equipment

   c. Higher maintenance costs

   d. Decreased cabling costs

12

6. Any new technology faces problems simply because _____ .

   a. it has not been as thoroughly used and tested as a mature technology

   b. it is based on a weaker standard

   c. managers are unfamiliar with it

   d. old technology is always easier

7. All wireless technologies are clearly based on approved industry standards. True or False?

8. Wireless technology's greatest strength, allowing access without being connected to the network by wires, is also its greatest weakness. True or False?

9. Using IP phones always requires that a business contract to use a VoIP service provider. True or False?

10. There is a shortage of qualified IT professionals to install, support, and maintain wireless systems. True or False?

11. "Do we really need it?" is a question that must be asked first when adding a wireless infrastructure to a business. True or False?

12. Sometimes users fall into the trap of viewing only their department or unit instead of seeing the big picture of the entire organization. True or False?

13. The banking industry must have networks that have a _____ degree of security.

14. The task of assessing the current network can be helped by documenting the _____ network in detail.

15. A(n) _____ seeks to gain information about what vendors may have to offer and are general in their scope.

16. Determining a project's cost in relationship to its benefits is known as _____ .

17. A(n) _____ cost is a cost that may continue to be paid over an extended period of time.

18. A(n) _____ should be performed by the company or by any vendor submitting a proposal for implementation of a WLAN.

19. List the three groups that should be involved in developing a plan and why they should be involved.

20. Why is it a mistake to turn the entire planning process over to external consultants? What is a better approach?

21. Describe a request for proposal (RFP).

22. What is a wireless access service provider (WASP), and what services can a WASP provide?

23. List three questions that can be answered by performing a wireless site survey prior to making a decision on WLAN implementation.

24. What is the advantage of a limited trial? What are some steps that should be taken during a trial?

HANDS-ON PROJECTS

Project 12-1: Researching VoWLAN Options

As the use of VoIP and WLANs grows, businesses of all sizes will be looking for ways to use both technologies to provide additional mobility to their staff, as well as to provide better customer service by making employees more available to their customers. Use the Internet to research the VoWLAN options available today. Write a one-page report and include one paragraph with your own thoughts about the additional equipment and features that might make this technology more attractive to any type of business.

Project 12-2: Researching Help Desk Setup

A help desk is a vital tool for providing continued maintenance and support for users of IT. Using a variety of sources, such as textbooks and the Internet, write a one-page paper about the type of help desk that you would set up for a law office employing approximately 100 staff. Include times of operation, number of support staff needed, and how the help desk would contact the technicians with a problem and continue to track that problem until it is resolved.

Project 12-3: Researching Education Resources and Certifications

A shortage of qualified IT staff in the high-tech industry is a critical area of concern. Use the Internet to research this problem and describe what is being done about it at the national and state levels. What are your suggestions for addressing this problem? Summarize your findings and recommendations in a one-page paper.

Project 12-4: Researching User Behavior

New technology almost always faces opposition from those people who are required to use it. Do some Internet and library research on user behavior. What are some of the ways to overcome user reluctance to adopt a new technology? What techniques would work for those who are opposed to any technology? What techniques would work for those who are just opposed to any change? Write a one-page paper on your findings.

12

Project 12-5: Considering a WLAN Implementation

Using the network at your school as a model, draw a diagram or floor plan and complete a table similar to Table 12-3 that describes the network. Include a narrative of the network history, as well as what changes are anticipated in the next 36 months.

If you have a wireless NIC that is compatible with a demo version of AirMagnet or similar software from another vendor, download the software, install it, and perform an initial site survey. You can check to see if your wireless NIC is compatible with AirMagnet on the company's Web site. You can obtain a demo version of AirMagnet Laptop and check their compatibility list at www.airmagnet.com/products/demo-download.php. Note that AirMagnet offers a variety of other products, including AirMagnet Surveyor, which is software specifically designed for this task. You can also perform a less sophisticated site survey using the wireless NIC software provided by the NIC manufacturer. Include in your report an analysis of any difficulties you may have encountered.

After completing your site survey, document the results of your signal strength and quality or speed/throughput, along with your recommendations for AP location, channels, antennas, and any other considerations, on the floor plan diagram.

Project 12-6: Selecting a Reseller or Consultant

Locate and identify four organizations in your area that install and service WLANs. Find out as much as you can about these organizations, and make a recommendation regarding which one you would hire if you were asked to take responsibility for the implementation of a wireless network to serve the students in your training institution or department. What were the different companies' strengths and weaknesses? How did they compare with one another? Write a one-page paper on your conclusions.

CASE PROJECTS

The Baypoint Group (TBG) needs your help with a WLAN proposal. GHS is a chain of sporting good stores that cater to the sport of soccer. Because GHS has grown in popularity, it now has nine stores in the area. GHS is considering implementing a wireless technology that will link all of its stores through wireless broadband service. The chain would install WLANs in each store and provide its employees with PDAs for better customer service. GHS is unsure how to start this process. They have asked TBG for help, and TBG has turned to you.

Project 12-1: Educating the Customer on WLAN Implementation

Create a presentation for GHS that explains the steps necessary to implement a wireless technology infrastructure, beginning with evaluating the needs and ending with providing support. Your presentation should last about 20–25 minutes. Use PowerPoint to create your slides.

Project 12-2: Devising a Support Strategy

GHS management is ready to start the process after hearing your presentation. They feel that one of the barriers they must overcome is providing support for their users. GHS does not have a centralized help desk; instead employees help each other and the IT staff does a limited amount of instruction, just enough to get the user through his or her problem. GHS would like your opinion on how to set up a help desk and what services it should provide. Create a short (five-minute) PowerPoint presentation about what a help desk does, its advantages and disadvantages, its challenges, and some tips on using a help desk for GHS.

OPTIONAL TEAM CASE PROJECT

Use the Internet to locate news articles and company press releases on one example each of wireless LAN, MAN, and WAN implementations. Review and note some of the challenges encountered and some of the expected or resulting benefits of the project. If possible, contact the organization or vendor and obtain additional information on the challenges and benefits. Your three-person team should write a one-page report for each LAN, MAN, and WAN implementation, and then present your analysis to the rest of the class. Your instructor will coordinate the timing and specific cases discussed and decide whether teams will be allowed to present a report on the same real project or will have to select a different one. Allow at least 5 to 10 minutes for the class to ask questions at the end of your presentation and be prepared to answer questions about ROI, technical support, what process and criteria were used to select the vendor, or whether the entire project was handled by internal staff. Your team's report should also include your own conclusions about the project's benefits.

12

A

WIRELESS# CERTIFICATION EXAM OBJECTIVES

The Wireless# certification is the entry-level wireless certification for the information technology industry, administered by Planet3 Wireless, Inc. Your Wireless# certification will get you started in your IT career by ensuring you have a solid base of applicable knowledge of:

- Wi-Fi
- Bluetooth
- WiMAX
- ZigBee
- Infrared
- RFID
- VoWLAN

The Wireless# Web site is located at www.cwnp.com/certifications/wsharp.

1 Wireless Technologies and Standards

1.1 Define the roles of the following organizations in providing direction and accountability within the wireless networking industry.

Objective	Chapter	Heading
IEEE	3	Understanding Standards
Wi-Fi Alliance	1, 7, 8	Various
ZigBee Alliance	5	IEEE 802.15.4 Low Rate WPANs
Bluetooth SIG	5	IEEE 802.15.1 and Bluetooth
WiMAX Forum	9	IEEE 802.16 WiMAX
Infrared Data Association (IrDA)	5	Infrared Technology (IrDA)

1.2 Define the characteristics of Wi-Fi technology.

Objective	Chapter	Heading
Range	7	Access Points
Frequencies/channels used	7	Physical Medium Dependent Standards
Power saving modes	7	Power Management
Data rates and throughput	7	IEEE 802.11b Standards, Media Access Control Layer
Dynamic rate selection	7	Access Points
Roaming functionality	7	Infrastructure Mode
Infrastructure and ad hoc modes	7	Infrastructure Mode, Ad Hoc Mode
SSID / network names	7	Association and Reassociation

1.3 Summarize the basic attributes and advantages of the following wireless LAN standards, amendments, and product certifications.

Objective	Chapter	Heading
802.11a	8	IEEE 802.11a
802.11b	7	IEEE 802.11b
802.11g	8	IEEE 802.11g
Wi-Fi® certification	8	Note under IEEE 802.11e
WMM® certification	8	Note under IEEE 802.11e
WPA / WPA2® certification	8	Note under Wi-Fi Protected Access

1.4 Summarize the characteristics, basic attributes, and advantages of ZigBee.

Objective	Chapter	Heading
Frequencies	5	ZigBee Protocol Stack
Power requirements	5	Power Management in ZigBee Networks
Topology models	5	ZigBee Network Topologies
Security features	5	Security in ZigBee and 802.15.4 WPANs
IEEE 802.15.4 standard	5	IEEE 802.15.4 Low-Rate WPANs
ZigBee stack	5	ZigBee Protocol Stack

A

1 Wireless Technologies and Standards

1.5 Summarize the characteristics, basic attributes, and advantages of WiMAX.

Objective	Chapter	Heading
Fixed vs. mobile and frequencies used	9	WiMAX Protocol Stack
Data rates, throughput, range, and line-of-sight parameters	9	WiMAX Protocol Stack
Quality of Service (QoS) and security features	9	Modulation and Error Correction
Different wireless MAN standards— 802.16-2004, 802.16e, ETSI Hiper-MAN, Wi-Bro	9	Standards Family Overview, WiMAX Coexistence (ETSI HiperMAN), IEEE 802.16 (WiBro)

1.6 Summarize the characteristics, basic attributes, and advantages of Bluetooth.

Objective	Chapter	Heading
Frequencies used	5	Bluetooth Protocol Stack
FHSS hop rates and adaptive frequency hopping support	5	Bluetooth Protocol Stack
Data rates, throughput, and range	5	Bluetooth Protocol Stack
Power classification	5	Bluetooth Protocol Stack

1.7 Summarize the characteristics, basic attributes, and advantages of Infrared technology.

Objective	Chapter	Heading
Frequencies used	5	Infrared WPANs
Data rates, range, and line-of-sight parameters	5	Infrared WPANs
Protocol types	5	Infrared WPANs
Interfering sources	5	Infrared WPANs
Different wireless PAN specifications— Serial Infrared (SIR), Medium Infrared (MIR), Fast Infrared (FIR), Ultra Fast Infrared (UFIR), Infrared Simple (IrSMP), Infrared Financial Messaging (IrFM), Infrared Transfer Protocol (IrTRAN-P)	5	Infrared WPANs

1.8 Summarize the characteristics, basic attributes, and advantages of VoWLAN.

Objective	Chapter	Heading
Wireless VoIP phone characteristics	12	VoWLAN
Wireless VoIP SOHO router characteristics	12	VoWLAN
Wireless VoIP SOHO router operation	12	VoWLAN

1.9 Summarize the characteristics, basic attributes, and advantages of RFID.

Objective	Chapter	Heading
RFID system requirements	11	RFID System Components
RFID tag types	11	RFID Tags
RFID hardware components	11	RFID System Components

2 Hardware, Software, and Installation

2.1 Identify the purpose, features, and functions of the following wireless network components. Choose the appropriate installation or configuration steps in a given scenario.

Objective	Chapter	Heading
Access Points	7	Access Points
Wireless LAN Routers	7	WLAN Applications
Wireless Bridges	8	Expanding WLAN Functionality
Wireless Repeaters	8	Expanding WLAN Functionality
WLAN Switch	8	Expanding WLAN Functionality
Wireless VoIP Gateway	12	VoWLAN
Wireless Media Gateway	8	Other WLAN Expansion Hardware
Power over Ethernet Devices	7	Access Points

2.2 Identify the purpose, features, and functions of the following client devices. Choose the appropriate installation or configuration steps in a given scenario.

Objective	Chapter	Heading
CardBus PC cards	7	WLAN Components
USB / USB2 devices	7	WLAN Components
Compact Flash devices	7	WLAN Components
SDIO devices	7	WLAN Components
PCI devices	7	WLAN Components
MiniPCI devices	7	WLAN Components
Client utility software and drivers	7	WLAN Components
Bluetooth connectivity devices	5	IEEE 802.15.1 and Bluetooth
Wireless IP Phone	12	VoWLAN
Wireless Gaming Adapter	8	Other WLAN Expansion Hardware
Wireless Print Server	10	WiMAX Security
Wireless IP Camera	7	Case Project 7-1
Wireless Hotspot Gateway	8	Other WLAN Expansion Hardware
Wireless Presentation Gateway	8	Other WLAN Expansion Hardware

2.3 Identify the purpose, features, and functions of the following types of antennas. Choose the appropriate installation or configuration steps in a given scenario.

Objective	Chapter	Heading
Omni-directional / dipole	4	Antenna Sizes and Shapes
Semi-directional	4	Antenna Sizes and Shapes

3 Radio Frequency (RF) Fundamentals

3.1 Define the basic units of RF measurements.

Objective	Chapter	Heading
Milliwatt	3	Gain and Loss
Decibel (dB)	3	Gain and Loss
dBm	3	Gain and Loss
dBi	3	Gain and Loss

A

3 Radio Frequency (RF) Fundamentals

3.2 Identify factors which affect the range and speed of RF transmissions.

Objective	Chapter	Heading
Line-of-sight requirements	3, 4, 5, 6, 7, 8, 9, 10, 11	Various (see also note under IEEE 802.11a)
Interference (Baby monitors, spread spectrum phones, microwave ovens, bright sunlight)	3, 4, 5, 6, 7, 8, 9, 10, 11	Various (see also note under IEEE 802.11a)
Environmental factors	3, 4, 5, 6, 7, 8, 9, 10, 11	Various (see also note under IEEE 802.11a)

3.3 Define and differentiate between the following wireless technologies.

Objective	Chapter	Heading
DSSS	2	Direct Sequence Spread Spectrum
OFDM	6, 8	UWB Phy, Orthogonal Frequency Division Multiplexing
FHSS	2	Direct Sequence Spread Spectrum
Infrared	2	Infrared Light
MIMO	8	802.11n

3.4 Define the concepts which make up the functionality of RF and spread spectrum technology.

Objective	Chapter	Heading
OFDM/DSSS Channels	8	Channel Allocation
Co-location of DSSS and OFDM systems	8	Channel Allocation
Adjacent-channel and co-channel interference	8	Channel Allocation
WLAN / WPAN co-existence	5, 6	Coexistence with Other Standards

4 Applications, Support, and Security

4.1 Identify proper procedures for installing and configuring common WLAN applications.

Objective	Chapter	Heading
Small Office, Home Office	7	IEEE 802.11b Standard
Extension of existing networks into remote locations	8	Expanding WLAN Functionality
Building-to-building connectivity	8	Expanding WLAN Functionality
Flexibility for mobile users	8	Expanding WLAN Functionality
Public wireless hotspots	7	Case Project 7-1
Mobile office, classroom, industrial, and healthcare	7	WLAN Applications
Short distance device connectivity	8	Expanding WLAN Functionality
Municipal connectivity	8	Expanding WLAN Functionality
VoWLAN	12	VoWLAN
RFID	11	RFID Applications

4 Applications, Support, and Security

4.2 Identify and describe common ZigBee applications.

Objective	Chapter	Heading
Building Automation and Residential / Light Commercial Control	5	IEEE 802.15.4 – Low-Rate WPANs
Industrial Control	5	IEEE 802.15.4 – Low-Rate WPANs
Personal Health Care	5	IEEE 802.15.4 – Low-Rate WPANs
PC & Peripherals	5	IEEE 802.15.4 – Low-Rate WPANs
Consumer Electronics	5	IEEE 802.15.4 – Low-Rate WPANs

4.3 Identify and describe common WiMAX applications.

Objective	Chapter	Heading
Campus and Wireless ISP Broadband	9	WiMAX Applications
Wireless Access (Point-to-Multipoint)	9	WiMAX Applications
Wireless Voice and Data Backhaul (Point-to-Point)	9	WiMAX Applications
Security / Surveillance	9	WiMAX Applications
Enterprise Private Networks	9	WiMAX Applications

4.4 Identify and describe common Bluetooth applications.

Objective	Chapter	Heading
Computer peripherals (GPS receivers, printers, keyboards, mice, digital cameras)	5	IEEE 802.15.1 and Bluetooth
Mobile audio (Cell Phones, MP3 Players, Headsets)	5	IEEE 802.15.1 and Bluetooth
Mobile data devices (PDAs)	5	IEEE 802.15.1 and Bluetooth
Unique devices (automotive diagnostics, wireless sensor links, gaming devices)	5	IEEE 802.15.1 and Bluetooth

4.5 Identify and describe common Infrared applications.

Objective	Chapter	Heading
PDA data communication and synchronization	5	Infrared WPANs (IrDA)
Point-of-Sale systems	5	Infrared WPANs (IrDA)
Laptop computer data communication	5	Infrared WPANs (IrDA)
Financial Messaging (IrFM)	5	Infrared WPANs (IrDA)

4 Applications, Support, and Security

4.6 Identify and describe the following wireless LAN security techniques. Describe the installation and configuration of each.

Objective	Chapter	Heading
SSID hiding	8	WLAN Security
WEP	8	WLAN Security
WPA-Personal	8	WLAN Security
WPA2-Personal	8	WLAN Security
RADIUS	8	WLAN Security
802.1X/EAP	8	WLAN Security
Passphrases	8	WLAN Security
MAC Filtering	8	WLAN Security
Push-button Wireless Security	8	WLAN Security
Virtual Private Networking (VPN)	8	WLAN Security

4.7 Identify procedures to optimize wireless networks in specific situations.

Objective	Chapter	Heading
Hardware placement	4, 8, 9, 12	Various
Hardware selection	4, 8, 9, 12	Various
Identifying sources of interference	4, 7, 8, 9, 10, 11	Various
Network utilization	5, 6, 7, 8, 9, 10, 11	Various
Appropriate security protocols	5, 6, 7, 8, 9, 10, 11	Various

4.8 Recognize common problems associated with wireless networks and their symptoms, and identify steps to isolate and troubleshoot the problem. Given a problem situation, interpret the symptoms and the most likely cause. Problems may include:

Objective	Chapter	Heading
Decreased throughput	3, 4, 5, 6, 7, 8, 9, 10, 11	Various
No connectivity	3, 4, 5, 6, 7, 8, 9, 10, 11	Various
Intermittent connectivity	3, 4, 5, 6, 7, 8, 9, 10, 11	Various
Weak signal strength	3, 4, 5, 6, 7, 8, 9, 10, 11	Various
Device upgrades	3, 4, 5, 6, 7, 8, 9, 10, 11	Various

B

HISTORY OF WIRELESS COMMUNICATIONS

Studying the history of a topic does not always evoke thrills and excitement. In fact, the question "Who cares about the past?" is often asked when studying history is even mentioned. However, there are several benefits to studying the history of a technology such as wireless communications. First, our current technology wasn't discovered overnight, like stumbling upon a previously unknown island in the ocean. There are always several smaller steps that take place to lead up to the development of the new technology. Tracing the development of these earlier discoveries can help us better understand how the final technology actually functions. Being able to see how a technology was created piece-by-piece, just as the early inventors did, can help us see how each piece fits with the next development and to understand how the technology actually works.

Another advantage of studying the historical development of technology is that it reveals how the device was accepted and used by society. This shows what value society placed on that technology and is a good predictor of how it will be used in the future. In short, studying the past helps us understand where we are headed.

Finally, historical study helps us better appreciate the technology. Some of today's great technological marvels were the result of years of painstaking trial and effort by some of the great minds of earlier days. How they persevered as early trailblazers without knowing exactly where they would end up is a testimony to their character and helps us better appreciate what we have before us today.

EARLY DEVELOPMENTS

The word *telegraphy* comes from a Greek word that means *writing in distance*. Telegraphy is a system of communication that can transmit signals that represent coded letters and numbers or other signs of writing over long distances. Telegraphy can be divided in acoustic (sound), optical (sight), and electrical transmissions.

Acoustic telegraphy has very ancient origins. Greek historians tell how the Persian king Darius I in 500 BC could send news from the capital city to the outlying provinces of the empire by means of a line of shouting men positioned on hills. This kind of transmission was determined to be 30 times faster than normal couriers carrying the information. Julius Caesar in 50 BC said that the nation of the Gauls could call to war their entire army in only three days just by using the human voice.

Early optical telegraphy consisted of fire at night and smoke or reflections from shiny objects during the day to transmit signals. A device called a hydraulic telegraph was used by the Caraginese around 500 BC. It consisted of two large vases placed on distant hills. The vases were filled with water and had a floating vertical pole at the center with coded letters attached to it. Messages were sent by rising or lowering the pole (by emptying or adding water to the vases) to move the coded letter to a certain point.

An optical telegraph was developed by Claude Chappe in 1792. Coded signals were based on the different positions of three wooden interlinked arms that rotated at the top of a fixed vertical pole. The central arm (called a regulator) was longer than the other two arms (called indicators). The indicator arms could rotate freely around a center and be positioned at 45 degree angles. A book 92 pages long contained 92 different words on each page (for a total of almost 8,500 words). The arms of the optical telegraph were moved to indicate the page number and the word number of the particular word that was to be transmitted. The optical telegraph was officially adopted by the French government and several other European states.

The discovery of electrical current led to the introduction of electrical telegraphy in the early 1880s. Samuel Morse toured Italy in 1830 as a well-known painter. When he was sailing back to the United States, the concept of a telegraph based on *electromagnetism* came to him. Electromagnetism is a magnetic force created by a current of electricity. His first telegraph receiving instrument was constructed from a wooden clock motor that provided the power to move a paper tape under a pen. The pen was moved by an electromagnet that was driven from a telegraph line. A canvas stretcher from his painting supplies was used as a frame to support the device. He received a patent for his telegraph invention in 1838, the same year he completed his last two paintings. In 1844, Morse sent the famous words from the Bible, "What hath God wrought!" on his telegraph from the U.S. Capitol Building in Washington, D.C., to Baltimore, Maryland.

Morse tried without success to obtain European patents for his telegraph. In addition, he invented a code now known as the Morse code for use with his telegraph instrument.

NOTE

B

James Maxwell, a Scottish physicist, was also very interested in electromagnetism. In 1861 he developed a mathematical model for a hypothetical medium that consisted of a fluid that could carry electric and magnetic effects. Maxwell theorized that if the fluid became elastic and a charge was applied to it, this would set up a disturbance in the fluid, which would produce waves that would travel through the medium. It was calculated that these waves would travel at the speed of light. Maxwell published his work in 1873.

In 1888, the German physicist Heinrich Hertz discovered radio waves, which are a form of electromagnetic radiation. This discovery confirmed Maxwell's theory. He devised a transmitter that radiated radio waves, and detected them across the length of his laboratory using a metal loop with a gap at one side. When the loop was placed within the transmitter's electromagnetic field, sparks were produced across the gap. This proved that electromagnetic waves could be sent out into space and could be remotely detected. Although people had seen the effects of radio waves before, nobody had realized what they were.

Radio waves were originally called "Hertzian waves."

NOTE

Radio

Guglielmo Marconi was born in Bologna, Italy, in 1874. By age 21 he had already performed simple experiments that had convinced him it was possible to send signals using electromagnetic waves. His first successes were at short distances, only about 330 feet (100 meters) between his house and the end of the garden.

Scientists and other experts at that time believed that electromagnetic waves could only be transmitted in a straight line, and then only if there was nothing in the way. They thought that the main obstacle to radio transmission was the curvature of the earth's surface. Marconi was convinced that transmission was possible between two distant points even if they were separated by an obstacle. He placed his transmitter near his house and the receiver almost 2 miles (3 kilometers) away behind a hill. Overseeing the receiver was Marconi's servant, Mignani, who was holding a rifle. His responsibility was to fire a rifle shot when the signal was received. From his house, Marconi pushed the key of the transmitter three times and then heard the answer of a distant gunshot. His experiment proved that electromagnetic waves had traveled a distance and overcome an obstacle. With the completion of his experiment in 1895, Marconi had demonstrated that wireless telegraphy, also known as radio communications, was possible.

The word *radio* comes from the term *radiated energy*.

NOTE

Marconi found little enthusiasm for his invention in Italy. He presented his device to the Italian government, only to be told by an Italian minister that it was "not suitable for telecommunications!" However, in England, where his mother was born, Marconi received support and financial backing and was able to patent his invention. In 1897, the British Ministry of Posts gave him money and technicians to continue his experiments and the transmission distances gradually became longer, up to 60 miles (100 kilometers).

In 1901, Marconi set up a transmitting station in England, and a receiving station was built on the other side of the Atlantic Ocean on the island of Newfoundland. For three hours every day, a signal was transmitted while Marconi experimented with newer and larger types of antennas suspended from light kites. On December 12, 1901, a signal was received at Newfoundland. For the first time, electromagnetic waves had crossed the Atlantic Ocean, traveling a distance of 2,175 miles (3,500 kilometers). Although Marconi did not know it at the time, the success of his experiment was due to the presence of the *ionosphere*. The ionosphere, a layer of the upper atmosphere (between 40 to 310 miles or 60 to 500 kilometers above the Earth), plays a fundamental role in all radio communications. The ionosphere reflects electromagnetic waves like a mirror and allows a radio signal to travel far distances.

The ionosphere was discovered by an English physicist, Edward Appleton, in 1924.

NOTE

Marconi quickly put his work on wireless telegraphy to practical use. In 1899 for the first time, a distress signal was sent from a shipwrecked boat to a station on land using wireless telegraphy, enabling its passengers to be rescued. Marconi also visited the United States and helped the U.S. Navy set up communications between its cruisers. In 1903, while sailing from England to the United States, Marconi established the first press agency. News information was flashed to the ship by wireless transmissions. This information was then printed onboard the ship as part of a newspaper.

Marconi continued to refine his wireless telegraphy devices. In 1904, he built a rotating device that led to the development of horizontal antennas, which permitted a tremendous increase in the strength of received signals. He later patented this device. In 1934, he demonstrated how a ship, in case of fog and in total blindness, could safely find the entrance of a harbor using wireless signals. In 1935, he performed distant search experiments that would eventually lead to the invention of radar.

Marconi also studied microwaves, early television technology, and started research on the therapeutic use of radio waves called Marconitherapy.

NOTE

Marconi died in Rome in 1937. To remember his great contribution to wireless telegraphy, radios all around the world observed a minute of silence on that date.

In 1909, Marconi was awarded the Nobel prize for physics.

NOTE

TELEVISION

The idea of transmitting pictures and sound over distance occupied the minds of dreamers for centuries. Yet unlike radio, television was not created by one individual at one specific point in time. Instead, television evolved over a period of 50 years based on the discoveries and efforts of many scientists and visionaries.

The basic process of television involves transmitting images by converting light to electrical signals. This is known as *photoelectric technology*. Early attempts to send still images down a telegraph wire in the mid 1800s were based on *electrochemical technology*. In 1842, Alexander Bain proposed a facsimile telegraph transmission system based on electrochemical technology. Bain proposed that metallic letters of the alphabet could be transmitted chemically. Electrified metal letters could be scanned by a pendulum device and reproduced at the other end of the telegraph wire by a synchronized pendulum contacting a piece of chemical paper.

Historians normally associate Bain's ideas with the modern day facsimile (fax) machine.

NOTE

Bain's proposal was improved upon in 1847 when F. Bakewell of Great Britain patented a chemical telegraph. Bakewell replaced the pendulums with synchronized rotating cylinders. By 1861, handwritten messages and photographs could be sent over telegraph lines.

In 1873, Louis May, a British telegrapher, discovered the basics of photoconductivity. He found that selenium bars, when exposed to light, were a strong conductor of electricity. He also found that the conduction of electrical current would vary depending on the amount of light hitting the bars. A later discovery revealed that changes in electrical voltage produced by selenium when scanning a document could magnetically control a pencil at the receiving end of the transmission. By 1881, Shelford Bidwell successfully transmitted silhouettes using both selenium and a scanning system. He called the device the scanning phototelegraph.

The first working device for analyzing a scene to generate electrical signals suitable for transmission was a scanning system proposed and built by Paul Nipkow in 1884. The scanner consisted of a rotating disc with a number of small holes (*apertures*) arranged in a spiral in front of light sensitive selenium. As the disc rotated, the spiral of 18 holes swept across the image of the scene from top to bottom in a pattern of 18 parallel horizontal lines. This had the effect of dividing the picture into 18 lines of dots or picture elements (*pixels*). For reproduction of the scene, a light source, controlled in intensity by the detected electrical signal, was projected on a screen through a similar Nipkow disc that rotated in synch with the pickup disc.

NOTE The Nipkow disc device was capable of transmitting about 4,000 pixels per second.

This was known as the world's first electromechanical television system. However, Nipkow could not build a reliable working system because he was unable to amplify the electric current created by the selenium to drive a receiver. Nevertheless, Nipkow demonstrated a scanning process for the analysis of images by dissecting a complete scene into an orderly pattern of pixels that could be transmitted by an electrical signal and reproduced as a visual image. This became the basis for present-day television.

With improvements in technology, mechanical television later became practical. In 1928, television signals were being sent from London to New York. By 1932, the first home mechanical television sets were available and over 10,000 sets were sold. These first sets delivered a crude picture consisting of a cloudy 40-line image (compared to 525 lines on today's televisions) on a six-inch square mirror. The sets cost between $85 and $135.

NOTE North America's first television station, W3XK in Wheaton, Maryland, was started in the 1930s.

Most historians generally credit Vladimir Zworykin as the "father of television." A Russian immigrant, Zworykin came to the United States after World War I and went to work for Westinghouse. From 1920 until 1929, Zworykin performed some of his early experiments in television. He developed the first practical TV camera tube known as the *iconoscope* in 1923. Zworkin's iconoscope (from the Greek for *image* and *to see*) consisted of a thin film coated with a photosensitive layer of potassium hydride. His kinescope picture tube formed the basis for subsequent advances in the field. With this crude camera tube and a kinescope as the picture reproducer, he had the essential elements for electronic television. By 1931, with the iconoscope and kinescope well developed, electronic television was ready to be launched.

A lesser-known early electronic television pioneer was Philo Farnsworth. At age 19, Farnsworth persuaded an investor to secure venture capital for an all-electronic television system. Farnsworth established his laboratory first in Los Angeles and later in San Francisco. It was there in 1927 that Farnsworth gave the first public demonstration of the television system he had dreamed of for six years. He was not yet 21 years old. Farnsworth was quick to develop several of the basic concepts of an electronic television system and was granted many patents.

By 1939, widespread commercial electronic television broadcasting started in the United States. The National Broadcasting Company (NBC) started regularly scheduled broadcasts in the New York area to only 400 sets. In 1941, the American Federal Communications Authority set the standards for broadcast television. With the start of World War II, however, television production stopped in the United States.

At the end of the war, there was a two-year delay in the development of television as the Federal Communications Authority considered proposals for color television systems. In 1947, all proposals for color television were rejected. Black and white sets, however, were manufactured in large quantities. In 1946, there were only 7,000 televisions in the United States. By 1950, there were over 10 million sets.

It took until 1954 for the National Television System Committee (NTSC) to set the standard for color broadcast television. They settled on a system that was compatible with existing black and white TV sets. Color was achieved by inserting the color information inside the black and white signal. The color standard specified 625 lines at 25 frames per second.

By 1970, television had become the primary information and entertainment medium in the world. Today it is estimated that there are close to a billion television sets worldwide. However, the standards for television broadcasting are not universal. There are 15 different variations of broadcasting standards used around the world.

RADAR

Radar has been hailed as one of the greatest scientific developments of the first half of the 20th century. Although radar is usually associated with detecting airplanes in the sky, or ships on the ocean, it actually is used in a variety of different ways. Some of these include:

- Radar is used extensively in weather forecasting and to provide early warning for severe weather. A radar system known as NEXRAD (NEXt Generation Weather RADar) can gauge the size, intensity, wind speed, and direction of storms, the amount of water vapor in clouds, and can detect high-level circular wind patterns that cause tornadoes.

- Radar is used to help archaeologists excavate ancient sites. Radar can be used from space satellites and airplanes to scan entire regions for possible archaeological sites. The radar waves can penetrate earth, sand, and volcanic ash that cover ancient sites. When the waves strike rock or metal, the echo is reflected back. This helps archeologists determine the best location to dig.

- Radar helps engineers study highway tunnels for potential hidden dangers. Radar can be mounted on a truck and driven through a tunnel that is built under a body of water. Radar can quickly and accurately scan the tunnel for leaks.

- Located on a space shuttle, radar can be used to locate stagnant pools of water in areas of dense foliage on Earth. With this information, the stagnant water, which can harbor insects carrying disease, can be located and drained.

- Radar has also helped provide information about the universe. It is used to locate comets, map stars, and probe planets that cannot be seen with a regular telescope.

NOTE   *Radar* is an acronym for *RAdio Detection And Ranging*.

Radar is an active remote sensing system that operates on the principle of echoes. When a person in a room yells out, her voice is sent out as sound waves and is reflected back by the walls to the ears of the listener. Instead of sound waves, radars use radio waves because radio waves travel faster, farther, and are reflected better than sound waves. Radio waves travel at the speed of light (186,000 miles or 300,000 kilometers per second).

Radar performs three primary functions:

- It transmits microwave signals (called the *pulse*) toward a target.

- After reaching an object, it is reflected back and the radar receives a return portion of the transmitted signal (called the *backscatter*), as seen in Figure B-1.

- It observes the strength, behavior, and the time delay of the returned signals and produces a *blip* on a screen, as seen in Figure B-2.

NOTE   A radar display shows a map-like picture of the area being scanned. The center of the picture corresponds to the radar antenna and the radar echoes are shown as bright spots on the screen. The distance of the spot from the center of the screen indicates how far away the object is.

The blips produced on a screen will vary depending upon the object reflecting the waves. Sophisticated radar can identify not only an airplane in the sky but also its type, manufacturer, and whether it is friend or foe.

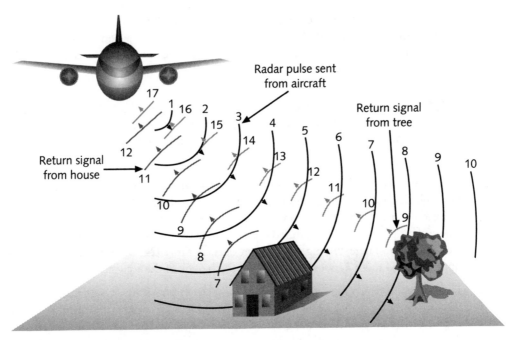

Figure B-1   Radar pulse and backscatter

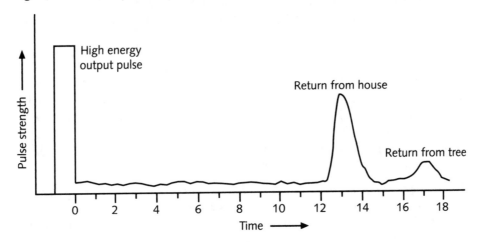

Figure B-2   Radar blips

A special type of radar known as Doppler radar is frequently used today by meteorologists to locate tornados and microbursts, which are downdrafts of air traveling at very high speeds. Doppler radar takes advantage of the *Doppler Effect*. The Doppler Effect is when the frequency of an electromagnetic wave is changed as the wave hits a moving object. Unlike regular radar, Doppler radar sends out waves at multiple sets of frequencies. Upon striking the target, the wave is reflected back at a different frequency from the transmitted wave. The radar compares the frequency of the returned echo with that of the transmitted wave. When the difference is calculated, the speed of the object, which caused the shift in frequency, can be calculated. Wind patterns are shown on the radar display in different colors. The faster a wind is moving, the brighter its color.

NOTE Doppler radar is also used by law enforcement agencies to locate speeding motorists. Most police radar guns have a split-screen display window, which shows both the speed of the target and the speed of the patrol vehicle.

The development of radar dates back to the discoveries of the 1860s and 1870s, when James Maxwell developed the equations that outlined the behavior of electromagnetic waves, and Heinrich Hertz discovered radio waves. Several years later, a German engineer named Christian Huelsmeyer proposed the use of radio echoes to avoid collisions in marine navigation. The first successful radio range-finding experiment occurred in 1924, when the British scientist Edward Appleton used radio echoes to determine the height of the ionosphere.

The first practical radar system was produced in 1935 by the British physicist Robert Watson-Watt. By 1939, England had established a chain of radar stations along its southern and eastern coasts to detect aggressors in the air or on the sea. About the same time, two British scientists were responsible for the most important advance made in the technology of radar during World War II. Henry Boot and John Randall invented an electron tube that was capable of generating high-frequency radio pulses with large amounts of power.

SATELLITES

A *satellite* is any object that orbits or revolves around another object. For example, the moon is a satellite of the Earth, and the Earth is a satellite of the Sun. Man-made satellites provide communications capabilities around the world, transmitting television signals, telephone calls, faxes, computer communications, and weather information. Satellites can be sent into space through a variety of launch vehicles.

The theory of satellites dates back to 325 years before the first man-made satellite was ever launched. Sir Isaac Newton in the 1720s was probably the first person to conceive the idea of a satellite. Newton illustrated how an artificial satellite could be launched from the Earth. He pictured the Earth with a high mountain and a cannon on top of the mountain firing shots parallel to the ground. Each time the cannon was fired more gunpowder was used and the shot went farther before striking the ground. Because the Earth is round, the shots would curve around it. According to Newton's theory, with enough gunpowder, a shot could eventually go fast enough to circle the earth completely and come back to the mountaintop.

During World War II, the German military made great strides in the development of rocket technology. However, even the best rocket technology of that day could not achieve an earth orbit. In 1945, Arthur C. Clarke, a science fiction author, wrote an article that envisioned a

B

network of communications satellites. Three satellites could be placed into space at 22,000 miles (35,400 kilometers) so as to orbit the planet every 24 hours. These satellites would be able to transmit signals around the world by transmitting in a line-of-sight with other orbiting satellites. At the time of his writing, the idea was not well received.

NOTE   Satellites of today that follow this same orbit are said to reside in the "Clarke Belt."

NOTE   The economic feasibility of satellites in the early days was hotly debated. At a cost of over $1 billion for a satellite, there were serious questions regarding its return on investment.

On October 4, 1957, the Soviet Union launched Sputnik 1. Sputnik 1 was described as "a radio transmitter in a 23-inch polished aluminum ball." Sputnik was equipped with transmitters to broadcast on two different frequencies, and it circled the globe every 90 minutes. After 18 days its battery was exhausted and the transmitting ceased, and almost three months later Sputnik 1 was incinerated as it fell from orbit back into Earth's atmosphere. A month after Sputnik 1, the Soviets launched Sputnik 2 and its passenger, Laika, a dog who has the distinction of being the first living creature to enter orbit.

The United States followed with its own launch of Explorer 1 in early 1958. The first communications satellite was launched later that same year. The Signal Communication by Orbital Relay (SCORE) satellite broadcasted a Christmas message from President Dwight Eisenhower of "Peace on earth, good will toward men" as it orbited the Earth for 12 days until its batteries failed. A succession of Soviet and American launches resulted in larger and more sophisticated satellites reaching orbit. In 1961, Yuri Gegarin became the first human in orbit.

NOTE   The United States and Soviet Union launched six satellites in 1958, 14 in 1959, 19 in 1960, and 35 satellites in 1961. In 1962, the United Kingdom and Canada launched satellites of their own, in addition to the 70 satellites launched by the United States and Soviet Union.

After the initial launches, the benefits and prestige associated with satellite communications made satellites a popular item. The National Aeronautic and Space Administration (NASA) confined itself to experiments with *mirrors* or passive communications satellites while the U.S. Department of Defense was responsible for *repeater* or active satellites that amplified the received signal at the satellite and provided a much higher quality of communications. In 1960, NASA launched Echo 1, a passive reflector satellite with no amplification possibilities. The Echo satellites were basically large metallicized balloons that served as passive reflectors of radio signals. At the time of its launch, it was thought that passive reflector satellites could serve a purpose in communications, but the technology was soon abandoned because the reflected signal was so weak.

In 1960, the American Telephone and Telegraph Company (AT&T) filed a request with the Federal Communications Commission (FCC) for permission to launch an experimental communications satellite. The U.S. government reacted with surprise because there had never been such a request and there was no policy in place to regulate satellites. AT&T designed, built, and even paid for the launches with its own funds, reimbursing NASA for its use of the rockets. The Telstar I and II spacecraft were prototypes for a constellation of 50 medium earth orbit (MEO) satellites that AT&T was working to put in place. Telstar was the first modern communications satellite to be placed in orbit. However, when the U.S. government later decided to give the monopoly on satellite communications to a consortium, AT&T's satellite project was halted.

NOTE   The first words transmitted over satellite were not as memorable as Alexander Bell's "Watson, come here I need you!" or Samuel Morse's "What hath God wrought?" The first transmitted words were, "Will everybody please get off this line?" So many people were trying to be the first to hear the transmission that the circuit was being overloaded!

In 1964, an international organization known as Intelsat (INternational TELecommunications SATellite Organization) was formed. Intelsat was a consortium of over 130 governments and organizations. Intelsat launched a series of satellites with the goal of providing total earth coverage (excluding the North and South Poles) by satellite transmission. This was achieved by 1969. Today Intelsat has 19 satellites in orbit that are open to use by all nations. The Intelsat consortium owns the satellites, but each nation owns their own Earth receiving stations.

NOTE   Intelsat completed its global coverage just days before the first men walked on the moon in 1969, enabling half a billion people around the world to watch the landmark event.

NASA led the next new wave of communications satellite technology with the launch of Advanced Communications Technology Satellites (ACTS) in 1993. ACTS pioneered the use of several new developments, such as on-board storage and processing and all-digital transmission, which make satellite transmission more reliable.

The explosive popularity of cellular telephones advanced the idea of always being connected no matter where you were located on Earth. Several companies committed themselves to providing a solution by using satellites in low earth orbit (LEO). The most ambitious of these LEO systems was Iridium, sponsored by Motorola. Iridium planned to launch 66 satellites into polar orbit at altitudes of about 400 miles (650 kilometers). Iridium's goal was to provide communications services to hand-held telephones around the world in 1998. However, Iridium declared bankruptcy in 1999. The total cost of the Iridium system was in excess of $3 billion dollars.

NOTE

Iridium originally planned to have 77 satellites, and thus was named after the 77th element in the periodic charts. However, when the plans were scaled back to only 66 satellites, the name Iridium continued to be used because Element 66 has the less pleasant name Dysprosium.

CELLULAR TELEPHONES

In the 1930s and 1940s, two-way car radios were installed and used by police, utility companies, government agencies, and emergency services. However, these two-way car radios had several disadvantages and were not very convenient to use. In 1946 in St. Louis, AT&T and Southwestern Bell introduced the first American commercial mobile radio-telephone service to private customers. *Mobiles*, as they were called, used the newly issued vehicle radio-telephone licenses granted to Southwestern Bell by the FCC. They operated on six channels. However, interference soon forced Bell to use only three channels.

NOTE

In a rare exception to the Bell System common practice, subscribers to this first system could actually buy their own radio sets and were not required to use AT&T's equipment.

With two-way car radios, a central transmitter with one antenna could serve a wide area. This is illustrated in Figure B-3. However, this system could not be used with mobiles. The reason is that car-mounted transmitters were not as powerful as the central antenna and thus their signals could not always be transmitted all the way back. To overcome this limitation, smaller receivers with antennas were placed on top of buildings and on poles around the city, creating smaller *cells*, or ranges of service areas. When a person used his mobile, the conversation that he heard was transmitted on one frequency by the central transmitter to the moving car. When the user spoke on his mobile, however, that transmission was sent on a separate frequency that the nearest receiver antenna picked up. In other words, messages were received on one frequency from the central transmitter but messages were sent to the nearest receiver on a separate frequency. When the car moved from one cell to another that was served by a different receiver, the switch between cells was known as a *handoff.* This is illustrated in Figure B-4.

As innovative as mobiles were, there were still several serious limitations. The first limitation was a lack of available frequencies. Mobiles required two frequencies to make a transmission, one frequency to transmit on and one to receive. A single radio-telephone call took up as much frequency space as a radio broadcast station. In the late 1940s, there was very little unused transmission space available. And because the FCC gave priority to emergency services, government agencies, utility companies, and services it thought helped the most people, this left only a tiny amount of frequencies available for mobiles. Most mobile telephone systems could not accommodate more than a total of 250 users, with only a handful actually being able to transmit at one time.

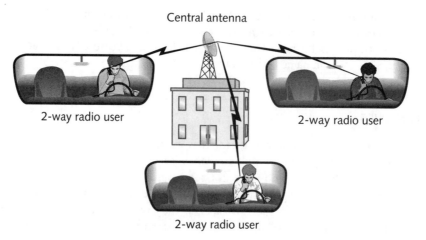

Figure B-3   2-way car radios

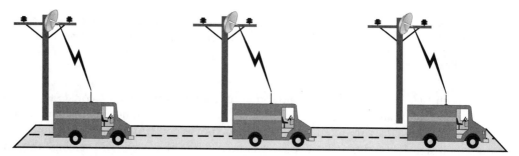

Figure B-4   Mobiles using cells

NOTE

At this time the technology for the mobiles was not refined and they actually required six times the amount of frequency that would be needed today.

The second limitation was that waves at lower frequencies travel great distances, sometimes hundreds of miles when they skip across the atmosphere. Although high-powered transmitters gave mobiles a wide operating range the signals could also be detected in adjacent cities. Telephone companies could not reuse their channels in nearby cities due to this potential interference; they required at least 75 miles between mobile systems.

Despite the limitations, mobile service was highly desired. Every city that offered mobiles had lengthy waiting lists. By 1976, only 545 customers in New York City had Bell System mobiles but 3,700 customers were on the waiting list. Some individuals were on waiting lists for up to 10 years. Although allocating more frequency would have solved the problem, the FCC did not do so. Even as late as 1978 all mobile carriers nationwide had just 54 channels.

NOTE The first modern cellular telephone systems in the early 1980s used 666 channels.

Although mobiles had limitations and were only used by very few people, they nevertheless launched the basic concept of cellular phones. Designers realized that by using small cells they could use lower-powered transmitters. They also determined that if they could have each cell use a different frequency, then by reusing these frequencies they could substantially increase the traffic capacity of mobile phones. At that time, however, the technology to do so did not exist. Nevertheless, the concepts of using cells and frequency reuse laid the foundation for cellular telephones 50 years later.

In 1969, the Bell System developed a commercial cellular radio operation using frequency reuse. The unusual setting for this venture was on trains running from New York City to Washington, D.C., using pay telephones. Passengers could make telephone calls onboard while the trains were moving at 100 miles an hour. Six channels were reused in nine zones along the 225-mile route. A computerized control center in Philadelphia managed the system. Thus the first cell phone was a pay phone.

In July 1978, AT&T and Illinois Bell started a pilot project in Chicago of analog-based cellular telephone service. Ten cells covering 21,000 square miles made up the Chicago system. This first equipment test began using 90 Bell System employees, and after six months it was opened to the general public. This early cellular telephone proved that a large cellular system could work.

Advanced Mobile Phone Service (AMPS) began setting up analog cellular telephone operations in other parts of the world. An 88-cell system in Tokyo began in December 1979, and a system in Mexico City with one cell started in August 1981. Europe saw cellular service introduced in 1981, when the Nordic Mobile Telephone System began operating in Denmark, Sweden, Finland, and Norway. This was the first multinational cellular system.

Initially, U.S. cellular telephone development did not keep up with the rest of the world. The most significant reason was the breakup of the Bell System by the U.S. federal court system and the FCC's 1981 regulations that required the Bell System or a regional operating company, such as Bell Atlantic, to have competition in every cellular market. However, the popularity of cellular soon began to spread across the nation along with the development of an analog cellular infrastructure. The American cellular phone industry grew from less than 204,000 subscribers in 1985 to 1,600,000 in 1988.

Roaming from one city or state in the United States was easy because the U.S. system was based on an analog cellular system. In contrast, it was almost impossible to roam in Europe. During the 1980s, a plan was launched to create a single Europe-wide digital mobile service with advanced features and easy roaming. This network started operating in 1991. In the United States, there was no such movement because the analog system was working well.

Today cellular telephone deployment is worldwide, but development remains concentrated in three areas: Scandinavia, the United States, and Japan.

Glossary

1/3 rate Forward Error Correction (FEC) — An error correction scheme that repeats each bit three times for redundancy.

1-bit tags — RFID devices that do not include a chip or memory and cannot store an EPC. 1-bit tags are only used to activate an alarm at retail store entrances as a means of preventing theft.

2/3 rate Forward Error Correction (FEC) — An error correction scheme that uses a mathematical formula to add extra error correction bits to the data sent.

2.5 Generation (2.5G) — An interim step between 2G and 3G digital cellular networks. 2.5G sends data at a maximum of 384 Kbps.

3G (third generation) — A digital cellular technology that sends data at up to 2 Mbps and is expected to synchronize all of the different specifications used around the world into one universal standard.

4-pulse position modulation (4-PPM) — A modulation technique that translates two data bits into four light impulses.

16-pulse position modulation (16-PPM) — A modulation technique that translates four data bits into 16 light impulses.

802.11 standard — An IEEE standard released in 1990 that defines wireless local area networks at a rate of either 1 Mbps or 2 Mbps. All WLAN features are contained in the PHY and MAC layers.

802.11b standard — A 1999 addition to the IEEE 802.11 standard for WLANs that added two higher speeds, 5.5 Mbps and 11 Mbps. Also known as Wi-Fi.

8-PSK — A modulation technique in which the phase of the carrier is shifted in 45 degree increments and 4 bits can be transmitted per phase change.

access control list (ACL) — A list of addresses of other devices from which the device that maintains the list expects to receive frames.

active antenna — A passive antenna with an amplifier built-in.

active mode — A state in which a Bluetooth device actively participates on a channel.

active scanning — The process of sending frames to gather information.

active tags — RFID tags that include a battery.

ad hoc mode — A WLAN mode in which wireless clients communicate directly among themselves without using an AP.

adaptive array processing — A radio transmission technique that replaces a traditional antenna with an array of antenna elements.

adaptive frequency hopping (AFH) — A feature added by Bluetooth version 1.2 that further improves compatibility with 802.11b by allowing the master in a piconet to change the hopping sequence so that it will not use the frequency channel occupied by 802.11b in the piconet area.

advanced antenna system (AAS) — An antenna that can transmit multiple simultaneous signals in different directions to stations that fall within the range of each of the antennas.

Advanced Encryption Standard (AES) — The latest encryption standard, developed by the National Institute of Standards and Technology (NIST) to replace the United States data encryption standard (*see* DES).

Advanced Mobile Phone Service (AMPS) — The standard used for 1G analog cellular transmissions based on FDMA.

American National Standards Institute (ANSI) — A clearinghouse for standards development in the United States.

American Standard Code for Information Interchange (ASCII) — An arbitrary coding scheme that uses the numbers from 0 to 255.

amplifier — A component that increases a signal's intensity.

amplitude — The height of a carrier wave.

amplitude modulation (AM) — A change in the height of the cycle.

amplitude shift keying (ASK) — A binary modulation technique in which 1 bit has a carrier signal while a 0 bit has no signal.

analog modulation — A method of encoding an analog signal onto a carrier wave.

analog signal — A signal in which the intensity (amplitude or voltage) varies continuously and smoothly, over a period of time.

antenna — A copper wire, rod, or similar device that has one end up in the air and the other end connected to the ground through a receiver.

antenna pattern — A graphic that shows how a signal radiates out of an antenna.

antenna polarization — An indication of the horizontal or vertical orientation of the sine waves leaving an antenna.

associate request frame — A frame sent by a client to an AP that contains the client's capabilities and supported rates.

associate response frame — A frame returned to a client from the AP that contains a status code and client ID number.

association — A mechanism for a device to join a network.

asynchronous connectionless (ACL) link — A packet-switched link that is used for data transmissions.

attenuation — A loss of signal strength.

authentication — A process that verifies that the client device asking to join the piconet has permission to access the network.

automatic retransmission request (ARQ) — An error correction scheme that continuously retransmits until an acknowledgment is received or timeout value is exceeded.

backhaul — A company's internal infrastructure connection.

backscatter — The type of modulation used by passive RFID tags. Backscatter is a reflection of radiation in which the tag reflects the signal sent by an interrogator while modulating it with the data to be transmitted.

bandpass filter — A filter that passes all signals that are between the maximum and minimum threshold.

bands — Sections of the radio frequency spectrum.

bandwidth — The range of frequencies that can be transmitted.

Barker code (chipping code) — A bit pattern used in a DSSS transmission. The term "chipping code" is used because a single radio bit is commonly referred to as a "chip."

Base 2 number system — See binary number system.

Base 10 number system — See decimal number system.

base station (BS) — The transmitter connected to the carrier network or to the Internet.

baseband — A transmission technique that treats the entire transmission medium as only one channel.

Basic Service Set (BSS) — A WLAN mode that consists of wireless clients and one AP.

baud — A change in a carrier signal.

baud rate — The number of times that a carrier signal changes per second.

beacon — A frame that signals the beginning of a superframe and contains information about the type and number of time slots contained in the superframe.

beacons — RFID tags that are battery powered and transmit on a periodic basis.

binary number system — A numbering system commonly used by computers that has a base number of 2 and uses the digits 0 and 1.

Binary Runtime Environment for Wireless (BREW) — A thin software interface layer that resides on a wireless device and creates a runtime environment.

binding — The process of establishing a relationship between endpoints in a ZigBee network.

biphase modulation — Modulation that uses a half-cycle positive analog pulse to represent a 1 and a half-cycle negative analog pulse to represent a 0.

bit — A binary digit; an electronic 0 or a 1 based on the binary number system.

bits per second (bps) — The number of bits that can be transmitted per second.

blocker tag — A type of Class 1 passive RFID tag that can be used to disable unauthorized readers from accessing the information from a selective group of tags by sending so many responses that a reader cannot differentiate between the blocker tag and a legitimate tag.

Bluetooth — A wireless standard that enables devices to transmit data at up to 1 Mbps over a maximum distance of 33 feet.

Bluetooth radio module — A single radio transmitter/receiver (transceiver) that performs all of the necessary transmission functions.

BREW (Binary Run-Time Environment for Wireless) — A programming language used to display text, graphics, and animations on cellular telephone screens.

broadband — A transmission technique that sends multiple signals at different frequencies.

buffering — The process that the AP uses to temporarily store frames for clients that are in sleep mode.

burst — A transmission containing data to or from a single SS or a broadcast transmission from the BS.

byte — Eight binary digits (bits).

cable modems — A technology used to transmit data over a television cable connection.

cards — A small block of a WML document.

carrier sense multiple access with collision avoidance (CSMA/CA) — A device access mechanism in which all devices must listen to the medium to determine if the channel is free before transmitting.

carrier signal — A transmission over a radio frequency that carries no useful information.

carriers — Telephone, cable TV, and other communication providers who own the wires and transmission towers that carry voice and data traffic.

CDMA2000 1xEVDO — The 3G digital cellular technology that is a migration from CDMA2000 1xRTT.

CDMA2000 1xEVDV — The 3G digital cellular technology that is a migration from CDMA2000 1xEVDO.

CDMA2000 1xRTT — A 2.5G digital cellular network technology that is a migration from CDMA (1xRTT stands for 1-times Radio Transmission Technology).

cell — A smaller area of a mobile network.

certificate authority — An organization that supplies security keys and authenticates users.

challenge-response strategy — A process used to check if the other device knows a shared identical secret key.

channel access methods — The different ways of sharing resources in a network environment.

channel time allocation (CTA) — Periods of time allocated by the PNC to a specific device for prioritizing communications in a WPAN. *See also* management channel time allocation (MCTA).

channel time allocation period (CTAP) — The superframe component used for communications between the PNC and other devices.

channels — Another name for frequencies.

child piconets — Separate piconets with their own ID; the child PNC is a member of the original or parent piconet.

chipless tags — RFID devices that use embedded fibers to reflect a portion of the RF waves emitted by a reader. The reflected portion of the RF waves is unique and can be used as an identifier.

circuit switching — Signal switching that is achieved through a dedicated and direct physical connection between two transmitting devices.

Class 0 — A class of RFID tags that are read-only.

Class 1 — A class of RFID tags that are read/write.

Code Division Multiple Access (CDMA) — A technique that uses spread spectrum technology and unique digital codes to send and receive radio transmissions.

collision — The scrambling of data that occurs when two computers start sending messages at the same time in a shared frequency.

compact flash (CF) card — A small expansion card that is used with PDA devices.

compact HTML (cHTML) — A subset of HTML that is designed for mobile devices.

Complementary Code Keying (CCK) — A table containing 64 8-bit code words used for transmitting at speeds above 2 Mbps. This table of codes is used instead of the process of adding a Barker code to the bit to be transmitted.

consortia — Industry-sponsored organizations that have the goal of promoting a specific technology.

constellation diagram — a graphical representation that makes it easier to visualize signals using complex modulation techniques such as QAM. It is generally used in laboratory and field diagnostic instruments and analyzers to aid in design and troubleshooting of wireless communications devices.

contention access period (CAP) — A mechanism used to communicate commands or any asynchronous data that may be present in a superframe. The CAP is also used to allow devices that are not yet part of a piconet to send a request to the PNC to join the piconet.

continuous wave (CW) — An unmodulated sine wave sent by the reader to power the passive tag so that it can transmit a response.

control channel — A special frequency that cellular phones use for communication with a base station.

control frames — MAC frames that assist in delivering the frames that contain data.

coupling — A connection between a reader and a tag.

crosstalk — Signals from close frequencies that may interfere with other signals.

customer premises equipment (CPE) — The WiMAX devices that are installed in a customer's office or home.

cycle — An oscillating sine wave that completes one full series of movements.

cyclic redundancy check (CRC) — A common technique for detecting data transmission errors.

Data Encryption Standard (DES) — The encryption standard used in the United States until the adoption of AES (*see* Advanced Encryption Standard).

data frames — MAC frames that carry the information to be transmitted to the destination clients.

Data Link layer — The layer responsible for the transfer of data between nodes in the same network segment and that also provides error detection.

dB dipole (dBd) — The relative measurement of the gain of an antenna when compared to a dipole antenna.

dB isotropic (dBi) — The relative measurement of the gain of an antenna when compared to a theoretical isotropic radiator.

dBm — A relative way to indicate an absolute power level in the linear Watt scale.

de facto standards — Common practices that the industry follows for various reasons.

de jure standards — Standards that are controlled by an organization or body.

decibel (dB) — A ratio between two signal levels.

decimal number system — A numbering system that has a base number of 10 and uses the digits 0–9.

deck — A WML document.

denial-of-service (DoS) — A type of security attack on a networked device in which the attacker sends so many frames to a single device that the device is unable to communicate with other devices.

destroy password — A code programmed into an RFID tag during manufacturing that can be used to permanently disable the tag.

detector — A diode that receives a light-based transmission signal.

device discovery — The process of querying other devices on the network to identify their location and the number of devices connected.

dibit — A signal unit that represents two bits.

diffused transmission — A light-based transmission that relies on reflected light.

digital certificates — A special message signed by a certification authority, used for security and authentication.

digital convergence — The power of digital devices, such as desktop computers and wireless handhelds, to combine voice, video, and text-processing capabilities, as well as to be connected to business and home networks and to the Internet.

digital modulation — A method of encoding a digital signal onto an analog carrier wave for transmission over media that does not support direct digital signal transmission.

digital signal — Data that is discrete or separate.

digital subscriber lines (DSL) — A technology used to transmit data over a telephone line.

dipole — An antenna that has a fixed amount of gain over that of an isotropic radiator.

direct sequence spread spectrum (DSSS) — A spread spectrum technique that uses an expanded, redundant code to transmit each data bit.

directed transmission — A light-based transmission that requires the emitter and detector to be directly aimed at one another.

directional antenna — An antenna that radiates the electromagnetic waves in one direction only. As a result, it can help reduce or eliminate the effect of multipath distortion, if there is a clear line of sight between the two antennas.

directional gain — The effective gain that a directional antenna achieves by focusing RF energy in one direction.

disassociation — A mechanism used by devices to leave a network.

disassociation frame — A frame sent by the new AP to the old AP to terminate the old AP's association with the client.

distributed coordination function (DCF) — The default access method for WLANs.

distributed coordination function interframe space (DIFS) — The standard interval between the transmission of data frames.

dynamic rate selection — A function of an AP that allows it to automatically select the highest transmission speed based on the strength and quality of the signal received from a client NIC.

eighth-wave antenna — An antenna that is 1/8 of the wavelength of the signal it is designed to transmit or receive.

electromagnetic interference (EMI) — Interference with a radio signal; also called noise.

electromagnetic wave (EM wave) — A signal composed of electrical and magnetic forces that in radio transmission usually propagates from an antenna and can be modulated to carry information.

Electronic Industries Alliance (EIA) — U.S. industry vendors from four areas: electronic components, consumer electronics, electronic information, and telecommunications.

Electronic Product Code (EPC) — A standardized numbering scheme that can be programmed in a tag and attached to any physical product.

emitter — A laser diode or a light-emitting diode that transmits a light-based signal.

encryption — The process of encoding communications to ensure that the transmissions cannot be easily intercepted and decoded.

enhanced data rate (EDR) — A feature of the Bluetooth version 2.0 specification that allows it to support data rates of 2 and 3 Mbps by adding two new modulations, while remaining fully backward compatible with Bluetooth versions 1.1 and 1.2.

Enhanced Data rates for GSM Evolution (EDGE) — A 2.5G digital cellular network technology that boosts GPRS transmissions.

EPCglobal Inc. — An organization entrusted by industry worldwide to establish RFID standards and services for real-time, automatic identification of information in the supply chain of any company, anywhere in the world.

European Telecommunications Standards Institute (ETSI) — A standards body that is designed to develop telecommunications standards for use throughout Europe.

Extended Service Set (ESS) — A WLAN mode that consists of wireless clients and multiple APs.

Extensible Authentication Protocol (EAP) — A collection of protocols used by IEEE 802.1x for network authentication between a wireless device, an AP, and a RADIUS server.

Extensible Markup Language (XML) — A definition language that uses tags to describe the data.

Federal Communications Commission (FCC) — The primary U.S. regulatory agency for telecommunications.

filter — A component that is used to either accept or block a radio frequency signal.

First Generation (1G) — The first generation of wireless cellular telephony that transmitted at 9.6 Kbps using analog circuit-switched technology.

fixed wireless — A wireless last mile connection.

fragmentation — The division of data to be transmitted from one large frame into several smaller frames.

frame — A Data Link layer packet that contains the header and trailer required by the physical medium.

free space loss — The signal loss that occurs as a result of the tendency of RF waves to spread, resulting in less energy at any given point, as the signal moves away from the transmitting antenna.

free space optics (FSO) — An optical, wireless, point-to-point, line-of-sight broadband technology.

frequency — A measurement of radio waves that is determined by how frequently a cycle occurs.

frequency division duplexing (FDD) — A mechanism that uses one frequency for uplink and another for downlink (*see also* TDD).

Frequency Division Multiple Access (FDMA) — A radio transmission technique that divides the bandwidth of the frequency into several smaller frequency bands.

frequency hopping spread spectrum (FHSS) — A spread spectrum technique that uses a range of frequencies and changes frequencies during the transmission.

frequency modulation (FM) — A change of the number of waves used to represent one cycle.

frequency shift keying (FSK) — A binary modulation technique that changes the frequency of the carrier signal.

Fresnel zone — An elliptical region spanning the distance between two directional antennas that must not be blocked more than 40% to prevent interference with the RF signal.

full-duplex transmission — Transmissions that enable data to flow in either direction simultaneously.

full-function device — A device used in 802.15.4 (ZigBee) networks that can connect to other full-function devices and has the capability of routing frames to other devices in a ZigBee network. It can also connect to endpoint or child devices. Full-function devices can maintain a connection to multiple devices.

full-wave antenna — An antenna that is as long as the length of the wave it is designed to transmit or receive.

gain — A relative measure of increase in a signal's power level.

General Packet Radio Service (GPRS) — A 2.5G network technology that can transmit up to 114 Kbps.

geosynchronous earth orbit (GEO) satellites — Satellites that are stationed at an altitude of 22,282 miles (35,860 kilometers).

Gigahertz (GHz) — 1,000,000,000 Hertz.

ground-plane — A metal disc or two straight wires assembled at 90 degrees used to provide a reflection point for monopole antennas that are not mounted on or near the surface of the ground.

GSM (Global Systems for Mobile communications) — One of three multiple access technologies that make up the 2G digital cellular system that uses a combination of FDMA and TDMA.

guaranteed time slots — Reserved periods for critical devices to transmit priority data.

half-duplex transmission — Transmission that occurs in both directions but only one way at a time.

half-wave antenna — An antenna that is half as long as the wavelength of the signal it is designed to transmit or receive.

handoff (or hand-off) — The transition that occurs when a client device connects with a new access point and disconnects from the previous one. Also, the ability of a device to move from one master or PNC to another without getting disconnected from the network in a network that extends beyond the communications range of each device that controls the communications.

help desk — A central point of contact for users who need assistance using technology.

Hertz (Hz) — The number of cycles per second.

high-pass filter — A filter that passes all signals that are above a maximum threshold.

HiperLAN/2 — A proposed high-speed WLAN that is similar to the IEEE 802.11a standard.

hold mode — A state in which the Bluetooth device can put slave units into a mode in which only the slave's internal timer is running.

hopping code — The sequence of changing frequencies used in FHSS.

horn antenna — A two-dimensional directional antenna typically used for microwave transmission; it resembles a large horn with the wide end bent to one side.

Hypertext Markup Language (HTML) — The standard language for displaying Web pages.

i-mode — An Internet access system for digital cellular telephones.

IEEE 802.11a — A standard for WLAN transmissions developed in 1999 for networks with speeds up to 54 Mbps and beyond.

IEEE 802.11a/b/g standards — A group of standards developed by the Institute of Electrical and Electronic Engineers that allows WLAN computers to transmit data at speeds ranging from 1 Mbps to a maximum of 54 Mbps. 802.11a transmits at 1 or 2 Mbps; 802.11b at up to 11 Mbps; 802.11g at 54 Mbps. These transmit in the 2.4 GHz unlicensed frequency band. 802.11a also transmits at up to 54 Mbps but in the less crowded frequency band of 5 GHz.

IEEE 802.11e — A standard for WLAN applications that requires QoS and provides for improvements in the capabilities and efficiency of the protocol.

IEEE 802.11g — A standard for WLAN transmissions for networks with speeds up to 54 Mbps using the ISM band.

IEEE 802.11i — An enhancement to 802.11 that deals with security weaknesses of the original standard.

IEEE 802.16 Fixed Broadband Wireless — A set of standards, some established and some still under development, for fixed and mobile broadband wireless communications that allows computers to communicate at up to 75 Mbps and at distances of up to 35 miles (56 km) in a point-to-point configuration. This group of standards also allows the use of both licensed and unlicensed frequencies.

IEEE 802.1X — A standard to increase the security of IEEE 802 WLANs.

impedance — The opposition to the flow of alternating current in a circuit. Represented by the letter "Z" and measured in ohms, impedance is the combination of resistance, inductance, and capacitance of the circuit.

impulse modulation — A digital transmission technique employed by UWB in which the polarity of a single analog pulse (one-half of a sine wave) represents a binary digit 1 or 0.

Independent Basic Service Set (IBSS) — A WLAN mode in which wireless clients communicate directly among themselves without using an AP.

Industrial, Scientific and Medical (ISM) band — An unregulated radio frequency band approved by the FCC in 1985.

infrared light — Light that is next to visible light on the light spectrum that has many of the same characteristics as visible light.

infrastructure mode — A WLAN mode that consists of wireless clients and one AP.

inquiry procedure — A process that enables a device to discover which devices are in range and determine the addresses and clocks for the devices.

Institute of Electrical and Electronics Engineers (IEEE) — A standards body that establishes standards for telecommunications.

Integrated Services Digital Networks (ISDN) — A technology that transmits data over telephone lines at a maximum of 256 Kbps.

interframe spaces (IFS) — Time gaps used for special types of transmissions.

intermediate frequency (IF) — The output signal that results from the modulation process.

International Organization for Standardization (ISO) — An organization to promote international cooperation and standards in the areas of science, technology, and economics.

International Telecommunications Union (ITU) — An agency of the United Nations that sets international telecommunications standards and coordinates global telecommunications networks and services.

Internet Architecture Board (IAB) — The organization responsible for defining the overall architecture of the Internet, providing guidance and broad direction to the IETF. The IAB also serves as the technology advisory group to the Internet Society, and oversees a number of critical activities in support of the Internet.

Internet Engineering Task Force (IETF) — A standards body that focuses on the lower levels of telecommunications technologies.

Internet Society (ISOC) — A professional membership organization of Internet experts that comments on policies and practices and oversees a number of other boards and task forces dealing with network policy issues.

IrDA — An acronym for the Infrared Data Association and also a set of specifications for wireless infrared communications.

isochronous — The channel time in synchronous transmissions.

isotropic radiator — A theoretical perfect sphere that radiates power equally in all directions; impossible to construct.

J2ME (Java 2 Micro Edition) — A variation of the Java programming language designed for use in portable devices such as PDAs and cellular phones.

Java — An object-oriented programming language used for general-purpose business programming and interactive Web sites.

Java 2 Micro Edition (J2ME) — A subset of Java specifically developed for programming wireless devices.

jitter — The maximum delay variation between two consecutive packets over a period of time.

Kilohertz (KHz) — 1,000 Hertz.

last mile connection — The link between the customer's premises and the telephone company, cable TV company, or an ISP.

latency — Delays caused by signals that must travel over a long distance. Also, the amount of time delay that it takes a packet to travel from source to destination device.

license exempt spectrum — Unregulated radio frequency bands that are available in the United States to any users without a license.

light spectrum — All the different types of light that travel from the Sun to the Earth.

line of sight (LOS) — The direct alignment as required in a directed transmission.

link budget — The process of calculating the signal strength between the transmitter and receiver antennas to ensure that the link can meet the receiver's minimum signal strength requirements.

link manager — Special software in Bluetooth devices that helps identify other Bluetooth devices, creates the links between them, and sends and receives data.

local multipoint distribution service (LMDS) — A fixed broadband technology that can provide a wide variety of wireless services.

Logical Link Control (LLC) — One of the two sub-layers of the IEEE Project 802 Data Link layer.

loss — A relative measure of decrease in a signal's power level.

low earth orbit (LEO) satellites — Satellites that orbit the Earth at an altitude of 200 to 900 miles (321 to 1,448 kilometers).

low-pass filter — A filter that passes all signals that are below a maximum threshold.

management channel time allocation (MCTA) — Time periods used for communication between the devices and the PNC.

management frames — MAC frames that are used to set up the initial communications between a client and the AP.

man-in-the-middle attack — A security attack in which a hacker captures frames, alters them, and then retransmits them to the intended receiver or another device on the network.

master — A device on a Bluetooth piconet that controls all of the wireless traffic.

Media Access Control (MAC) — One of the two sub-layers of the IEEE Project 802 Data Link layer.

medium earth orbit (MEO) satellites — Satellites that orbit the Earth at altitudes between 1,500 and 10,000 miles (2,413 to 16,090 kilometers).

Megahertz (MHz) — 1,000,000 Hertz.

mesh networking — A network topography in which each device connects to all other devices within range.

message integrity — A process of adding certain encrypted random data to each communications session so that the receiver can verify that the message has not been tampered with, after being transmitted.

message integrity check — A combination of variable and static data items that ensure that encrypted data has not been altered.

message integrity code (MIC) — A code composed of a subset of the data, the length of the data, and the symmetric key, used by the receiving device to verify that the data has not been tampered with during transmission.

microbrowser — A tiny browser program that runs on a WAP or WAP2 cell phone.

microwaves — Part of the spectrum from 3 to 30 GHz.

Mini PCI — A small card that is functionally equivalent to a standard PCI expansion card used for integrating communications peripherals onto a notebook computer.

mixer — A component that combines two inputs to create a single output.

mobile telecommunications switching office (MTSO) — The connection between a cellular network and wired telephones.

modem (MOdulator/DEModulator) — A device used to convert digital signals into an analog format, and vice versa.

modulation — The process of changing a carrier signal.

modulation index — The amount that the frequency varies.

monopole antenna — An antenna built of a straight piece of wire, usually a quarter of the wavelength with no ground point or reflecting element.

motes — Remote sensors used for collecting data from manufacturing equipment or for scientific research that can communicate using wireless technology.

multichannel multipoint distribution service (MMDS) — A fixed broadband wireless technology that transmits at 1.5 Mbps over distances of 35 miles (56 kilometers).

multipath distortion — The same signal being received from several different directions and also at different times.

multiple in, multiple out (MIMO) — A technology that uses multiple antennas (usually three or four) and also uses reflected signals (multipath) to extend the range of the WLAN by attempting to correctly decode a frame from multiple copies of it received at different times (multipath reflections).

narrow-band transmissions — Transmissions that use one radio frequency or a very narrow portion of the frequency spectrum.

neighbor piconets — Separate piconets that have their own PNC, but that depend on the original piconet's PNC to allocate a private block of time when their devices are allowed to transmit.

network interface unit (NIU) — A device that connects an LMDS modem to a LAN or telephone system.

noise — Interference with a signal.

nomadic user — A user that moves frequently but does not use the equipment while in motion.

non-line-of-sight (NLOS) — When the transmitter antenna cannot be seen from the receiver end, or vice-versa.

non-return-to-zero, invert-on-ones (NRZ-I) — A binary signaling technique that changes the voltage level only when the bit to be represented is a 1.

non-return-to-zero (NRZ) — A binary signaling technique that increases the voltage to represent a 1 bit, but provides no voltage for a 0 bit.

non-return-to-zero-level (NRZ-L) — See polar non-return to zero.

null data frame — The response that a client sends back to the AP to indicate that the client has no transmissions to make.

Object Name Service (ONS) — An EPCglobal Inc. service, modeled after DNS, that can assist in locating information about a product, over the Internet.

official standards — See de jure standards.

offset quadrature phase shift keying (O-QPSK) — A transmission technique used in 802.15.4 that uses two carrier waves of the same frequency but with a phase difference of 90 degrees between them. This technique modulates even numbered chips in the in-phase wave and odd numbered chips in the other (Q-Phase), using quadrature amplitude modulation, before combining the waves for transmission.

omnidirectional antenna — An antenna that sends out the signal in a uniform pattern in all directions.

one-dimensional antenna — A straight length of wire or metal connected to a transmitter at one end.

orthogonal frequency division multiple access (OFDMA) — A multiple access technique, based on OFDM, that divides the frequency channel into 1,536 data subcarriers.

orthogonal frequency division multiplexing (OFDM) — A transmission technique in which the frequency band is divided into a number of frequencies (called sub-frequencies or channels) that do not interfere with each other.

oscillating signal — A wave that illustrates the change in a carrier signal.

packet — A smaller segment of the transmitted signal.

packet acknowledgment (ACK) — A procedure for reducing collisions by requiring the receiving station to send an explicit packet back to the sending station.

packet switching — Data transmission that is broken into smaller units.

paging procedure — A process that enables a device to make an actual connection to a piconet.

PAN coordinator — The 802.15.4 device that controls access to the piconet and optionally the timing as well.

parabolic dish antenna — A high-gain directional antenna that emits a narrow, focused beam of energy and is used for long-distance outdoor links.

park mode — A state in which a Bluetooth device is still synchronized to the piconet but it does not participate in the traffic.

passband — A minimum and maximum threshold.

passive antenna — The most common type of antenna. Passive antennas can only radiate a signal with the same amount of energy that appears at the antenna connector.

passive scanning — The process of listening to each available channel for a set period of time.

passive tags — The most common type of RFID tag. They do not include a battery and are powered by the electromagnetic energy in the RF waves transmitted by the reader. Passive tags never initiate a transmission and must wait for a reader to interrogate them.

patch antenna — A semi-directional antenna that emits a wide horizontal beam and an even wider vertical beam.

peer-to-peer mode — A WLAN mode in which wireless clients communicate directly among themselves without using an AP.

personal digital assistant (PDA) — A handheld computer device used for taking notes, making appointments, creating to-do lists, and communicating with other devices.

phase — The relative starting point of a wave, in degrees, beginning at zero degrees.

phase modulation (PM) — A change in the starting point of a cycle.

phase shift keying (PSK) — A binary modulation technique that changes the starting point of the cycle.

physical layer (PHY) — The layer that is responsible for converting the data bits into an electromagnetic signal and transmitting it on the medium.

piconet — A small network composed of two or more Bluetooth devices that contains one master and at least one slave exchanging data using the same channel.

piconet coordinator (PNC) — A device that provides all of the basic communications timing in an 802.15.3 piconet.

pizza box antenna — A small antenna used for MMDS systems.

PN code — Pseudo random code; a code that appears to be a random sequence of 1s and 0s but actually repeats itself. Used in CDMA cellular telephone technology.

point coordination function (PCF) — The 802.11 optional polling function.

point-to-multipoint wireless link — A link in which one central site uses an omnidirectional antenna to transmit to multiple remote sites, which may use omnidirectional antennas or directional antennas to maximize the distance and the quality of the signal.

point-to-point wireless link — The most reliable link between two antenna sites using directional antennas to maximize the distance and the signal quality.

polar non-return-to-zero (polar NRZ) — A binary signaling technique that increases the voltage to represent a 1 bit, but drops to negative voltage to represent a 0 bit.

polling — A channel access method in which each computer is asked in sequence whether it wants to transmit.

power management — An 802.11 standard that allows the mobile client to be off as much as possible to conserve battery life but still not miss out on data transmissions.

power over Ethernet (PoE) — A technology that provides power over an Ethernet cable.

pre-shared key — A 128-bit key used by WPA.

privacy — Standards that ensure that transmissions are not read by unauthorized users.

probe — A frame sent by a client when performing active scanning.

probe response — A frame sent by an AP when responding to a client's active scanning probe.

profile — An extension of the XML language.

profiles — Sets of predefined WiMAX connection parameters that include the frequency channel, bandwidth of the channel, and transmission mechanism (OFDM, OFDMA, etc.).

Protocol Adaptation Layer (PAL) — A set of protocol implementation rules that will enable wireless FireWire at 400 Mbps based on an 802.15.3a/WiMedia platform.

public key infrastructure (PKI) — A unique security code that can verify the authenticity of a user.

quadbit — A signal unit that represents four bits.

quadrature amplitude modulation (QAM) — A combination of phase modulation with amplitude modulation to produce 16 different signals.

quadrature phase shift keying (QPSK) — A digital modulation technique that combines quadrature amplitude modulation with phase shift keying.

quality of service (QoS) — A feature of some PANs that allows devices to request more channel access time in order to prioritize high-volume, time-sensitive traffic such as a voice stream.

quarter-wave antenna — An antenna that is one-fourth as long as the wavelength of the signal it is designed to transmit or receive.

radio frequency communications (RF) — All types of radio communications that use radio frequency waves.

radio frequency identification (RFID) — A technology that uses electronic, flexible tags, equipped with microprocessor chips and memory, to identify products. RFID tags can store significantly more information than the current barcode system.

radio frequency spectrum — The entire range of all radio frequencies that exist.

radio modules — Small radio transceivers built onto microprocessor chips that are embedded into Bluetooth devices and enable them to communicate.

radio wave (radiotelephony) — An electromagnetic wave created when an electric current passes through a wire and creates a magnetic field in the space around the wire.

reader — The RFID device that captures and processes the data received from the tags.

reassociation — The process of a client dropping a connection with one AP and reestablishing the connection with another.

reassociation request frame — A frame sent from a client to a new AP asking whether it can associate with the AP.

reassociation response frame — A frame sent by an AP to a station indicating that it will accept its reassociation with that AP.

recurring costs — Costs that continue to be paid over a period of time.

reduced-function device — In ZigBee networks, a device such as a light switch, or lamp that can only connect to one full-function device at a time and can only join the network as a child device.

repeater — A device commonly used in satellite communications that simply repeats the signal to another location.

request for information (RFI) — A document sent to a vendor to gain general information about a vendor's products or solutions to a problem.

request for proposal (RFP) — A detailed planning document with precise specifications for the products and services.

Request to Send/Clear to Send (RTS/CTS) — An 802.11 protocol option that allows a station to reserve the network for transmissions.

return on investment (ROI) — The profit or advantage of an action.

return-to-zero (RZ) — A binary signaling technique that increases the voltage to represent a 1 bit, but the voltage is reduced to zero before the end of the period for transmitting the 1 bit, and there is no voltage for a 0 bit.

RFID device — A small tag placed on product packaging and boxes that can be remotely activated and read by remote sensors. The data about the product is then transferred directly to an information-processing system for inventory control, location, and counting.

roaming — The automatic transfer of the RF signal when moving from one cellular network to another network.

robust security network association (RSNA) — A grouping of several security functions to protect data frames by providing mutual authentication between client devices and access points, controlled access to the network, establishment of security keys, and key management.

RSA — An encryption algorithm developed in 1977 by Ron Rivest, Adi Shamir, and Leonard Adleman.

satellite radio — A pay-for-service high-quality radio broadcast system that transmits digital programming directly from satellites to a network of ground-based repeaters and that holds the signal regardless of the listener's location.

scanning — The process that a client uses to examine the airwaves for information that it needs in order to begin the association process.

scatternet — A group of piconets in which connections exist between different piconets.

scintillation — The temporal and spatial variations in light intensity caused by atmospheric turbulence.

Second Generation (2G) — The second generation of cellular telephony that uses circuit-switched digital networks.

secure digital (SD) card — A small expansion card that is used with PDA devices. SD cards are smaller than CF cards. *See also* compact flash (CF) cards.

semi-active tag — RFID tags that include a battery that is only used when the tag is interrogated. The batteries in semi-active tags usually last for several years.

sensory tags — RFID devices that include a thermal or other kind of sensor and can record information about the environmental conditions to which a product has been exposed during transportation or storage.

sequential freshness — A security service available in 802.15.4 used by the receiving device that ensures that the same frames will not be transmitted more than once.

service discovery — The process of sending a query to other devices on the network to identify their capabilities.

Service Set Identifier (SSID) — A unique identifier assigned to an AP.

short interframe space (SIFS) — A time gap used for immediate response actions such as ACK.

Short Message Services (SMS) — A delivery system for short, text-based messages sent between wireless devices such as cellular telephones and pagers.

sidebands — The sum and the differences of the frequency carrier that serve as buffer space around the frequency of the transmitted signal.

signal-to-noise ratio (SNR) — The measure of signal strength relative to the background noise.

simplex transmission — Transmission that occurs in only one direction.

sine wave — A wave that illustrates the change in a carrier signal.

slave — A device on a Bluetooth piconet that takes commands from the master.

sled — An external attachment for a PDA that permits external cards to attach to the device.

sleep mode — A power-conserving mode used by notebook computers.

slotted terminating adaptive protocol (STAC) — The communications protocol used by passive RFID tags that work in the 13.56 MHz HF band.

smart antennas — A new type of antenna that uses a signal processor and an array of narrow beam elements to track the user and send most of the RF energy in the direction of the mobile receiver to prevent interference and avoid wasting RF energy.

smart labels — Another name for flexible RFID tags that include a microprocessor chip and memory.

Smartphone — A device that combines a cellular phone with the capabilities of a personal digital assistant (PDA). These devices provide the user with the ability to enter appointments in a calendar, write notes, send and receive e-mail, and browse Web sites, among other functions.

sniff mode — A state in which the Bluetooth device listens to the piconet master at a reduced rate so that it uses less power.

spatial diversity — The sending of parallel beams during free space optical transmissions.

spectrum conflict — The potential for technologies using the same frequency bands to interfere with each other to the extent that they sometimes perform poorly when used within close range of each other.

spread spectrum transmission — A technique that takes a narrow signal and spreads it over a broader portion of the radio frequency band.

subnets — A smaller unit of a network.

subscriber station (SS) — In a WiMAX network, either a CPE device that attaches to a LAN or a laptop computer.

super high frequency (SHF) — Part of the frequency spectrum from 3 to 30 GHz.

superframe — A mechanism for managing transmissions in a piconet. The superframe is a continually repeating frame containing a beacon, contention access periods, channel time allocation periods, and management time allocation periods. Using the superframe is optional in 802.15.4 WPANs.

switching — Moving a signal from one wire or frequency to another.

symbol — A data unit that can represent one or more bits.

synchronous connection-oriented (SCO) link — A symmetric point-to-point link between a master and a single slave in the piconet that functions like a circuit-switched link by using reserved slots at regular intervals.

system profile — A combination of the basic WiMAX profile and one of the transmission profiles.

T1 — A technology to transmit data over special telephone lines at 1.544 Mbps.

tags — Devices that include an antenna and a chip containing memory and can store information about products, such as the manufacturer, product category, and serial number, along with date and time of manufacturing.

Telecommunications Industries Association (TIA) — A group of more than 1,100 members that manufacture or supply the products and services used in global communications.

temporal key integrity protocol — A security protocol used in WPA that provides per-packet key-mixing

Third Generation (3G) — Digital cellular wireless generation of cellular telephony with speeds up to 2 Mbps.

time division duplexing (TDD) — A mechanism that divides a single transmission into two parts, an uplink part and a downlink part (*see also* FDD).

Time Division Multiple Access (TDMA) — A transmission technique that divides the bandwidth into several time slots.

time slots — The measurement unit in a PLCP frame. The length of a time slot is predefined by the standard or specification for a particular system.

traffic encryption key (TEK) — The security key used to encrypt the data in a WiMAX network.

traffic indication map (TIM) — A list of the stations that have buffered frames waiting at the AP.

transponders — Another name for RFID tags.

trellis code modulation (TCM) — A method of encoding a digital signal in a way that permits single bit errors to be detected and corrected.

tribit — A signal unit that represents three bits.

triple-play — The support of transmission of video, voice, and data on the same network.

truck-rolls — Support technician visits to a site.

two-level Gaussian frequency shift keying (2-GFSK) — A binary signaling technique that uses two different frequencies to indicate whether a 1 or a 0 is being transmitted in addition to varying the number of waves.

UART (Universal Asynchronous Receiver/Transmitter) — A microchip that controls a computer's interface to its attached serial devices through a serial port or IrDA port.

Ultra Wide Band (UWB) — A wireless communications technology that allows devices to transmit data at hundreds of megabits per second at short distances (up to a few feet) and at up to 150 feet (50 meters) at lower speeds. The transmissions use low-power, precisely timed pulses of energy that operate in the same frequency spectrum as low-end noise, such as that emitted by computer chips and TV monitors.

Unlicensed National Information Infrastructure (U-NII) — An unregulated band approved by the FCC in 1996 to provide for short-range, high-speed wireless digital communications.

unregulated bands — See license exempt spectrum.

upfront costs — Costs that are necessary to start a project.

virtual private network (VPN) — A secure, encrypted connection between two points.

Voice over Internet Protocol (VoIP) — A technology that allows voice telephone calls to be carried over the same network used to carry computer data.

voice over wireless LAN (VoWLAN) — In WLANs that support QoS, it is possible to support telephone calls over the same wireless connection.

voltage — Electrical pressure.

wake superframe — The superframe designated by the PNC in which devices that are in power save mode will wake up and listen for frames addressed to them.

wavelength — The length of a single RF wave, measured from the starting point of the sine wave to the starting point of the next sine wave or from any point in a wave (usually the peak) to the same point on the next wave.

Wideband CDMA (W-CDMA) — The 3G digital cellular technology that is a migration from EDGE.

Wi-Fi — A trademark of the Wi-Fi Alliance, often used to refer to 802.11b WLANs that pass the organization's interoperability tests.

Wi-Fi Protected Access (WPA) and **WPA2** — A security enhancement introduced by the Wi-Fi Alliance, in advance of the 802.11i standard, to deal with the security flaws in WEP.

WiMAX — Worldwide interoperability for microwave access.

WiMAX Forum — An industry organization dedicated to promoting the implementation of 802.16 by testing and certifying equipment for compatibility and interoperability.

WiMedia Alliance — An association of manufacturers and interested organizations formed to promote the implementation of the IEEE 802.15.3 standard and provide various support activities.

Wired Equivalent Privacy (WEP) — The IEEE specification for data encryption between wireless devices that prevents eavesdropping.

wireless access point (access point or AP) — A device that receives and transmits signals back to wireless network interface cards.

Wireless Application Protocol (WAP or WAP2) — A standard for transmitting, formatting, and displaying Internet data on cellular phones. WAP can display only text. WAP2 supports HTML and can display color and pictures.

wireless application service provider (WASP) — An organization that can design, create, and deliver a complete wireless application.

wireless bridge — A networking component that connects two wired networks or extends the range of a WLAN.

wireless communications — The transmission of user data without the use of wires between devices.

wireless high-speed unlicensed metro area network (WirelessHUMAN) — A WiMAX specification based on OFDM, specifically designed for use in the 5 GHz U-NII band.

wireless local area network (WLAN) — A local area network that is not connected by wires but instead uses wireless technology. Its range extends to approximately 100 meters and has a maximum data rate of 54 Mbps, by current standards. Today's WLANs are based on IEEE 802.11a/b/g standards.

wireless metropolitan area network (WMAN) — A wireless network that covers a large geographical area such as a city or suburb. The technology is usually based on the IEEE 802.16 set of standards, and can span an entire city, covering distances of up to 35 miles (56 km) between transmitters and receivers or repeaters.

wireless metropolitan area networks (WMANs) — A group of technologies that provide wireless connectivity across a substantial geographical area such as a large city.

wireless network interface card (wireless NIC) — A device that connects to a PC to transmit and receive network data over radio waves. It includes an antenna for wireless communication between networked devices.

wireless personal area network (WPAN) — A group of technologies that are designed for short-range communications, from a few inches to about 33 feet (10 meters). Due to its limited range, WPAN technology is used mainly as a replacement for cables. *See also* piconet and UWB.

wireless residential gateway — A combination of several technologies that permit home users to have wireless capabilities and also allow Internet and printer sharing and provide better security than connecting a computer directly to the Internet.

wireless site survey — The task of measuring the signal strength and quality in several locations around the office to determine how many APs will be required, how many and which channels will be used, as well as identifying interference sources and security needs.

wireless switching — Construction of a wireless network with devices that incorporate all of the functions of an AP and can control multiple dumb 802.11 radios.

wireless VoIP phones — The telephone handsets that connect to a WLAN's AP, permitting use of the WLAN for telephone calls.

wireless VoIP SOHO routers — Devices that can be connected to a DSL or cable modem and provide both a WLAN and telephone services through the user's Internet connection.

wireless wide area network (WWAN) — A network that can encompass geographical area, even the entire world. WWANs use cellular phone technologies.

WirelessMAN-SC (single carrier) — A WiMAX specification that uses a single carrier and is intended for point-to-point connections in the 10 to 66 GHz bands.

WirelessMAN-SCa (single-carrier access) — A WiMAX specification that uses a single carrier and is intended for point-to-point connections in the 2 to 11 GHz bands.

yagi antenna — A directional antenna that emits a wide, less-focused beam and is used for medium-distance outdoor applications.

ZigBee Alliance — An association of manufacturers and interested organizations formed to promote the creation of a global standard for wireless devices used in monitoring and control applications.

Index